Packard Gold Portfolio 1946-1958

Compiled by
R.M. Clarke

ISBN 1 870642 198

Cover photo by Bud Juneau courtesy of The Packard Club.
1947 Clipper Custom. Owner Terry Knoepp.

Distributed by
Brooklands Book Distribution Ltd.
'Holmerise', Seven Hills Road,
Cobham, Surrey, England

BROOKLANDS BOOKS

BROOKLANDS BOOKS SERIES

AC Ace & Aceca 1953-1983
AC Cobra 1962-1969
Alfa Romeo Alfasud 1972-1984
Alfa Romeo Alfetta Coupes GT.GTV.GTV6 1974-1987
Alfa Romeo Guilias Berlinettas
Alfa Romeo Giulia Berlinas 1962-1976
Alfa Romeo Giulia Coupés 1963-1976
Alfa Romeo Spider 1966-1987
Aston Martin Gold Portfolio 1972-1985
Austin Seven 1922-1982
Austin A30 & A35 1951-1962
Austin Healey 100 1952-1959
Austin Healey 3000 1959-1967
Austin Healey 100 & 3000 Collection No. 1
Austin Healey 'Frogeye' Sprite Collection No. 1
Austin Healey Sprite 1958-1971
Avanti 1962-1983
BMW Six Cylinder Coupés 1969-1975
BMW 1600 Collection No. 1
BMW 2002 1968-1976
Bristol Cars Gold Portfolio 1946-1985
Buick Riviera 1963-1978
Cadillac Automobiles 1949-1959
Cadillac Automobiles 1960-1969
Cadillac Eldorado 1967-1978
Cadillac in the Sixties No. 1
Camaro 1966-1970
High Performance Camaros 1982-1988
Chevrolet 1955-1957
Chevrolet Camaro Collection No. 1
Chevelle & SS 1964-1972
Chevy II Nova & SS 1962-1973
Chrysler 300 1955-1970
Citroen Traction Avant 1934-1957
Citroen DS & ID 1955-1875
Citroen 2CV 1949-1982
Cobras & Replicas 1962-1983
Cortina 1600E & GT 1967-1970
Corvair 1959-1968
Daimler Dart & V-8 250 1959-1969
Datsun 240z 1970-1973
Datsun 280Z & ZX 1975-1983
De Tomaso Collection No. 1
Dodge Charger 1966-1974
Excalibur Collection No. 1
Ferrari Cars 1946-1956
Ferrari Cars 1962-1966
Ferrari Cars 1969-1973
Ferrari Dino 1965-1974
Ferrari Dino 308 1974-1979
Ferrari 308 & Mondial 1980-1984
Ferrari Collection No. 1
Fiat-Bertone X1/9 1973-1988
Ford Falcon 1960-1970
Ford Mustang 1964-1967
Ford Mustang 1967-1973
High Performance Mustangs 1982-1988
Ford RS Escort 1968-1980
Honda CRX 1983-1987
High Performance Escorts MkI 1968-1974
High Performance Escorts MkII 1975-1980
Hudson & Railton Cars 1936-1940
Jaguar Cars 1957-1961
Jaguar Cars 1961-1964
Jaguar Cars 1964-1968
Jaguar MK2 1959-1969
Jaguar E-Type 1961-1966
Jaguar E-Type 1966-1971
Jaguar E-Type V12 1971-1975
Jaguar XKE Collection No. 1
Jaguar XJ6 1968-1972
Jaguar XJ6 Series II 1973-1979
Jaguar XJ6 & XJ12 Series III 1979-1985
Jaguar XJ12 1972-1980
Jaguar XJS 1975-1980
Jensen Cars 1946-1967
Jensen Cars 1967-1979
Jensen Interceptor Gold Portfolio 1966-1986
Lamborghini Cars 1964-1970
Lamborghini Cars 1970-1975
Lamborghini Countach Collection No. 1
Lamborghini Countach & Urraco 1974-1980
Lamborghini Countach & Jalpa 1980-1985
Lancia Stratos 1972-1985
Land Rover 1948-1973
Land Rover Series II & IIa 1958-1971
Land Rover Series III 1971-1985
Lotus Cortina 1963-1970
Lotus Elan 1962-1973
Lotus Elan Collection No. 1
Lotus Elan Collection No. 2
Lotus Elite 1957-1964
Lotus Elite & Eclat 1974-1981
Lotus Turbo Esprit 1980-1986
Lotus Europa 1966-1975
Lotus Europa Collection No. 1
Lotus Seven 1957-1980
Lotus Seven Collection No. 1
Maserati 1965-1970
Maserati 1970-1975
Mazda RX-7 Collection No. 1
Mercedes 230/250/280SL 1963-1971
Mercedes 350/450SL & SLC 1971-1980
Mercedes Benz Cars 1949-1954
Mercedes Benz Cars 1954-1957
Mercedes Benz Cars 1957-1961
Mercedes Benz Competition Cars 1950-1957
Metropolitan 1954-1962
MG Cars 1929-1934
MG TC 1945-1949
MG TD 1949-1953
MG TF 1953-1955
MG Cars 1957-1959
MG Cars 1959-1962
MG Midget 1961-1980
MG MGA 1955-1962
MGA Collection No. 1
MGB Roadsters 1962-1980
MGB GT 1965-1980
Mini Cooper 1961-1971
Morgan Cars 1960-1970
Morgan Cars 1969-1979
Morris Minor Collection No. 1
Old's Cutlass & 4-4-2 1964-1972
Oldsmobile Toronado 1966-1978
Opel GT 1968-1973
Packard Gold Portfolio 1946-1958
Pantera 1970-1973
Pantera & Mangusta 1969-1974
Plymouth Barracuda 1964-1974
Pontiac Fiero 1984-1988
Pontiac GTO 1964-1970
Pontiac Firebird 1967-1973
High Performance Firebirds 1982-1988
Pontiac Tempest & GTO 1961-1965
Porsche Cars 1960-1964
Porsche Cars 1964-1968
Porsche Cars 1968-1972
Porsche Cars in the Sixties
Porsche Cars 1972-1975
Porsche 356 1952-1965
Porsche 911 Collection No. 1
Porsche 911 Collection No. 2
Porsche 911 1965-1969
Porsche 911 1970-1972
Porsche 911 1973-1977
Porsche 911 Carrera 1973-1977
Porsche 911 SC 1978-1983
Porsche 911 Turbo 1975-1984
Porsche 914 1969-1975
Porsche 914 Collection No. 1
Porsche 924 1975-1981
Porsche 928 Collection No. 1
Porsche 944 1981-1985
Porsche Turbo Collection No. 1
Reliant Scimitar 1964-1986
Rolls Royce Silver Cloud 1955-1965
Rolls Royce Silver Shadow 1965-1980
Range Rover 1970-1981
Rover 3 & 3.5 Litre 1958-1973
Rover P4 1949-1959
Rover P4 1955-1964
Rover 2000 + 2200 1963-1977
Rover 3500 1968-1977
Rover 3500 & Vitesse 1976-1986
Saab Sonett Collection No. 1
Saab Turbo 1976-1983
Singer Sports Cars 1933-1934
Studebaker Hawks & Larks 1956-1963
Sunbeam Alpine & Tiger 1959-1967
Thunderbird 1955-1957
Thunderbird 1958-1963
Thunderbird 1964-1976
Toyota MR2 1984-1988
Triumph 2000-2.5-2500 1963-1977
Triumph Spitfire 1962-1980
Triumph Spitfire Collection No. 1
Triumph Stag 1970-1980
Triumph Stag Collection No. 1
Triumph TR2 & TR3 1952-1960
Triumph TR4.TR5.TR250 1961-1968
Triumph TR6 1969-1976
Triumph TR6 Collection No. 1
Triumph TR7 & TR8 1975-1982
Triumph GT6 1966-1974
Triumph Vitesse & Herald 1959-1971
TVR Gold Portfolio 1959-1988
Volkswagen Cars 1936-1956
VW Beetle 1956-1977
VW Beetle Collection No. 1
VW Golf GTi 1976-1986
VW Karmann Ghia 1955-1982
VW Scirocco 1974-1981
Volvo 1800 1960-1973
Volvo 120 Series 1956-1970

BROOKLANDS MUSCLE CARS SERIES

American Motors Muscle Cars 1966-1970
Buick Muscle Cars 1965-1970
Camaro Muscle Cars 1966-1972
Capri Muscle Cars 1969-1983
Chevrolet Muscle Cars 1966-1972
Dodge Muscle Cars 1967-1970
Mercury Muscle Cars 1966-1971
Mini Muscle Cars 1961-1979
Mopar Muscle Cars 1964-1967
Mopar Muscle Cars 1968-1971
Mustang Muscle Cars 1967-1971
Shelby Mustang Muscle Cars 1965-1970
Oldsmobile Muscle Cars 1964-1970
Plymouth Muscle Cars 1966-1971
Pontiac Muscle Cars 1966-1972
Muscle Cars Compared 1966-1971
Muscle Cars Compared Book 2 1965-1971

BROOKLANDS ROAD & TRACK SERIES

Road & Track on Alfa Romeo 1949-1963
Road & Track on Alfa Romeo 1964-1970
Road & Track on Alfa Romeo 1971-1976
Road & Track on Alfa Romeo 1977-1984
Road & Track on Aston Martin 1962-1984
Road & Track on Auburn Cord & Duesenberg 1952-1984
Road & Track on Audi 1952-1980
Road & Track on Audi 1980-1986
Road & Track on Austin Healey 1953-1970
Road & Track on BMW Cars 1966-1974
Road & Track on BMW Cars 1975-1978
Road & Track on BMW Cars 1979-1983
Road & Track on Cobra, Shelby & Ford GT40 1962-1983
Road & Track on Corvette 1953-1967
Road & Track on Corvette 1968-1982
Road & Track on Corvette 1982-1986
Road & Track on Datsun Z 1970-1983
Road & Track on Ferrari 1950-1968
Road & Track on Ferrari 1968-1974
Road & Track on Ferrari 1975-1981
Road & Track on Ferrari 1981-1984
Road & Track on Fiat Sports Cars 1968-1987
Road & Track on Jaguar 1950-1960
Road & Track on Jaguar 1961-1968
Road & Track on Jaguar 1968-1974
Road & Track on Jaguar 1974-1982
Road & Track on Lamborghini 1964-1985
Road & Track on Lotus 1972-1981
Road & Track on Maserati 1952-1974
Road & Track on Maserati 1975-1983
Road & Track on Mazda RX7 1978-1986
Road & Track on Mercedes 1952-1962
Road & Track on Mercedes 1963-1970
Road & Track on Mercedes 1971-1979
Road & Track on Mercedes 1980-1987
Road & Track on MG Sports Cars 1949-1961
Road & Track on MG Sports Cars 1962-1980
Road & Track on Mustang 1964-1977
Road & Track on Peugeot 1955-1986
Road & Track on Pontiac 1960-1983
Road & Track on Porsche 1951-1967
Road & Track on Porsche 1968-1971
Road & Track on Porsche 1972-1975
Road & Track on Porsche 1975-1978
Road & Track on Porsche 1979-1982
Road & Track on Porsche 1982-1985
Road & Track on Rolls Royce & Bentley 1950-1965
Road & Track on Rolls Royce & Bentley 1966-1984
Road & Track on Saab 1955-1985
Road & Track on Toyota Sports & G T Cars 1966-1986
Road & Track on Triumph Sports Cars 1953-1967
Road & Track on Triumph Sports Cars 1967-1974
Road & Track on Triumph Sports Cars 1974-1982
Road & Track on Volkswagen 1951-1968
Road & Track on Volkswagen 1968-1978
Road & Track on Volkswagen 1978-1985
Road & Track on Volvo 1957-1974
Road & Track on Volvo 1975-1985

BROOKLANDS CAR AND DRIVER SERIES

Car and Driver on BMW 1955-1977
Car and Driver on BMW 1977-1985
Car and Driver on Cobra, Shelby & Ford GT40 1963-1984
Car and Driver on Datsun Z 1600 & 2000 1966-1984
Car and Driver on Corvette 1956-1967
Car and Driver on Corvette 1968-1977
Car and Driver on Corvette 1978-1982
Car and Driver on Ferrari 1955-1962
Car and Driver on Ferrari 1963-1975
Car and Driver on Ferrari 1976-1983
Car and Driver on Mopar 1956-1967
Car and Driver on Mopar 1968-1975
Car and Driver on Pontiac 1961-1975
Car and Driver on Porsche 1955-1962
Car and Driver on Porsche 1963-1970
Car and Driver on Porsche 1970-1976
Car and Driver on Porsche 1977-1981
Car and Driver on Porsche 1982-1986
Car and Driver on Saab 1956-1985
Car and Driver on Volvo 1955-1986

BROOKLANDS MOTOR & THOROUGHBRED & CLASSIC CAR SERIES

Motor & T & CC on Ferrari 1966-1976
Motor & T & CC on Ferrari 1976-1984
Motor & T & CC on Lotus 1979-1983
Motor & T & CC on Morris Minor 1948-1983

BROOKLANDS PRACTICAL CLASSICS SERIES

Practical Classics on Austin A40 Restoration
Practical Classics on Land Rover Restoration
Practical Classics on Metalworking in Restoration
Practical Classics on Midget/Sprite Restoration
Practical Classics on Mini Cooper Restoration
Practical Classics on MGB Restoration
Practical Classics on Morris Minor Restoration
Practical Classics on Triumph Herald/Vitesse
Practical Classics on Triumph Spitfire Restoration
Practical Classics on VW Beetle Restoration
Practical Classics on 1930S Car Restoration

BROOKLANDS MILITARY VEHICLES SERIES

Allied Military Vehicles Collection No. 1
Allied Military Vehicles Collection No. 2
Dodge Military Vehicles Collection No. 1
Military Jeeps 1941-1945
Off Road Jeeps 1944-1971
V W Kubelwagen 1940-1975

CONTENTS

ACKNOWLEDGEMENTS

In a recent survey we found that out of every two books we sell one goes to a home containing at least one other Brooklands title. These buyers know what to expect and we hope that they are not disappointed with this Packard anthology.

For those adventurous first time buyers we should explain that nothing original lies between these covers. We are in a way explorers trying to unearth lost stories on historic vehicles so that we can make them available again for those who's interest is drawn towards the old car hobby.

During the 30 years of compiling this series, some 10,000 road tests and other articles have been included in the 400 titles that make up our list. We print only small quantities of each book which, in the main are aquired by enthusiastic owners.

Packard was a great marque and we regret that this book on the face of it has an unhappy ending. Some comfort can be drawn however from the wonderful legacy left to us by the company in the form of a string of classic models which each year grace concours and auto shows from coast to coast and beyond.

Our special thanks go to Bud Juneau and his collegues in the Packard Club who came so speedily to our rescue with the delightful photograph reproduced on our front cover.

We also owe a debt of gratitude to the publishers of the journals from which our stories are taken. We are sure that Packard devotees will wish to join with us in thanking the management of Auto Age, Autocar, Auto Catalog, Auto Show, Autosport, Auto Sports Review, Car Life, Hot Rod, Mechanix Illustrated, Motor, Motor Age, Motor Life, Motor Trend, Motorsport, Popular Science, Product Engineering, Science and Mechanics, Special Interest Autos, Speed Age, Wheels and Your Car for their generosity and ongoing support.

R.M. Clarke

Side view of the 1946 Packard Clipper. Below, new styled radiator grille has been incorporated in the new models.

New Packard Models Introduced

Clipper Eight and Deluxe Clipper Eight to be featured in four-door sedan styles

THE Packard Motor Car Co. has announced that the first public showings of their new models would be made at regional dealer meetings scheduled in early November.

Owing to the problems of initial production, output for the rest of this year will be concentrated upon two basic models—the Clipper Eight and the Deluxe Clipper Eight, both mounted on 120 in. wheelbase chassis. These will be available in four-door sedan bodies only. Full details of other models and additional body styles will be given later. According to George T. Christopher, president, production during the rest of this year would be about 8000 cars; later production will be augmented to include models in four price ranges.

The initial models feature the familiar Packard straight eight engine —8-cyl., in-line, L-head, 3¼ in. bore by 4¼ in. stroke, 282 cu. in. displacement, developed hp. is 125 at 3600 rpm. The engine remains the same in specification details but incorporates two major features. One is the adoption of the Moraine Div., Durex No. 300 sintered type precision bearing for the main and connecting rod bearings. Bearing coating is a thin section high lead babbitt.

The other feature marks the first use of the Perfect Circle Type 86 oil ring, representing the culmination of development work dating back to prewar years. It has a coil expander spring instead of the flat formed springs commonly employed. Among the claims for this ring are the following:

1. Uniform radial pressure distribution through the application of the principle of circumferential expansion. The radial pressure of the ring results from the compression of the long, soft, coil spring.

2. Loss of unit pressure as the ring wears is very low

CONTINUED ON PAGE 43

MI Tests the New Cars

PACKARD

Tom McCahill, MI's automotive expert, inspects the engine of the new 1946 de luxe Packard Clipper.

Full view of the new 1946 Packard Clipper "8." Note the absence of rear wheel fender shells.

THE 1946 Packard Clipper "8" is similar in most respects to the 1942, pre-war model. Its radiator grille has been redesigned and it has larger bumpers, but otherwise its appearance is almost the same. On the car I tested—which incidentally was the automobile presented, figuratively only, to the "Little Flower," former Mayor La Guardia, by the Committee of Mayors, I was pleased to find that the 1942 rear wheel fender shells had been left off. These infernal contraptions in the writer's opinion added little to the appearance but much to tempers when a flat was experienced, especially at night. I trust this is not just another war casualty that will be replaced as soon as more material is available.

Rated as a medium-priced automobile, the 1946 Clipper is definitely on the high side of that bracket, but there is no disputing the fact that the buyer receives his money's worth in comfort and performance. I was immediately impressed with the abundant power and ease of control. On pick-up tests, the Packard gets away like a bee-stung rabbit, which is only natural when you consider that the Clipper "8" engine has a horse-power rating of 33.8 and develops 125—a powerful automobile engine in any league. On my favorite test hill I started at the bottom doing less than 10 miles an hour in high, then opened the throttle wide without shifting gears. Instantly the car gathered speed as if jet-propelled and I was forced to break speed before reaching the halfway mark. The Clipper has all the pick-up, speed and hill climbing quality anyone could wish for. I kept remembering that its power plant is the little brother of the giant Packard engines which drove our PT boats in the Pacific.

At this writing, the Clipper is only being made with an 8-cylinder engine which is in reality the Packard "120" model of past years. This year's engine crankshaft bearings have been improved through war research and now consist of a steel shell with a copper-nickel matrix which is impregnated with a new and longer wearing babbitt material, developed to withstand rugged, abusive war use. The piston rings are also different; the oil-control rings are coil spring expanded in a manner which assures uniform radial pressure—entirely different from some rings which have several peak pressure points.

The front wheels of the Clipper are individually sprung by low-frequency coil springs. Springs of low frequency react slower than other types when subjected to bumps or rough roads and this retarded action smoothes the ride. The brakes are hydraulic of the self-energizing type. This means that the two brake shoes in each wheel are movably connected at the bottom by a coupling. When the brakes are applied, forcing the shoe against the drum, the turning drum sets up a similar motion, known as a wrapping action in the shoes, and this uniformly increases the braking pressure at every point. This type of brake action is not only positive but assures a longer life for the brake shoes.

The steering gear is new and minimizes turning effort. The gear is a triple-tooth worm type and the roller is mounted on a double row of needle bearings that extend the complete width of the roller. The arm-building Packards of the past have faded into history; the 1946 model handles with the ease of a bicycle.

As in 1942, Packard again features the so-called fade-away fenders. Admittedly this enhances overall appearance as they blend into the body without a break—but I can't help but think what a financial catastrophe would result if you tangled with a taxi or truck. In the old days if you mangled a fender on the garage door or ripped it on a fellow motorist's bumper, it simply meant buying a new fender, reasonably priced and a cinch to install; but if this should happen on a Clipper you would soon know the full meaning of that word, as your bank roll would be clipped like a fresh-shorn lamb.

The hood or bonnet opens in the old-fashioned way from each side, and I think Packard should feature this hold-out in design, for it makes it a lot easier to make adjustments without experiencing the Jonah feeling of crawling into a whale's mouth. The sedan roof is only 64 inches high, which is low for a car this size, but it maintains ample comfort and seating height inside. The over-all car width is a foot more than the height which promotes excellent roadability.

While on the subject of roadability I must mention the Packard roll-control bar, as it makes this car one of the finest for the road ever built in this country. The roll-control bar is fastened near the front wheels of the Clipper and is designed so that it passes through rubber-cored brackets on each side of the frame. When one side of the car rises from swinging around a curve or traversing uneven roads, a twisting action is set up in the bar that

CONTINUED ON PAGE 26

How this Packard "slings the mud" in its pre-production mud-road test! The diagram shows the "Comfort-Aire" ventilation system, which provides good circulation even in a rainstorm.

MI Tests The '48 PACKARD

McCahill answers the question, "Is it worth the price increase?"

PACKARD claims it's the first of the entire industry to come out with a complete line of 1948 cars! Please pass the nuts to the gentleman who just muttered, "So what?" To date, Studebaker is still the only one of the old line outfits who's really done any major changing since VJ Day and that was done back in 1946. At this writing, all Hudson's activity has stopped for a promised complete change-over, and if advanced publicity is correct it will be the number two company bringing out an entirely different-looking automobile.

Packard has made some changes, however. They have dropped the six-cylinder passenger line completely and have added more horsepower to their smaller straight-eight line. The bodies have been changed somewhat, but if you can find sensational improvements in appearance, you have better eyes than I have. I took one of the new 145 hp super-8 convertibles for a spin and I am truly unhappy to report that I wasn't thrilled in the least. This job is a push-button executive's dream, as it appears to have just about everything short of automatic pilot control. There are buttons which raise and lower each individual window as desired. There is another button for moving the front seat backward or forward without taxing your leg muscles and all these buttons are within easy reach of the driver. The instrument panel, resembling the organ at the Radio City Music Hall, is one of the most impressive I've seen that was not in a B-29. It is really luxurious. Chrome, piano-key-like controls permit the driver to do any one of a number of things by merely pushing his finger on the right key. He has at his fingertips the option of going into over-drive or into automatic gear shifting, too. This new Packard might be better named the "Look! No-hands-or-feet Model!"

Getting back to the body, there are no rear fenders as the body now goes over the rear wheels, but this is hardly a new wrinkle: look at your Kaisers and Frazers. For many years a distinctive Packard feature has been the broken-line profile of the hood, diminished last year; this has disappeared completely, leaving the forward contour without its former trade-mark appearance. The convertible is neat and good looking with lots of room inside, but it's doubtful if any little boys on the curb are going to exclaim, "Gee, whiz! Look at that!" when one goes by, because in my book it is just another convertible. It sells for approximately thirty-six hundred dollars, delivered in New York, and that, my friends, is a lot of dough to lay out for any car, no matter how many push buttons and controls it has.

There are many indications that the heavy cream has already been pretty well absorbed in the high-priced field and it is very doubtful if a car offering anything short of sensational looks and performance will prove popular in the high-bracket markets from now on.

The convertible I had out is the smallest Packard convertible in the line. It has a 145-hp engine on a 120-inch wheelbase, which, by American standards, puts it on the medium short side for length and on the long side for horsepower. It performs well though not sensationally and its riding qualities are excellent. I may be wetter than a forty-cent duck, but I can't help feeling that this new Packard is definitely not the last trick that Packard has up its sleeve. These new models were brought out without a single day's loss of production and though the engines are different and a few alterations are apparent.

I feel that Packard may be playing the game cozy with the other major manufacturers, waiting for someone to make a real move. I also believe that as soon as one of the big three makes a break, and comes out with a truly different car, then all hell will break loose in Detroit. The three major companies will all be out within a month of each other with radical design changes called 1949 or even 1950 models, and when this happens Packard won't be far behind with a brand new Packard. •

Push-buttons do everything imaginable. McCahill seems to be overwhelmed by the instrument panel!

Interior of the Station Sedan can be hosed and scrubbed, for plastic fabrics, more durable than leather, have been used throughout.

Body now goes over the rear wheels, and the grille is a part of the front-end design. The long front bumper passes air to engine.

1948 Packard Station Sedan

by Bill Williams, *Associate Editor*

driveReport

PACKARD CALLED it the Station Sedan because it used mostly sedan body stampings. Everything ahead of the rear doors, and even the doors themselves and the rear fenders, were interchangeable with the Packard 8 sedan. The Station Sedan's roof and rear panels were unique, but they mated with the standard sedan's floor and body sides.

The Packard wagon's tailgate also fit into the same-width and -depth opening as the sedan's decklid. That's what, in fact, makes the body so tapered toward the rear. It's a characteristic that also leaves the Station Sedan's tailgate smaller than the 1973 Pinto wagon's.

The 1948-50 Pregnant Packard, whose pudgy lines seem to suit the wagon better than that era's sedans, has an unusual styling history. Edward Macauley, Packard's design vice president, was crazy about sports cars. He admired Dutch Darrin's conversions of the early 1940s and was instrumental in giving factory support to the Packard-Darrin project. Ed Macauley had also built himself a series of Packard sportsters. One, called the Phantom, was begun in 1941, then modified in 1944 and again in 1947 to take on lines very similar to the Pregnant Packard. The Phantom became, in effect, a drivable test bed for Ed Macauley's ideas. Behind the scenes and very instrumental in both the 1941 Clipper and Phantom designs was Werner Gubitz, a man who apparently did much of Packard's real design work but, being shy and retiring, never got much credit.

Ed Macauley was no car designer but he had a good sense of proportion. John Reinhart, who was Packard's chief stylist from 1947 to 1951 (and who later did the Lincoln Continental Mark II under William Clay Ford), recalls the Pregnant Packard's design history this way:

"Ed Macauley was a good friend, a very fine man and one of the last true gentlemen in the industry. What happened was this. The Clipper was taken over to Briggs Mfg. Co. around 1946. [Briggs stamped and built Packard bodies at that time.] There, Al Prance, Briggs' chief designer, filled in the areas between the front and rear fenders with clay. And that became the 1948 Packard. They didn't like the front end so they put a lower grille on it. The idea was to save money by reworking as few of the old Clipper's panels as possible, but before they got through with it, they'd redone almost everything, so they didn't save much after all. I think all they saved were the roof and decklid. Of course, some of the inner panels were held over—inner doors, cowl, floor, etc."

Ed Macauley then pushed for a station wagon for 1948 even though most other company executives weren't anxious to see one. Packard's most recent station wagon, the 1941 model, had sold only about 600 units, and that seemed par for an average year. Macauley, though, urged building the 1948 wagon with mostly sedan stampings, and despite lingering objections, he rammed it through. Result: a handsome wagon that suffered from cramped cargo space because of its sedan heritage.

Packard's 1948-50 Station Sedan turned out to be one of the two most expensive wagons of its day. It was even one of the more expensive Packards. Only the Custom 8s, Packard limousines, and 7-passenger sedans cost more. The Buick Roadmaster wagon was the Station Sedan's only price rival, and by 1950 even the Roadmaster cost $13 *less*.

Yet despite the Station Sedan's high price, it used Packard's smallest engine and spanned its shortest wheelbase. Also, during its entire 3-year production run, the car never changed. The 1949-50 Station Sedans are almost indistinguishable from 1948 models. The surest way to tell them apart is to look under the hood at their patent plates. The body number begins with 22 for 1948 models and has a 9 suffix for the early '49s. Late 1949s begin with 23, and the 1950 models have a 5 suffix.

Packard's Station Sedan *looks* like a woody, but it uses an all-steel body with bolted-on wooden ribs over simulated woodgrain panels. These painted-on panels were originally applied by rolling graining ink onto a colored enamel ground coat, then sealing the two with a clear, synthetic baked enamel. This wasn't the Di-Noc method, although the factory did suggest using Di-Noc decals if the sheetmetal had to be completely refinished (as in an accident). The factory also recommended restoring the wooden ribs every year or so by sanding them lightly, applying a toxic wood sealer (to kill fungus that might cause wood rot), then applying one of several recommended varnishes. The wooden cargo deck and inner tailgate needed similar periodic restoration. So despite being basically an all-steel wagon, the Station Sedan demanded as much upkeep as real woodies.

Many enthusiasts believe that Plymouth introduced the first all-metal production station wagon in 1949. *Its* first, yes, but *the* first, no. Packard beat Plymouth by some 18 months, but the 1946 Willys Jeep wagon beat Packard by two years. But then Chevrolet beat even Willys by 11 years. Chevy offered an all-steel wagon on a pickup chassis in 1935, and even that probably wasn't the first.

By today's standards, the Station Sedan's cargo area seems ludicrously tiny. With the second seat upright, the deck measures 42.75 inches long by 45.5 wide by 32.5 high. This comes out to 36.6

Except for roof and rear quarters, Packard's all-steel wagon uses sedan sheetmetal, applied wooden ribs.

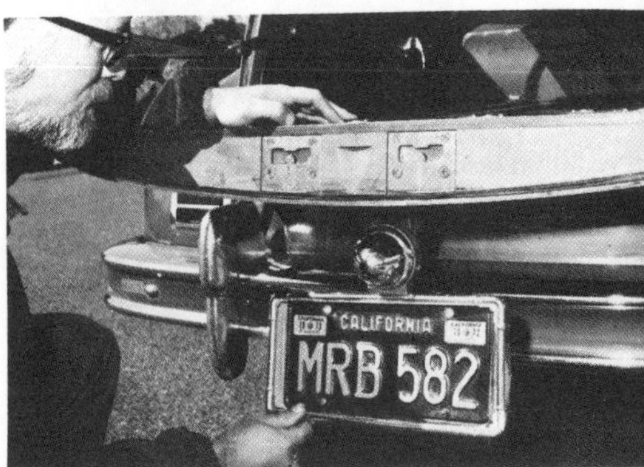

With tailgate open, license plate and light flip down. Open gate gives 25 inches of additional cargo floor.

DETROIT PUBLIC LIBRARY

Ed Macauley, Packard's styling director, built series of Phantom customs that became base for '48 design.

Since wagon's rear opening fits into sedan's former trunk, it's fairly tiny—smaller than Pinto wagon's.

Tapering rear section looks unusually sporting for so utilitarian a vehicle. Lack of drip rail over rear liftgate causes leaks and rust.

All Station Sedans used Packard's new small 8. Bill Geyer's wagon has overdrive, which gives good flexibility, effortless highway cruising.

While 1949-50 Packards went to podded tail lamps, wagons stuck with 1948 lens all 3 years.

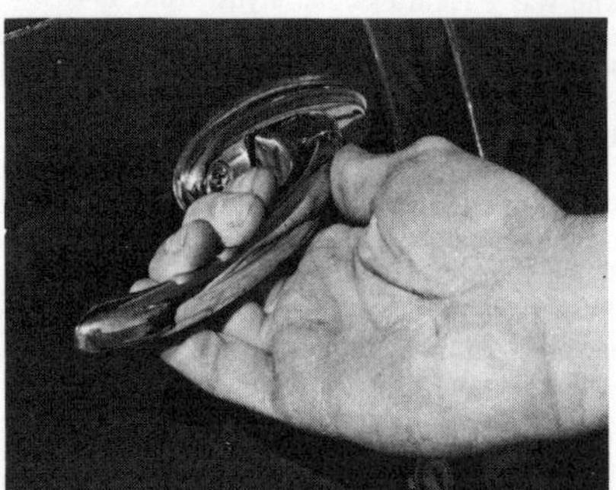

Pull-type handles make doors easy to open even if you have both arms full of grocery bundles.

Rear suspension uses anti-sway bar and inverted shackles. Wagon has more leaves than sedan.

Packard Station Sedan *continued*

cubic feet or some 24 cubic feet *less* than inside the 1973 Pinto wagon with its second seat flat. In the Packard, you can leave the tailgate down for an added 25 inches of floor length. With the Station Sedan's second seat down, cargo volume rises to 63.0 cubic feet or about 2.5 *more* than in the Pinto wagon. Neither has provision for a third seat. The Station Sedan's spare tire rests underneath the stainless-steel-ribbed plywood cargo deck, and there's some extra hidden storage space beneath the second seat.

A major problem with the Station Sedan is that it leaks. All of them leak, and they leaked even when new. Since there's no rain gutter above the hinged rear window, water drips in when the liftgate is raised. After the rubber weatherstripping dries out around the fifth door, dew and rain easily seep in and eventually rot the cargo deck floor, the sheetmetal below the tailgate, and the bottom hinges. So it's rare today to find a Station Sedan without cancer of the rear floor area.

An early 1948 press release said that the Station Sedan's durable plastic-and-wood interior could be hosed out for quick cleaning. I can't imagine anyone actually doing that; I hope no one ever did. I found the wagon's upholstery sturdy looking and comfortable. All Station Sedans came with tan plastic/leatherette seats with woven plastic inserts. The rear-seat cushion flips up from the rear and rests on end against the back of the front seat. Then the rear-seat backrest unsnaps (a leather strap and eyebuckle hold it) and lengthens the cargo deck.

Packard's engineering in almost every area was very straightforward, conventional, and *rugged*. The only far-out piece of engineering for the Pregnant series involved the Ultramatic. I place emphasis on *rugged* because Packard used one of the strongest X-member frames in the industry—an absolutely stable platform for an equally rigid body. Siderails were fully boxed behind and ahead of the big X, and the X itself was U-section with double gussets at each leg. Add to that five crossmembers plus a one-piece steel floor with pressed-in bracing and welded-on cowl and trunk, then braced and cross-braced sides, and you've got a monolithic structure. Packard bodies were thoroughly insulated with six different sorts of asphaltic compounds and padding—jute, celotex, fiberboard, asbestos, and flocking plus combinations.

The Station Sedan's 288-cid L-head engine became one of two re-engineered 8s for 1948 Packards, the other displacing 327 cid. Both were derived from the old 282, introduced in 1936. Chief research engineer Forest McFarland told SIA that Packard's decision to redesign the 282 into the new 288 and 327 came so the company could use common tooling and a minimum of different machining operations. The cylinder block was new but served both engines. All Packard engines now shared 3.5-inch pistons. Cylinder heads were common, although the 327 had greater clearance volume. Bore/stroke ratios became more nearly square. But the overriding consideration remained that Packard's smallest 8 (the 288) and its medium 8 (327) could be manufactured with common tools, from the same castings, and on the same production lines.

I should explain the various Packard series and designations at this point, because they've still got most people confused. First, please understand that Packard went along with conventional year-model dates (1948, 1949, etc.) only because everyone else did. But so far as the factory was concerned, year-model dates meant relatively little, and changes were heralded by series numbers. Packard's First Series began in 1923, and the Pregnant Packard, which bowed in Aug. 1947 as a 1948 model, kicked off the 22nd Series. The so-called 1949 Packard, introduced in Nov. 1948, simply continued the 22nd Series and looked almost the same. Except for a solid front bumper, there were no special changes at the beginning of the 1949 model year.

But in May 1949 came the celebration of Packard's 50th anniversary, so the company announced the 23rd Series that month. Styling changed very slightly *(see chart)*, the Ultramatic transmission bowed, and a lot of fanfare and advertising attended Packard's Golden Jubilee. But when other automakers announced their 1950 models that October, Packard simply glided by with the 23rd Series, leaving it unchanged from mid-1949. After 1951, though, when the newly restyled bodies appeared to become the 24th Series, Packard's series changed year by year in step with other year models.

Within the 22nd and 23rd Series, Packard offered three distinct lines. Least expensive was the simple Packard 8 on a 120-inch wheelbase. This used the new 288-cid, 130-bhp engine. Above that came the Super 8 on the same wheelbase but with the 327, 145-bhp 8. Then at the top stood the Custom 8 on a 127-inch chassis, using a completely different,

Packard engineered a new 288-cid block for 1948 (shown), and it shared most components with also-new 327. Both derived from previous 282.

Packard's Electromatic clutch (arrow shows vacuum cylinder) rarely worked right. Most owners disconnected it. Ultramatic arrived in 1949.

Standard on Custom 8s, cormorant was available in lesser series, as were 3 other mascots.

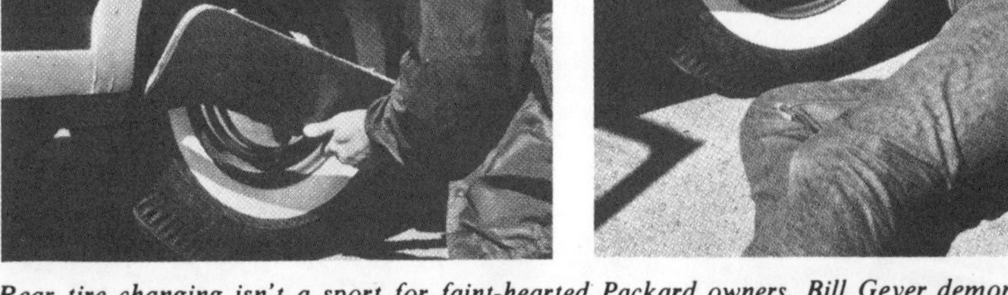

Rear tire changing isn't a sport for faint-hearted Packard owners. Bill Geyer demonstrates his technique by removing the two wingnuts that hold skirt on. To see them, Bill has to lie prone.

Spotter's Guide to Pregnant Packards

-1948: Introduced Aug. 1947 as Packard's 22nd Series. **Identity clues.** Bumper forms lower grille opening. Flush tail lights with horizontal chrome dividers. Full-length chrome strips along rocker panels—one strip on Packard 8s and Super 8s, two strips on Custom 8s. Custom 8s also have eggcrate grilles front and rear.

-1949: Early 1949s were continuation of 22nd Series but had solid front bumpers. Body number 9 on patent plate. In May 1949, Packard's 23rd Series introduced (50th anniversary models). **Identity clues:** Solid front bumper. Horizontal trim spear runs full body length midway up doors. Chrome tail lamp pods. Custom 8s again have eggcrate grilles fore & aft, shared with new Super Deluxe. No suffix number on patent plate.

-1950: Continuation of 23rd Series. No visible differences from later 1949 models. Suffix number on patent plate became 5.

REPRINTED WITH PERMISSION FROM
Special Interest Autos June-July 1973
Box 196, Bennington, Vermont 05201
special interest autos
A Publication from Hemmings Motor News

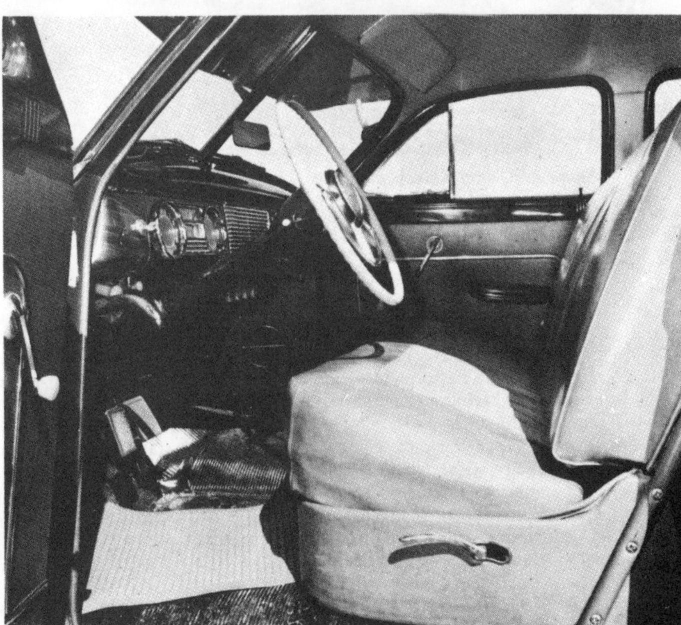

Uninspired gauge cluster makes all dials visible but seems out of keeping with tenor of that era's most expensive wagon. Upholstery is plastic.

Rear seat folds flat to nearly double deck space. Hasps lock seatback in place. Small valuables can be hidden in bins under bottom cushion.

Lovely wooden cargo deck uses stainless-steel ribs to protect finish. Factory said deck could be hosed out, but only a madman would do it.

Packard's smooth, soft ride means mushy suspension, which gives lots of lean in cornering. It's stable on the road, with plenty of brakes.

Spare rests under deck planking. This means you have to unload cargo for spare tire or tools.

Rear window locks with wingnuts. Fumes don't enter while driving with rear window open.

GM-like front suspension makes upper A-arms double as levers for indirect shock absorbers.

Packard Station Sedan *continued*

9-main, 356-cid 8 at 160 bhp, with hydraulic lifters and quite a few refinements in body, chassis, interiors, and trim. Yet even the Custom 8 used the same basic body as the lower lines, because the seven more inches of wheelbase came ahead of the cowl and showed up strictly in hood length.

Within the Packard 8 and Super 8 lines lay standard and deluxe trims. Body styles included a fastback 2-door club sedan, notchback 4-door touring sedan, the Station Sedan in the smallest line only; then the two sedans plus a convertible in the Super and Custom 8s; and finally 7-passenger sedans and limousines in Super and Custom 8s on 141- and 148-inch wheelbases respectively.

Packard's board chairman during the 22nd Series' development was Alvan Macauley, Ed Macauley's father. Alvan was a strong, capable gentleman whose tenure (1916-48) paralleled the company's good years. He ruled benignly from a huge office in Packard's main building in Detroit that covered nearly a whole floor. Alvan Macauley always kept a roaring fire going, and he traditionally served coffee and donuts to visitors, be they employees or outsiders. His manner was friendly, worldly, and of the old school. He wouldn't be rushed, which perhaps helps explain the Series system—it was more important to get out a new car when it was ready than when the calendar dictated. Alvan Macauley's rather leisurely pace set the tone for the whole company, and former employees still remember the low pressure and Packard's freedom from tight deadlines.

Alvan Macauley retired in Mar. 1948, and his place was temporarily taken by Max Gilman and then by George T. Christopher, a man quite unlike Macauley. Christopher had come up through Packard's manufacturing vice presidency and had fought the battles of postwar steel procurement. Those battles left him considerably less relaxed than Macauley had been. Colleagues describe Christopher as ambitious, pushy, hard-headed, not generally liked, but a man who did get things done. Under Christopher, Packard turned its first profits since WW-II. In 1949, his first year in office, Christopher saw the Ultramatic unveiled, the Golden Jubilee celebrated, and a record production of 116,995 cars.

SPECIFICATIONS

1948 Packard Station Sedan 4-door wagon

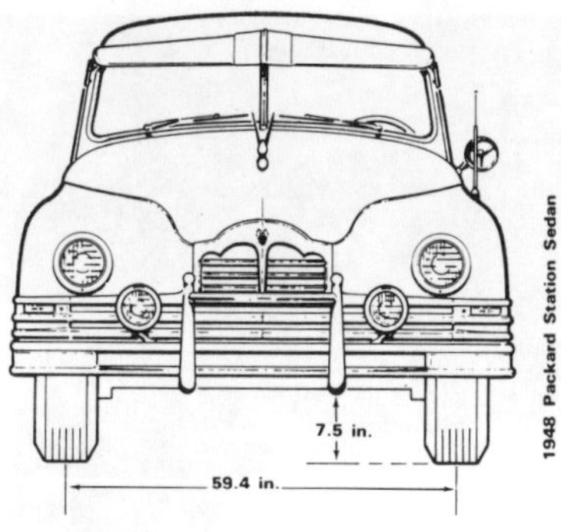

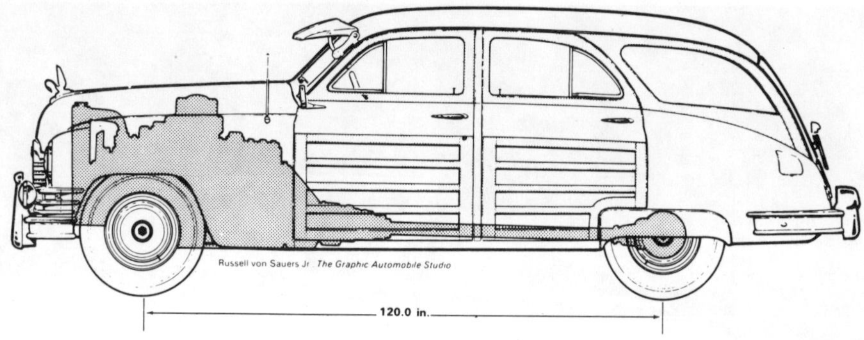

Price when new . . . . . . $3425 f.o.b. Detroit (1948).

Current valuation* . . . . Xlnt. $3542, gd. $1550, fair $530.

Options . . . . Radio, power antenna, heater, visor, Electromatic clutch, overdrive, fog lights, cormorant, whitewalls.

ENGINE

Type . . . . L-head, in-line 8, water cooled, cast-iron block, 5 mains, full pressure lubrication.
Bore & stroke . . . . 3.5 x 3.75 in.
Displacement . . . . . . 288.64 cid.
Max. bhp @ rpm . . . . 130 @ 3600.
Max. torque @ rpm . . 226 @ 2000.
Compression ratio . . . 7.0:1.
Induction system . . . . Carter 2-bbl. downdraft carb.
Electrical system . . . . 6-volt battery/coil.
Exhaust system . . . . . Cast-iron manifold, single exhaust.

CLUTCH

Type . . . . Single dry plate, woven asbestos lining.
Diameter . . . . 10.0 in.
Actuation . . . . Mechanical foot pedal plus electro-vac assist.

TRANSMISSION

Type . . . . 3-speed manual with overdrive, all synchro, column shift.
Ratios: 1st . . . . 2.03:1.
2nd . . . . 1.28:1.
3rd . . . . 1.00:1.
Overdrive . . . 0.61:1.
Reverse . . . . 2.65:1.

DIFFERENTIAL

Type . . . . Hypoid, Hotchkiss drive.
Ratio . . . . 4.10:1.
Drive axles . . . . Semi-floating.

STEERING

Type . . . . Worm & 3-tooth roller.
Turns lock to lock . . . . 3.5.
Ratio . . . . 26.2:1.
Turn circle . . . . 44.0 ft.

BRAKES

Type . . . . 4-wheel hydraulic drums, internal expanding.
Drum diameter . . . . . 12.0 in.
Total lining area . . . . . 171.5 sq. in.

CHASSIS & BODY

Frame . . . . Box & U-section steel siderails with central X-member, 5 crossmembers.
Body construction . . . All steel, wood overlays.
Body style . . . . 4-door, 6-pass. station wagon.

SUSPENSION

Front . . . . Independent SLA, coil springs, hydraulic lever shocks, torsional stabilizer bar.
Rear . . . . Solid axle, semi-elliptic leaf springs, tubular hydraulic shocks, anti-sway bar.
Tires . . . . 7.00 x 15 tube type, 4-ply whitewalls.
Wheels . . . . Pressed steel discs, drop-center rims, lug-bolted to brake drums.

WEIGHTS & MEASURES

Wheelbase . . . . 120.0 in.
Overall length . . . . . . 204.6 in.
Overall height . . . . . . 64.1 in.
Overall width . . . . 77.5 in.
Front tread . . . . 59.4 in.
Rear tread . . . . 60.5 in.
Ground clearance . . . 7.5 in.
Curb weight . . . . 4075 lb.

CAPACITIES

Crankcase . . . . 6 qt.
Cooling system . . . . . 4.5 gal.
Fuel tank . . . . 17 gal.

FUEL CONSUMPTION

Best . . . . 16-18 mpg.
Average . . . . 12-14 mpg.

* Courtesy **Antique Automobile Appraisal,** Prof. Barry Hertz.

But all wasn't rosy under Christopher. According to FORTUNE Magazine, he under-produced the 1948 models and found his dealers screaming for more. Dealers had plenty of customers that year but no cars. On the other hand, they still had lots of leftover '47 Packards that they couldn't sell, and Christopher wasn't about to give any fancy allowances.

Then for 1949, Christopher told everyone he planned to produce 200,000 cars, and anxious dealers, believing him, began expensive expansion programs. They enlarged their showrooms, service areas, and so forth. But despite everyone's high hopes, Packard's 1949 registrations fell 19,000 cars short of production, and even at that, production was only half the 200,000 Christopher had talked about. So dealers were again stuck with leftovers.

Feeling unappreciated, Christopher resigned in Oct. 1949, which put Packard's reins in the hands of Hugh J. Ferry. Ferry had been the company's treasurer for the past 23 years. He served as a capable stopgap president, his most important moves being to commission the radical restyling of 1951 and to seek out a replacement for himself. This last turned out to be James J. Nance.

Bill Geyer met me in Elk Grove, Calif., in his 1948 Station Sedan. You'll recall that Bill kindly lent SIA his 1954 Dodge D-500 convertible for a similar driveReport in SIA #8. I'd seen his Packard wagon before, so when we decided to do our survey of woodies (*preceding article*), I immediately thought of Bill's Station Sedan.

This car shows 70,855 original miles, and Bill, who's a legislative consultant in Sacramento, is its third owner. He bought the wagon from a hobbyist who outbid him at the auction of the original owner's estate. The Station Sedan's interior is especially well preserved, with no signs of water seepage into the cargo area. The exterior looks nearly new, too.

As in most Station Sedans, this one came with almost every option Packard offered in 1948. The cormorant was one of four hood ornaments listed. It was standard on Custom 8s and optional on lesser models. Also available were the "goddess of speed," irreverently known as the boy with the donut; the "Egyptian," which looked like a fancified 1949 Ford hood ornament; and the "flying wing," a low streak of chrome on the Packard 8's nose.

Bill's wagon has overdrive and the Electromatic clutch. His over-

CONTINUED ON PAGE 175

P R O D U C T

BODY on the 1948 Packard Convertible has front fender lines extended through one-piece doors to meet rear fenders.

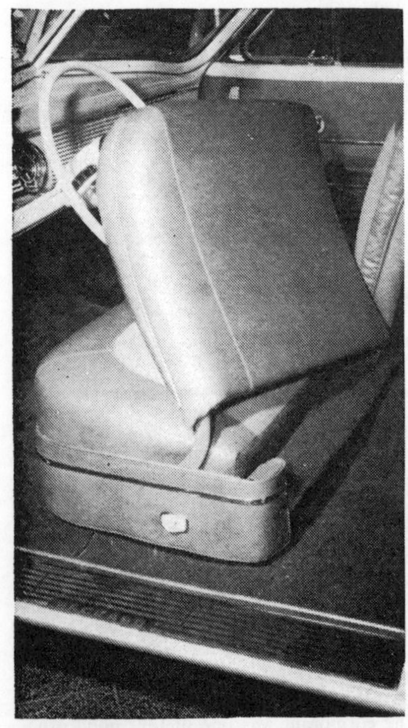

2 FRONT SEAT adjustment is also hydraulically operated by a push button control. Front seat backs are pivoted so that they tip forward and away from the doors, giving room for back seat entrance. Floor is welded steel.

3 ALL INSTRUMENTS on the instrument panel are located in front of the driver. Light reflection from the panel at night is reduced by using filters on panel lights in conjunction with fluorescent painted numerals and pointers on the dials. Radio mounts in the center of the panel. The functions of the various switches are die cast in the control knobs. Circuit breakers are used throughout the electrical system except for fuses in the circuits of the radio and heater. Instrument vision is improved by two spoke steering wheel.

Body Styling And Engine Design Details of the 1948 Packard

Body styling, new 145 hp engine and many improvements in overall design feature the 1948 Packard Convertible. The car has a wheelbase of 120 in. and an overall length of 205 inches. Windows, top and front seat adjustment are hydraulically operated. A twin duct ventilating system has individual controls for regulating the flow of fresh air to the front seat compartment.

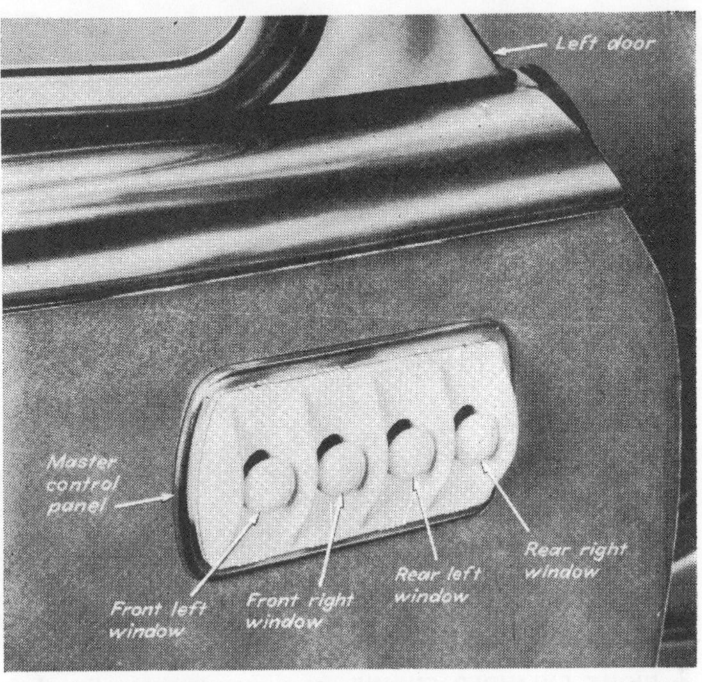

1 ALL WINDOWS are hydraulically operated by pushbutton controls. Controls are individually placed for each passenger. A master control panel is located beside the driver on the left hand door. Upholstery is vinyl plastic and bedford cord construction. The plastic material is used for the interior finish on the double panelled doors. Safety glass windows are outlined with chromium trim. Top is raised and lowered hydraulically.

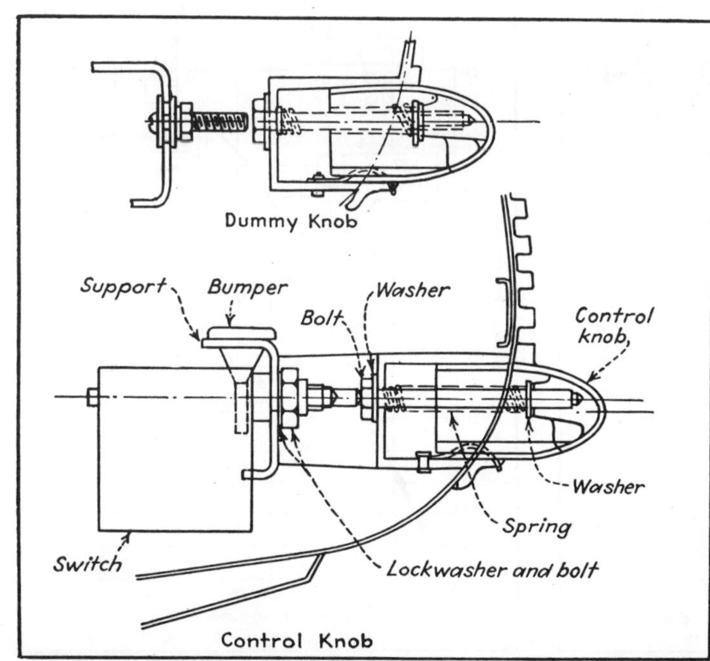

4 CONTROL KNOBS that operate the switches for the lights and accessories stay in trim alignment whether in "on" or "off" position. Switches are mounted on a bracket behind the die cast instrument panel. The control keys operate the switch through a bolt threaded into the knob. After the switch has been operated, a spring returns the knob to its original position. Dummy knobs are mounted in spaces where no switch is required.

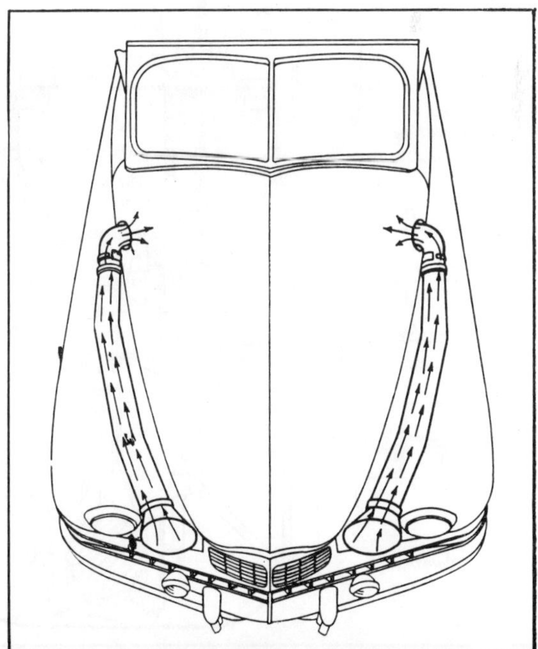

5 FRESH AIR VENTILATION is provided by two welded sheet metal 5 in. dia. ducts. Air enters ducts through the grill and is forced through screened openings at each side of the driver's compartment under the instrument panel. Each duct has individual control knobs on the panel for regulating the amount of fresh air.

6 EIGHT CYLINDER ENGINE has a compression ratio of 7.0 to 1. Former engine had 6.85 to 1 ratio. Cylinder block has been strengthened by rib section additions that were determined from stresscoat analysis. Redesigned manifold gives better fuel distribution by being level when engine is mounted in car. Water pump shaft has been shortened to decrease deflection and reduce wear. Valve diameters have been increased and induction hardened camshaft redesigned. Valve guides are manganese phosphate coated to eliminate former finishing operation after assembly. Cast iron camshaft sprocket is hardened to reduce wear. Coil has been moved from heat wall and is now mounted on engine. Steering gear ratio has been changed from 20.4 to 26.2 to 1, for easier steering.

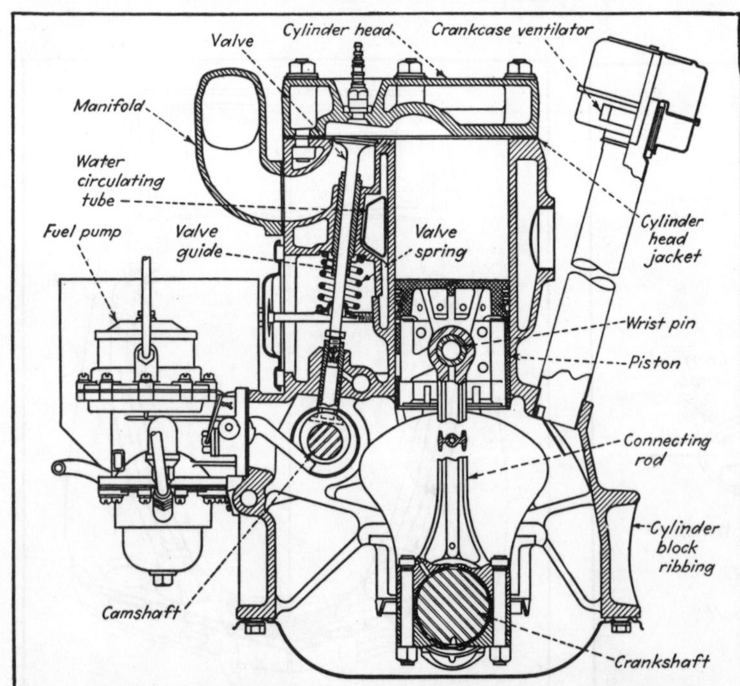

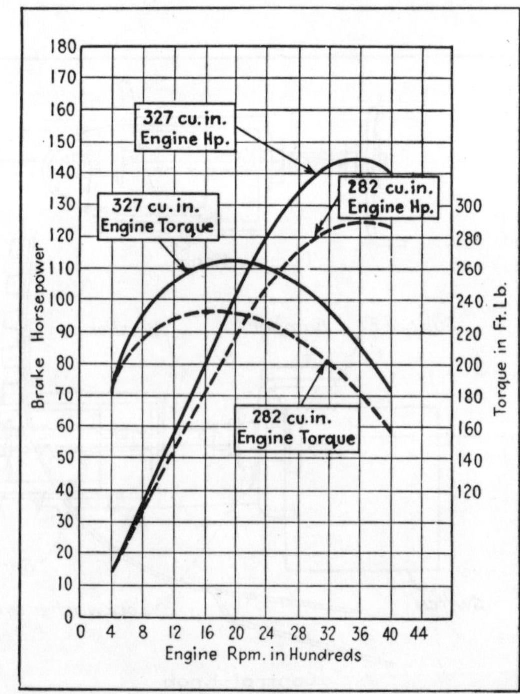

7 VERTICAL SECTION through engine shows moving components. Engine is an L-head type with cylinders cast en bloc. Gasket area between cylinder and block has been increased. Water circulation has been improved by increased size of brass circulating tube section. Crankshaft rod bearing diameter has been increased from 2 3/32 in. to 2¼ in. to reduce loading. Main and connecting rod bearings are a copper nickel matrix with impregnated lead base babbit.

8 NEW ENGINE has 327 cu in. displacement and develops 145 hp at 3,600 rpm. Maximum torque is 266 ft lb at 2,000 rpm. Former engine has 282 cu in. displacement. It developed 125 hp at 3,600 rpm. Maximum torque was 234 ft lb at 1,750 rpm. Axle ratio was changed from 4.1 to 1, to 3.9 to 1 for new engine.

Comfort and Convenience – U.S. Style

THE PICTURES : British semaphore-type traffic signals have been fitted, and this car, which was on the Packard stand at the Earl's Court Show last autumn, has a non-standard emblem which is among listed extras for the car. The lower pair of lamps is used as fog lamps. The radio aerial is raised and lowered by a suction-operated relay.

● The fuel tank filler cap is concealed, but not lockable, though again it can be as an extra. A spanner is needed to deal with the shallow rear wheel shields. The four-light style, once a typically European design, is now common in U.S. cars ; the rear window is not so large as in some American cars.

● The lid of the vast luggage compartment (below) is self-supporting and a light is switched on when it is opened at night. Anti-drumming material is applied prolifically to the interior of the locker.

QUITE apart from their sheer size as full six-seaters in comparison with the average British car, the current American products, of which little has been seen in Great Britain since the war, are interesting as a comparison with British cars of the way in which the user has been studied. In detail features there are perhaps now wider divergences in this respect between the approach in the two countries than used to apply before the war.

A case in point is the latest Packard, one of America's finest cars and one of its oldest makes, which has a decided tradition, although Americans themselves would probably scorn the use of such a word in connection with motor cars. *The Autocar* has recently had an opportunity of inspecting and trying on the road an example of the current 1949 Packard Eight by arrangement with the British concessionaires, Leonard Williams and Co. (1940), Ltd., Great West Road, Brentford, Middlesex.

In engine size and wheelbase this is the smallest of the current Packards, at 4.7 litres and 10ft respectively, and it has a side-valve straight eight engine, a design which, with the exception of one or two examples of six-cylinder engines offered for comparatively short periods, in lower-priced models, has been typically Packard over many years. It has independent front suspension by coil springs. The body is an extremely roomy four-door saloon. Overdrive transmission is fitted, giving a cruising ratio of 2.96 to 1, as compared with the ordinary direct drive top gear ratio of 4.1 to 1, the other ratios of the three-speed gear box being high. The car weighs approximately 37½ cwt.

It must be noted that the price, delivered in New York, is 3,059 dollars (approximately £767), inclusive of the equipment carried by the car that has been seen and tried, and with right-hand drive. The basic factory price without additional equipment is 2,417 dollars, so that a car of this size and luxury, with the name Packard attached to it, can be bought in the U.S., shorn of trimmings, and with its native left-hand drive, for approximately the equivalent of £600.

It is obvious with the U.S. cars generally that what would be called a fully equipped car in Great Britain embodies as standard a number of features treated in America as additions to the basic list price. On the Packard items of extra cost, included in the total price already quoted, were a reversing light, under-bonnet lamp, luggage compartment light, radio, heater, plated exhaust deflector on the tail pipe, seat covers, windscreen washer, bonnet ornament or mascot, and even the shallow rear wheel shields, which are standard, however, on the Custom Eight, biggest and most expensive model of the range. A lockable fuel tank filler is another extra available, as also are a vanity mirror for attaching to the passenger's sun vizor, the special type of rear-view prism mirror which can be adjusted by a touch of the finger to minimize glare from behind at night, and, an interesting offering that seems to comment on the overall size and vision from the modern American car, an external driving mirror.

It is, however, the additional equipment which has a strong appeal, especially to passengers. In the first place, the heater and ventilating system is typically elaborate and effective. The main heater radiator and two-speed fan unit is mounted under the front seat, from which position back seat passengers receive benefit. There is also a separate fan, mounted above the base of the steering column, for circulating warm air for de-misting and de-icing the windscreen, and this secondary unit can circulate warm air round the driver's ankles, a valuable arrangement when it is not required to warm the whole car. Two controls regulate the entry of fresh air through panels set in the scuttle sides. With the change to right-hand drive in the car concerned, only cold fresh air enters thus, and plenty of it when required, but with left-hand drive fresh air can be admitted and warmed before circulation.

Quality Reproduction

An exceedingly good eight-valve radio with press-button control is fitted, possessing a tone range which would be more than acceptable for domestic purposes and which is notably in advance of the reproduction usually obtained in the somewhat difficult conditions applying to car radio. A suction-operated control raises and lowers the aerial.

Another additional item of equipment is a Trico screen spray. When the control for the suction-operated screenwipers is turned in the opposite direction to that for bringing the wipers into operation, fine water sprays are directed on to the screen, enabling it to be cleared of the fine mud film which is a decidedly annoying feature of driving on wet roads when it is not actually raining, besides being useful for removing dead insects.

American and British ideas differ in regard to provision for the carrying of books, packages, maps and so forth, and the shelf which is a common British feature beneath the instrument board seems to be unknown in American cars, which also

DETAIL FEATURES OF A CURRENT PACKARD STRAIGHT EIGHT, ONE OF AMERICA'S CLASS CARS

do not usually have door pockets. In the Packard, for compensation, there is a lockable compartment of useful size in the left of the facia, whilst behind the back seat, beneath the rear window, is a very useful shelf for the convenience of back-seat passengers.

When either front door is opened, lights placed immediately under the facia are illuminated, and these can be switched on separately at other times for map reading. The roof light in the rear compartment is operated by opening either rear door as well as by an over-riding switch. The instruments are illuminated by "black lighting," the figures and needles standing out in luminous green against a purple background in a way which is attractive as well as effective. A detail which causes interest at filling stations is that as petrol is put in, a warning whistle comes from a device known as the Ventalarm, incorporated in the tank filler neck, as a safeguard against overfilling. Easy removal of the whole bonnet is a feature. Normally, it opens from the side, in one piece.

Door Locking Details

The Americans have developed a different door-locking technique from that on British cars, and this Packard is a typical instance. All doors can be locked from inside by means of a press-down knob, but one cannot lock oneself out of the car, for when the door handle is operated to open the door this locking control is overridden. Both forward doors have key locks, and, for instance, the driver can lock the right-hand door by means of the press-button mentioned, get out by the left-hand door, lock that by means of the key and then subsequently re-enter the car by using the key on the right-hand door. Only a half-turn of the key is needed for either locking or unlocking. There are various circumstances of parking in which this arrangement proves valuable, especially with a wide single-piece front seat and cloth upholstery with which it is not really convenient for the driver to slide himself along to get out of the car by the opposite door.

The starter motor is operated by full depression of the throttle pedal, only when the ignition is switched on,

Specification in Brief

PRICE, with four-door touring sedan body with additional equipment, $2,984 f.o.b. Detroit. Basic price, $2,417 = £604 approx.

ENGINE : 39.2 h.p., 8 cylinders, side valves, 88.9 × 95.2 mm, 4,720 c.c. Five-bearing counterbalanced crankshaft with torsional vibration damper.

BRAKE HORSE-POWER: 130 at 3,600 r.p.m. **COMPRESSION RATIO:** 7.00 to 1.

MAX TORQUE : 226 lb ft at 2,000 r.p.m. 21.2 m.p.h. per 1,000 r.p.m. on top gear.

OVERALL GEAR RATIOS : 2.96 (overdrive), 4.1, 6.27 and 9.96 to 1.

TRANSMISSION : Single-plate semi-centrifugal clutch. Open propeller-shaft to hypoid bevel rear axle.

WEIGHT : 37 cwt 2 qr 10lb (4,210lb). **LB per C.C. :** 0.89. **B.H.P. per TON :** 69.17.

TYRE SIZE : 7.00 × 15in on bolt-on steel disc wheels. **LIGHTING SET :** 6-volt.

TANK CAPACITY : 15½ Imperial gallons : approximate fuel consumption range, 12-16 m.p.g.

BRAKES : Hydraulic front and rear. **STEERING :** Worm and roller.

SUSPENSION : Independent coil spring front, with anti-roll bar; half-elliptic rear springs with lateral stabilizer.

TURNING CIRCLE : 44ft (L and R). **MINIMUM GROUND CLEARANCE :** 7 11/16in.

MAIN DIMENSIONS : Wheelbase, 10ft 0in. Track, 4ft 11 11/32in (front) ; 5ft 0 15/32in (rear). Overall length, 17ft 0⅝in ; width, 6ft 5 15/32in ; height, 5ft 4 1/16in.

and return from the overdrive to ordinary top gear can be made by full depression of the throttle pedal through a solenoid-operated relay. On the Packard the overdrive comes into operation at about 25 m.p.h., and goes automatically out of action at approximately 20 m.p.h.

The eight-cylinder engine was found to be delightfully smooth and quiet right through the range, and maximum speed was in the order of a genuine 90 m.p.h. at a speedometer reading of 100. The riding is soft, as would be expected. There is reasonable control of the suspension for fast cornering by means of an anti-sway bar in front and what Packard term a fifth shock absorber, forming part of a lateral stabilizer connected between the rear spring bracket on one side and a frame cross-member on the other side. The steering is light right down to manœuvring speeds, and, of course, low geared, four and a half turns of the wheel being required from lock to lock. Clutch action is so smooth that the eight-cylinder engine will start the car without protest on top gear on the level, provided that reasonable care is taken in releasing the pedal. The steering column gear change is very smooth and light, by means of a slightly cranked lever.

The doors remain open at these positions under the control of check devices. No use is made of the thickness of the doors to provide pockets for maps and books. Loose covers were fitted over the cloth upholstery. The rotary door latches will be noticed.

Golden Anniversary Packard Models

A New Torque-converter Transmission Offered on the Largest of Three Straight-eight Models

ULTRAMATIC is the name which Packard have coined for their newly introduced transmission, which marks a further step forward in the development of torque converter installations. Standardized initially on the largest of their three straight-eight models, it is to be built in gradually increasing numbers which at a later date will allow it to be offered as an optional extra on other models.

Three stages are incorporated in an Ultramatic Drive unit to handle varied road conditions, the most important being the hydraulic torque converter. This is a relatively simple version of a device which is rapidly gaining popularity, comprising a centrifugal oil pump impeller unit on the engine flywheel, an output turbine, a vaned reaction member located on a free-wheel clutch which allows it to overrun in one direction only, and a secondary turbine providing extra torque for acceleration or hill climbing.

This particular torque converter design uses aluminium alloy castings for its main functional parts. If the car is accelerated away from a standstill with the throttle snapped wide open, it will initially let the engine run at about 1,600 r.p.m. and will deliver to the rear axle approximately 2.4 times engine output torque. As the car gains speed, the engine r.p.m. will rise very gradually, and output torque to the rear axle will drop, until at 50 m.p.h. the engine will be doing slightlv over 2,000 r.p.m. on virtually a direct drive.

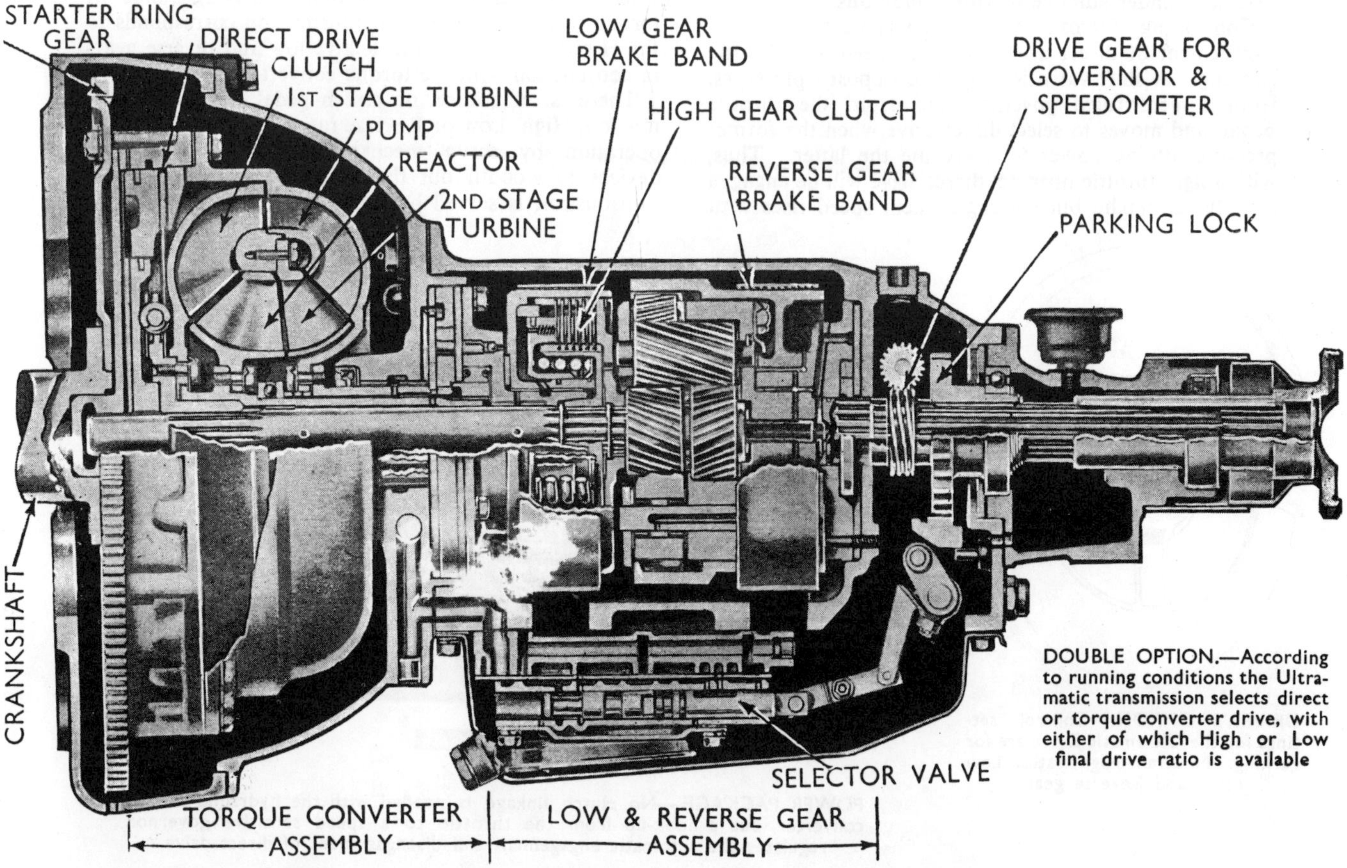

STARTER RING GEAR
DIRECT DRIVE CLUTCH
1ST STAGE TURBINE
PUMP
REACTOR
2ND STAGE TURBINE
LOW GEAR BRAKE BAND
HIGH GEAR CLUTCH
REVERSE GEAR BRAKE BAND
DRIVE GEAR FOR GOVERNOR & SPEEDOMETER
PARKING LOCK
CRANKSHAFT
SELECTOR VALVE
TORQUE CONVERTER ASSEMBLY
LOW & REVERSE GEAR ASSEMBLY

DOUBLE OPTION.—According to running conditions the Ultramatic transmission selects direct or torque converter drive, with either of which High or Low final drive ratio is available

POPULAR LINE.—Low-priced model of the Packard range is the two-door Club Sedan, on the 135 b.h.p. (British rating 39 h.p.) straight eight chassis with synchro-mesh transmission.

Between the torque converter and the propeller shaft an epicyclic gear train is located which, as on another recently standardized American transmission, provides a reverse drive and also an emergency low gear. The latter is not required in ordinary driving, but is available to provide engine over-run braking down steep hills, prompt re-starts on freak gradients, or the utmost acceleration at speeds below 50 m.p.h.; ordinarily, a multi-plate clutch locks the epicyclic gear train into a single unit.

The real innovation on the Packard is the third component of the Ultramatic drive, a friction clutch which can be engaged to give a solid drive without any slip in the hydraulic torque converter. Direct drive is automatically engaged during much ordinary open road driving, to eliminate any annoying sudden rise and fall in engine r.p.m. in response to throttle movements, and to save petrol by reducing the number of engine revolutions made per mile of road.

Fluid or Solid Drive

This clutch is a single plate type, cork lined and operating in oil like the torque converter whose two halves it can link. Engagement is by a special controlled feed of pressure oil, acting through the medium of an annular piston, and takes place positively and automatically under suitable driving conditions.

Controlling factors in the engagement and disengagement of direct drive are road speed and throttle opening. A shift valve is subject to opposed pressures, from a centrifugal governor and from the throttle pedal, and moves to select direct drive when the former pressure attains power to overcome the latter. Thus, with a light throttle opening, direct drive will be engaged at only 15 m.p.h., but the engagement speed rises with throttle pressure until at full throttle a speed of 55 m.p.h. must be attained before governor pressure suffices to select direct drive.

Once direct drive is engaged, it remains in use either until the car is slowed to 15 m.p.h., or until the driver opens the throttle fully at some speed between 15 and 50 m.p.h. To a driver, Ultramatic drive will have much in common with an overdrive unit, in that an upward change from acceleration to cruising ratio is delayed during hard acceleration, while below 50 m.p.h. it is possible to kick-down on the throttle pedal and regain accelerating gear.

The driving controls of the new Packard have been kept closely in accord with those used with the other quantity-produced torque converter transmission of to-day, comprising a steering column lever moving an indicator along a 5-position quadrant. Markings on this quadrant are P—N—H—L—R, a safety switch (the only electrical component in the system) rendering the electrical engine starter inoperative unless the lever is in the P or N position.

On this quadrant both P and N represent "free engine" positions with no power transmitted to the road wheels; N, however, corresponds to a true neutral gear, in which the car can coast, whereas P engages a pawl to lock the propeller shaft and hold the car stationary where it is parked. The ordinary driving range of torque converter and direct transmission corresponds to the H setting, while L and R give low and reverse gears in conjunction with the torque converter.

There is, of course, no clutch pedal with this transmission, High, Low or Reverse ratios being brought into operation by servo mechanisms which incorporate devices to smooth out their engagement. The whole transmission is served by a pair of Gerotor oil pumps,

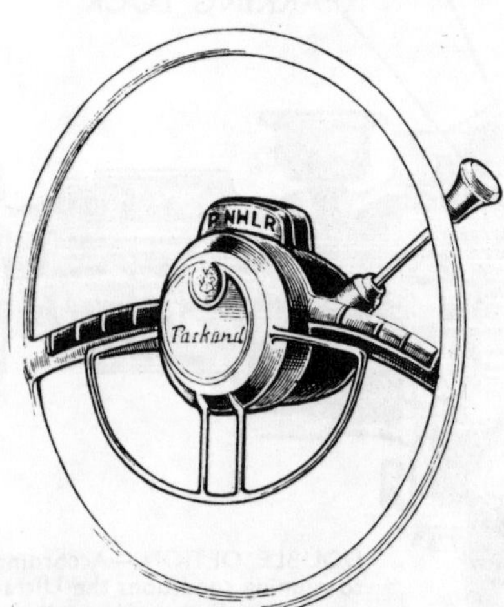

DRIVER'S OPTION.—Control settings for the Ultramatic Drive are for Parking, Neutral, High ratio, Low ratio, and Reverse gear.

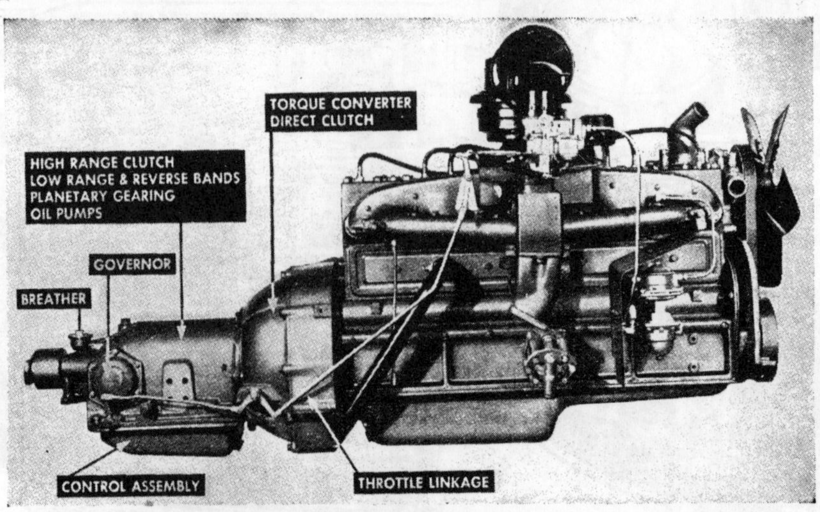

POWER PACKAGE.—No clutch linkage is needed with the hydraulic torque converter, but a hook-up from the throttle to a speed sensitive governor regulates the automatic engagement and disengagement of direct drive.

on input and output shafts respectively, the circulation system incorporating an oil cooler. The speed-sensitive governor is a non-electric centrifugal unit, rotating bob weights adjusting the setting of an oil pressure regulating valve in accordance with car speed.

As has been said, use of this new transmission is at present confined to the "Custom" model Packard, on which it is standardized Smaller cars of the range are as yet still being equipped with three-speed synchromesh gearboxes, which may optionally be supplemented by kick-down overdrive units.

Apart from the new transmission, which represents a notable step forward in the torque converter field, the models which celebrate Packard's 50th year in the automobile industry incorporate evolutionary, as distinct from revolutionary, changes. Fourteen different body styles are offered, each in any of nine colours, closely resembling 1949 designs, although certain models incorporate much-enlarged rear windows.

Straight-eight engines of 3½-in. cylinder bore are used in all models, but three lengths of stroke provide a range of power outputs. The smaller models use five-bearing crankshafts, the long-stroke Custom model which alone has hydraulic self-adjusting tappets boasts a nine-bearing crankshaft weighing 104 lb. Power outputs of all engines have been slightly increased by a torque-boosting camshaft modification, and durability is claimed to have been improved by new piston and ring assemblies and heavier-duty steel-backed crankshaft bearings. In contrast to the current American trend towards ever higher compression ratios, Packard claim that their side-valve engines with 7-1 compression ratio do not require the "premium" price high-octane fuels now marketed in U.S.A.

Chassis Details

Chassis on all models are laid out with X-braced box-section side members, special frames being used for cars equipped with convertible coachwork to compensate for reduced body stiffness. Front suspension is by hydraulically damped coil springs, linked by an anti-roll torsion bar, with wishbone linkages for wheel location. The hypoid-geared rear axles support the chassis by means of half-elliptic leaf springs, 54¾ ins. long, which take drive reactions. Rear springs have rubber-bushed shackles, and composition inserts separate their leaves, a transverse stabilizer rod and fifth shock absorber correcting for any resultant lack of lateral rigidity.

Interesting detail alterations have recently been introduced into the bodies, such as seat cushions which may be adjusted to a spring strength suiting the owner. Convertible coachwork on the Super and Custom chassis uses electro-hydraulic power for raising and lowering the roof and windows, also for seat adjustment, the latter two features being optional extras on 4-door closed cars. Where this extra electrical equipment is installed on a car, the dynamo output capacity is stepped up from 40 amps to 45 amps, on a 6-volt system.

The policy of gradual design evolution has allowed Packard to put their Golden Anniversary models into production without delays. Dealers from all parts of North America collected 2,000 gold-painted examples of their latest lines as long ago as May 3.

PACKARD DATA

Model	Eight	Super de Luxe	Custom
Engine Dimensions:			
Cylinders	Straight 8	Straight 8	Straight 8
Bore	89 mm.	89 mm.	89 mm.
Stroke	95.3 mm.	108 mm.	117.5 mm.
Cubic capacity	4,720 c.c.	5,360 c.c.	5,840 c.c.
Piston area	77 sq. ins.	77 sq. ins.	77 sq. ins.
Valves	Side	Side	Side
Compression ratio	7.0 to 1	7.0 to 1	7.0 to 1
Engine Performance:			
Max. power	135 b.h.p.	150 b.h.p.	160 b.h.p.
at	3,600 r.p.m.	3,600 r.p.m.	3,600 r.p.m.
Max. b.m.e.p.	—	123 lb./sq. in.	120 lb./sq. in.
at	—	2,000 r.p.m.	2,000 r.p.m.
B.h.p. per sq. in. piston area	1.75	1.95	2.08
Peak piston speed ft. per min.	2,250	2,550	2,780
Engine Details:			
Carburetter	Dual downdraught	Dual downdraught	Dual downdraught
Ignition	6-volt coil	6-volt coil	6-volt coil
Sparking plugs	10 mm.	14 mm.	—
Fuel pump	Mechanical	Mechanical	Mechanical
Fuel capacity	14 gallons	16¼ gallons	16½ gallons
Oil capacity	11½ pints	11½ pints	11½ pints
Cooling system	Pump and fan	Pump and fan	Pump and fan
Water capacity	3¾ gallons	4 gallons	4 gallons
Electrical system	6-volt, 40-amp. generator	6-volt, 40-amp. generator	6-volt, 40-amp generato
Battery capacity	100 amp.-hrs.	100 amp.-hrs.	120 amp.-hrs.
Transmission:			
Clutch	Semi-centrifugal 10" single dry plate	Semi-centrifugal 10½" single dry plate	Ultramatic drive (Torque converter
Gear ratios:			
Overdrive	—	2.96 to 1	—
Direct drive	3.9 to 1	4.1 to 1	3.54 to 1
2nd	5.96 to 1	6.27 to 1	6.44 to 1
1st	9.44 to 1	9.92 to 1	—
Rev.	12.34	13.0 to 1	5.80 to 1
Prop. shaft	3" open; needle roller universals	3" open; needle roller universals	3' open; needle roller universals
Final drive	Hypoid bevel	Hypoid bevel	Hypoid bevel
Chassis Details:			
Brakes	Self-energizing hydraulic	Self-energizing hydraulic	Self-energizing hydraulic
Friction lining area	172 sq. ins.	—	208 sq. ins.
Suspension:			
Front	Coil I.F.S.	Coil I.F.S.	Coil I.F.S.
Rear	Semi-elliptic leaf	Semi-elliptic leaf	Semi-elliptic leaf
Shock absorbers	Hydraulic	Hydraulic	Hydraulic
Wheel type	Steel disc	Steel disc	Steel disc
Tyre size	7.60 × 15	8.20 × 15	8.20 × 15
Steering gear	Worm and 3-tooth roller	Worm and 3-tooth roller	Worm and 3-tooth roller
Dimensions:			
Wheelbase	10 ft. 0 in.	10 ft. 7 ins.	10 ft. 7 ins.
Track:			
Front	4 ft. 11½ ins.	5ft. 0 in.	5 ft. 0½ in.
Rear	5 ft. 0½ in.	5ft. 1 in.	5 ft. 1 in.
Overall length	17 ft. 0¾ in.	17 ft 7¾ ins.	17 ft. 9¼ ins.
Overall width	6 ft. 5½ ins.	6 ft. 5½ ins.	6 ft. 5½ins.
Overall height	5 ft. 4 ins.	5 ft. 3 ins.	5 ft. 3½ ins.
Ground clearance	7 ins.	—	—
Turning circle	44 ft.	45 ft.	45 ft.
Dry weight	34 cwt.	34½ cwt.	35½ cwt.
Performance Data:			
Piston area, sq. ins. per ton	45.3	44.7	43.4
Brake lining area, sq. ins. per ton	101	—	117
Top gear m.p.h. per 1,000 r.p.m.	21.2	(Overdrive) 28.6 m.p.h.	23.9 m.p.h.
Top gear m.p.h. at 2,500 ft./min. piston speed	85 m.p.h.	(Overdrive) 101 m.p.h.	77.5 m.p.h.
Litres per ton-mile, dry	3,940	(Direct 3rd) 4,520	4,130

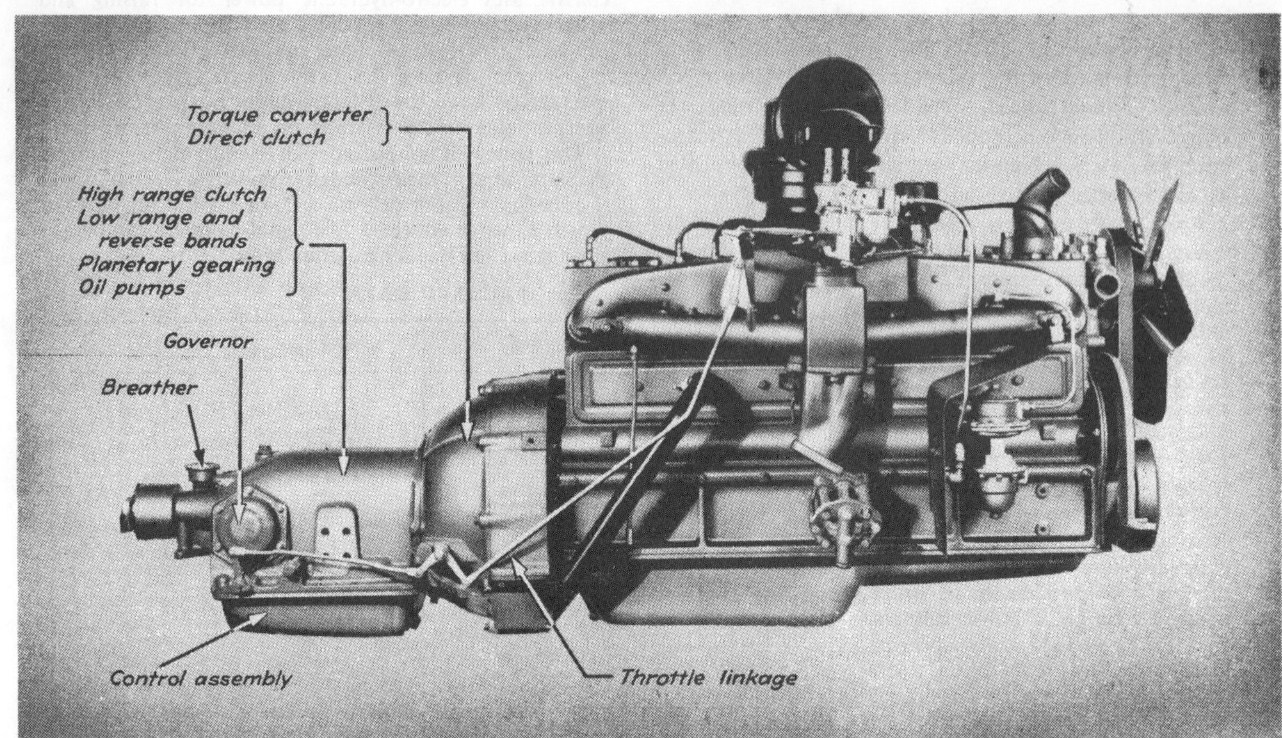

PACKARD TRANSMISSION has two clutches—one forward and the other to the rear of the torque converter. The high range clutch connects the converter directly to the drive shaft. This clutch bypasses all gearing so that converter alone must provide the multiplication of engine torque needed to start and accelerate the car. The direct drive clutch is located between the engine and the torque converter turbine. Car speed and throttle position control the engagement of the direct drive clutch, which rigidly connects engine to rear wheels and allows converter to "float".

Packard's Ultramatic Drive

The torque converter in Packard's automatic transmission is intended only for acceleration. At cruising speeds, a direct-drive clutch completes a mechanical connection between engine and rear wheels. This renders the torque converter inoperative, preventing wasteful slip and oil churning after the coupling point is reached. The driver's control of the direct drive clutch is similar to his control of the fourth speed in overdrive cars. At speeds between 15 and 56 mph, a momentary release of the gas pedal causes the direct drive clutch to engage. Within this same range of speeds, the driver can disengage this clutch and return to converter operation by pushing the pedal to the floor. Above 56 mph, the direct drive clutch is engaged regardless of throttle setting. During deceleration, the car stays in direct drive until speed drops to 13 mph. Thus, the engine aids braking.

LIGHTED LAMP behind the sector letters tells driver what position the controls are in. Cars with Ultramatic have no clutch pedal or gear shift lever. Engagement of the direct-drive clutch depends on throttle opening and car speed. For every throttle position there is a definite speed at which clutch operates automatically—unless the driver chooses to exercise his control over clutch before that point is reached.

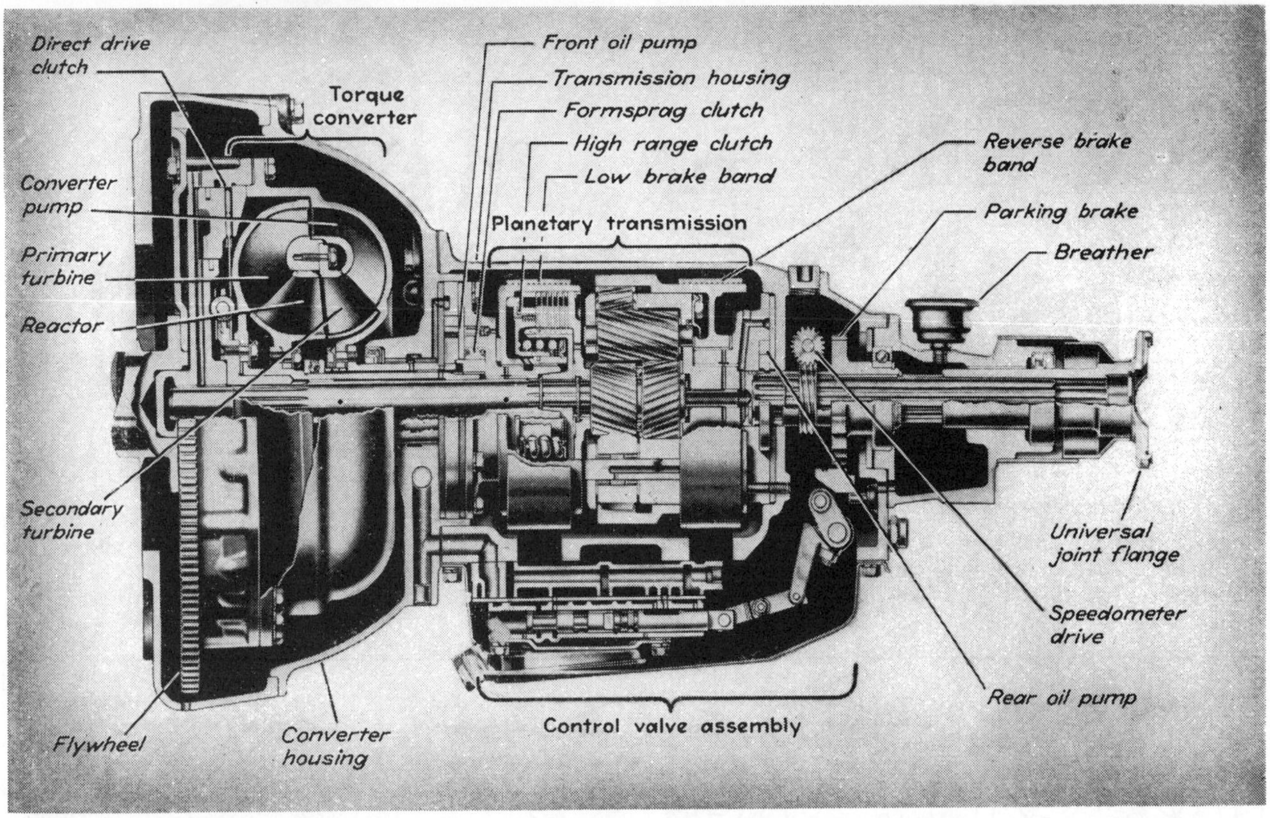

TO SIMPLIFY CONSTRUCTION, the rotor units are flanged and bolted to hubs which engage with quill shafts. These quill shafts extend back to the planetary transmission. The converter pump rotor is attached to a quill shaft that acts as a seal and outboard bearing for the unit. This shaft also drives the front oil supply pump. A second quill shaft inside the first carries the reactor and extends through the pump to an overrunning clutch. The direct drive clutch disk and the turbine are both fixed to the hub which is splined to the transmission input shaft.

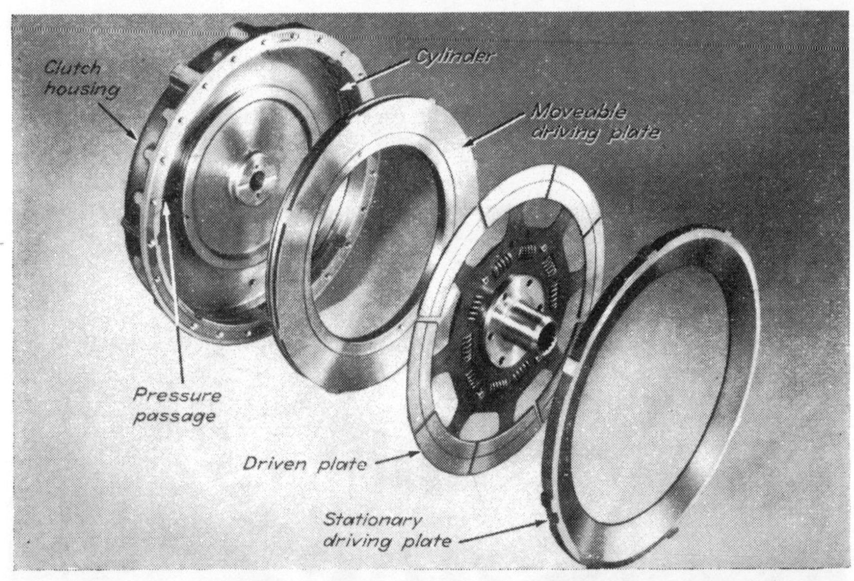

HOUSING of direct clutch rotates with the flywheel. For engagement, oil passes through hollow transmission input shaft, then through radial pressure passage into clutch cylinder. The oil shifts the moveable driving plate, forcing the driven plate against the stationary driving plate. Then, engine torque is transmitted directly to the driven plate which is splined to the input shaft.

MORSE-FORMSPRAG overrunning clutch holds reactor stationary at low speeds, allows it to turn with turbine and pump after coupling point is reached. (*continued on next page*)

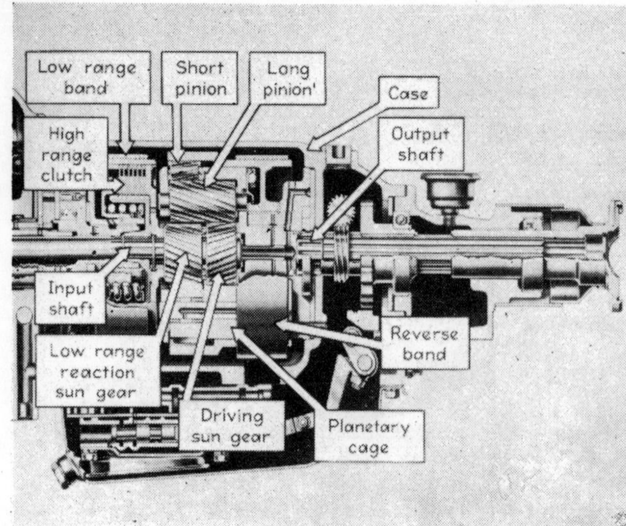

HIGH RANGE CLUTCH, when engaged, locks the low range reaction sun gear to the clutch hub that is splined to the input shaft and driving sun gear. This locks the planetary system which then rotates with the input shaft.

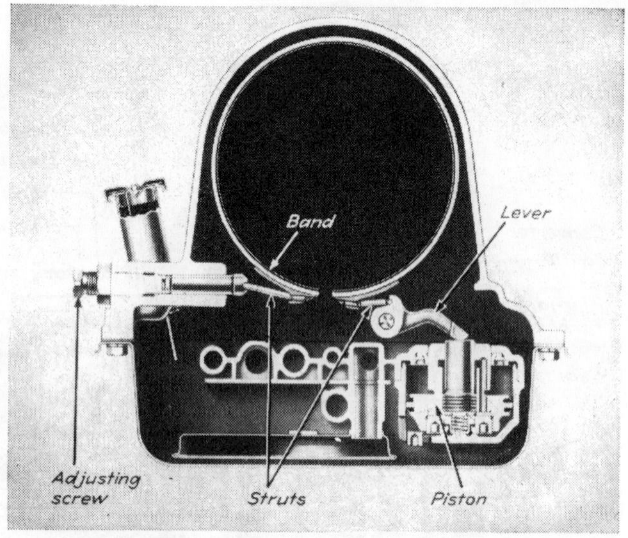

LOW RANGE BAND holds the low range reaction sun gear when gear reduction is required. One end of the band is held in position by an adjustable strut while the other end is operated by the piston of the hydraulic unit.

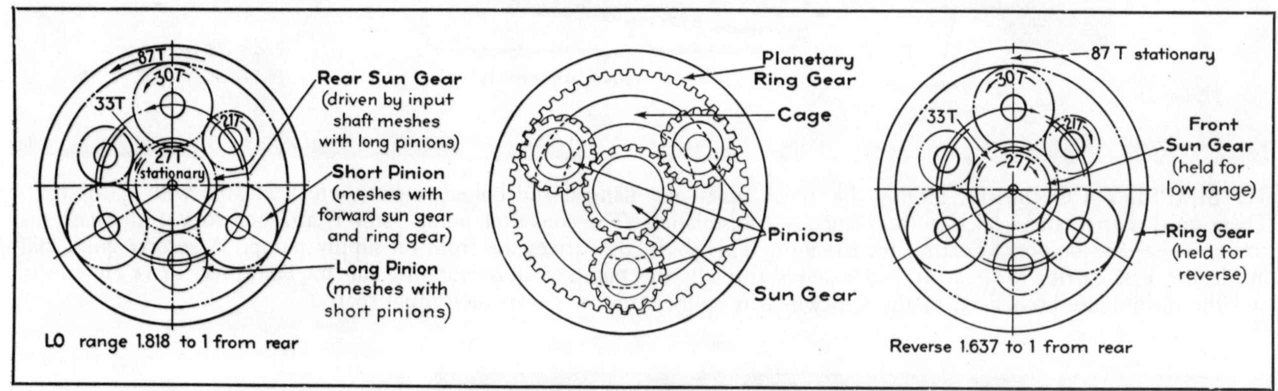

WHEN REAR SUN GEAR is rotating and the pinion cage is stationary, the long pinions turn counterclockwise and the short pinions clockwise. If the forward sun gear is held, the short pinions will walk the planetary cage around clockwise at a reduced speed. Releasing the forward sun gear and holding the ring gear causes short pinions to walk the cage counterclockwise inside the ring gear, giving reverse at a reduced speed.

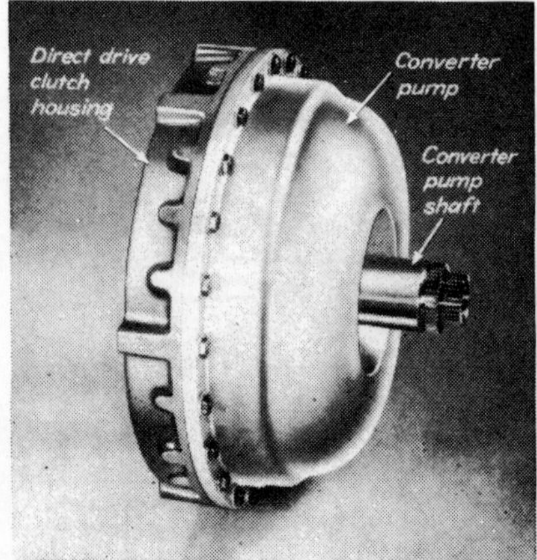

DIRECT DRIVE clutch housing and converter pump are assembled as a unit and bolted to flywheel.

TURBINES, converter pump and reactor are mainly sand cast from aluminum. This represents a considerable cost saving over entirely plaster cast units. The finish of the sand castings is smooth enough for efficient performance.

New Packard Takes McCahill for a Ride

Here's an official photo release showing the Golden Anniversary Packard going through a test—without McCahill at the wheel.

Ease of handling is more important than performance, officials at Packard say, but Tom McCahill wonders if that's really true.

SINCE kicking an old lady in the teeth is considered bad form in many circles, I'll try to go easy with the Golden Anniversary Packard.

This time I'm going to ask you readers to draw your own conclusions. I'll lay all the cards on the table and tell you exactly how much I know about this job. And this isn't much, because I wasn't allowed to give the car a regular test.

This story starts last winter when I was in California. There I received a special delivery from MI's editor telling me that Packard has the latest in automatic transmission and asking me to test it on my way east. In April, when I was in Detroit, I called the factory. "Sorry, no regular test," a company official told me, but I could "see" the car. I answered that my only interest was in giving the Packard the same test I gave all other cars. The company official assured me I could do just this on the Packard proving grounds on June 1. So I waited.

I phoned from Indianapolis May 31 to remind the Packard people I was on my way and would go directly to the proving ground. They told me to call again in the morning for verification—to make sure a car would be available.

In Detroit my proving ground test was stalled. I was advised to come to the factory for a talk with Forest McFarland, chief research engineer, who would take me for a ride in the car. I smelled a mouse and that smell was getting stronger by the minute. When I entered the factory, I was practically sure the Packard people weren't going to permit any real test. This was quickly confirmed during lunch with a

Dashboard, top, reveals no major changes, except for absence of clutch. Grilled circle on floor is ventilator.

That wishful look in Tom's eyes, center, indicates his longing to give this new Packard a real McCahill test.

Luggage compartment of the convertible, right, is roomy. Redesigned stop-lights now have built-in turn indicators.

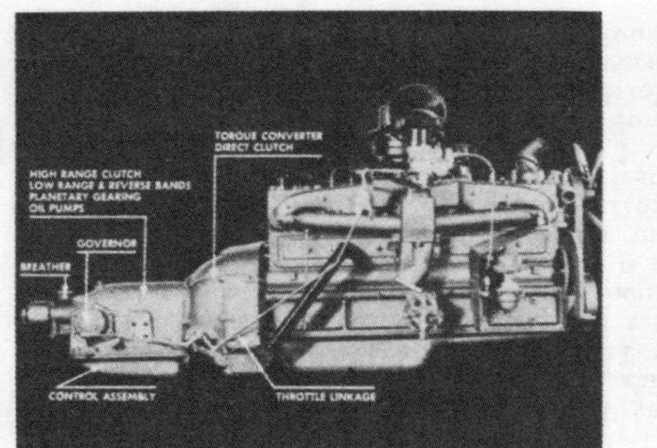

Torque converter for acceleration with positive mechanical drive for cruising makes Ultramatic Drive "very responsive," according to Packard press releases.

company public-relations officer who was ducking like a ruffed grouse in a forest.

Maybe it was a coincidence but it did seem strange that no car was available for a test since Packard had known for more than a month *exactly* when I was coming to try out their new model. I was told that the new Ultramatic drive was only on the large Packards and that there were only four around. Three were making a company test run and couldn't be disturbed. The fourth was being prepared for a Society of Automotive Engineers meeting. I would be allowed to drive this one—but *not* on the proving grounds.

In the interest of MI's readers, I tried another tack. I told the public-relations man I frankly thought Packard was afraid to let me test the car because I might find it a tomato. This brought no response.

After lunch, McFarland showed up with a beautiful convertible. Off we drove, heading for Belle Isle. The car ran, the wheels seemed to stay in place, but it was a highly unimpressive ride.

Once on the Isle and in a strict 20-mile-an-hour zone with cops always in sight, McFarland let me drive this wonder car. I repeated that this was no good for MI, that I needed a place where I could really run this goat to find out if it was any damn good. I told him I needed my own stopwatch acceleration figures and general performance data. McFarland replied:

"From a sales and merchandizing standpoint, Packard feels the public is more interested in riding comfort and ease of handling than in acceleration figures and high-speed performance, and therefore, the company never releases such figures."

This may be true. I don't know. But I feel that when a guy lays out close to $5000 for a 160-hp, 4600-pound convertible he would like to know that a kid on a whizzer bike won't be able to pin his ears back on breaking from a light. As for comfort, I did succeed in finding my way into two bad ruts and the Packard took them slightly better than a 1949 $2000 car.

I made at least a dozen additional stabs to get a real test, saying I would make my own timing checks as usual. It was no dice. For the test—such as it was—I put the Ultramatic drive into high range and shot the throttle to the floor. This reminded me of a show I saw at the old New York Hippodrome when I was a kid. They had a fire engine on the stage with a steam pumper snorting flames from a funnel and four white horses were supposedly pulling it. They ran like mad on a treadmill as bells rang and people shouted.

Well, the Packard was revving up but we weren't going anywhere fast. The public-relations man shouted,

"Here comes a cop."

Sure enough, a little police car whizzed by, doing all of 20 mph. It was like making a test in Times Square. People were all over the road in bathing suits and cars were parking all over the place. Testing was out. At one point, I think I did get this equippage up to 35 mph. But then more cops loomed up. I slowed down and headed back for the factory, never less impressed with any car.

The anniversary gimmick with Packard is the new Ultramatic drive. This, they readily admit, is very similar to Buick's Dynaflow with one addition—direct drive at speeds above 15 miles an hour. The Ultramatic is controlled with throttle toe-tip pressure, similar to overdrive in other cars.

Incidentally, the only thing I did get out of McFarland, after practically getting down on one knee and singing "Mammy," was that the new Packards performed just about equal with the new Buicks—according to McFarland.

I can see nothing to be gained by going into detail about all the multiple wonders of the new Ultramatic. These features have now been written up in most of the trade publications and it is doubtful if any MI reader will try building a similar device at home. In short, the Ultramatic is just another type of automatic, hydraulic transmission, boasting a direct-drive feature.

McFarland says Packard feels ease of handling—meaning automatic shifting—is more important than performance. I wonder. Some of the

New Packard

more complicated automatic transmissions cost more to manufacture per car than do engines, because of precise and elaborate multiple gearing. I wonder if some buyers wouldn't rather have this extra cost shoved into improved engines and all-around car quality. For example, why shouldn't a car be delivered with all four wheels balanced? Not one in 50,000 is. This would cost peanuts on a large scale, would greatly increase the handling and safety factors of all cars and would extend tire life.

A balanced wheel is one that has no high points of weight around its circumference. An unbalanced wheel is caused by any one of a number of factors, such as distortion wheel, a heavy spot in the tire, and, quite often, a tube valve. Anything aside from equal weight distribution around the entire wheel and tire produces an eccentric, or wobble, that causes wheel shimmy, tire wear and poor handling qualities at higher speeds. Four such unbalanced wheels can prove a definite menace to the car's roadability.

To balance a wheel, several methods are employed including an electric wheel balancer and a mechanical unit. Any faults in off-center weight distribution can easily be counteracted by the addition of lead weights inserted in the tire rim at strategic spots. Naturally, this must be done with correct wheel-balancing equipment. Ninety per cent of all tires and wheels delivered on cars today are unbalanced to some degree. But as this error is rarely noticed at moderate speeds, nearly all cars on the highway today are actually traveling on four unbalanced wheels.

I'll tell you why I don't think such things as balanced wheels are added. Joe Blow who buys a car thinks wheel balancing is just another juggling act for a television show. Therefore it definitely doesn't have the "merchandizing appeal" (to quote McFarland).

Personally, I feel most manufacturers today are like blind moles running after each other in a tunnel. What one does, all must do.

I wonder just how many buyers are really interested in these extra-tariff automatic transmissions? How about sending me a penny postal card, saying yes or no on automatic transmissions. Maybe we can find out the real score. If you do, I'll see that every manufacturer hears how you feel about it.

In summing up, the Golden Anniversary Packard is just about the same as last year's offering, plus the new transmission. Though only available in the biggest jobs now, it supposedly will be on all models in a year. •

MI Tests The New Packard

CONTINUED FROM PAGE 6

tends to keep the rising side down on the same level with the opposite side, so the entire car stays on an even keel. To try this out I took a sharp curve doing better than 50 miles an hour, and was amazed at how much it felt like driving a speed boat, which as you know, always leans into a curve.

The Packard Clipper boasts many little refinements not practical from a commercial standpoint in a really low-priced car; for example, the lighted turn indicator, the twin electric windshield wipers, and the counterbalanced trunk hinges of flat-coil springs which make opening easy.

You must bear in mind that the 125 horsepower engine will not be as economical to operate as smaller engines, and repairs, when they come, will run higher.

The Packard Clipper is a fine automobile, luxurious in appointments and finish, and it will meet all comers in performance. If you are looking for a car in the top medium-priced bracket I recommend that you personally investigate the Packard Clipper "8."

The mechanical specifications are as follows:

Wheel base	120 inches
Overall length	208 7/16 inches
Overall width	76 1/8 inches
Overall height	64 inches
Shipping weight, 4-door sedan	3560 lbs.
Engine, L-head type	
Rated horsepower	33.8
Developed horsepower	125.36 rpm's
Engine suspension, rubber mounted	
Torque	230 lbs. at 2000 rpm's
Bore	3¼ inches
Stroke	4¼ inches
Piston displacement	282 cu. inches
Cylinders	8 in.-line
Compression ratio	6.85 to 1
Engine weight, with clutch and transmission	791 lbs.
Gasoline capacity	20 gals.
Choke, automatic	
Carburetor heat control, thermostat	
Brakes, hydraulic	
4-door sedan:	
Front seat width	58 inches
Front seat door to door	62½ inches
Rear seat width	50½ inches
Front seat depth	18½ inches
Rear seat depth	19 inches
Headroom front	36⅞ inches
Headroom rear	37 inches
Leg room from edge of front cushion	20¾ inches
Leg room from edge of back cushion to foot rest	22 inches
Steering wheel to top of cushion	5¾ inches
Trunk capacity	17.2 cu. ft.

Super Eight

De Luxe Eight 4-Door Touring Sedan

PACKARD

PACKARD MOTOR CAR COMPANY

Detroit, Michigan

Eight Club Sedan

Custom Convertible

Packards for 1951

THE Packard range for 1951, announced in Detroit last week-end, comprises three series of cars, with completely new low-built bodywork of striking modern style and high compression straight eight engines. The six-cylinder engines have been dropped.

The 200 series, the smallest cars of the range, have a wheelbase of 10ft 2in, and 4,719 c.c. eight-cylinder engines, with five-bearing crankshafts. When supplied with synchromesh and overdrive transmission the power is 135 b.h.p. on a 7 to 1 compression ratio; but if fitted with the optional Ultramatic torque converter transmission, compression ratio is increased to 7.5 to 1, giving 138 b.h.p. The larger cars, the 300 and 400 series, are fitted with a larger eight-cylinder engine with nine-bearing crankshaft, developing 150 b.h.p. on a 7 to 1 compression ratio; but when the torque converter transmission is used, compression ratio is increased to 7.8, claimed to be the highest in American production.

The Ultramatic transmission, consisting of torque converter and planetary gear box with friction clutch to lock the converter for economical cruising, is expected to be ordered on about 90 per cent of cars sold. Engines have hydraulic vibration dampers.

Styling of all models is entirely new. Bodies are lower and roomier and it is claimed that overall height has been cut by about two inches without loss of head room. By bringing rear seats right forward of the wheel arches, hip room has been increased by nearly one foot to 62in. Body styles include a three-passenger business coupé, two- or four-door saloons, convertibles and hard top coupés, in a choice of eleven colours.

The Packard automatic ventilation system has been improved and is now said to provide a complete change of air in one minute with all windows shut and the car stationary.

The chassis are similar to those of the previous models and have deep X bracing in the centre, pierced so that the propeller shaft can pass through the middle. Front suspension is by coil springs and wish-bones with telescopic dampers and the rear suspension is by half-elliptic springs which now have composition inserts between the leaves.

Most luxurious car in the Packard range is the 400, with torque converter transmission and 155 b.h.p. engine. Overall height is reduced, the bonnet line is lowered five inches, but bodies are more roomy than ever. Screen pillars are cut down to minimum thickness. Tyres are 15×7.60in.

The lowest-priced series in the new Packard range is the 200, with 4,179 c.c. engine giving 138 b.h.p. Despite the modern styling, traditional Packard details have been retained. The bonnet panel still incorporates hard shoulder lines; the arrow motif, which once ran alongside the bonnet, now forms the rubbing strip on the side of the car and the red hexagons still appear on the wheel discs.

SPECIFICATIONS

Engine.—"200": 8 cylinders, side valves, 88.9×95.5 mm, 4,179 c.c., 138 b.h.p. on 7.5 to 1 compression ratio. "300" and "400": 8 cylinders, side valves, 88.9×107.9 mm, 5,358 c.c., 155 b.h.p. on 7.8 to 1 compression ratio.

Transmission.—Three-speed gear box with optional overdrive or torque converter with planetary gear box and friction clutch to lock converter.

Suspension.—Coil springs and wish-bones with anti-roll bar at front; half-elliptics rear. Direct acting hydraulic dampers.

Brakes.—Packard self-servo hydraulic.

Dimensions.—"200": Wheelbase: 10ft 2in. Track (front) 4ft 11$\frac{13}{32}$in; (rear) 5ft 0$\frac{23}{32}$in. "300" and "400": Wheelbase: 10ft 7in. Track (front) 5ft 0$\frac{3}{32}$in; (rear) 5ft 0$\frac{47}{64}$in. Length: 18ft 1¾in. Width: 6ft 6in. Height: 5ft. 2½in.

Prices.—Not yet available.

New carburetor in '51 Packard is pointed out to Wilbur Shaw by William H. Graves, vice president of engineering, at Packard Proving Ground in course of inspection of new cars. Engine has 3-point rubber suspension and hydraulic vibration damper. Blower beneath Graves' hand can provide pressurized fresh air to passengers at low car speeds during warm weather.

Point of maximum fender height is marked by upright stick, showing good right-side visibility from driver's seat. Windshields have maximum width of more than 56 in. Fore-aft adjustment of front seat is 4½ in. Headroom in front is 36 in., rear 35. All body mountings float in rubber. Fuel tank on "200" has been enlarged to take 20 gals., boost of 3 over the equivalent 1950 model.

CLOSE-UP of the '51 Packard

By Devon Francis
PS PHOTOS BY W. W. MORRIS

THE first automobile company in the U. S. to place a straight-eight L-head engine in mass production—back in 1921—last month introduced the highest compression in the industry in standard-sized cars. The '51 Packard, as Wilbur Shaw remarks in his *Report from the Driver's Seat* in this issue (page 100), is available with a ratio of 7.8-to-1.

With a new type of automatic spark control and a leaner mixture in these new engines, Packard expects to get from two to three more miles from a gallon of gasoline at speeds between 20 and 45 m.p.h. Above that, they will deliver about a mile more to the gallon than at present.

Packard now offers a greater choice of horsepowers without increasing the number of engine models on its production line. Here's how:

For 1950 the company offered engines of 135, 150, and 160 hp. For 1951 there are still only three basic engines, one of 288 cu. in. displacement, one of 327, and a third of 327 but with nine instead of five main bearings. The horsepowers available—135, 138, 150, and 155—spring from compression ratios ranging from 7-to-1 to 7.8-to-1. Premium fuel is a must for engines with 7.5 and 7.8 ratios.

The company has also completely re-done its models. The entire frame and body, including the side rails, roof rails and pillars, are built of box-section steel for greater rigidity, weight-saving, and safety. This is evident in the ultrathin windshield pillars.

The Ultramatic transmission (PS, June '49, p. 139) has undergone refinement. Its oil cooler, for instance, has been removed from the engine radiator and mounted below the water pump. This improves accessibility and is greater insurance against oil-line leakage. The governor in the control system has new

Clean, light frame of "200" model is on a wheelbase of 122 in., 2 in. greater than on 1950 model it replaces. Wheelbase of "300" and "Patrician 400" models (replacing 1950's Super and Custom) remains unchanged at 127 in. All models have almost 9 in. ground clearance.

To reduce hood height to 43.8 in., water pump and fan were lowered. Lowering pump also insures cooling even when water level is low.

Classic Packard lines are retained despite restyling. This sedan is in "200" series. Rear window on this series is doubled in size. Instrument panel is recessed to prevent glare from incident light.

gearing, and bearings have been steel-backed to increase their life. Pistons in the control system are bigger.

The styling is brand new. You'll have to give the new Packards a double take to recognize them. Yet you get the feeling that Packard has gone back to that familiar dignity of line the car had when it was known as one of the few fine vehicles in America and one that didn't greatly change its looks from year to year.

Over-all heights are reduced two inches without a sacrifice of ground clearance. Incidentally, it's without a sacrifice of headroom in getting in and out, either. In two of the models, the "300" and "Patrician 400," the area of the rear window is two and a half times as great as it was in the 1950 models. Leg room and hip room are boosted. Overall lengths are increased—and the length is in the body, not in the hood.

Finally, the new Packards give you an extraordinary amount of visibility. I am accustomed to driving in New York traffic, and seeing what's around me to the front, sides, and back is the first design requisite to safety. The hood line has been lowered a full 4½ inches. There's no trouble in seeing what's in front of you unless it's right under the wheels. And the windshield and window areas are as good as, if not better than, any of the new cars on the road, size considered, with the possible exception of the Studebakers with the wrap-around glass.

Heat-sealed plastic inset paneling on rear of front seat is stain- and scuff-proof and is designed to outlast car itself. To increase softness of ride, rear springs are ½ in. wider.

By moving brake pedal to the left, designers make it available to either right or left foot. Wilbur Shaw commented, "With practice, the left foot is bound to become the braking foot."

Packard for '51 has four lines of cars. The "200" comes in sedans and a business coupe. This is the smallest of the company's cars and is the one pictured with Wilbur Shaw on the cover. The "200" also comes in a de luxe version and will include a hard-top convertible after the turn of the year. Next in size is the "300," a four-door sedan. The fanciest of the lot is the "Patrician 400" sedan. END

Manufacturers gradually are realizing that American motorist, nomadic at heart, needs storage space. Packard's luggage compartment has been boosted from 19½ cubic feet to 30-plus.

Hood-release lever on the '51 Packard is inside grille because of breakage trouble with cable from driving compartment. It sacrifices engine-compartment theft protection, however.

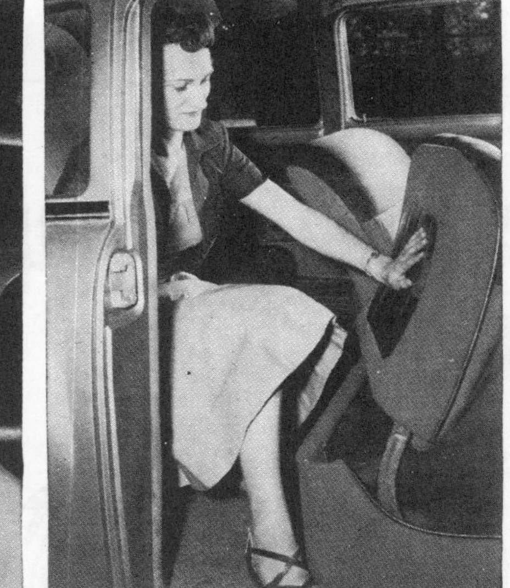

Ample entryway is provided for rear-seat passengers in two-door sedans. Body paneling is Fiberglas-padded to reduce road noise. Except in "200" series, seat cushions are foam rubber.

REPORT FROM THE DRIVER'S SEAT . . .

Cover by Reynold Brown

Take a Ride In the '51 Packard

This is the "Patrician 400," the fanciest entry in the company's 1951 stable. Under that low hood she's got 155 hp. The crankshaft in this straight-eight engine has nine main bearings.

I opened up the Packard on the Proving Ground track with Bill Morris and his camera in the back seat. The speedometer needle in the picture below is *past* the 110-m.p.h. mark. The photo at the bottom shows how a second speed run looked from the infield. The car is a "300" sedan.

By Wilbur Shaw

PS PHOTOS BY W. W. MORRIS
ON LOCATION AT PACKARD PROVING GROUND

> ***EDITOR'S NOTE:** For his first* Report from the Driver's Seat, *Wilbur Shaw takes you to the famous Packard Proving Grounds in Utica, Mich. Climb aboard, and America's best known man behind the wheel will take you for a drive in the 1951 models. Other reports will come in succeeding months.*

WHEN Packard invited me to try out its new models, in deepest secrecy, I jumped at the chance. It offered three "firsts" with one jump:

A grand old name for my first assignment as automobile reporter for POPULAR SCIENCE.

A first whack at some brand-new cars, one of them with the highest compression ratio in the industry in standard-size cars—7.8 to 1.

A first work-out on the Packard Proving Ground private speed track. Ever since Leon Duray was clocked at 148 miles an hour in a 90-cu.-in. Miller back in 1928, I've wanted to turn a fast lap on that track. I figured it had to be something special for Duray to post a record that has stood for 22 years.

I was tickled to get a crack at these new cars because Packard's always had a name for advanced engineering, ever since the old Twin-Six. To tell the truth, I also brought along some misgivings, after I heard they'd boosted the compression. A lot of the wise boys don't think a straight eight likes high compression. The crankshaft's so much longer than a V-8's, they say, that it's likely to develop whip at speed. I wanted to see for myself.

Before I drove the new cars, Bill Graves, Packard engineering v.p., took me on a get-acquainted tour of the Proving Ground in the "200."

I wanted to get a running record of my comments on this car. So I took along a recording set and put it on the seat alongside of me. The gimmick on my head that looks like it was swiped from a doctor's office holds the mike. I was surprised at some of my own comments while driving.

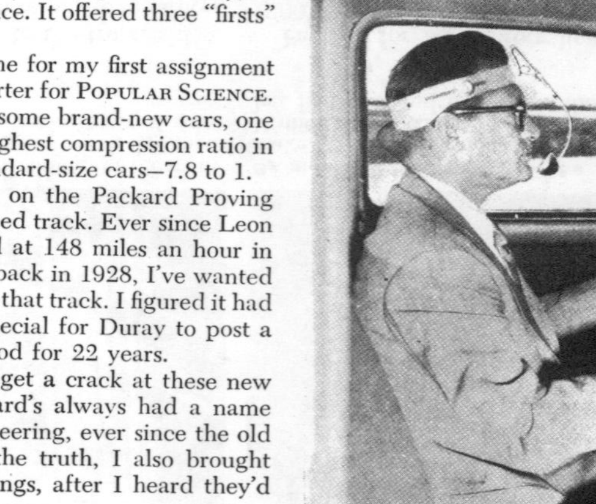

On the way back I couldn't resist the temptation to do a half-lap on the track. We went up to 90 miles an hour on the speedometer without giving the "200" a chance to really get its wind.

Trying Out Ultramatic

The "300" was next. It was a beaut. A heavier car with a 5-inch longer wheelbase. A two-pedal job—just a brake and accelerator. With the Ultramatic transmission the clutch pedal is gone.

Like most automatics, the Ultramatic creeps a little when you are trying to stand still with the selector lever in driving range. That may bother some drivers until they get used to holding with the brake.

Like the "200," the "300" is nicely appointed inside. The visibility is wonderful. The hood has been lowered to reduce the blind spot on the road in front of the car; and *you can even see your right fender!* Windshield pillars are very narrow. If you can't see out of these cars, you're blind and shouldn't be driving.

The "300" with Ultramatic has 155 hp. at 3,600 r.p.m. and she runs at 7.8-to-1 compression. That's squeezing it pretty tight for a passenger car, especially one with an L-head engine. L-heads usually don't take to high compression as well as overhead-valve jobs. But the boost ought to increase power and relative fuel mileage, provided they can maintain volumetric efficiency.

Crankshaft Is Stiffened

Packard's put *nine* main bearings, instead of the usual five, in the engine of their "Patrician 400" line. With the crankshaft beefed up, they figure to march right on up with compression ratios as better fuels become available.

One thing's for sure: they're going to have to keep carbon out of *any* of these high-compression engines, whoever makes them, or they'll cackle like a bunch of hens.

With Devon Francis, of the POPULAR SCIENCE editorial staff, and Bill Morris, the magazine's chief photographer, in the back seat, I drove toward the test course. On the way I did a little commenting:

I'm going to do a half-lap on the track just for fun. This job moves away as though we had steam for power. The engine speed required to get torque is a bit strange to me, but this is a characteristic of all torque-converter types of transmissions.

What I like is that you can get into direct drive in high range at practically any speed merely by easing off on the accelerator. In direct drive you have a mechanical connection between the engine and rear wheels.

They've done a nice job with this power plant. I can't resist pushing it a little. Registering 95. We haven't even reached the turn. For a car of this weight, with three of us aboard, that's moving right along.

We had to pull off on the inside and stop, before crossing the track to the rough ground. This was a safety measure on a busy track.

Could Use a Spinner

Here's one of those switchback turns. Whew! That's rough! But when I give her her head she straightens up. I've never liked those motormen's knobs that people put on steering wheels. But I could use one now.

There's a bit of a chuckle in the steering gear going over the washboard. Matter of adjustment.

Here are the thank-you-ma'ams and dipsa-daisies. They're lulus! We're going fast enough . . . this is fast . . . she's taking it like a well-mannered boat in rough water. . . . This car has a good, solid feel, that's for sure.

Now, I'd like to pause here to say that these new torque-converter transmissions are just as new to me as they are to the average motorist. Remember, in racing cars we try to keep as many things *off* a car as we possibly can.

We headed for the killer-hill because I wanted to see what Packard's Ultramatic would do under these tough conditions.

This time, with three of us in the car and about a 15-m.p.h. run, we sailed up over that hill in high without a whimper. At the top I *reversed* momentarily to start backing down. Then I put the selector lever in *drive* position and let the car down, using forward driving power as braking power.

Transmission During Roll-Back

I've often wondered what would happen if an inexperienced person got stopped with one of these transmissions on a steep grade. Now I know about the only thing you could do wrong during a roll-back would be to put the lever in reverse and bang up the back.

After lunch Bill Morris wanted to get some speed pictures on the track. I was anxious, I admit, to see how it would perform in the speed department. I'm certainly not an advocate of high speeds on the highway. Let's get that clear. But speed is a rough measurement of power. And plenty of power lets people cruise at a reasonably high speed without punishing their engines.

Devon and Bill Morris, with his camera, got into the back seat.

I don't propose to make any acceleration tests with this car. It's not a hot rod. It's moving away from a full stop smoothly. These torque converters at the present state of the art are no match in acceleration for a good mechanical transmission. Correction—I mean with the lever in driving range. If you want a jackrabbit start, put her in low for the first spurt. Then flip her to "Drive." But, for me, that sort of thing outside of competition is silly.

Are you fellows set? Let's stretch this baby out.

110 m.p.h. and Going Up

There's your 100. We're still in the first turn. We're coming off the bank. We ought to find a few more knots now. We are. There it is! Got it, Bill? Hear me, back there? Got it, Bill? It's 110 on the speedometer. Going up, too. Let's see if she'll hold that through the turn. Yup! That's probably a good, honest 100, allowing for normal instrument error.

We actually picked up some more speed even though the speedometer didn't show it. There's a smell to speed, if you've driven races. You can feel it in your engine revs and the way the terrain goes by.

It was such a soft ride that you couldn't even feel the expansion strips in the track. I swayed back and forth over the longitudinal strips to see how the car would react. She was stable.

As we slowed to a walk I glanced at the heat indicator. She wasn't sweating. There was no indication of temperature rise under the full-throttle running that she had done.

As we drove back to the office Bill Morris, running his fingers through his big shock of white hair, commented: "That's the fastest ride I've ever had on wheels."

For me, it wasn't the fastest, but it was one of the pleasantest. I'd finally driven that magnificent Packard track, and in a fine automobile END

I told Bill Graves that I wasn't anxious to push his new car beyond its limits. That would be plain punishment. But he said to go right ahead. So I did. Here the car is performing a Herculean feat—holding fast on a better-than-35-percent grade with only the churning blades of the automatic transmission to support it. The oil trail is from backing down the hill after a previous run when oil dripped from the transmission breather due to the unnatural slant of the car. Nobody would ever ask a car to do this much. The picture really doesn't do the hill justice.

This Month's Shaw-ism

The greatest safety device that will ever be used in an automobile is the knob a driver hangs his hat on.

Wilbur Shaw

Optional Heads Simplify Engine Production

GLASS AREA is 26 percent greater than that of previous models. The Patrician "400" series, above, features wrap-around rear window.

Body design of the Packard 1951 line of automobiles is completely new. Greatly increased glass area, lower hood and extended rear deck are the main styling changes. The cars are lower, longer and have trunk space almost double that of last year. Rear seats of some models are almost 12 in. wider. As in the past, Packard offers three series of models. Series "200" has a 122 in. wheelbase while the "300" and "400" series are on a 127 in. wheelbase. The adoption of high compression engine design has resulted in production economies, while increasing the number of power plants from which the customer can choose. Formerly, there were three Packard engines of 288, 327 and 356 cu. in. piston displacement. All engines had a 7 to 1 compression ratic. The largest of these has been discontinued, and the two remaining are available with either standard or high compression heads. Thus, there are four power plant combinations developing 135, 138, 150 and 155 hp at 3,600 rpm. The compression ratio of the 155 hp engine is 7.8 to 1, which is claimed to be the highest in the auto industry for full-size cars. Prominent interior styling detail is the use of biscuit-design, leather-like vinyl plastic in the back of the front seat, harmonizing with fabrics used on cushions and door trim. For maximum engine quietness, the Patrician "400" series cars are equipped with asbestos lined mufflers. This series also is equipped with a wrap-around rear window, while all series feature a one-piece curved windshield. Defroster outlets run the entire width of the windshield. The instrument panel has been simplified by the substitution of red warning lights for the ammeter and oil pressure indicator.

INTERIOR CHANGES include drawer-type glove compartment and red warning lights replacing battery charge and oil pressure meters.

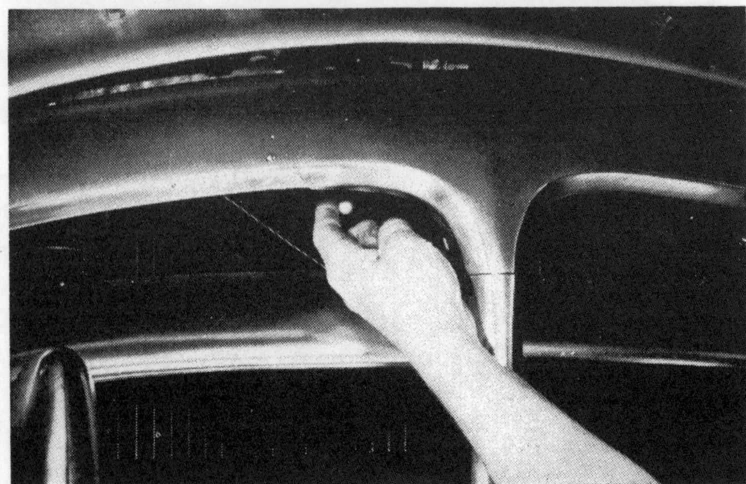

HOOD LOCK RELEASE is accessible through front grille. Hood hinges are at the back rather than at the sides as previously. Grille retains traditional Packard design theme.

OPTIONAL HEAD raises compression ratio of the larger engine to 7.8 to 1 and boosts power to 155 hp. These figures compare with 7.0 to 1 compression ratio and 150 hp for standard engine. The torque converter oil cooler is now mounted directly on the engine to eliminate need for flexible tubing between engine and chassis.

WATER PUMP has been moved down to allow lower hood and cowl. New location assure satisfactory operation of pump even when cooling system water level is low.

DIP-STICK PORT is now above engine ledge to lessen possibility of entry of dirt when oil level is checked. Starter is solenoid actuated and is mounted high for easy servicing.

MOTOR TRIALS

PACKARD 200 IS THE ONE TO BEAT FOR COMFORT AND PERFORMANCE

by Walter A. Woron

PHOTOGRAPHS BY THOMAS J. MEDLEY

A DISCUSSION between editor and tech editor about accessibility of various engine components wound up with conclusion that there is plenty of working room to get at all the accessories

MOST of you no doubt remember the famous Packard slogan, "Ask the man who owns one." Packard Motor Co. had a reason to use it once, but now they have even more cause to use such a slogan. It's a cinch that any '51 Packard owner is justifiably proud of the comfort and performance of his car.

We've been exposed to manufacturer's claims and enthusiasm for a long enough time to look upon them with some reservation, and this was naturally so in the case of the '51 Packard. But now that the motor trial of the Packard 200 with Ultramatic is a thing of the past, we know why the Packard Motor Company is so enthused about its product.

On the morning that we were to begin the Packard motor trial, we arrived at Earle C. Anthony, Inc. (1000 So. Hope St., Los Angeles, Calif.), where we had a pleasant chat with George Wagner, Resident Manager. He introduced us to Tracy E. Reigelman, Service Manager of the company, who, in turn, showed us some interesting aspects of the Ultramatic.

The Packard test car was a 200 series Deluxe four door sedan, equipped with the 138 bhp engine and Ultramatic transmission. It had been amply broken in, was tuned perfectly and rode on 15x7.60 tires.

Usually, any Packard is thought of as a large car, but the model that we tested is affectionately called "baby" by the Packard people, having a wheelbase of only 122 ins. Even so, the car is still a big car.

Detailed Test Report

TRANSMISSION: The Ultramatic, which we were giving a test as much as we were the car itself, is a combination of hydraulic torque converter, planetary gearset, and friction clutch. For all normal driving, the gearshift control is set in H (high) and left there. The transmission is operating in torque converter up until 15-17 mph (for normal acceleration, higher speeds for faster acceleration), at which speed the clutch automatically engages, causing the crankshaft to link up directly to the driveshaft. Any downshift that becomes necessary can be made by additional throttle pressure, provided you're below 50-55 mph (above these speeds, you're always in direct drive). L (low) is used for extremely hard pulls, added acceleration or braking. At any speed below 50-55 mph you can move the gearshift selector from H to L for immediate braking. This is decidedly advantageous down a steep incline, for in L the transmission won't shift to a higher range until *you* make a selector change.

In place of the Ultramatic transmission, which is optional ($185 extra) on the Packard 200 series, you can have a conventional transmission, with or without overdrive ($100 extra). If you don't mind shifting, you'll get better performance (including improved gas mileage) by using the conventional transmission with overdrive.

BEHIND THE WHEEL: What can be said for vision, legroom, headroom, feel of the seat and wheel is all visible in the accompanying photographs. All of these features are above par.

TOP SPEED: We were mildly surprised and gratified by the top speed reached with the Packard 200 test car. The one-way fastest time (95.74 mph) was the highest yet recorded on any motor trial, as was the average of four runs (93.17 mph). The Ultramatic-equipped Packard has a rear axle ratio of 3.9, which is not overly high.

STEERING: Controllability of the Packard is quite good: at no speed or condition of the road does it feel that you might lose control. The one slight objection here is the fact that in going around sharp corners at particularly high speeds there is a tendency of the body to lay over because of the soft springing. Outside of this, the steering ratio is quite satisfactory. The 22½-foot turning radius certainly makes the Packard an easy car to park.

ACCELERATION: As with all automatic transmission-equipped cars which we test, we made acceleration checks using only the high range and then checks starting in the low range and shifting to the high range. And again, as with all previous cars tested, we found that we could improve acceleration by using the latter method. The shift from L to H was tried at several different speeds, but the best shift point was found to be around 45 mph (speedometer reading). The averages

FILLING up with Mobilgas Special gasoline prior to acceleration, economy and top speed runs

of the different conditions are shown in the Table of Performance (page twenty-seven).

FUEL CONSUMPTION: This factor of the Packard is not the car's best selling point, for as with all big cars, fuel consumption averages are anything but outstanding. Even so, the over-all average for the motor trial (not counting acceleration and top speed runs) was 14.35 mpg. At speeds up to 45 mph on the highway fuel consumption is quite satisfactory; however, at higher speeds on the highway and in traffic, consumption increases noticeably (see Table of Performance).

BRAKES: The self-energizing hydraulic brakes of the Packard provide a positive, smooth stop, but some brake fade was noticeable after severe and constant usage (such as during our brake checks). Ordinarily, the brakes would not get this hard treatment.

Appearance and Mechanics

There has been a slow reversal of thought that the streamlined body is the most efficient, with Packard following along with the "functional" body on their 1951 models. With their design, however, Packard has maintained high esthetic values and has achieved, in the opinion of your editor and technical editor, a body design that is one of the best of the current offerings.

The entire car appears to be well put together and is solidly constructed. And not only does the car *appear* to be well put together, you can *feel* it as you drive or ride along. The fit of major components is very good.

The box-section with X-member frame is suspended in front with coil springs and wishbones, and in the rear with long (54⅜ ins.), wide (2½ ins.) longitudinal leaf springs. An anti-sway bar is used in front and tubular shocks are used all the way around.

Interior appointments and upholstery of the Packard 200 are top quality, while the seat, wheel and dash are all well set up (see photographs).

One of two engines is available on the Packard 200—both of them being in-line eights, with the same bore (3½ ins.) but different strokes (3¾ vs. 4¼ ins.). The standard 288 cu. in. engine has a compression ratio of 7:1, but when Ultramatic-equipped, is provided with a 7.5:1 c.r., which ups bhp ouput by three. The optional 327 cu. in. engine, using a 7.8:1 c.r. gives 155 bhp @ 3600 rpm, and is the engine that is standard on the Packard 300. A heavier crankshaft (by 8½ lbs.) is also used on this latter engine, both using five main bearings. (The Patrician 400 engine—basically the same as the 300—uses a *nine*-bearing crankshaft.)

Trend Trials Number

In continuing our policy of giving each tested car a Trend Trials Number, we have arrived at a figure of 32.4 for the Packard 200, Ultramatic-equipped. This figure is a combination of fuel cost per year, cost per bhp and normal maintenance cost, which

CONTINUED ON PAGE 43

FLASHING BY at top speed is the Packard 200 on its fastest run (95.74 mph) through the ¼-mile trap. Control and ride at top speed is remarkable. At high cruising speeds (around 80) the Packard 200 feels as most cars do at 60 mph

STEERING control on dirt is good and car virtually floats over bumps and railroad tracks

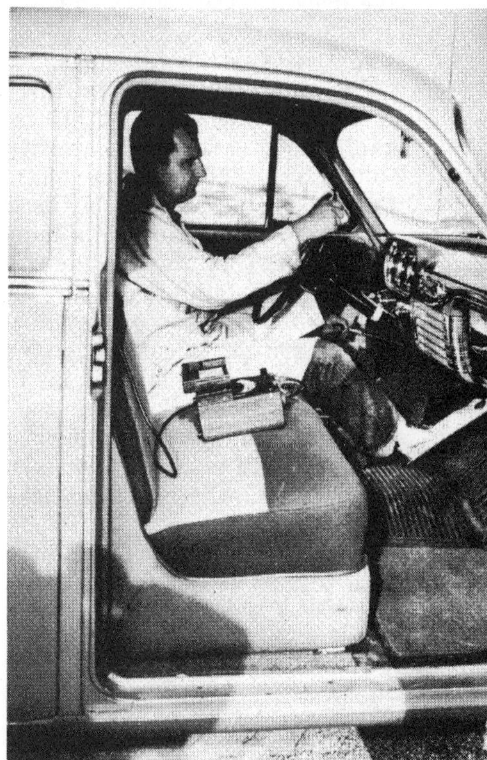

DON FRANCISCO, MT Tech Editor (above) shows that there is plenty of headroom and legroom behind wheel. Instrument panel is well set up—all instruments being visible at a glance and all controls being within easy reach. Seat provides unusual amount of comfort and wheel is set at an angle that makes it no chore to drive the car

"SHOWCASE" vision (left), as seen from rear through rear window toward windshield. Front corner posts are narrow and left one is in location that does not cause blind spot. Windshield is nearly five feet wide; combination of seat position and raised front fenders makes judging of distances no problem in traffic

Packard Pulls Out The Stops On Style

New Models for 1951 Hit High Note in Design Harmony

Packard pulled the stops wide open on body design harmony for its three 1951 lines and the resulting melody is not likely to be sweet music to competition. While the 1951 models set a new high in modernism for normally conservative Packard, the dignity imposed by its quiet slogan, "Ask the Man Who Owns One," is retained.

The new lines include three series, the "200," and "200" deluxe, "300" and the Patrician "400." The "200" series offers three body types—a business coupe, two-door sedan and a four-door sedan. The "200" deluxe line includes two- and four-door sedans, and a soft-top convertible, with a hard-top to come.

The "300" series is available in a four-door sedan. Both the "200" series and the "300" series will be equipped with unimesh transmissions, with the Ultramatic—torque converter type transmissions—available at extra cost. The Patrician "400" series, available in four-door sedan models, will have Ultramatic as standard.

Engines in the new lines have been redesigned. The engines in the "200" and "200 deluxe series are L-head, 8-cylinders in-line with aluminum alloy, steel strut pistons. Displacement is 288 cu. in. Bore and stroke 3½ x 3¾ inches. Compression ratio is 7.0 to 1. Brake horsepower is given as 135 at 3600 rpm. The five main bearing crankshaft weighs 95 pounds. Main and connecting rod bearings are removable. Spark plugs are 14 mm. The oil capacity is 7 quarts. Optional high compression heads for use with Ultramatic equipped cars provide a ratio of 7.5 to 1, and step the horsepower up to 138 at 3600 rpm.

Engines for the "300" and "400" series are basically the same, except for dimensions. The bore and stroke of the latter engine is 3½ x 4½ inches, giving a displacement of 327 cu. in. The crankshaft weighs 103½ pounds. Hydraulic tappets are used instead of the adjustable type. This engine is rated at 150 hp at 3600 rpm. Optional high compression heads, for use with Ultramatic, boosts the compression ratio to 7.8 to 1, and the horsepower to 155 at 3600. Oil capacity 7 quarts.

The "200" and "200" deluxe series are mounted on 122-inch wheelbase chassis and have a bumper to bumper length of 209⅜ inches. The "300" and "400" series are mounted on 127-inch wheelbase chassis and have a bumper to bumper length of 217¾ inches. Bodies are 62½ inches from roof to road and an average of 78 inches wide.

Packard Patrician "400" provides better visibility front and rear. The hood line has been lowered and upper line of fenders emphasized to assist in parking or driving through tight places. One piece curved windshield is used. Car at top of page is the Packard "300".

Clear vision to the rear is provided by the wrap-around rear windows. The trunk capacity is 30 cubic feet. Flared rear fenders are tipped with chrome trim. Bumper provides special protection for the rear of the fenders.

Few people would be likely to deny the 1951 Packard the right to be called impressively handsome, though reaction to car appearance is a highly individual process. White-wall tyres, popular in the U.S.A., are fitted at extra cost.

DATA FOR THE DRIVER

PACKARD 200 DE LUXE

PRICE, with saloon body, right-hand drive and Ultramatic transmission, \$2,684 (at factory). With extras as tested, \$3,013 = £1,076 8s at \$2.80 = £1.

ENGINE: 39.2 h.p. (R.A.C. rating), 8 cylinders, side valves, 88.9 × 95.25 mm, 4,720 c.c. Brake Horse-power: 135 at 3,600 r.p.m. Compression Ratio: 7 to 1. Max. Torque: 230 lb ft at 2,000 r.p.m. 21.25 m.p.h. per 1,000 r.p.m. on top gear.

WEIGHT (running trim with 5 gallons fuel): 35 cwt 2 qr 7 lb (3,983 lb). Front wheels 55 per cent; rear wheels 45 per cent. LB per C.C.: 0.84. B.H.P. per TON: 76.5.

TYRE SIZE: 7.60 × 15in on bolt-on steel disc wheels.

TANK CAPACITY: 16½ English gallons. Approximate fuel consumption range, 13-16 m.p.g. (21.7-17.7 litres per 100 km).

TURNING CIRCLE: 43ft 0in (L and R). Steering wheel movement from lock to lock: 5¼ turns. LIGHTING SET: 6 volt.

MAIN DIMENSIONS: Wheelbase, 10ft 2in. Track 4ft 11½in (front); 5ft 0 23/32in (rear). Overall length, 17ft 5⅜in; width, 6ft 5⅝in; height, 5ft 2 11/16in. Minimum Ground Clearance: 7½in.

ACCELERATION

Overall gear ratios	From steady m.p.h. of 10-30 sec	20-40 sec	30-50 sec
High Range—3.9 to 1 to 9.36 to 1	5.9	7.2	9.3
Low Range—7.098 to 1 to 17.035 to 1	4.7	5.8	7.0

From rest through gears to:—

	sec	sec		sec	sec
30 m.p.h.	†5.5	7.2	60 m.p.h.	*18.2	21.2
50 m.p.h.	*12.1	15.5	70 m.p.h.	*25.1	28.4
			80 m.p.h.	*37.3	—

* On Low range. † Using Low and High ranges. Other figures from rest on High range.

SPEEDS ON GEARS

(by Electric Speedometer)	M.p.h. (max)	K.p.h. (max)
Low	55	89
High	90	145

Speedometer correction by Electric Speedometer:—

Car Speedometer		Electric Speedometer m.p.h.
10	=	9.0
20	=	18.5
30	=	27.0
40	=	36.75
50	=	45.0
60	=	54.0
70	=	63.5
80	=	72.5
90	=	80.5
100	=	89.5

WEATHER: *Dry, cold; fresh wind.*

Acceleration figures are the means of several runs in opposite directions.

Described in "The Autocar" of September 1, 1950.

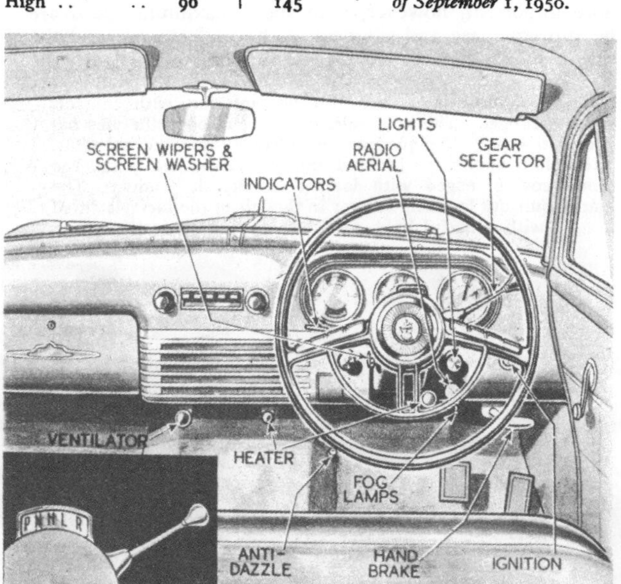

No. 1424 : PACKARD 200 DE LUXE TOURING SALOON

IN *The Autocar* of December 22, 1950, road impressions appeared resulting from a comparatively brief run on the latest 1951 model Packard 200 with Ultramatic automatic transmission. It has now been possible to carry out a full-scale Road Test extending over some 600 miles, by arrangement with the well-known Packard British concessionaires, Leonard Williams and Co. (1940), Ltd., on a demonstration car that came into this country in connection with the last Earls Court Show. As already described, the transmission system available on the Packard is one of the most modern types, basically comprising two speeds of epicyclic (or planetary) pattern combined with an hydraulic torque converter, which in addition to its function of multiplying engine torque for hill-climbing and acceleration over the lower ranges of speed, acts also like a fluid coupling in providing a smooth start from rest without risk of stalling the engine.

This example of the 24th Series Packard, though the smallest and least expensive model in the range, is a car of impressive size, with an overall length of nearly 17ft 6in, and is typical of the U.S. scale of values in the generosity of the power given by its straight eight engine and in the spaciousness of both seating and luggage capacity. Basically, in its own country it is not expensive, costing approximately £850 with left-hand drive, the Ultramatic transmission being optional equipment at extra cost.

To have done with the ordinary clutch pedal and gear lever somehow seems especially appropriate with this type of car, designed to give a most comfortable form of transport in the hands of those to whom ease of control is of great appeal. It is, also, of course, designed primarily for use on roads that are very much easier as regards both grading and radius of bends than applies in most of Great Britain.

With the automatic transmission control of the car, especially in congested road conditions, is sufficiently simplified to enable a greater degree of the driver's concentration to remain available for dealing with hazards and with both hands on the sterling wheel. This cannot but be a safety factor, the effect of which is not nullified, when there is an excellent power-to-weight ratio, as on the Packard, by the driver's not having the same direct control over the gear ratio of the moment as with a conventional transmission.

With the engine running, the now typical pointer, travelling over a quadrant indicator under the steering wheel and operating an hydraulic pump, is set to the H or High position. As the throttle pedal is depressed the car moves smoothly away and in this particular instance the torque converter takes charge up to approximately 21 m.p.h. on an

Extensive use of chromium is made in front, although the windscreen frame is of stainless steel. The fog lamps are an extra fitting, alongside them are the front units of the U.S. winking traffic indicator lights, whilst the parking lamps beneath the sealed beam head lamps are an English addition.

ROAD TEST: continued

The four-window body style, now common among American models, was once a European "smart car" prerogative. The huge curved rear window of the Packard is well observed here, also the rear deck enclosing the luggage compartment, which is not much shorter than the bonnet.

easy throttle opening on a level road, when the torque converter clutch that is an important feature of the Packard locks up and a positive drive, not subject to hydraulic slip, is obtained. If full throttle is applied, again on a level road, this changeover does not occur below approximately 48 m.p.h.

There is a Low position (at L on the indicator), intended chiefly to provide additional engine braking and to deal with a really severe hill or an appreciable gradient on which the car has been severely baulked. Also this range can be used by an enterprising driver to give more acceleration in getting away from rest, or from the lower speeds, than is available on the comparatively limited engine revs, and therefore power output, imposed by the governing effect of the torque converter. For a great part of the time in open-road driving the car runs on the direct drive, the torque converter taking charge again only under road and traffic conditions where a change of gear would be suggested, or become necessary, with a conventional transmission. It is possible, however, at speeds not exceeding approximately 50 m.p.h., to introduce the converter for increased acceleration by depressing the throttle pedal firmly on the floor and allowing a brief pause.

If the Low range is engaged at, say, 35-40 m.p.h., an inescapable jerk occurs at the moment of transition, but such usage is to be regarded as abnormal. The Low range can be introduced without jerk when, for instance, the car is rolling up to a traffic light about to change to green, for then a cushioning effect is available from the torque converter functioning as a fluid coupling. Such methods are largely, however, to be looked on as specialized handling as practised by a European driver accustomed to thinking of gears as performance aids, and throughout a day's motoring in the thickest traffic, or on main roads with gradients up to about 1 in 7, there is not the slightest need to move the pointer from H other than when leaving the car stationary.

As a safety measure against the engine's being started in a position where the car would at once move, the starting motor will operate only in the (Neutral or Parking) positions of the selector lever. At P, a position that can be engaged only when the car is at rest, a latch is introduced to lock the transmission positively and hold the car stationary even in lieu of the hand brake. The transmission is singularly free from noise under all conditions and at no time is there any trace of epicyclic gear whine. Under the bonnet is a separate cooler, connected into the main engine cooling system, for the 10 Imperial quarts of oil used in the Ultramatic transmission.

Packard's continue to use a side-valve straight eight engine. In the model 200 it is of 4.7 litres by European reckoning, and when the Ultramatic is fitted as an alternative to the synchromesh and overdrive which are also still available, a high compression ratio of 7.5 to 1 is normally used to give 138 brake horse power instead of 135 with the 7 to 1 compression that in America goes with the orthodox transmission. Such an engine is under a handicap on fuel such as the approximately 72-octane Pool spirit on which it has been tested on this occasion, and the car tried had the 7 to 1 compression, plus a thicker cylinder head gasket than is standard, it still being necessary to retard the ignition setting to keep clear of pinking. Therefore, by no means the full power and liveliness of the engine were available. None the less, there is a fine feeling of smooth power once on the direct drive, and from 30 m.p.h. onwards the acceleration and climbing are about as would be expected with an engine of this size.

No one speed is better than another and the Packard can be driven as fast as at any rate English roads allow, up to the maximum of 90 m.p.h. true speed indicated by the usual test instruments, and it could probably exceed that figure by several m.p.h. given a sufficient stretch of road. Far more important, however, than sheer maximum speed are the supreme ease and silkiness of the performance and the way in which the car will trickle through traffic "on" the

Doors remain firmly in the fully opened position under the control of a check device. The unusual thickness of the rear door seen end on arises from the rear wing fairing being extended into the door panel. Hinged extractor panels are provided in addition to the drop windows. The panelled trim on the back of the front seat is in leather and on the doors in cloth.

A neat, almost plain, grey finished interior, with controls well arranged. The gear selector is seen above the steering column boss; the quadrant is softly illuminated at night. The cloth upholstery is fitted with extremely neatly tailored loose covers, edged with leather—a British product. The large pull-out lockable drawer in the left of the facia is fitted with a useful light, switched on automatically.

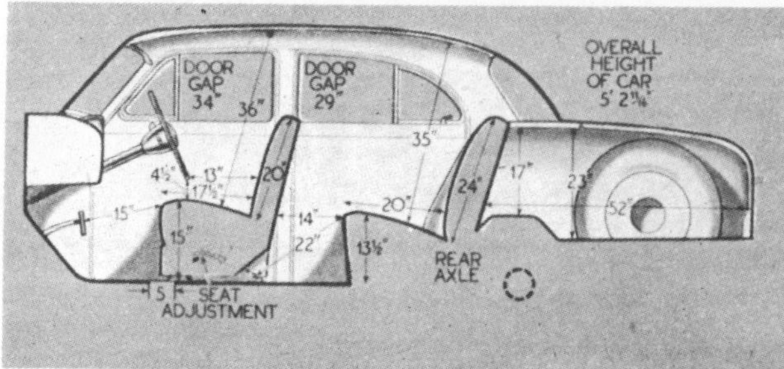

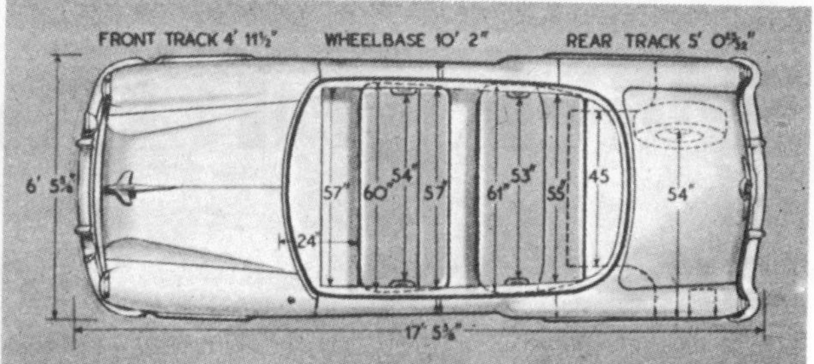

Measurements in these scale body diagrams are taken with the driving seat in the central position of fore and aft adjustment and with the seat cushions uncompressed.

throttle pedal, with infinite flexibility and no risk of stalling the engine.

A matter to which one becomes used to some extent is the very low ratio of the steering, even among contemporary American cars that have been sampled. The objective of light control at low speeds is achieved, a subject even more important in congested American cities than in this country, but naturally not the maximum precision or ability to deal with an emergency is imparted by steering that requires so much turning. It has strong castor action, the wheel spinning back after a right-angle turn.

Hydraulically operated brakes deal well with the speed of the car. Marked temporary fading was experienced when testing for maximum performance, when many brake applications in close succession are called for from speeds up to the maximum—conditions where some degree of this phenomenon is common with current cars.

Suspension is by coil springs independently in front and by half-elliptic leaf springs at the rear. The effect is typically soft and there is some roll under fast cornering on the type of bends that English roads introduce so frequently; also, even with the tyre pressures set correctly, tyre squeal sets in rather easily, and sometimes unexpectedly. A certain amount of vertical motion occurs, but riding in all seats is extremely comfortable.

An immediately favourable impression is gained of the driving position from the fact that the bonnet does not present any noticeable obstruction to vision, whilst both wings, or fenders, as our friends across the Atlantic call them, are fully visible. The driver would feel happier at night, in rain, if the windscreen were closer, but the pillars are not obtrusive and rearward vision is remarkably good, the window being extended round the quarters and rivalling the windscreen in area. The large-diameter steering wheel is at a good angle and comfortably thin in the rim. The one-piece front seat is readily adjustable by a smooth movement controlled by an easily reached lever at the side of the cushion.

Controls are one fewer in number than commonly, as the starting motor is engaged through the throttle pedal. Ammeter and oil pressure gauge are replaced by warning lights. The instruments are beautifully illuminated at night, and there is that most valuable provision, a rheostat switch permitting the lighting to be graduated from full brilliance to virtually nothing. When the same switch is turned in the opposite direction useful lights are switched on under the facia, these coming on automatically when the front doors are opened, as does the roof light in the rear compartment when the rearward doors are opened.

An example on the Packard of ingenious minor controls on American cars is the control on the side of the enclosed head of the steering column, which, turned in one direction brings into operation the suction-driven screenwipers, and in the other direction causes the screen washer to function. A booster pump in conjunction with the camshaft-operated fuel pump maintains a constant vacuum to prevent the wipers from drying up at full throttle. A really clean sweep is obtained by the twin blades on the markedly curved screen and their speed can be varied. The radio aerial can be raised and lowered by an electro-hydraulic control.

The upholstery is in cloth, provided in this car with well-fitting covers in a bright modern fabric. There is a great amount of leg room in all seats, as might be expected. This model does not have a central armrest in the rear seat and the interior finish is somewhat plain, certainly free from the over-decoration sometimes applying to U.S. cars. As is current American practice, either or both forward doors can be locked by the same key and it is necessary to use one of the two keys to open the lid of the enormous luggage locker, which has no separate handle. With the changeover to right-hand drive the original American heater and ventilation equipment, which is usually extremely efficient, had had to be sacrificed and an ordinary recirculating heater fitted.

The head-lamp beam was very fair. With automatic mixture control, starting from cold was quick and it was possible to drive straight off without a trace of hesitation.

A luggage locker to make envious all those who have struggled with stowing the family's holiday baggage in smaller cars! It is provided with a really effective dome light in the lid. The exhaust pipe is fitted with the American version of a fishtail, an extra, as also is the reversing light, which operates in conjunction with the gear control.

The bonnet is spring balanced in the open position and proves unexpectedly light to lift. An unusual box-like effect is given to the L-head engine by its uncompromisingly flat cylinder head as seen externally. The efficient six-volt battery (a 17-plate 100 ampère-hour pattern) is seen on the right. A well-placed under-bonnet lamp is provided.

Packard Packs Pep

by Bill Callahan

Redesigned 1951 Series 200 Shows Excellent Acceleration Characteristics for Big Car

In addition to its complete revision in styling for 1951, Packard has packed an unusual amount of pep into its new "200" series for a car of its size. Those who have not driven this new line are in for surprises. Handling and ride characteristics are good, with a high degree of stability in cornering in spite of the soft springing. Steering ratio is normal in relation to other American cars of similar proportions which of course leaves room for improvement.

Interior appointments in the roomy, quiet bodies are well balanced and in good taste. Controls are conveniently located and vision in all directions is excellent and unobstructed. Body panels, hoods, bumpers and all parts are sturdy and reassuring. Trunk compartments are very generous in size.

Ultra-Matic drive, in the model road tested, functioned smoothly and efficiently. There is positive action in this mechanism and a complete simplification of control that should appeal strongly to those who like the automatics. Like similar torque converter types, Ultra-Matic produces a whirring sound even in higher speeds which is more noticeable than the sounds produced by conventional gear-sets. On the other hand, the Ultra-Matic was free of excessive heat.

The most surprising factor in the "200" performance is the unusual acceleration for a car of this size and weight. Using the higher speed driving range on the quadrant, the "200" will pick up to 30 m.p.h. from a standing start in 6.8 seconds. It will rev up to 50 m.p.h. in 11.8 seconds and hit 60 m.p.h. in 15.3 seconds. By using the low gear range for acceleration, the "200" can be pushed up to 30 m.p.h. from a standing start in 5.2 seconds. It will hit 50 m.p.h. in 9.5 seconds and 60 m.p.h. in 13 seconds flat.

For those who want to reach 60 m.p.h. more quickly, the trick is to start in low and rev up to 50 m.p.h. This can be done in 9.5 seconds. By manually shifting into the high range at 50 m.p.h., the "200" climbs from zero to 60 m.p.h. in 12.5 seconds. On this basis, even in normal drive the "200" will not be left behind in getaway and when operated in the lower range for starting, it is not an easy car to catch.

In addition to good acceleration the "200" has equally good deceleration characteristics. It can be brought to a stop from 30 m.p.h. in 40 feet; from 50 m.p.h. in 98 feet; and from 60 m.p.h. in 139 feet. The generally accepted good stopping performance for the average car is about 47 feet at 30 m.p.h. and 131 feet at 50 m.p.h. This puts the Packard brake considerably above average.

While the car road tested had relatively low mileage on the clock and therefore discouraged prolonged driving at anywhere near top speed, we would peg the "200's" top at somewhere in the neighborhood of 95 to 96 m.p.h. Gasoline consumption was slightly on the high side but again this may have been effected by the newness of the car.

Packard has three distinct engines in its 1951 line. The "200" series engine is an L-head, eight in line, with a displacement of 288 cubic inches. Bore and stroke 3½ x 3¾ inches. Compression ratio: 7 to 1. Brake horsepower 135 at 3600 r.p.m. Crankshaft weight 95 pounds. Five main bearings with removable main and connecting rod bearing. The high compression head for use with Ultramatic Drive gives a 7.5 to 1 compression ratio and has a brake horsepower of 138 at 3600 r.p.m.

The "300" series engine is an L-head, eight in line, with displacement of 327 cubic inches. Bore and stroke 3½ inches x 4¼ inches. Compression ratio: 7 to 1. Brake horsepower 150 at 3,600

PACKARD

r.p.m. Crankshaft weight 103½ pounds. Five main bearings with removable main and connecting rod bearings. This engine also has hydraulic valve tappets. An optional high compression head for use with Ultramatic Drive gives a 7.8 to 1 compression ratio and develops 155 at 3,600 r.p.m.

The "400" series engine differs from the "300" in that it has a bore and stroke 3½ inches x 4½ inches which is ¼" more stroke than the "300." It has a compression ratio: 7.8 to 1 and develops 155 hp at 3,600 r.p.m. Crankshaft weight 105 pounds. Nine main bearings are used instead of the five for the "200" and "300" series. Hydraulic valve tappets are used in the "400" engine also.

New Packard

CONTINUED FROM PAGE 5

by virtue of the very low spring rate of the coil spring.

3. A very light ring cross section which results in a high degree of flexibility and conformability.

4. Effectiveness, particularly at high speeds, without high unit pressure. Unit pressure is comparable to that of conventional rings without expanders.

While chassis details remain the same as before, one of the major improvements is the adoption of a new model steering gear of the worm-and-triple-tooth roller type. The roller is mounted on a double row of needle bearings while the worm is mounted on two tapered roller bearings. This unit is said to provide unusual steering ease.

A new die-cast radiator grille and lower radiator emblem enhance outward appearance. The new models follow the general lines of the prewar Clipper model.

Packard Motor Trials

CONTINUED FROM PAGE 37

should help a person decide if a car is a good buy. Since the number given the Packard 200 (equipped with Ultramatic) is the first one given a car in this price category ($2501-2700) a comparison is difficult, but the lower the number, the better the buy and on this basis the Packard is a good buy.

You would have to be shopping for a medium-high priced car before you could consider buying the Packard 200, but if you have an appetite for luxury—and can afford it—you definitely should not overlook this car. The Packard 200 has comfort, class and an all-around roadability that is hard to beat.

WHEN counterbalanced trunk lid is raised, it exposes a spacious (32½ cu. ft.) compartment

TABLE OF PERFORMANCE

DYNAMOMETER TEST	
1200 rpm (full load) 25 mph	37.5 road hp
2000 rpm (full load) 41.5 mph	61 road hp
2850 rpm (full load) 63 mph	80 road hp
ACCELERATION TRIALS (SECONDS)	
Standing start ¼-mile	:22.74 (H)*; :21.04 (L-H)**
0-30 mph	:07.87 (H); :06.01 (L-H)
0-60 mph through gears	:20.66 (H); :17.31 (L-H)
10-60 mph in high	:18.13
30-60 mph in high	:13.28

*Shift using HIGH only. **Shift using LOW, then to HIGH.

TOP SPEED (MPH)	
Fastest one-way run	95.74
Average of four runs	93.17
BRAKE CHECK	
Stopping distance at 30 mph	32' 11"
Stopping distance at 45 mph	96' 2"
Stopping distance at 60 mph	236' 0"

FUEL CONSUMPTION (MPG)	
At a steady 30 mph	19.59
At a steady 45 mph	15.44
At a steady 60 mph	13.57
Through light traffic	15.68
Through medium traffic	12.49
Through heavy traffic	11.34

SPEEDOMETER CHECK	
At 30 mph indicated 31 mph	3.3% error
At 45 mph indicated 48 mph	6.7% error
At 60 mph indicated 65 mph	8.3% error

GENERAL SPECIFICATIONS

ENGINE	
Type	L-head, in-line 8
Bore and Stroke	3½x3¾
Stroke/Bore Ratio	1.07:1
Cubic Inch Displacement	288
Maximum Bhp	138 @ 3600 rpm (with Ultramatic) 135 @ 3600 rpm (with conventional)
Bhp/Cubic Inch	.479
Compression Ratio	7.5:1 (with Ultramatic) 7:1 (with conventional)

DRIVE SYSTEM

Transmission — Conventional three speed; Ratios: Low—2.43:1, Second—1.53:1, Third—1:1, Reverse—3.17:1

Ultramatic Ratios: Low—4.37:1, High—2.4:1, Direct—1:1, Reverse—3.94:1

Rear Axle—Hotchkiss drive, hypoid axle, Ratio: 3.9:1

DIMENSIONS	
Wheelbase	122 ins.
Overall Length	209⅜ ins.
Overall Height	62½ ins.
Overall Width	77⅝ ins.
Turning Radius	22½ ft.
Weight (Test Car)	4090 lbs.
Weight/Bhp Ratio	29.6:1
Weight/Road HP Ratio	51.1:1
Weight Distribution (Front to Rear)	55/45%

IF YOU want more performance from the Packard 200, you can get it for an additional $65. This low amount will give you the 155 bhp engine (standard with 300 series with Ultramatic) in place of this 138 bhp, in-line 8 engine

Testing the PACKARD "300"

Packard wearing chains blasts its way through a snowdrift at a speed of 70 mph.

By JULIAN LEGGETT

IF AN automobile has what the customer wants, there's no better way to find it out than to subject it to a scientific test under extreme winter conditions. And that's why the third in this SCIENCE AND MECHANICS series of car performance reports includes an *extra*—road tests on cars put through their paces in sub-zero weather, complete with severe icing and heavy snow, at the Motor Vehicle Research laboratory near Epping, N. H. The weather meant rough going for the test crew and members of our advisory committee who ran the tests, but their efforts make the tests far more significant to you car buyers who will have to do much bad weather driving.

Then, too, when the time came to subject the 1952 Packard "300" 4-door sedan to impartial engineering analysis by the independent Motor Vehicle Research organization, Packard's engineers challenged us by saying: "Give it the works!" And that's exactly what the test drivers did. Here are a few samples of what the "300" was called upon to do: start at 15° F. *below* zero after standing out all night; plunge through huge piles of snow and through mud-and-water troughs; take jumps so high that all four wheels were off the ground at the same time; speed over railroad cross-ties—a bone-rattling test of body construction; take skidding turns on a snow-covered, icy circular track and make "panic" stops to demonstrate how effective its brakes were. Packard engineers can be proud of the results.

(Top right) Packard takes a jump test at 58 mph. Note front wheels off ground. (Bottom right) coming out of the jump, front wheels did not bottom on this test and there was no lurch or sway as front shocks recovered nicely.

When started after standing overnight at 15° below zero, the Packard's engine caught after only 7 revolutions of the crankshaft. In a second test, it took only 5 revolutions to start the Packard with the temperature at 9 below zero. Incidentally, the door didn't suffer from frost in the door locks after standing out overnight—they opened without difficulty. With the temperature at 6 above, tests showed the heating system warmed the car interior to 100° F., or 94° above the outside temperature. That means Packard is a tight car, bodywise. Of course, you wouldn't want to maintain such a high temperature under normal driving conditions—but that's easily regulated.

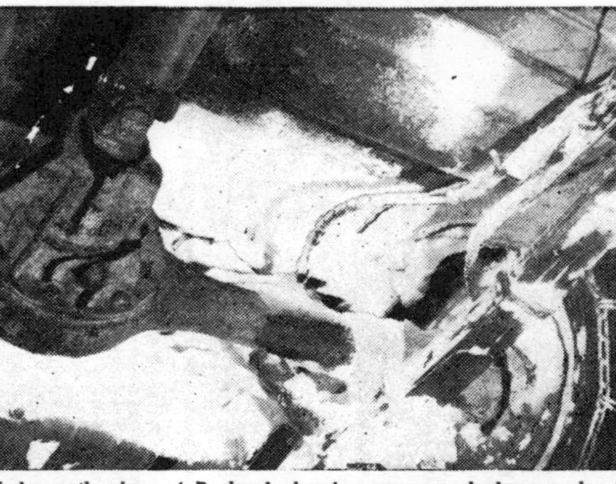

Underneath view of Packard showing snow packed up under it from rough weather runs. The snow did not freeze brake lines and failed to affect performance.

Demonstrating tightness of Packard body as well as efficiency of heater: thermometer at left shows outside temperature of 6 above zero; inside the car, the thermometer at right registered 100, after starting up and running heater in cold car for 25 minutes.

Jumping the Packard and running it along railroad cross-ties and through a mud-and-water trough, the springing and shock absorbing system, as well as the general stability of this 3,875-pound car (unloaded), showed up as excellent, as did the sturdiness of the body. Test drivers were particularly impressed with the car's rapid recovery from severe bumps without rebound—a nice feature to have handy if you happen to drive off the pavement and hit a sharp drop-off.

After the run through the mud-and-water trough, an examination of the engine showed that the pan and shrouding deflected so well that there was no water on top of the block nor on the wiring. The Ultramatic automatic transmission was tested in a mud hole, deep enough to cover the wheels to the hubs, and a gentle application of power brought the car out of the mud easily, although neither chains nor special tread tires were used. (This Ultramatic transmission is, by the way, one of the few automatic transmissions approved for the tough 8-mile Mt. Washington, N. H., climb.) Test drivers reported there was no noticeable click or hesitation in shifting, even when shift was down to a lower speed.

Henry Pratt, a member of the advisory board, drove this Packard about 600 miles before the

Here's the pedal pressure unit, used on the brake tests, attached to the Packard. The brakes on this car produced an exceptionally good percentage of efficiency, on both "panic" and normal stops.

Packard "300" Performance

DATE OF FINAL TEST: December 11, 1951

MAKE OF CAR: Packard "300" 4-door sedan

DRIVERS: Henry W. Pratt, A. J. White, Wm. H. Wells, Leonard B. Bell

WEATHER CONDITIONS (prevailing on last day of test, at which time tabular results given below were obtained. Additional road and track tests, made under extremely severe weather conditions, are reported in the text): Temperature: 44° F., humidity: 49%, wind velocity: 11 mph, wind direction: W

ROAD SURFACE: Asphalt-covered crushed rock

MILEAGE AT START OF INSTRUMENTS TEST: 1152

GAS USED IN TESTS: Amoco Ethyl

OIL USED: Amoco Permalube **VISCOSITY:** 10

TEST DATA

	Miles Per Hour				
GASOLINE MILEAGE: (checked with velocity flow meter, gas volume meter, 5th wheel and Mile-O-Meter vacuum gage—runs made with 4 occupants)	20	30	40	50	60
1st Run, North ....(mpg)	19	17	16½	16	14½
Reverse Run, South.........(mpg)	19¼	16½	16	15½	14¾
Average of both Runs......(mpg)	19⅛	16¾	16¼	15¾	14⅝
Manifold Vacuum	19"	17"	17"	15½"	15"
	60%	70%	60%	55%	50%
	17-18"	16"	15½"	16"	13"
	40%	30%	40%	45%	50%
ACCELERATION: (checked with dampened pendulum meter and timed electrically)	Low Range		High Range		
From standstill to speed specified.	2⅗ sec.	4⅘ sec.	7 sec.	8 sec.	14⅕ sec.
	from 0 to 70 mph took 14¼ sec.				
HILL CLIMBING: (checked with pendulum performance meter)	Low Range		High Range		
Steepest grade possible..........	31%	22%	16¼%	12%	10%
	steepest grade at 70 mph was 8½%				
BRAKE EFFICIENCY: (checked with decelerometer and Sioux pressure cylinder) Minimum allowable is 50%, which means car can be stopped in 26 feet while going 20 mph.	All panic stops				
% of efficiency..................	91%	95%	95%	94%	91%
Stopping distance in feet from speed specified	16¾	—	—	—	—
Pedal pressure in lbs. (for panic stops)	40	44	43¼	38	40
TOP SPEED: (checked with radar timer and 5th wheel)...........	Speedometer—103.5; Actual 96.25				
SPEEDOMETER ERROR:	¾	½	¾	1¼	3¼
	Speedometer error at 70 mph was 4¼				
BRAKE HORSEPOWER: (checked with pendulum performance meter and dynamometer)	76 horsepower — rear wheel full load—1 in. vacuum—2000 rpm.				

MOTOR VEHICLE RESEARCH herewith certifies that these are the true and accurate findings in tests conducted on the automobile named under the conditions specified.

A. J. White,
Motor Vehicle Research,
Gale Hall Engineering, Inc.

SPECIFICATIONS

a. ENGINE: 8-cylinder, L-Head valves; bore: 3½"; stroke: 4¼"; brake hp: 155 @ 3600 rpm; compression ratio: 7 to 1; torque: 270 Foot Pounds @ 2000 rpm

b. TRANSMISSION: (type) Ultramatic Torque Converter; Rear axle ratio: 3.9 to 1

c. EXTERIOR: Wheelbase: 127"; overall length: 217¾"; overall width: 77¹¹⁄₁₆"; overall height, 62²⁹⁄₃₂"; weight (ready for road): 3875 dry lbs.

d. INTERIOR:
Headroom: front seat 36"; back seat 36³⁄₁₆"
Legroom: front 43¹³⁄₁₆"; back 46½"
Hiproom: front seat 62¾"; back seat 62"

e. STEERING:
Turning circle 30'9"
Lock to lock sprung—6 turns; unsprung—5 turns

f. VISIBILITY:
Windshield area: 97.7 sq. in.
Driver's eye to road over left fender—38' 11"
Driver's eye to road over hood center—37' 11"
Driver's eye to road over right fender—35' 9"
Rear window area: 1117 sq. in.

g. MISCELLANEOUS:
Battery: 6 volts; Capacity 100 amps
Location: mounted under hood in left fender shield
Tire size: 8.00 x 15; Tire pressure: Factory specs. 24 lbs. operated @ 28 lbs. all around
Luggage capacity: 36 cu. ft.
Springing: Front—coil; Rear—semi-elliptic
Special Features: Defroster louvers run full width of windshield

Drivers' Observations

ROADABILITY: Steering wheel response is excellent and this car doesn't sway or cramp up a bit on the worst curves. Only once was a little chatter noticed on one very sharp, high speed turn. Recovery from an intentional spin was exceptionally good. On the straightaway, there was no wander and the tracking ability of this car was excellent. Front end balance is good but car does seem a little light in front end at very high speeds.

RIDING COMFORT: Very good. On the most extreme jump test, recovery of front shocks was excellent, even though car bottomed with a very strong force. Noticed some steering wheel post vibration on the most severe jump test. Front seat wouldn't tire average driver who sat erect but its back might need to be tucked up a bit higher for those who slump. Front arm rest seemed a bit high to this 5 ft. 9 in. driver, crowding his left elbow. Rear arm rest seemed a bit low to average size passenger.

HARMONIC BALANCE POINT (best cruising speed): 70 mph.

INSTRUMENTS: Well-located and easy to read. It was particularly easy to pick up speedometer reading without hunting for it.

ACCESSORIES: Spare tire and tools are easy to get at. Luggage compartment is very roomy, has well-counterbalanced lid that opens on turn of key and pushes up with practically no effort, and compartment has good interior light. Finish looks hand-rubbed, has no "orange-peel" effect from spraying. Heating system is extremely efficient. Rear view mirror needs darker glass to reduce glare.

OTHER REMARKS: Wish they'd position front air conditioning intake so it wouldn't pick up CO from cars ahead in heavy traffic or tunnel but this location seems to be common on most cars. Lift on shift lever is so slight it might be easily bumped into Reverse from Drive position, which is not good but is typical of automatic transmissions. There's so much vision in this car it feels as if you are riding without a top.

performance tests to bring its mileage up to that required for a fair performance trial. Here are some of his comments: "My first impression was that it was a *big* automobile. I had to become accustomed to looking over the broad hood and a pair of fenders that looked very wide, but after I drove it a few miles, this impression left me. What I especially liked was the ability of the brakes to perform with such ease and with such effectiveness. About the only fault I could find was the rear view mirror, which picked up the horizontal lines in the car's upholstery and tended to confuse the man at the wheel, particularly at night."

Those Packard brakes are vacuum-powered, therefore require but slight pedal pressure, and drivers reported no sidesway, even in panic stops. In emergency stops from 50 *mph*, the braking efficiency was registered at 94%. This compares with the minimum allowable efficiency in many states of 50%, which means that a car traveling 20 *mph* can be stopped in 26 feet on a first-class, dry road surface. Packard's 94% was achieved with a pedal pressure of only 38 pounds—amazingly low for panic stops. The test crew raised the question of whether the car would lose its braking power if the engine stalled and cut off the manifold vacuum. This point was quickly settled by driving at 50 *mph*, then killing the vacuum and emptying the vacuum tank. When the brakes were applied, their efficiency was high, far exceeding safety requirements. In fact, about all that was lost was the softness of pedal pressure. Test drivers remarked that brakes on the particular car tested might be adjusted a little so rear ones would take hold just a little before front ones—it was the other way around during the initial tests. Otherwise they labeled the braking operation as "smooth as silk" and requiring only "a feather touch."

Conditions were not ideal for speed tests on the open road, but the Packard reached 103.5 *mph*, speedometer reading, or 96.24 by radar timing, which is more accurate. Since the road surface did not lend itself to record trials, the powerful engine was not even tuned before the run. The long, low overhang on this car would make it rough for cross-country work but then, like almost all cars today, it wasn't designed for off-the-road use.

Note to some of those who supply Packard with parts—you should try harder to match the job Packard does on the car itself. That solenoid on top of the starter wasn't good and starter wouldn't work at lower than 15° below zero, until the solenoid was replaced. Spark plug setting on arrival was 22, and it should have been 27. Points specified at 16 were set at *10 minus* on arrival. But these are minor problems of service and adjustment common to all new cars, and they don't detract from what the test drivers found to be a remarkably good automobile.

Here is the Packard riding the cross-ties, a tough test for any car. At a certain speed (not the one at the time this photo was taken), the test driver reports he could hardly tell that car wasn't on a pavement.

As for accessories, the testing crew particularly liked the pushbutton operated radio antenna (who wants to get out on a freezing night to lower the antenna before going into the garage?), the windshield wiper control on the steering column which was easy to get at and adjust, and the defroster louvers running the full width of the windshield. They also liked the roomy bin-type glove compartment, which doesn't act like Fibber McGee's closet when you open it, and the two ashtrays in front—one on the driver's and one on the passenger's side.

But the important thing was the fine performance as demonstrated throughout the 2,000 some miles of driving tests. This 155 *hp* Packard did all right for itself—and then some. Pricewise, at this writing, the Packard "300" sells for about $3,094 F.O.B. Detroit, plus $189 for the Ultramatic transmission and $76.58 for the special heater-defroster, both listed as extras.

ADVISERS ON TEST PROCEDURES

To make sure that each of these new car performance tests is scientifically sound and completely unbiased, Motor Vehicle Research, the independent testing laboratory which is a subsidiary of Gale Hall Engineering Co., of Boston, Mass., receives advice and supervision on technical procedures from the following recognized authorities:

PROFESSOR DEAN FALES
Chassis construction authority, Massachusetts Institute of Technology, Boston, Mass., and member, National Technical Committee of the Contest Board, American Automobile Association.

DR. JOHN M. COLONAS
Chief engineer, Commercial Filters Corp., South Boston, Mass.

HENRY PRATT
Automotive lubrication expert, American Oil Co. (a subsidiary of Standard Oil Co. of Indiana), Boston, Mass.

LEONARD BELL
Ignition expert, Mallory Electric Co., Detroit, Mich.

DR. R. F. BUCHAN
Clinical director, Prudential Life Insurance Co., Newark, N. J., authority on safety.

FRANK THILOW
Service and lubrication engineer, American Oil Co., Baltimore, Md.

DR. FREDERICK N. DUBE
Authority on vision, Manchester, N. H.

LAWRENCE E. ASHWORTH
Instruments engineer, United States Gauge Co., Boston, Mass.

VICTOR NIELSEN
Authority on motor wheel alignment and equipment, Bear Mfg. Co., Rock Island, Ill.

The beautiful sleek, low slung three-passenger Packard Pan American captured top honors at the International Motor Sports Show in New York as the car with the most outstanding design and engineering achievement.

An ALL-AMERICAN sports car, the 1952 Packard Pan American . . . adjudged the 'most outstanding design and engineering development' at the International Motor Sports Show in New York . . . is being studied by the factory for possible future production.

The sleek, low-slung three-passenger car, styled by Richard Arbib, consultant to the Henney Motor Company, Inc. of Freeport, Ill., possesses ample luggage space, roominess and serviceability.

Unlike foreign counterparts, the Pan American is wide, and with a low center of gravity, is built on a 122 inch wheelbase Packard convertible chassis. Overall length is 221 inches.

The overall height is 53 inches with the top raised, and 36 inches to the top of the door. A well behind the front seat holds the recessed top and is covered by a metal lid.

Exterior door buttons are flush with the body, blending into a chrome moulding that sweeps along the top of the door. The seat, fashioned with contrasting oyster white and dark green genuine leather, is one piece with an arm rest in the center of the back for use when only two passengers are riding. The rest disappears into the back when not in use.

Powerplant is a Packard 327 Thunderbolt engine; carburetion and cylinder head modifications have resulted in 175 horsepower. The hood air scoop is functional in feeding air to the carburetor and a triple stack dresses up the exhaust tube at the rear.

Chrome plated wire spoke wheels are used throughout with the spare tire rear-mounted. Regular wheel lugs are used instead of European quick change knock-off hubs.

Instrument panel is finished in top-grain leather and similar trim on the steering wheel, door handles and dash knobs complement the Pan American's interior decor. ☆ ☆

Hugh J. Ferry, left, Packard president receives prized trophy from show manager Fred Pittera, center. Show Queen Shirley Talbott, right, helped make presentation official.

Exterior covering of seat is a contrasting oyster white and dark green genuine leather. Instrument panel is also finished in leather with a similar trim on steerwheels and door handles.

Each month our Missouri-minded expert gives an unbiased report of the cars he tests. This month Ted Koopman drives the beautiful new 1952 Packard.

Ted Koopman Photo

Ted Koopman Photo

TESTING THE PACKARD FOR 1952

By TED KOOPMAN

ASSOCIATE EDITOR, SPEED AGE

FOR MORE than 50 years the world challenging slogan "Ask The Man Who Owns One," has illustrated the printed word's far reaching influence, and though the Frenchman says, "Demandez a l'homme qui en possede un," the German, "Frage den mann welcher einen besitzt" or the Spaniard, "Pregunte al hombre que possee uno," each associates his words with Packard and fine motor cars.

Packard, Peerless and Pierce Arrow—three great names in automotive Americana to stir the imagination of all who knew them—and in the 1952 models, Packard, the surviving member of the famous trio, perpetuates their traditional high standards.

Cappy Capwell Photo

Ted Koopman Photo

The graceful curves and folded wings of the flamingo hood ornament are truly beautiful and its position, set back from the front, greatly reduces the danger of obstructing front view vision.

Beneath the hood is a compact installation of engine and accessories; a far cry from the huge four-cylinder engine of the 1910 Model 30 Packard which I learned to drive.

Well do I recall the progressive type transmission with its long, polished brass gear shift lever; contrasted with this ingeniously efficient Ultramatic transmission it is a jolt to realize how we have accepted the meteoric development of the automobile without recognizing its material effect on the social pattern of modern living, or how deeply we are obligated to those responsible for its existence.

Despite the contrast in design, there are several features common to old and new. Each represents the highest development of engineering in its era—each reflects a perfection of detail that overlooks no essential component, while in each car the superior quality of material and workmanship is evidence of intensive research and infinite attention to detail that set them apart from the majority of cars.

The convenient location of fixtures and operating controls; the quality and design of both interior and exterior hardware—are all the result of careful and intelligent planning. The superior handling of the front suspension and the effectively balanced chassis and its excellent riding characteristics are not the result of hit and miss engineering. Their performance is as predetermined; in fact, the entire assembly is engineered and constructed to a high degree of mathematical prediction.

Through the years, Packard has retained two distinctive features in the hexagonal red hub center and the curved top radiator with its lateral declivities extending to the vertical sections of the shell. With the passing of the exposed radiator, the essence of the pattern was embodied in the grille and the functional red hub center became only symbolic.

The 1952 Packard line consists of two basic chassis, one of 122 inch and the other 127 inch wheelbase. The shorter carries an eight-cylinder, in-line engine of 288 cubic inches. Rated at 135 brake horsepower, and the Model 200 bodies. The 127 inch chassis employs the same type engine increased to 327 cubic inches with a brake horsepower rating of 150 and is fitted with the Model 300 body.

This same 127 inch chassis, when equipped with a higher compression engine having nine main bearings, is rated at 155 horsepower, and with a deluxe type 300 body, is called the Patrician, or 400 model.

The convertible and hard top or sport coupe are not available on either of the above combinations, but are furnished on the 122 inch chassis employing the 327 cubic inch engine and designated Model 250.

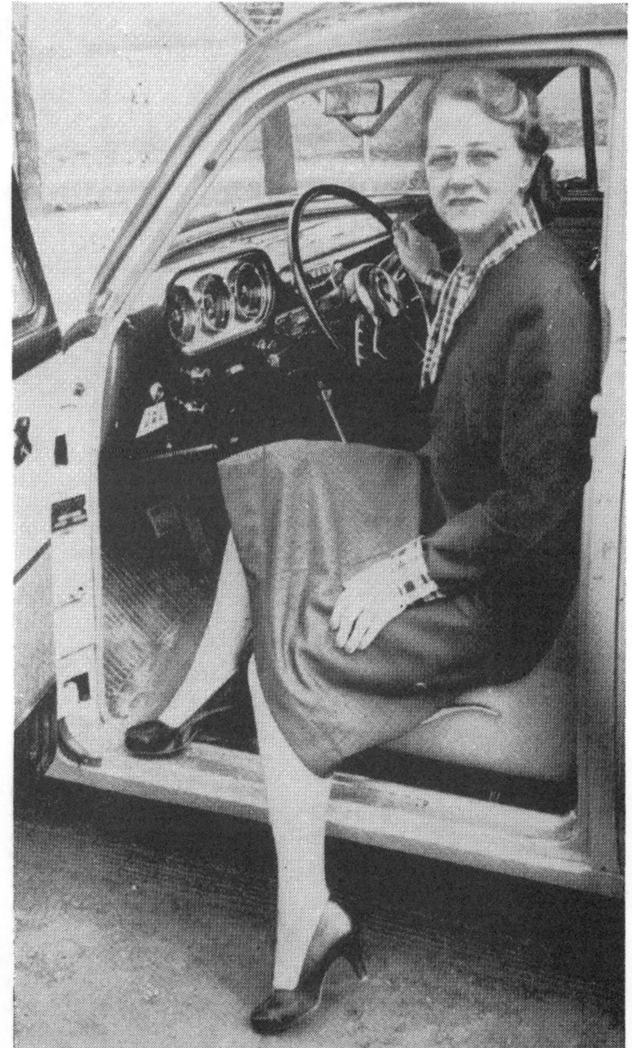

Ted Koopman Photo

Feminine test driver for the Packard was Mrs. Herford A. Smith of East Greenbush, N. Y. Mrs. Herford reported that the Packard practically drove itself through traffic.

Cappy Capwell Photo

During break-in period, veteran test driver Ted Koopman, keeps a constant check on the running gear. He makes repeated stops to assure himself that when it comes time for the running of the actual tests the car will be in perfect operating condition.

All models have the three-speed synchro-mesh transmission as standard equipment and the overdrive and Ultramatic units are optional for all models. The 200 engine has adjustable steel tappets, but the hydraulic lifters as used in the 300 engine are available as an optional choice at a small increase in cost.

The 200 model offers both two and four-door sedans, but only the four-door is furnished in the 300 and 400 series. The standard models avoid the use of non-functional chrome and are exceptionally trim in appearance, but the addition of chrome knickknacks on the deluxe and 400 models break up the graceful longitudinal body lines and create an illusion of stubbiness.

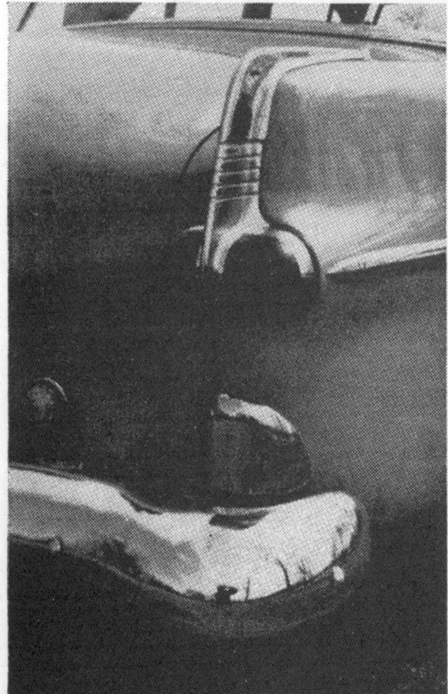

Ted Koopman Photo

The original taillight design is both distinctive and functional and identifies the 1952 Packard among all other cars.

The 300, four-door sedan is exceptionally sleek and beautifully proportioned with an overall appearance excelled by no other '52 car.

The recent trend towards full width frontal areas is not conducive to attractive grilles although the Packard suffers less in this respect than the majority of cars. It seems odd that manufacturers, racing for extreme horsepower output, should utilize frontal designs requiring tremendous power to overcome air resistance and thus cancel power increases. This also applies to the square rear end design with its excessive air drag. In instances where the fenders are above the rear deck level, smoke tests have demonstrated even greater air drag.

Doubtless, this faulty aerodynamic design accounts for the poor high speed performance of many late model cars and their exceptionally high gas consumption at speeds over 60 MPH.

Equipped with Ultramatic transmission and Packard's new power brake, driving this 300 model is effortless, with practically no correctional steering required at any speed, regardless of road contour or wind turbulence. For normal driving the automatic transmission gives smooth and effective operation, but doesn't permit utilizing the peak performance latent in this outstanding car.

The front seat isn't as comfortable for driving as one might wish, and why this is so, is difficult to determine. Possibly, a slightly wider seat with greater height at the front edge might be the answer. From a standpoint of passenger comfort, the seat is excellent, with ample leg room for the largest person.

The rear seat is roomy and comfortable but its position in relation to the rear window frame, directly over the passenger's head, poses the danger of striking against this solid frame when vertical motion is excessive. Although serious injury might not result, it wouldn't be pleasant.

The narrow, drop arm rest when retracted is uncomfortable for the person seated in the middle and I believe a wider section, similar to that employed by Hudson offers greater all around comfort and convenience. The added width brings the cushion separation to either side of the middle passenger, providing comfort equal to the outer positions, and when lowered, provides greater lateral support for the one or two passengers occupying the seat.

Other than these minor points, the body is exceptionally well dimensioned and offers the utmost in luxury and convenience. Door openings are large and head room permits access without undue stooping.

Vision is excellent with the position and lighting of instruments giving no reflection on the windshield at night; controlling the map lights with the single headlight switch is also extremely convenient.

The highpoint of design is the glove compartment, or more properly, the drawer. The outward appearance is no different from the usual drop front compartment, but there the similarity ends, for instead of tilting forward, the entire front pulls forward revealing a drawer with the dimensions of the average compartment, with ample capacity and automatically lighted.

Another innovation is the wiper and windshield washer control, located very conveniently on the left side of the steering column.

In general, the design follows conventional and accepted practices, although Packard's adherence to the in-line engine has been somewhat controversial. It is undeniable that the V8 design offers greater crankshaft rigidity at a minimum of cost and while Packard's nine-main bearing crank is equally rigid, the cost is considerably greater.

The V8 appears to have a further edge in fuel distribution and cooling as well as requiring less room for installation.

The 300 model sedan I used had but 30 miles on the odometer when I left Packard headquarters. Before attempting performance checks, I drove it a couple hundred miles in normal business use to bring total mileage on leaving for Lake Placid, New York, to 361.

Ted Koopman Photo

The sloping hood gives unusual road vision and its curved frontal portion blends well with the arched grille.

Except for the optional power brake, only minor changes have been made in the 1952 model. In reality this brake is more a power assist brake, for with the pedal acting directly on the master cylinder, braking action is possible without the introduction of vacuum but when utilized, it provides approximately 60% of the required pedal pressure.

This gives feather weight braking pressures and requires careful application to prevent over-braking. In operation, the heel is not lifted, but pivots as the toe swings from throttle to brake pedal thus permitting a much quicker shift under emergency conditions with a reduction in reaction lag between visual conception and physical application.

The delicate touch is quickly acquired, and under normal driving conditions it is the easiest and most efficient brake I've ever used. In an emergency my foot instinctively slams down the pedal with a resulting stop that would throw a passenger through the windshield.

That is my only criticism of this type brake; how universal this overbraking in emergencies becomes, may decide the future of the power brake as standard equipment.

That it is meeting with some resistance is disclosed by the fact that one dealer informed me he would accept no cars thus equipped. However, I believe it should be given a fair trial before being condemned as undesirable.

I had driven the 1951 Packard equipped with Ultramatic transmission, but not to any great

Cappy Capwell Photo

Although struck with devastating force, the Packard's heavy body construction absorbed much of the impact without damage to frame. Ted Koopman sustained minor injuries in this crash, but the Packard's door in remaining closed prevented serious injury.

extent, and while the unit gives smooth and effortless operation, acceleration in driving range is sluggish with the torque converter apparently churning wildly yet going no place. Starting in the low range offers a different picture and a zero to 30 spurt requires less than five seconds.

As a kick down gear, it hasn't the effective drive of third speed in a standard transmission and overdrive, and offers less economy in cruising ranges. Thus the person who uses a car for city and suburban travel, will be served better with the Ultramatic, while for fast cross country travel, the synchro-mesh transmission with overdrive would seem more desirable.

During the round trip to Lake Placid, temperature variations developed the need of both ventilating and heating, as well as defrosting or perhaps demisting would be more correct. The unit in the Packard furnished a blast of cool air that is really effective and the same may be said of its heating qualifications, while the full width defroster openings are a big improvement over the usual narrow slots.

In a car having a body as wide as this one, the control of the right hand window becomes a problem when riding alone, as operating the window adjustment crank requires a reach that endangers driving control. Complete safety requires a stop to make the necessary adjustment. The use of remote mechanical control of at least that window would become a safety measure as well as one of convenience.

The upholstery in this car was patterned in black and gray stripes and was used in the area behind the rear seat with the result that the rear window resembled a TV set out of adjustment, with black and white lines wiggling across the screen. Thus vision through the rear view mirror was constantly interrupted by these moving reflections, which at their worst, completely blocked its use, but by placing my topcoat over this striped covering, the difficulty was eliminated.

I found the front seat somewhat tiring to my throttle leg, and a light sweater, rolled up and placed under my knee provided the support necessary for driving ease.

In making this test trip, it was not my intention to set new records for cross country travel yet, I was curious to the extent of learning the car's capacity to take real road punishment. Regardless of the roughness or twisting of the roads, the faster I drove the better it handled and the action of the front suspension was tops. Steering through the tightest turns was effortless and the body remained level both transversely and lengthwise, since the dampening of the rear springs held it to a minimum of vertical motion.

The ability of this car to change direction without the usual body tilt is one of its outstanding features; anyone who has spent a day in the average car, fighting to maintain equilibrium while

Standard Specifications 1952 PACKARD 300 4 Door Sedan

Width of front seat measured 5 inches from back	57 inches
Width of back seat measured 5 inches from back	55½ inches
Depth of front seat cushion	18½ inches
Depth of rear seat cushion	19 inches
Height of front seat cushion	14 inches
Height of rear seat cushion	13-27/32 inches
Front seat horizontal adjustment	4⅞ inches
Vertical distance wheel to seat	5⅛ inches
Head room front seat	36 inches
Head room back seat	35-3/6 inches
Leg room front seat	43-13/16 inches
Leg room rear seat	46½ inches
Width of trunk at top	55⅜ inches

Engine Specifications

ENGINE:	
Number of cylinders	8
Arrangement	in-line
Bore	3½ inches
Stroke	4¼ inches
Displacement	327 cubic inches
Taxable horsepower	39.2
Brake horsepower	150 @ 3600 RPM
Maximum torque	270 @ 2000 RPM
Compression ratio (standard)	7 to 1
Compression ratio (optional)	7.8 to 1
PISTONS:	
Make	own
Material	Aluminum alloy
Features	Split skirt—plated
Weight	19.575 ounces
Compression rings	2
Oil rings	1
CONNECTING RODS:	
Material	Steel forging
Length C. to C.	7-11/16 inches
Weight	36 ounces
CRANKSHAFT:	
Material	Steel forging
Weight	104 pounds
Number main bearings	5—optional 9
Connecting rod journal dia.	2.250 inches
VALVE TIMING:	
Intake opens	15° BTC
Intake closes	43° ABC
Exhaust opens	53° BBC
Exhaust closes	4° ATC
Firing order	1-6-2-5-8-3-7-4
MISCELLANEOUS:	
Oil capacity including filter	7 quarts
Gas capacity	20 gallons
Water capacity with heater	20.5 quarts
Spark plugs	14 mm

Chassis

FRAME:	
Type	Channel rails; cross and X brace
WHEELBASE:	127 inches
TREAD:	
Front	60 inches
Rear	61-7/32 inches
WEIGHT:	
Shipping	3875 pounds
Curb	4205 pounds
Overall Length	217¾ inches
Overall Width	77-11/16 inches
Overall Height	62-29/32 inches
REAR AXLE:	
Type	Semi-floating
Gearing	Hypoid
Ratio Conventional	3.9
Overdrive	4.1
Automatic	3.54
TRANSMISSION:	
Conventional:	
Number forward speeds	3
Overdrive	yes
Ratios: first	2.43
second	1.53
third	1.00
over-drive	.722
reverse	3.16
Automatic Type:	Ultramatic
Number forward speeds	3
Down-shift possible up to	67 MPH
Ratios: first	Torque converter
second	Torque conv. plus 1.82
third	Direct
reverse	Torque conv. plus 1/64
FOOT BRAKES:	
Drum diameter	12 inches
Material	Centrifuse cast iron
Effective area	208.25 square inches
Percent effective rear	40%
Type	Hydraulic 2 shoe—power optional
Linings	Marshall—4112
STEERING:	
Type	Worm and 3 tooth roller
Turns, lock to lock	4¾ turns
Ratio	22.3
Wheel diameter	18 inches
Turning radius	22 feet-6 inches
ROAD CLEARANCE:	
At rear axle	8-21/32 inches
SUSPENSION:	
Front	Independent parallelogram
Rear	2 longitudinal-semi elliptic
Shock absorbers	Delco direct acting
TIRES:	
Standard	8.00 x 15

Performance Data

Top Speed

	Indicated	Actual
East-west run	105 MPH	98 MPH
Reverse	107 MPH	99 MPH
Average	106 MPH	98.5 MPH

Rate of Acceleration

0 to 30, low range only	4.35 seconds
0 to 60, low and drive	13.82 seconds
20 to 50, low and drive	9.56 seconds
30 to 50, kick-down	8.01 seconds
30 to 60, kick-down	9.71 seconds
40 to 60, kick-down	7.20 seconds

Speedometer Correction

Indicated	Actual
20 MPH	18½ MPH
30 MPH	28 MPH
40 MPH	37 MPH
50 MPH	46 MPH
60 MPH	56½ MPH
70 MPH	65 MPH
80 MPH	75 MPH
90 MPH	81 MPH
100 MPH	93 MPH
105 MPH	98 MPH

Dynamometer Test

1200 RMP	49 rear axle horsepower
2000 RPM	75 rear axle horsepower
3000 RPM	96 rear axle horsepower

Brake Test—Emergency Stop

From	Foot Brake (power)	Hand brake
30 MPH	21 feet	84 feet
40 MPH	64 feet	245 feet
60 MPH	104 feet	—

Withstood 25 panic stops from 40 MPH to zero without fade.

Fuel Consumption—Premium Gas

Steady 30 MPH	17.5 MPG
Steady 40 MPH	17 MPG
Steady 50 MPH	15 MPG
Steady 60 MPH	14.5 MPG
Heavy traffic	10.5 MPG
Average of 615 miles	14.3 MPG

All tests made with tire pressure 28 pounds. Dry roads; asphalt top. Temperature 60 to 65 degrees; wind negligible.

Other Cars Road-Tested by Speed Age

the body swings and sways, will appreciate the level riding qualities of the Packard.

Excessive body tilt is not only unpleasant for passengers, but is mechanically unsound and places undue loading on the outside wheels and tires as well as altering the steering geometry. On top of that, it looks bad to see an otherwise well behaved car, roll like a drunken alligator each time it negotiates a curve of any severity.

Running northwest from Fitchburg, Mass., to Rutland, Vt., the roads are narrow and winding with some very sharp grades. Scattered showers with wet roads made cornering treacherous, but the excellent balance of the chassis permitted my going through these turns as though the road was dry.

Through the mountainous country, speeds were maintained regardless of grades, the automatic transmission shifting to give the most efficient gear ratio. Since this unit does not go into free wheeling it is also extremely effective for down-hill braking.

Having completed slightly over 1,500 miles under every type of driving conditions found in this New England area, the Packard handled in a manner equal to the best of our American production cars, and the only point that might be challenged is its tendency to float slightly at high speeds.

As this takes place only at relatively high speed and even then not to extreme, I hardly think it should be called detrimental to the car's performance.

Taking all its qualifications into consideration, my judgment classifies this car as excellent and except for its shortcomings in seating arrangement, it would be classed outstanding. The break-down is as follows:

Overall rating ....Excellent
Ease of handling, riding and cruising performance ....Outstanding
Roadability on rough and crooked roads....Outstanding
Body stability in directional change ....Outstanding
Mechanical operation...Excellent
Visibility ....Excellent
Driving position and fatigue potential .....Fair
Passenger comfort .....Good
Overall safety factor....Good
Braking efficiency and freedom from fade...Excellent

Record of Lake Placid Trip

Left Newton, Mass., at 5 a.m. to

	Miles
Fitchburg, Mass.—1 hour	47
Keene, N. H.—40 minutes	36
Bellows Falls, Vt.—30 minutes	23
Rutland, Vt.—1 hour, 10 minutes	52
Whitehall, N. Y.—35 minutes	24
Ticonderoga, N. Y.—40 minutes	29
Westport, N. Y.—45 minutes	26
Keene, N. Y.—25 minutes	21
Lake Placid, N. Y.—20 minutes	14
Saranac Lake, N. Y.—12 minutes	10
Keene, N. Y.—35 minutes	24
Pottersville, N. Y.—1 hr., 5 min.	44
Glenns Falls, N. Y.—1 hr., 5 min.	39
Saratoga Springs, N. Y.—35 min.	19
Albany, N. Y.—55 minutes	34
Pittsfield, Mass.—50 minutes	37
Springfield, Mass.—1 hr., 15 min.	56
Newton, Mass.—1 hr., 40 min.	80

Total mileage—615 miles.

Elapsed time—23 hours, 40 minutes.

Actual driving time—14 hours, 17 minutes.

Newton to Saranac—282 miles; 6 hours, 17 minutes......46.5 MPH

Saranac to Newton—333 miles; 8 hours ....41.5 MPH

Average for total distance...44 MPH

Gasoline consumed: 43 gallons. Average ....14.3 MPG

While visiting with Mr. and Mrs. Herford A. Smith of East Greenbush, N. Y., I asked Mrs. Smith to drive the car and pass her opinion on to SPEED AGE readers. As her driving experience covers 25 years over roads where mud in the spring and snow in the winter, coupled with the constant heavy traffic, challenge one continually, her judgment is sound.

"I liked the way the seat fitted me, it was practically tailor-made and although I had the feeling of pitching forward when I first got in the car, when I started to drive this impression vanished. The brakes are superb with a minimum of effort.

"The glove compartment caught my fancy since its contents are so accessible. The high windshield made the front seat very warm when driving into the sun and I believe a sun visor is essential to comfort, and although the cool air fan helped, I don't like the added whirring noise.

"This Packard handled very easily and practically drove itself through traffic, while the exceptional vision made parking a minor problem. I think it is a fine car and one I'd enjoy owning."

Safetywise, the Packard rates somewhat higher than average, with the interior about the usual style except for the two-spoke steering wheel which gives a driver more chance of escaping chest injuries in event of collision.

The brakes should be classed as adjuncts to safety and whether their potential for dangerous over-braking will offset their safety gains, only future developments will determine.

The safety type rims are valuable and by holding the tire on the rim after a blowout, may easily prevent a roll-over.

The exterior surface is free from danger spots and the well located and designed door handles offer little if any danger. The hood ornament is safer than on previous models where the wings were extended, rather than folded back, and being located away from the extreme front of the hood, it may be considered comparatively less dangerous.

Seldom does Fate administer misfortune with one hand while tempering it with the other. In this instance, however, the misfortune—having the car seriously damaged in collision—is outweighed by having opportunity to describe at first hand the Packard's structural resistance to impact and its bearing on passenger safety.

Tests completed, I was driving to Boston to return the car, and while stopped at a traffic signal, a heavy fuel tank truck—apparently out of control—crashed into the car, opposite the left rear door, with the truck traveling an estimated 35 miles an hour, the impact was frightful and I sat with shoulders hunched, while around me rose the sounds of destruction.

The car lifted as though to roll over; at the same time spinning wildly in a counter-clockwise direction; then returning to a level position. It continued its spin to come to rest headed in the opposite direction. Somewhat dazed, I looked around expecting to find the entire rear portion of body torn from the chassis. To my amazement, it was intact and I was able to unlatch and open the door beside me.

The body was a crumpled ruin of folded and twisted metal from the edge of the left front door to the extreme tip of the tail, and with the fender driven down over the tire, movement was impossible. The trunk had been twisted, with the lid sprung open, and while the large rear window had been forced away from the frame, it was intact.

The only glass to suffer was in the door receiving the brunt of the impact, and that, while cracked in a thousand and one places, had not shattered. The unusually heavy body metal had absorbed much of the force of collision without transmitting it to the frame.

All the doors had remained closed and this no doubt can be attributed to the quality hardware employed throughout the body, and this fact alone is responsible for my miraculous escape without serious injury. Had the left front door sprung open, I would have landed in the street, possibly under the truck's wheels.

As it was, while no injury was apparent at the time, the following day developed considerable lameness and tender portions of anatomy.

After the usual formalities, an attempt was made to free the rear wheel but only with the aid of two bumper jacks could we move the heavy metal jammed against the wheel. Unable to clear it completely, I ran slowly to a nearby garage, where, with the help of a hydraulic ram, the wheel was given ample clearance, permitting normal operation of the car.

When a heavy truck travelling 35 MPH strikes a car broadside, it is only reasonable to expect the frame to be twisted so far out of line as to be undrivable. Here is a car able to continue on its way with the frame perfectly straight, wheels in line and steering normal. In fact, further examination failed to locate any mechanical damage to chassis, engine or drive units.

The body might be called a total loss and the secret of its protecting action is doubtless the slow crumbling effect of the heavy gauge metal which absorbed the tremendous force of the impact. As for its stability, I am certain the low center of gravity and wider than normal rear tread, prevented the completion of what started to be a roll.

The next time I am asked what car offers the greatest chance for passenger survival in case of collision, there can be little doubt as to my answer. ☆ ☆

Pan-American model, styled along continental lines, is low, has large air-scoop on the hood, a minimum of chrome, large window area and wire racing wheels.

PACKARD *Pan American*

CREATED especially for the 1952 International Motor Sports Show in New York, Packard's *Pan American* is a serious contender in the continental styling competition. Richard Arbib, engineering consultant, is the designer, and Henney Motor Co., the builder.

Sleek and sculptured, the *Pan American* stands a scant 36 inches with its top down. (Fifty-three inches with top up). Power plant is a Packard 175 h.p. "Thunderjet" engine with extra carburetion. Overall length is 221 inches on a 122-inch wheel base. Resting on a Packard convertible frame, the low-slung *Pan American* hugs the road like a lovesick sailor.

An unbroken flowing design line extends from the functional air scoop to the debonair externally-mounted spare wheel.

Without visibly striving for a streamlined flyer, the Henney Co. has produced a speedy-looking, powerful airborne beauty. Furthermore, this Freeport, Illinois company has shown ingenuity as well as good taste in the minor design features. There is a minimum of chrome on the smooth-flowing panels. Wire wheels,

Richard Arbib, well-known automobile stylist, spent much time designing and building the Pan-American. Here we see Dick checking the wheel and seat position.

At this point, with the front fender in position, it is arc-welded to the body.

Head-on view of the new Packard "Pan-American reveals air-scoop construction.

long recognized as a "must" on sports cars, have been used to enhance a feeling of lightness. Knifing out from the rear end triple exhaust stacks create the impression of movement even in repose.

PASSENGER comfort is a major consideration. Three persons can sit comfortably in the roomy front seat. When only two passengers are aboard, a center arm rest may be pulled from the seat-back for added comfort.

Behind the front seat is a "well" into which the convertible top may be folded when not in use. When the top is down, a metal lid, which conforms to body contour, covers the "well."

Exterior door buttons do not protrude or break the clean lines. Instead, the push buttons harmonize with the small chrome molding on door top.

Although anticipated production figures and costs were not available, the *Pan American* is an indication that Packard, like General Motors and Chrysler, is in the sports car business for keeps.

Guide lines painted by body expert aid him in the sculpturing of the rear fender.

Elongated rear deck of special Packard is checked for correctness of contour.

Luxurious interior upholstery and appointments include leather-covered dash.

PACKARD 300

An MT Research Report
By Walt Woron

Editor Woron stops on Donner Summit with Packard 300 on return from Lake Tahoe

Packard's new "Easamatic" power brakes make traffic driving a pleasure; highway roadability at high cruising speeds is good

SINCE THE TURN of the century, the phrase "Ask the man who owns one" has been familiar to automotive-minded persons. Synonymous with the name Packard is the pride of ownership exhibited by those persons who drive Packards, and they have good reason to be. Maybe the Packard isn't a "bomb" and maybe it doesn't handle like a sports car, but for the average motorist it provides good family transportation.

So that we could get an owner's reaction to our test car, the Packard 300, we took it on a weekend 1300-mile, round-trip jaunt from Los Angeles to Lake Tahoe. This route took us through all kinds of picturesque country, from desert at sea level through narrow-laned hairpin mountain passes at 8000-foot altitudes. For marathon driving runs of 10 hours' duration experienced on the Tahoe trip, the Packard proved itself to be a car that didn't appreciably tire either the driver or passengers.

Handling Good on Cruising Rides

Every type of road was encountered on the Tahoe trip, and our general reaction to Packard's handling qualities is good, especially on long, cruising rides. Steering wheel vibration and shock are only noticeable on washboard roads.

Going into tight corners, such as those experienced on narrow twisting roads up the sides of mountains, didn't give us any problem. Through high speed turns, the front end has a little tendency to "walk"; at normal speeds, this condition is never noticeable. The steering wheel returns to neutral quickly. The front end never breaks loose on any kind of turn, but at high speeds you can break the rear end loose on a sharp turn or on wet pavement. Railroad tracks, tar strips, shoulders, and edges of asphalt roads have no appreciable effect on steering wheel control. When standing still, with the combination of weight and low pressure tires and despite the high steering ratio, the wheel is hard to turn.

One outstanding characteristic of the '52 Packard is its ability to take corners without excessive body tilt, a tribute to the engineering of the suspension system and weight distribution of the body, which gives the overall ride a balanced, equalized effect, ideal for comfort on long trips.

Various Models Compared

Last year we tested the Packard 200 equipped with the 138-bhp engine and Ultramatic transmission (Febr. '51 MOTOR TREND). This year's test car, the Packard 300, seemed to have better roadability and cruising comfort, possibly due to the 290-pounds additional weight (4380 compared to 4090 pounds), five inches long wheelbase (127 compared to 122 inches), and the airplane-type, direct-acting, shock absorbers in the rear suspension system (not on the 200 model). The Packard 300 has a powerplant rated at 150 bhp @ 3600 rpm, and for those who like more power, an optional compression head (7.8:1 instead of 7:1) is available which boosts the power to 155 bhp.

On the Patrician 400, Packard's top luxury model, the 155-bhp powerplant Ultramatic transmission, and a lateral stabilizer on the rear suspension system is standard equipment. For those who still like the more economical, manual, gear-shifting arrangement, Packard's standard transmission is optional on the 200 and 300 series. Overdrive is available at extra cost on the standard transmission cars.

Performance Not Outstanding, But Adequate

A performance comparison of the '52 model 300 with the '51 model 200 proved to be an interesting but not altogether enlightening study. For instance, in the 0 to 30 mph acceleration tests, the 300 proved to be faster; but in the 0 to 60 mph tests, the 200 was faster by 1.1 seconds. Top speed of the 300 (97.8 mph) exceeded that of the 200 (95.6 mph) by 2.2 mph, while average fuel consumption at 60 mph was identical, with the average for both being 13.6 mpg.

"Easamatic" Power Brakes

Brake stopping distances should have indicated better performance for the 300

Two hands are required to operate latch release and lift hood; release is difficult to find; grille retains familiar Packard styling

Visibility to rear is good; interior appointments give look of the luxury class which has long been associated with the Packard

model since it is equipped with the Packard "Easamatic" power brakes (optional at $39.45 on all models), but the truth of the matter is that last year's brakes (self-energizing, hydraulic-type) on the 200 out-performed the power brakes, except for the stopping distance at the 60-mph speed.

Cold test figures, however, do not always tell the complete story. The "Easamatic" power brakes (exclusive with Packard) actually *do* make brake applications "almost as effortless as pressing the accelerator." Power braking has been standard equipment on trucks and buses for years; the difference in Packard's brake system, developed by Bendix Aviation Corp., is that the toe pressure required on the brake pedal increases gradually to give the driver the proper "feel" when applying brakes. In the event of vacuum boost failure, engine manifold pressure is still sufficient for an easy stop; with the engine off, the amount of pressure required would merely return to normal.

We especially like the positioning of the brake pedal at approximately the same distance from the floorboard as the accelerator. Thus, shifting of your entire leg when moving your foot from the accelerator to the brake pedal is unnecessary; a pivoting motion is all that is required.

The Packard brakes, unlike any other

PHOTOS BY JACK CAMPBELL

in the industry, operate through a simple unit combining power and brake master cylinders. The "Easamatic" brake system utilizes the same vacuum that runs the windshield wipers to do a third of the work. The light braking pressure requires careful application until the driver has the new "feel"; otherwise, overbraking may result, especially under emergency conditions. However, in our case, the delicate touch was quickly acquired and the reduction in effort undoubtedly helped to make our Tahoe trip one of the easiest and least tiring that we have ever taken.

Acceleration Not Startling

One noticeable point discovered on the long Tahoe trip was that in an attempt to pass other cars at a speed in excess of 60 mph, there is no surge of power when it is most needed. Although at speeds above 55 mph the Ultramatic is advertised as being in "solid, direct drive," a kick-down gear might be helpful here, or some means by which to improve the direct-drive acceleration. Actually, the synchro-mesh transmission with its more effective third-speed and overdrive would probably be more ideally suited for cross-country driving than the Ultramatic, but of course, not as convenient. By today's standards of performance in competitive cars, the Packard's acceleration is relatively poor.

Sleek, Graceful Body Lines

Studying the body lines of the various Packard models is indeed a pleasure, for they are exceptionally well-proportioned, giving the appearance of sturdiness, balance, and large-car luxuriousness. The full width frontal areas with the high-crowned front fenders give a sense of unusual massiveness and, in addition, give the driver good visibility for parking. In these days of loss of distinctive identification, it is a tribute to Packard stylists that they were able to maintain a semblance of the familiar grille shape of past years.

The standard Packard models are devoid of excess chrome; however, this non-functional styling which the chrome affords on the deluxe models is in keeping with other makes of the same class. Especially distinctive are the rear fender louvers. Legroom, shoulder and headroom of the car's interior are excellent, with the foam-rubber seat cushions giving soft-ride comfort.

Interior Roomy, Seats Comfortable

The passenger compartment of any car becomes very familiar to you when you have been driving steadily for extremely

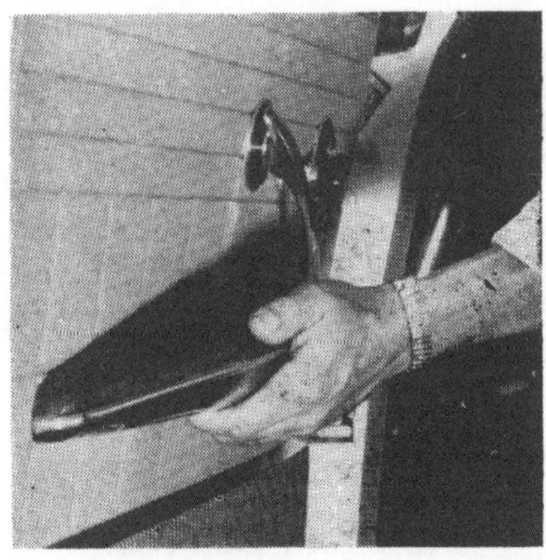

The armrests have undersize indentations for gripping to close doors; position of the hand is awkward as indicated in this view

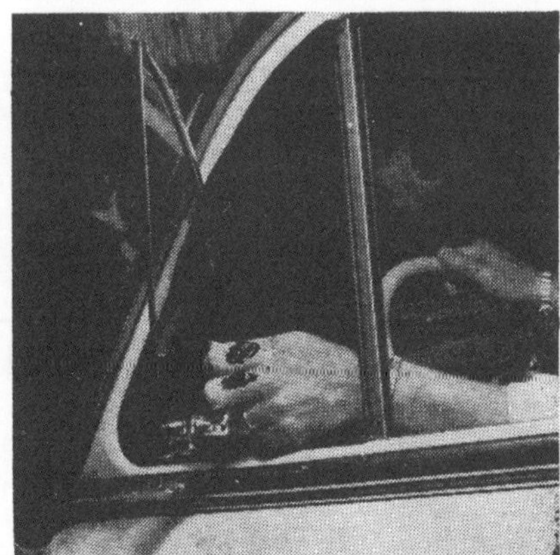

The windwings have to be opened manually instead of by crank. Most cars in the Packard price range have crank-operated wings

Wide doors and chair-height seats make getting in and out of car a simple procedure; seat comfort is exceptionally good

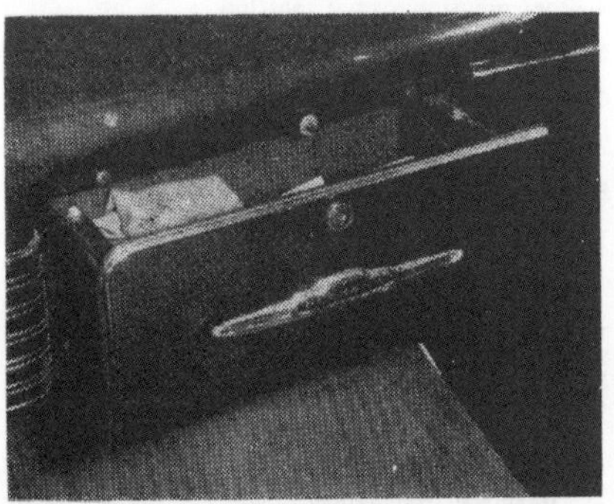

The innovation for Packard is the sliding drawer-type glove compartment; spilling of contents is definitely eliminated

Less leg work is required on Packard since pivoting of foot from accelerator is all that is required to operate low-set brake pedal

One of the industry's roomiest luggage compartments is incorporated in the Packard body design. Note taillight styling

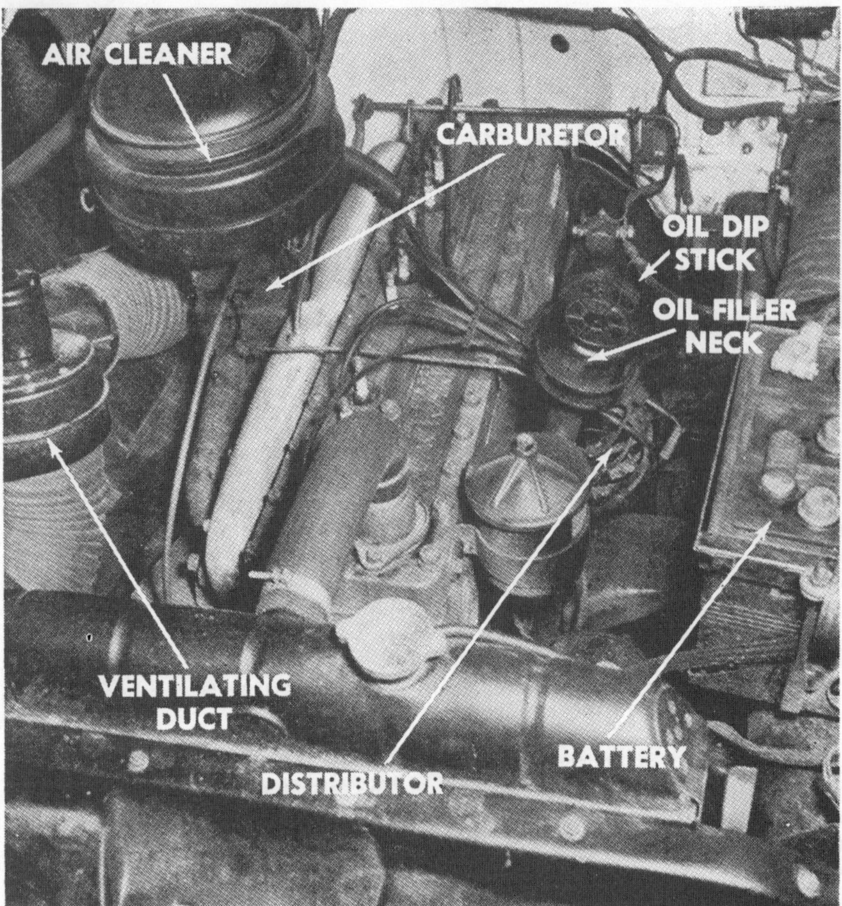

Packard's L-head, in-line, eight cylinder engine is rated at 150 bhp @ 3600 rpm; a high compression head, boosting ratio up to 7.8:1, is available for those who like more power

long stretches. The roominess and overall comfort of our test car on the Tahoe trip were a welcome relief to some cars that we have tested that didn't have these advantages. The chair-height seats made driving especially pleasant, and no complaints were heard from the passengers. We like the relative position of the seats to the dash and to the outside. The seats are firm but soft enough to be "just right" for maximum comfort. Vision to front and rear is excellent.

Door openings are large, allowing easy ingress or egress without undue stooping or maneuvering.

Armrests are a slight disappointment in that the aft section of them tapers to too narrow a width to be comfortable for resting your elbow. They are also awkward to use for closing the doors as the hand-grip indentation is on the underside of the armrests. The windwings have to be opened manually instead of by crank as are most cars in this price range. Ashtrays, however, are adequate with one for the driver and another on the extreme right of the dash for the passenger. The glove compartment is a drawer-type. The windshield wiper control is located conveniently on the left side of the steering column. The upholstery and general interior appointments are luxurious in design.

Instrument Panel Over-Simplified

While something can be said for keeping the number of instruments that a driver has to be bothered with to a minimum, in this case we feel that Packard has over-simplified their instrument panel. The only gauges on the panel are the fuel capacity and water temperature units with only red warning lights used for the oil pressure and battery charge. The metal-worked pattern behind the instruments' dials is very effective in providing the luxury look, but the dials themselves are not set up for legible reading, with not enough definition between the numerals and the background of the speedometer.

Reflections from the dash are practically nil. Only once on the entire trip to Tahoe

PACKARD 300 TEST TABLE

PERFORMANCE

CLAYTON CHASSIS DYNAMOMETER TEST

(All tests are made under full load conditions)

RPM	MPH	ROAD HP
2000	27	45
2600	45	74
2900	62 (maximum)	86

Per cent of advertised hp delivered to driving wheels—57.3.

ACCELERATION IN SECONDS

(Checked with fifth wheel and electric speedometer)

	H	L-H*
Standing start ¼ mile		:20.7
0-30 mph (0-37, car speedometer reading)	:06.9	:05.4
0-60 mph (0-74, car speedometer reading)	:20.8	:18.3
10-60 mph in High		:18.3
30-60 mph in High		:13.5

*Shift to High at 30 mph

TOP SPEED (MPH)

(Clocked speeds over surveyed ¼ mile)

Fastest one-way run	97.8
Average of four runs	96.3

FUEL CONSUMPTION IN MILES PER GALLON

(Checked with fuel flowmeter, fifth wheel and electric speedometer)

Steady 30 mph	17.5
Steady 45 mph	14.8
Steady 60 mph	13.6
Approximate average in traffic	14.8

BRAKE STOPPING DISTANCE

(Checked with electrically actuated detonator)

Stopping distance at:

30 mph	52 ft. 7 in.
45 mph	113 ft. 3 in.
60 mph	227 ft. 7 in.

GENERAL SPECIFICATIONS

ENGINE

Type	L-head, in line 8
Bore and stroke	3½x4¼
Stroke/bore ratio	1.22:1
Compression ratio	7:1
Compression ratio (optional high compression head)	7.8:1
Displacement	327 cu. in.
Advertised bhp	150 @ 3600 rpm
Piston travel @ maximum bhp	2550 ft. per min.
Bhp per cu. in.	.46
Maximum torque	270 lbs. ft. @ 2000 rpm
Maximum bmep	100.92 psi

DRIVE SYSTEM

Transmission: Ultramatic (torque converter with gears)

DIMENSIONS

Wheelbase	127 in.
Tread	Front—60, Rear—61¼ in.
Wheelbase/tread ratio	2.1:1
Overall width	77⅞ in.
Overall length	217¾ in.
Overall height	62⅞ in.
Turning radius	22 ft.
Turns, lock to lock	4¾
Weight (test car)	4380 lbs.
Weight/bhp ratio	29.2:1
Weight/road hp ratio	50.9:1
Weight distribution (front to rear)	2390-1990 or 54.5-45.5
Weight/sq. in. of brake lining area	21.03 lbs.
Leg room (measured diagonally from floorboard to front of seat to seat back)	Front—43¾ in., Rear—46½ in.
Head room (measured on 8-degree diagonal line from 5 in. forward of seat back to headlining)	Front 36 in., Rear 35³⁄₁₆ in.

INTERIOR SAFETY CHECK CHART

QUESTION	YES	NO
1. Blind spot at left windshield post at a minimum	X	
2. Vision to right rear satisfactory?	X	
3. Positive lock to prevent doors from being opened from inside?	X	
4. Does adjustable front seat lock securely in place?	X	
5. Minimum of projections on dashboard face?	X	
6. Is the emergency brake accessible to both driver and passenger?		X
7. Are cigarette lighter and ashtray both located conveniently for driver?	X	
8. Is rear vision mirror positioned so as not to cause blind spot for driver?		X
Total for Packard 300		75%

OPERATING COST PER MILE ANALYSIS

1. Cost of gasoline	$177.00
2. Cost of insurance	162.40
3. First year's depreciation	665.00
4. Maintenance	
a. Two new tires (8.00x15)	60.30
b. Brake reline	23.36
c. Major tune-up	13.65
d. Renew front fender	72.10
e. Renew rear bumper	59.85
f. Adjust automatic transmission, change lubricant	14.10
First year cost of operation in cents per mile	12.5c

Packard's new "Easamatic" power brakes require only toe pressure for rapid windshield-pitching stops. Over-braking, however, is a possibility until the driver becomes used to the light "feel." The brakes operate on a vacuum boost system principle, which is an ingenious system developed for Packard by the Bendix Aviation Corporation

did reflection occur and then only momentarily. This was from the small chrome strips from the two adjoining windshield strips. Actually, the paint on the dash gives a glossy appearance, yet it doesn't reflect sunlight. A welcome relief is the absence of chrome on the dash proper.

Summary

The Packard 300, while easy to drive long distances and easier to ride in, has not kept pace with other makes in the same price class performancewise. In this regard, Packard is known to be developing its own V-8 powerplant which may replace the old L-head, in-line, eight-cylinder engine possibly with the '53 or '54 models.

Acceleration is probably adequate for the type of driving the car is designed for, and the handling qualities are above-par, especially in regard to the car's cornering ability and highway cruising roadability. Packard's "Easamatic" power brakes will find favor with most drivers, especially with those who do considerable driving in heavy traffic, and with women. This item, which is optional equipment, should become very popular with Packard owners.

Fuel consumption figures indicate that the car is not an economical one, with the result that the cruising range suffers. A major consideration is in the owner's loss (depreciation) in trade-in value; on the basis of performance and the generally fine craftsmanship that go into each Packard, the MOTOR TREND Research Staff does not understand why this should be so. One thing is fairly certain; if you buy a Packard once, you will probably be satisfied to stay in the Packard line for some time to come.

—*Walt Woron*

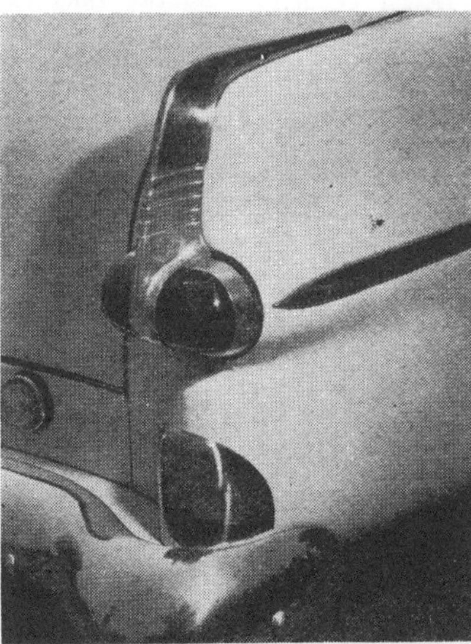

Taillight and rear fender design of Packard is pleasing to eye; in fact, entire body styling is considered by many to be good

Rear suspension system consists of 2½ inch wide semi-elliptic springs 54¾ inches long. Full length inserts are between the leaves

The low, sleek lines of the Packard Pan American are emphasized in this photograph. In addition to making the car a thing of beauty, this styling provides a low center of gravity, which means increased safety and comfort for the three passengers carried in the single wide seat.

presenting... *the*

The instrument panel is covered with top-grain leather, blending with that used on the seats and repeated in steering wheel trim.

NEWEST of Detroit's "dream" cars, the Packard Pan American has been attracting wide interest and excited acclaim in its first showings. So far, only two of these special jobs have been built. The first has been shown to the public in a New York exhibition and at the Michigan State Fair, and is now touring other shows around the country.

The experimental car has a completely customized body styled by Richard Arbib, and built by Henney Motor Co., although Packard officials are the first to point out its strong resemblance to the company's ordinary convertible. This is natural, since the basic body shell is the same in each case.

No definite plans have been made to put the Pan American into production, according to Fred J. Walters, Packard's vice president and general sales manager. However, several similar models are under construction, and will be unveiled at auto shows as soon as they are ready. Packard, like other companies, is well aware of the sharp upswing in the public's interest in European sports cars, and wants to be ready to enter that field if there appears to be a substantial market.

There's no telling what a car like the Pan American might cost the eventual purchaser. Production would undoubtedly be limited, and most estimates as to the price hover around $10,000.

Meanwhile, the car is a highly interesting product, mechanically as well as on the surface. It is powered by

The grille design retains the familiar Packard flavor, although it is highly modern and impressive. The air scoop on the hood is actually functional, directing air to the four-barrel carburetor. Wire wheels are not the foreign knock-off type, but bolt on in the Amerian manner.

Packard Pan American

AUTO AGE'S cover car may go into limited production in 1953. It'll be expensive, but clean styling and luxury features should attract attention

the Packard "Thunderbolt" engine, beefed up to achieve 185 horsepower (the main changes being in the carburetion and cylinder heads). The air scoop on the hood is functional, in addition to being a styling feature.

Chrome has been minimized throughout the Pan American's body to give the car a clean, smooth appearance. Where used, chrome pieces accent the basic forms of body sections, and are not mere ornamentation. For this, the designers deserve some sort of medal—but not a chromium one, obviously!

Wire wheels and a rear-mounted spare add to the car's custom appearance. A commendably low center of gravity has been achieved (at the cost of a rear seat, as seems customary with these dream jobs), making the car easy to handle and spectacular on corners.

Overall length of the Pan American is 220¼ inches from bumper to bumper, on a wheelbase of 122 inches. Overall width is 77¾ inches, and height to the top of the door is only 37½ inches.

The driving compartment is luxuriously furnished in leather, and an arm rest in the center of the seat can be hidden when not in use. The large luggage compartment is complemented by a package area behind the seat.

For the more technically minded, the engine is an L-head with eight cylinders in line. Bore is 3½ inches and stroke 4¼—a long way from square. With a compression ratio of 7.8 to one, the engine develops 185 brake horsepower at 4,000 rpm. That all-important carburetor is of the four-barrel type developed recently.

Suspension is more or less conventional, with leaf springs in the rear and coils in front. Transmission is Packard's Ultramatic.

The number of such sleek customs as the Packard Pan American to hit the highways, now or in the future, will probably be comparatively limited. But for its engineering and styling accomplishments, the company, one of America's leading independents, certainly deserves credit—and a chance to sell a few of these beauties!

Testing the PACKARD CLIPPER

Testing the Clipper Deluxe on a muddy track bounced water into the engine compartment, but water-proof ignition never faltered.

Packard's power-steering hydraulic assist unit attaches directly to steering linkage. Sand traps and muddy road tests point need for boot to protect cylinder arm.

THE *Clipper* is Packard's entry into a lower competitive price class ($2735 for the *Clipper* Deluxe 4-dr. sedan in 1953 against $3234 for a 4-dr. sedan in the "300" Packard line). Last year Motor Vehicle Research tested the Packard "300" and it did all right by itself. When we heard about the *Clipper*, we wanted to see how it stacked up for '53 with its new 8-to-1 compression ratio engine boosting horsepower to 160 (against 155 *hp* for the "300" in 1952), a 4-barrel carburetor and direct-acting power steering. Packard is still the only manufacturer sticking with their straight-8 engine while upping compression ratios into the 8-to-1 range.

The *Clipper* is a heavy car, weighing in at over 4000 lbs. with fuel and water, ready for business. When you're toting around that kind of poundage, you can usually count on two things—a smooth even ride with good roadability at high speeds and a slower getaway from stop signs with reduced gas mileage. Let's see how the *Clipper* did on these counts.

MVR engineers reported the *Clipper* was surefooted and took all kinds of roads with equal ease. The driver had that inner feeling of complete control over the car at all speeds that comes from excellent handling stability and the "road feel" characteristics of the power steering. The car is easy to drive and restful on long trips, with no wheel fight. Of course, the steering will seem sensitive to you if this is the first time you have driven a car equipped with the power type.

The speedometer and odometer on the particular car we tested certainly didn't do the car justice. They both read *low*—(the speedometer by nearly 10% at 60 *mph* and the odometer by about 15%). Speedometers and odometers usually read slightly high. To see how much a faulty speedometer can throw off acceleration readings, let's look at the standstill to 60 *mph* runs. The *Clipper* turned in a relatively slow 19.1 sec. time for this run according to the speedometer using H-drive only, or 17.8 secs. using L and shifting to H at 25 *mph*. In reality, when the *Clipper* reached 60 *mph* it was doing a true speed of 66.25 *mph*. On another test using the true speed indicator from the 5th wheel the time required to accelerate from 0 to 60 *true speed* was 16.90 secs. in High and 14.80 seconds in Low and High, shifting at 25 *mph*.

On the top speed run, the speedometer read 85 *mph*, but the *Clipper* was actually doing 97 *mph*.

The low reading odometer didn't give the *Clipper* credit for ground covered. On the 3-mile check when the odometer indicated exactly three miles, the car had actually traveled 3 miles *plus* 2,376 ft. which shows an odometer error of 15%. For an idea of how such an odometer error on the low side can put a crimp in your apparent gas mileage, let's look at the 5-gallon economy test. This is the test where an average driver takes off with a 5-gallon tank connected to the carburetor, mixing city-country driving in the ratio of 35-65% until the car rolls to a stop.

According to the car's odometer, the *Clipper* ran out of fuel after running only 70.3 miles for an uncorrected average of 14.6 *mpg*. But by allowing for the odometer error, the *Clipper* actually traveled about 81 miles for an average of 16.2 *mpg*, a fairly respectable average for a heavyweight and a 160-*hp*. engine.

Science at the Wheel — Packard Clipper Performance

START OF TESTS: December 17, 1952

MAKE: Packard Clipper 4-dr., Deluxe Sedan, 1953

WEATHER CONDITIONS (prevailing at time of recorded road tests): Temperature: 30-42° F. Humidity: 49-80%. Wind velocity: Calm to 8 **mph.** Wind direction: Calm, NE and NW. Barometer 30.41-30.42

ROAD CONDITIONS (for gas mileage, acceleration and brake efficiency tests): Asphalt covered crushed rock, clean and dry

MILEAGE AT START OF TESTS: 1186.9

MILES COVERED IN TESTS: 2113.1

GAS USED: Premium. **OIL USED:** SAE #10

TEST DATA

GASOLINE MILEAGE (checked with fuel velocity meter, gas volume meter, 5th wheel and conventional vacuum gage. Carried weight (passengers plus test equipment), 384 lbs. Average of two steady runs made in H-gear north and south on 2% grade at each speed. Tire pressure 24 lbs. cold all around, 5th wheel pressure, 21 lbs. cold. Speedometer correction not applied to miles-per-gallon readings):

MPH Speedometer	True Speed	Miles Per Gallon	RPM
20	23.1	17.5	890
30	33.55	17.75	1300
40	44.45	13.75	1725
50	55.35	13.0	2180
60	66.25	11.0	2600
70	78.35	10.5	3040

FUEL ECONOMY ACCELERATION TEST (both tests made in H-gear): On jack-rabbit start, car was started from standstill and brought to 60 mph as fast as possible, then held at 60 mph until one mile was covered, time 1 min. 9.40 secs. Fuel used, .145 gal. at approximate rate of 6.9 mpg. On feather-foot start (slow acceleration) car was started from standstill and brought to 60 mph and held at 60 mph until one mile was covered, time 1 min. 23.2 secs. Fuel used, .100 gal. at approximate rate of 10 mpg.

ACCELERATION (checked with dampened pendulum meter and timed electrically. Times subject to speedometer correction. Carried weight [passengers and instruments], 381 lbs. Figures are average of two successive runs at speeds specified):

MPH Speedometer	Gear Range	Average Time (Seconds)	MPH Speedometer	Gear Range	Average Time (Seconds)
0–20	L	2.74	0–60	L & H (shift at 25)	17.80
0–30	L	4.86		H only	19.10
0–40	L	7.50	10–50	H	11.20
0–50	L & H (shift at 25)	12.10	10–60	H	18.15
	H only	13.80	20–60	H	16.45

ACCELERATION FACTOR (roughly speaking, a measure of potential pick-up performance. Full throttle in gears indicated):

MPH Speedometer	Gear	Accelerometer Reading	Pull in lbs. per ton	Miles per hour per sec.	Feet per sec. per sec.
20	L	33.0	625	7.2	10.6
	H	23.75	471	5.4	8.0
30	L	25.0	489	5.5	8.1
	H	20.0	393	4.4	6.4
40	L	20.0	393	4.4	6.4
	H	16.0	320	3.5	5.2
50	H	12.0	240	2.65	3.85
60	H	8.25	165	1.75	2.55

TOP SPEED AND SPEEDOMETER CORRECTION (average of north and south runs in miles per hour with carried weight of 384 lbs. and indicated peak rpm of 3700. Tire pressure 24 lbs. cold, 5th wheel pressure 21 lbs. no wind):

MPH Speedometer	5th Wheel Check	Radar Time Check	RPM
85.0 Top Speed	97.08	97.0	3695
80	90.0	89.95	3500
70	78.35	78.40	3040
60	66.25	66.20	2600
50	55.35	55.25	2180
40	44.45	44.45	1725
30	33.55	33.25	1300
20	23.10	23.05	890

ODOMETER CORRECTION (checked with Veeder-Root counter and hairline magnifier, 6th and 7th wheels used with error checkout of 11 in. in 5000 ft. Indicated speed during tests, 15 mph. Tire pressures, 24 lbs. all around): Car's odometer—5,280 ft., true distance, 6,072 ft.; error 792 ft. Three-mile checkout error, 2,376.8 ft. short of true distance.

HILL CLIMBING (checked with pendulum performance meter. All tests at full throttle with 381 lbs. carried weight):

MPH Speedometer	Gear Range	Maximum Grade in %	MPH Speedometer	Gear Range	Maximum Grade in %
20	L	33.0	40	L	20.0
	H	23.75		H	16.0
30	L	25.0	50	H	12.0
	H	20.0	60	H	8.25

BRAKE EFFICIENCY (checked with decelerometer and Sioux pressure cylinder. Tire pressure 24 lbs. all around cold. Carried weight 565 lbs. Time between normal stops 2¾ min. average, between panic stops 3 min. average. Temperature, 27° F., barometer 30.41, humidity 80%. Asphalt covered crushed rock road surface, clean and dry. Normal stops all straight, no slewing; panic stops straight with all wheels locked except for early stops on fade tests when brakes were not burnished, later stops straight. Weight shift normal):

NORMAL STOPS

MPH Speedometer From	Pedal Pressure in Lbs.	Efficiency	Approx. Time in Secs.	Stopping Distance in Ft.
20	27.5	41.6	2.54	47.5
30	31.5	41.0	2.90	84.0
40	28.0	34.0	5.44	170.0
50	29.0	36.0	7.21	202.0
60	31.0	34.0	8.0	393.0

PANIC STOPS

MPH Speedometer From	Pedal Pressure in Lbs.	Efficiency	Approx. Time in Secs.	Stopping Distance in Ft.
20	45	83	1.0	20
30	53	81	1.11	49
40	49	75	1.31	83
50	38	73	1.41	164

REAR WHEEL HORSEPOWER (checked on dynamometer. Temperature in laboratory 57° F., under hood 91° F., barometer 30.41, humidity 49%, rear wheel tire pressure cold 24 lbs.): At an indicated 1950 rpm, with 1½ in. Hg vacuum in H-drive, developed horsepower at rear wheels was 56.075.

CAR FRICTION or HOLD-BACK (tractive resistance in lbs. per ton, checked on dynamometer):

Miles Per Hour (speedometer)	10	20	30	40	50	60	70	80
Declutched	40	48	60	80	105	180	210	240
Gear Clutched, ignition off	70	110	128	145	170	215	240	250

SPECIFICATIONS

ENGINE: 8-cylinder, L-head. Bore 3.50", stroke 4.25"; maximum brake horsepower rated 160 at 3600 rpm; compression ratio 8 to 1; maximum torque 295 ft.-lbs. at 2000 rpm; piston displacement 327 cu. in.; fuel specified, premium.

TRANSMISSION: Ultramatic automatic, gear ratio 3.23 to 1.

STEERING: Power assisted by direct acting hydraulic system. Turning circle, 43 ft. curb to curb, lock to lock 4½ turns sprung and unsprung.

EXTERIOR: Wheelbase 122"; overall length 213.09"; overall height 62.69"; overall width 77.88"; weight dry (no fuel, oil or water) 3745 lbs.; road clearance 7" at differential housing.

INTERIOR: head room, front seat 36", rear seat 35.19"; legroom, front seat 43.50", rear seat 43.75"; hip room, front seat 60", rear seat 59.50"; shoulder room, front seat 57.50", rear seat 56"; 4 in. manual seat adjustment, control handle at left of driver's seat.

VISIBILITY: Windshield area (1 piece curved) 989.2 sq. in. approx., rear window (1 piece curved) 968 sq. in. approx.. Driver's eye to road (5'8½" driver, seat in extreme rear position), over left front fender 33', over hood center 34', over right front fender 35'.

EQUIPMENT: Battery, 6 volts, 17 plates, 100 amp. hrs., located under hood. Tires 15 x 7.60", recommended pressure 24 lbs. all around. Luggage capacity, 30 cu. ft. 10-gallon pumping time, 52.21 secs., with no blowback or spillage. Filler tube in side of left fender. Springing, front independent coil, rear semi-elliptic leaf. Box X-type frame.

CAPACITIES: Fuel tank, 20 gals; crankcase 7 qts.; cooling system 20 qts., with heater 20½ qts. Ultramatic transmission 12 qts., differential 3.75 pts.

MOTOR VEHICLE RESEARCH herewith certifies that these are the true and accurate findings in tests conducted on the automobile named under the conditions specified.

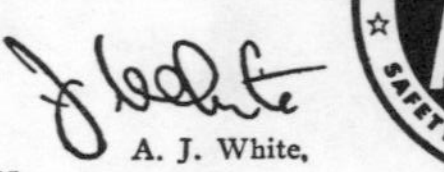

A. J. White,
Director,
Motor Vehicle Research

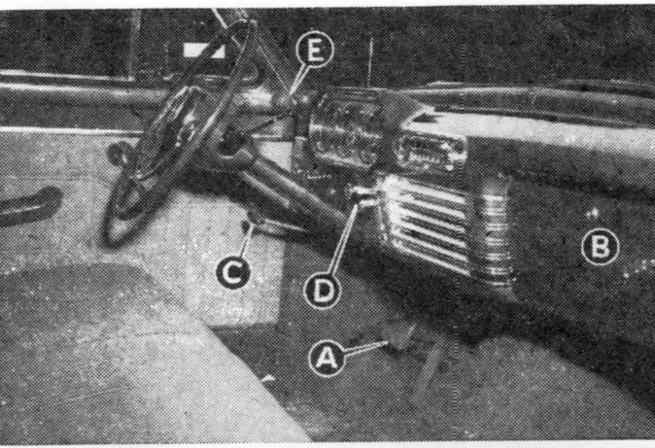

Interior arrangement of Deluxe Clipper—**A. wide** Easamatic **power brake pedal, B. pull-out bin type dash compartment drawer, C. T-handle emergency brake handle in the OUT position, D. heater controls work up and down, fan switch at bottom, E.** Ultramatic **transmission drive selector handle.**

In all the MVR tests, speedometer readings and odometer distances are used because they relate test data in terms you are familiar with or can check on your car when you get it. You would find it pretty difficult to find a car's true speed without a calibrated 5th wheel or a radar true-speed set-up like the one used at Motor Vehicle Research. We take the true speeds and distances for two reasons—to check on the accuracy of the car's instruments and for converting all performance data to a common base.

The *Ultramatic* transmission on this Packard is the same as on the *Clipper's* big brothers and was extremely smooth with no lurch between gears or when shifting from Low to High—the normal driving range. The quadrant arrangement with reverse on the right side might allow a youngster riding next to the driver to yank the car into a gear-clashing reverse. A soft green light illuminates the shift quadrant for night driving.

Service points are easily accessible under counterbalanced hood. A. heater blower fan, B. wiper blade motor, C. spark plug covers and waterproofed ignition system kept engine running even when sprayed directly with a water hose, D. accumulator for power steering unit, E. double catch for hood, both released through grill, F. 4-barrel carburetor.

Drivers' Observations

ROADABILITY: Good stability at high speeds and little sense of traveling fast. Steering response with power assist excellent but sensitive. Noticeable tire howl on curves, even at 30 *mph* on curves of short radius. Good recoverability from shoulder back to road. Excellent tracking ability and little wind wander. Noticeable vibration in steering wheel from 50 to 70 *mph*.

RIDING COMFORT: Heavy smooth ride, restful on long trips. Foam rubber cushion on front seats. Body well soundproofed with little engine noise reaching passengers. Doors, trunk and even hub caps coated with sound deadening material. Rear windows allow wide angle visibility but small rear vision mirror does not take full advantage of range. Windshield wipers leave large blind spots (see accompanying photo).

HARMONIC BALANCE POINT: (best cruising speed as determined by "feel of the car" to the driver). 53 *mph* in High.

INSTRUMENTS AND CONTROLS: Panel instruments operate smoothly and are well grouped for operation by the driver—including radio. Generally instruments were easy to read, but metallic finish is distracting. Ash trays are poorly positioned, driver's low and small directly over right leg. Passenger's ash tray located so wind from angle window blows ashes into front seat. Red lights indicate battery charging and oil pressure up instead of gages. No sharp edges on instrument controls, horn rim, ashtray, dash and underseat metals. T-handle handbrake easy to reach and operate, but difficult to release. Clock can be set and adjusted for fast or slow running without removing face. Horn ring around lower half of wheel. Shift lever close to wheel. Glove compartment pulls out as a drawer. Directional arrows blink in green with fairly loud clicking when turn signals are ON.

SPECIAL COMMENTS: Trunk lid counterbalanced and opens with key only—found open twice during first 150 miles of test. Luggage compartment roomy. Jack and handle and socket wrench come in simple corrugated carton—no place to store them when removed from carton. Heater controls seem to stick and are hard to operate unless pushed to right or left. Fan ON-OFF switch difficult to reach when controls are in down position. Floor mats are well padded, simulated carpet surface of rubber in front, carpet in rear. All doors are equipped with hold-open devices. Hood vibration found when testing the "300" Packard last year not present on this *Clipper*. Front seat travel 4" but control handle alongside driver's seat hard to reach when door is closed. Wing nut on spare tire removable by hand. Rear doors include safety buttons to keep children from opening them accidentally. Windows are easy to roll up or down. Changing tires and putting on chains are fairly easy when using a bumper jack. Cooling fluid was leaking around three head bolts on Chicago car, but no leakage noted on car which was tested at the Epping laboratory.

The "300" Packard tested last year was not equipped with power steering, so the *Clipper* afforded the MVR engineers the first chance to test the characteristics of Packard's version, in which the hydraulic assist cylinder connects directly to the turning linkage. The driver must supply only about 20% of the torque on the wheel and the hydraulic assist does the rest. Doing part of the work at all times, left enough of the "road feel" in the system for the driver to retain a good sense of control according to the MVR test drivers, who have, of course, driven many cars with power assisted steering. The fellow who has not tried it before may find it a little soft and sensitive until he gets used to it. Hence he should be extra cautious, especially at high speeds. One thing we noticed with the *Clipper* steering was the way the wheel held position at any point when we removed our hands momentarily. Not having to fight the wheel to hold it in position is restful on long trips, but it means you must turn the wheel back after rounding corners instead of letting the car straighten out of its own accord.

From a service standpoint, the starter, coil, generator, oil dip stick, power steering unit, spark plugs, radiator fan, heater blower and nearly all connecting lines are easily accessible under the hood. Both primary and safety hood latches are accessible through the grill—and it's a bit of a trick to release both catches until you get the hang of it. The engine of the car we drove in Chicago was unusually noisy with the hood up, but a heavy blanket of fiber glass under the hood partially muffled it from inside the car.

Road tests with a 27 ft. Rollahome trailer connected with Tour-Aid hitch (right) slowed the Clipper to a top speed of 59 mph but MVR engineers recommend a cruising speed of not more than 40.

Wiper blade pattern leaves large blind spots at windshield corners and around the rear view mirror.

Panic brake tests on the Clipper.

On the water penetration test, admittedly a toughie, where the car was flooded with water from two fire hoses without nozzles under 100 *psi* line pressure from 4 to 6 ft. away for 11 minutes, all vents and windows leaked as did the trunk lid. The total amount of water leaking inside was moderate.

How good is the *Clipper* for towing a house trailer? In a new test devised by MVR engineers, a 27 ft. *Rollahome* trailer (weight about 5,000 lbs.) was attached with a *Tour-Aid* hitch and put through a series of fuel economy and safety trials. On a 5-gallon test similar to the one made without the trailer, the *Clipper* ran 41.5 miles according to odometer or approximately 47.7 miles true for an average of 9.55 *mpg* true.

The added weight and low rear end changed driving characteristics considerably with some side sway noticed above 40 *mph*. *Clipper's* soft springs need beefing up for trailer towing. Acceleration from a standstill to 50 *mph* (uncorrected speedometer) with trailer slowed to 41.31 secs. using L and H, shifting at 25. Braking distances using both car and trailer brakes increased to 390 ft. when slowing from 50 *mph* in a normal brake test, an increase of approximately 93% over the stopping distance without the trailer. MVR engineers recommended that top speed for towing trailer be limited to 40 *mph*.

Quality Check

A check on such factors as how well the door, hood and trunk seams line up, operation of doors, windows, locks and controls, care in fastening upholstery, weatherstripping and appearance of chrome and other paint finishes indicates that this is a quality car, as you might expect. Such things as having no provision for holding down tools and incompletely flocked areas in trunk, foam rubber cushions in front only, and the like are not in our minds up to what should be Packard's standards.

The O. P. S. price on the 4-dr. Deluxe *Clipper* is $2,735 including all federal excise taxes, factory handling and dealer handling and delivery charges but not including transportation, state and local taxes or optional equipment. *Ultramatic* transmission costs $199, power steering $195 and *Easamatic* power brakes, $39.45.

MI Tests the '53 Packard

A fine old name in automobiles comes up with a fine new line of cars in a determined bid to regain the leadership it once held.

By Tom McCahill

Chief experimental engineer Earl Smith, head man at Packard proving grounds, shows Tom a Deluxe Clipper.

Packard Patrician was last year's 400 and is the most luxurious of Packard's regular line of cars in 1953.

SOME guy with a bloody nose once said: "If you can't beat 'em, join 'em." Well, Packard didn't beat 'em and it didn't join 'em—so somewhere in this maze of confusion lies a tale. Back in 1951, when Chrysler teed off with its 180-horsepower V8 engine, a step similar to blowing a hole in the dam, Packard was slow in following suit. Cadillac met the challenge first with 190 horsepower for 1952 (raised to 210 horsepower this year) and Lincoln in its 1953 models came up with a hot 205-hp mill.

Packard's Mayfair hardtop and convertible, the Cavalier and the Patrician 4-door sedans and the custom special 8-passenger executive sedan and corporation limousine all have 180 horsepower for 1953 with a straight-8 engine. The cheaper models, Clipper and Clipper Deluxe, aren't too far behind with 150 and 160 respectively. This is quite an advance for Packard but it still leaves them carrying the coat tails of the real big kids in performance and power. However, the Packard boys are going after a different type of buyer than the fellow who hops from car to car, always demanding the hottest performance.

Packard is out to get the steady luxury trade in the medium and high-priced market. They are building cars that will match any in America from the standpoint of material, quality and general appointments and they are as proud of their silent ride, free from body squeaks, as Lincoln is of its South of the Border accomplishments in the Mexican road race. Packard is just as enthused about its interior fabrics and comfortable seats as some other manufacturers are about their zero-to-60 time. But don't for a moment think that these '53 Packards are deadheads on the road because they definitely are not. The Mayfair will get right up to a true 100 when tuned right and I held one at this speed for many laps on Packard's justly world famous track.

Now, I was all set to do a whiz bang story about the '53 Packards because I truly feel they are fine cars and I was very much impressed with the general attitude of the engineers about their new top brass. It seems some Hotpoint electrical kids from Chicago have taken over the top management and when I was in Detroit all the old timers still on the payroll felt that these boys were going to get Packard back on the hit parade in jig time. I even found some of the engineers buying Packard stock and if that isn't a good sign, nothing is. But then, just as I was about to write this, I picked up a copy of another magazine—and that did it!

In this magazine two of Packard's old standbys, Chief Engineer Bill Graves and Chief Stylist Ed Macauley, did a Damon and Pythias act in an interview that sounded like a script from the Dark Ages. I don't know whether these two were serious but for the good name of Packard, I sincerely hope not. Their remarks were recorded by a competent reporter and here's more or less how they went:

On being asked a question about the future of the small car, Graves made a chump out of himself to this writer by taking the same tack as Chrysler's chief engineer took just a few weeks before—namely, that it costs practically as much to build a small car as a big one and for this reason he felt the small car future was limited. Look, Bill, a ten-carat diamond costs a thousand times what a 50-carat rhinestone costs—so what's the pitch? You may not believe it but it's quite possible to build a small car that has a lot more actual quality built into it than even a Packard. And I, for one, would like such a car. To further emphasize my point and to prove that there is a market for good

Aside from chrome trim, Packard Clipper looks like Deluxe job on the opposite page. Engine has 10 less horsepower.

Except for the convertible, every car in the Packard line this year has the same luggage capacity: 32 cubic feet.

Although the long-necked cormorant on the left generally is standard on the higher-priced Packards, and the modernistic emblem on the lower-cost cars, you can order either ornament.

small cars, last year Nash sold nearly twice as many little Ramblers as the total Packard output.

In another part of this interview, Graves remarked that small cars have poor mufflers. All I can say is, "Look, bub, open an MG muffler and compare it with yours." At one point Macauley spoke of riding in a new English Bentley but added that it didn't compare with Packard's cheapest model. He's so right—but not the way he meant it. In still another spot, Macauley stated that slow steering was okay and Graves said he felt stiffer suspension could cause more accidents through fatigue. You know why? Because, said Graves, sharp curves usually are unexpected and a driver needs to be wide awake. How's that again? I guess what he's saying is that lousy suspension keeps you on your toes.

The part where I really fell off the sled was where Graves, in ridiculing sports cars in general, said in effect that he didn't believe the best sports car could take a corner very much faster than a Packard. Well, Bill, pull up your chair and I'll tell you. On my test corner a 1952 Packard hardtop slid off course completely at any speed above 48 miles an hour. My Mark VII Jag could take it at 66 (and that's not a sports car) and a Mark 2 MG stays with it up to 68. Cars such as Oscas, Ferraris and Cunninghams can all do better than 70 on this corner that dumped a Packard off course at 48. In another spot, Macauley voiced the idea that the design of sports cars sacrifices handling. Yipes!

A little over a year ago I sat down at a conference table with these two. The entire discussion was about sports cars and should Packard build a real one. Now, I have no hurt feelings because they apparently didn't agree with me or didn't want to go to the expense. My whole beef is in their damning something they don't know how to build, as proven by the Packard Pan-American. I may be wrong but I feel these two old hands (in the interview referred to) were out to try and pull a little wool over somebody's eyes. And I'd like to put any other engineers in Detroit on notice, including Zeder of Chrysler, that as long as I have three keys left in my typewriter I'll go to the verbal mat with them whenever I feel they are trying to kid the American public.

Well, handicapped as I am with a vision of the 1956 Packards being powered by 16 mad squirrels, let's look over the 1953 line. The Clipper, last year's 200, is Packard's bid in the medium-priced field and it's a strong bid. Here is a car with a reasonably modest price tag, luxurious appearance and more than passable performance. The standard Clipper has a 150-horsepower engine and the Deluxe 160. These cars handle well by low American standards and frankly look like a lot more dough than most of their immediate competitors. Zero to a corrected 60 takes 15.6 seconds in the standard rig and 15.1 in the more powerful Deluxe job. Earl Smith, Packard's very able experimental engineering chief, suggested I test the Deluxe Clipper first with its 160-horsepower engine. This car will reach a top speed in the very high 90's. In fact, on one lap of the Packard trap coming off the high bank and whipping into the long straightaway, I got a timing of 99-plus between the half-mile posts. The smaller-engined Clipper gives up the ghost at 94 miles an hour, which is very fast but not sensational for 150 horsepower.

The Mayfair hardtop and the convertible are last year's model 300 but are now powered by a big 327-cubic inch straight-8 engine that develops 180 horses. In the hardtop, these jobs in still air will do an honest 100 miles an hour. In acceleration, using low and drive of the Packard Ultramatic, the zero to 60 time is slightly less than with the lighter Deluxe Clipper; the best time averaged 15.7.

The Mayfair is the real glamour barge of Packard's line and is a top quality rig from every angle. The paint jobs are excellent and the interior material and comfort leave little to be desired. I had a feeling when I was at Packard that this old line company was sort of considering an American Rolls-Royce approach, meaning top quality and more than passable performance. They are making a play for the so-called carriage trade in an attempt to get back Packard's former prestige of more than 30 years ago when everyone who was anyone owned a Packard Twin Six and only characters from under the railroad tracks would be found dead in a Cadillac.

The Grand Dame pitch is made with Packard's Patrician 400, a car which qualifies to carry the spare tire for a Rolls as a modern version of Cleopatra's barge. The 400 is a real tycoon's scooter and it has plenty of nooks and crannies to carry an extra supply of check books. In the looks department, the big styling change was lowering the wings on the radiator goose.

In summing up, I like the new Packards, the whole line. I'm sorry I got off on the wrong foot with Graves and Macauley but I find it hard to believe they really meant what they said. ●

If your eyesight is real good, you can see Uncle Tom in the rear-view mirror as he whips a new Packard around the test track.

SPECIFICATIONS

MODEL TESTED:
1953 Packard Deluxe Clipper 2-door sedan (with Ultramatic drive)

ENGINE:
8 cylinder, L-head; bore 3½ inches, stroke 4¼ inches; piston displacement 327 cubic inches; maximum torque 295 foot pounds @ 2000 rpm; brake horsepower 160 @ 3600 rpm; compression ratio 8 to 1

DIMENSIONS:
Wheelbase 122 inches; overall length 213 3/32 inches; tread 60¾ inches front, 60¾ rear; width 77⅝ inches; height 62¾ inches; weight 3,855 pounds; standard tire size 7.60x15; gas tank 20 gals

PERFORMANCE: (using Low & Drive)
0 to 30 mph, 5.3 seconds
0 to 50 mph, 10.4 seconds
0 to 60 mph, 15.1 seconds
0 to 70 mph, 20.6 seconds
Top speed, 99-plus mph

AN **MT RESEARCH** ROAD TEST REPORT

Packard Makes a Challenge

TO FIND THE ANSWERS to the many questions on the Packard, we could have taken the suggestion offered by Packard's famous slogan, and asked "the man who owns one" these questions: Why did you buy it? What do you like about it? Would you buy another Packard?

Asking these and endless other questions would have been a time-consuming job, and even a complete cross-examination (under bright, hot lights, if necessary) would have left us with one important question unanswered: Would we feel the same way about the Packard? We road tested a '53 Packard Cavalier, the lowest priced of the new big cars on which Packard is again lavishing its attention. (The less luxurious Clipper corresponds to last year's "200" series.) Then we put ourselves in the shoes of a Packard owner, and asked ourselves these questions to get the full story:

The Packard looks big, and somewhat "boxy." Is it hard to drive? For a large car (127-inch wheelbase, 217¾ inches overall), the Cavalier four-door sedan is very easy to drive. Power steering and gently responsive Ultramatic transmission take the work out of parking, and power brakes offer tip-toe stopping under normal conditions. Although we feel the steering wheel rim is a little small in diameter, it has well-defined finger grips on the underside, and its position (angle and relationship to seat height) is comfortable.

That shows you don't have a boxcar on your hands in city driving, but how does the car handle under other driving conditions? Driven conservatively, the Packard has average handling qualities—nothing outstanding, but good at normal highway speeds. No steering correction is needed on tight corners until the rear end begins to drift (at about 50 mph). The car is easily controlled in turns, and there is no feeling of "mushiness" in the steering. However, we have one complaint—typical of most power steering units, the Packard's steering wheel has poor return characteristics (unlike last year's car, which did not have power steering). If the wheel is turned more than a half circle going through a curve it will not return to a "straight wheel" position by itself as quickly as a non-power-assisted wheel. For a car of this size, the Packard uses a low steering gear ratio: the wheel requires only 4⅓ turns lock to lock.

Is the Packard's riding quality an asset to the car's bid for a favored spot in the "fine car" field? The Cavalier is not the most luxurious car of the Packard line (it's topped by "400" series models with more deluxe appointments), but it provides a ride equal to, or above, the cars in its class. The chair-height seats are very comfortable, and the seatbacks give good, firm support.

There's no "see-saw" sensation going through dips at average highway speeds, but the body sways from side to side more than usual on rutted roads and when coming out of streetcar tracks. Body lean is not bothersome in corners taken at low speeds, but over 40 mph, there's a great deal of heel-over.

What kind of gas mileage can you expect from the Packard? Never before considered an economy car (except in its reputation for long service), the '53 Packard showed considerable improvement in fuel economy over its last year's counterpart, the "300." Its increase from 14.8 mpg to 18.2 mpg at a steady 45 mph (using Mobilgas Special) puts it up with other cars in its own and even in lower price ranges.

Is Packard's performance up with others in its class? Packard has been considered a car powered for good highway speeds, rather than a car with lightning acceleration. Equipped with Ultramatic, it has somewhat slow pickup (standing start ¼ mile in 20.0 seconds, as compared to its class average of 18.45 seconds). A top speed average of 100.9 mph shows that the Packard is capable of highway cruising speeds that are entirely in keeping with those expected from a luxury car.

Is the interior up to the standard of a "fine car"? The term "fine car" has been applied to cars in every price class, and is probably as free a term as "big car," which is also used for nearly every car on the road. Even though it is overworked, the phrase is apt for the Packard interior. The Cavalier has not received the full treatment of Packard's luxury interiors, but it still rates above average in quality of material and workmanship. Upholstery and trim colors are pleasing to look at, and have the feel and appearance of richness and comfort.

After discussions with Dale Runyan, MT's interior appointments expert, the MT Research staff consensus was that upholstery materials were very good, and the interior workmanship excellent throughout. The Packard's chrome door handles and window cranks are sensibly located for convenient use, and are out of the way of elbows and knees. Electric window lifts can add extra luxury.

Carpeting is used in front and rear compartments, and a rubber scuff pad takes the abuse of the driver's heels. Carpet

Any size driver can make a quick check of the Packard's big gauges without dropping his eyes far from the windshield

Is the interior roomy? Here's how MT found the answer to that question. Our six passengers had ample room in the '53 Packard

Packard's intentions to recapture the top spot it held in the Thirties are quite clear. Will this old star shine brighter in the years to come?

Photos by Jack Campbell

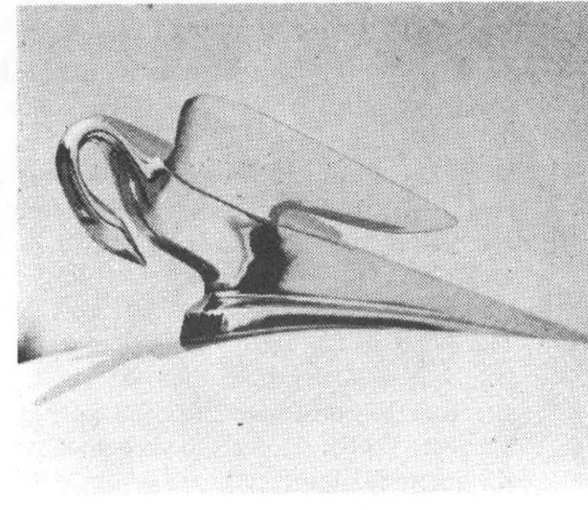

materials, like other interior furnishings, are of good quality material (as they should be in a luxury car), and their finish and neat edging show that Packard pays a little more attention to some details than other manufacturers.

How comfortable are the seats? Very, owing largely to the use of coil springs in their construction. The seatbacks are well covered with a durable ribbed material. Women will appreciate the ease with which the front seat can be moved. (For an extra charge, you can limit your effort to pushing a button.) Armrests add to comfort, and the one on the driver's door is ideally located for resting the elbow, yet it does not interfere with arm movement while driving.

Is there much room inside the car? Headroom is excellent for front-seat passengers and good for rear-seat passengers. The Packard rates "very good" for rear passenger legroom, and stretching your legs is no problem at all when you're sitting in the front seat. This combination of comfort and attractive, high quality material and workmanship should be a boon to Packard sales in its chosen field.

Has Packard overlooked interior safety in an effort to establish luxurious interiors? Glittering gadgetry is held to a bare minimum on the Packard dashboard. The panel's attractiveness comes from the use of conservative gunmetal blue and copper, used as a background for the instruments. Except for the ashtray knob and the glove compartment pushbutton, the right side of the dashboard is "clean." The center of the dashboard holds the radio grille; although it is a hard surface, it is not as hazardous as the radio control knobs might be in a collision. The only glare or reflection from the panel comes in the position, a glare spot just below the line of vision is reflected in the windshield from the top of the panel. There is no glare from the instruments at night.

Are the instruments easy to read? The Packard's instrument panel consists of three large dials placed in a row near the crown of the dashboard. The instruments are in a good position to be read with a quick glance, but the chrome numbers have a tendency to blend into their black background. The dial on the left holds the water temperature and fuel gauges. The speedometer is placed in the center dial, and a clock makes up the third dial. Where are the ammeter and oil pressure gauges? We slighted them in the instrument lineup because they aren't "readable" gauges—just warning lights. Perhaps keeping the number of gauges to a minimum is commendable in some ways, but we feel that all cars, high-priced or low-priced, should have more than just warning lights for instruments. With lights, the driver has no indication of how much the oil pressure has dropped in past months, and he can't tell if the battery is receiving a correct charge.

Are the controls easy to reach? The light switch, windshield wiper control, and other necessary controls are handy. The ignition key switch is to the left of the panel, and may seem awkward until you become used to it. The Packard's conventional T-handled emergency brake was fairly stiff in operation, and compared to others of the same type, rather hard to release.

Does the Packard have a good heating system? The heater and air vent controls are located on the instrument panel, to the right of the steering column. Although the lever-type controls are easy to use, they are not lit for night operation. Even without a boost from the blower fan, the heater provides plenty of warm air. The system works well for cooling, and at 45 to 50 mph, where it seems to hit its best point of operation, a large quantity of air is circulated throughout the car. At the time of this test, Packard did not offer air conditioning in any of the company's models, but if their re-entry into the big car field is to be complete (especially in the lim-

Wide rear door opens to spacious interior. Electric windows and power seat are extra

Cormorant ornaments have graced Packard hoods for many years. Taillights, fins, and wide deck lid chrome piece are new, but grille still echoes past Packard style

ousine class) we believe an announcement of a refrigerated cooling system will come in the near future.

Does the Packard have blind spots? Do you have to guess where the fenders are when you park? The Packard, unlike some cars of comparable size, has front fenders that can be seen by the driver. The hood has a fairly good slope, and the fenders are higher than those of many cars, but for the most part, it's the position of the seats that increases the view of the road ahead, and allows even the shortest driver a glimpse of the fenders. The chrome trim on top of the rear fenders can be seen from the driver's seat, and is a valuable guide in parking. All-around vision is excellent, because of the thin corner posts, a wrap-around rear window, and the wide, one-piece windshield. The rear-view mirror does not obstruct vision to the right front, but the windshield wiper sweep leaves a low blind spot in front of the driver. The blades are long and have a good sweep to the top and sides, but a blade one inch longer at the bottom would eliminate much of the blind spot.

Has the Packard straight-eight engine changed this year? Basically, the Packard engine is the same as last year's. Improvements include a new four-barrel carburetor, a higher compression ratio, redesigned combustion chambers and longer-wearing, chrome-plated piston rings. One of only three straight-eights remaining in the industry, the Packard engine boasts the highest compression ratio (8.0:1) and the highest horsepower output (180 @ 4000 rpm) of any Detroit-produced in-line eight. Although the company has used V-12 engines (retired in 1939) and six-cylinder engines (discontinued after 1947), it has relied for years on its straight-eight to power most of its models. This will probably change in the next year or two, when it is expected that Packard will introduce one of the several V-8 engines now under development.

Is the engine easy to work on? Except for the position of the generator (extremely low and below the battery and oil filter) all major engine components are readily accessible and all additional power equipment can be serviced without trouble. Our only suggestion is aimed at the construction of the power steering mechanism. The cylinder shaft is exposed, and we feel it should be covered in some manner to prevent wear and lessen the possibility of cylinder failure.

How good is the Packard's Ultramatic transmission? A loss of fuel economy when accelerating at low speeds is the price you pay (besides the initial $199 cost of Ultramatic) for having a car with a torque converter transmission. Packard's automatic transmission does have a favorable feature that allows the car to remain in direct drive in city driving at fairly low speeds, provided that the throttle is not depressed to the extent that a shift-down occurs. However, don't feel that just because of Ultramatic's low economy value, it should go the way of the V-12 engine, for this transmission has some traits that, for your purposes, may overshadow its drawbacks. The greatest advantage is, of course, that it eliminates the usual gear shifting, and replaces it with unusually smooth acceleration. Acceleration whine is at a minimum, and our test car was free of the clanks and clunks so often heard in automatics. The torque converter automatically locks out, making a mechanical connection, anywhere from 15 to about 57 mph, depending on how fast you are accelerating. Ultramatic, like similar transmissions, operates in either a DRIVE range for normal driving, or LOW range for additional pulling power or increased low-speed acceleration. This transmission has no hill-holding or anti-creep features, but it has an uncommon feather touch, and is extremely sensitive in operation, making the car easier to park than most automatic-drive cars.

Is it hard to stop this two-tonner? The average stopping distance (at 30, 45 and 60 mph) for cars in Packard's weight class is 123 feet. The Packard's average stopping distance is a little over 119 feet, or about average. Some fade occurred after acceleration tests were run, as well as during the brake checks. The power brakes need only a slight touch to bring the car to a stop at low speeds, but for high-speed panic stops, it's necessary to "stand" on the pedal. Because the brake pedal is close to the floor, you can move your foot from the accelerator to the brake pedal without lifting your heel from the floor. This should help to lessen braking distances in emergency stops because of some reaction time saved.

Is the Packard's long, wide rear deck any indication of actual trunk space? Definitely. Bulging deck lids often conceal protruding fender wells and gas filler pipes within a trunk, but in the case of the Packard, you can believe what you see. As we have mentioned in other road tests, MT's Research staff depends more on actual carrying space than on advertised cubic-footage to determine the size of the trunk. We were able to put all of our road test equipment in the Packard's trunk with room to spare, so perhaps for once we could have put a little faith in an advertised 30 cubic feet of space and not been disappointed.

Is Packard's construction on a par with other cars in its class? Body panels, bumpers, grille and chrome trim are all made of good quality metal, and were well put together on our test car. No uneven gaps were seen; panels were smooth and the paint was unblemished. A protective chrome strip is at the correct height to prevent damage to paint and panels in crowded parking lots, and the "bug-eye" taillights are placed so they can be seen from the sides of the car. The rear wheel cutouts are somewhat low for easy tire removal, and a bumper jack will be needed to raise the body high enough to remove the wheel.

Good workmanship was also apparent in door construction, and door jambs (a good place to look for signs of inferior workmanship) were smooth. The large-sized doors are opened by pushbuttons set in permanent handles, and a stop is provided at the full-open position. The width of the doors and the position of the seats allow easy entry and exit, and the doors are high enough to eliminate the need for excessive stooping before you step into the car.

Front-end repair costs should be kept to a minimum because of the use of separate grille pieces. However, keep the rear fenders of the car away from poles and walls, for the fenders are integral with the rear-quarter body section; repair costs may run high.

Do you think the Packard is a good buy? As shown in MT's resale chart three months ago ("How Often Should You Trade In Your Car?" June '53 MOTOR TREND), Packard has had a low resale value. However, we feel the Packard should be a durable car, and if you intend to keep a Packard for many years (and many people do), this point will not loom too large. Also (as with other independents) your Packard will be worth more as a trade-in on another Packard than it would be on a car produced by the Big Three.

The dollar-for-dollar value of the car depends primarily on the reason for which it is bought. You'll be getting your money's worth if you buy a Packard for comfort. You'll think it's a good buy if you paid for a roomy car that will provide pleasant traveling, with plenty of room for passengers and all their baggage.

What chance does Packard have of once again becoming the top seller in the fine car class? Although Packard may have dropped in sales since the late Thirties, it hasn't lost its name; and the name Packard means luxury, sturdiness, and prestige to many people. Regardless of what car they own now, those people who remember Packard in the pre-horsepower-race days may return to the fold *if* the company improves performance in its cars. As it is now, "regular" Packard buyers buy the car not for high performance, but for the other fine features the car offers them. Many new buyers would be attracted to it because of these features *and* improved performance.

Packard's intentions are quite clear. They've introduced a limousine in this year's line, and extended their models to cover all of the upper-medium and high-priced classes. In these moves, they've challenged cars that have held top spot in all these classes for many years. Whether Packard makes the grade is not so much a matter of the competition meeting the challenge, but of Packard being able to back it up. Sales figures, while they may rise, will probably not skyrocket this year, but there may be an old star with renewed luster by the end of 1954.

THE STORY IN FIGURES

1953 PACKARD (Equipped with Ultramatic Transmission)

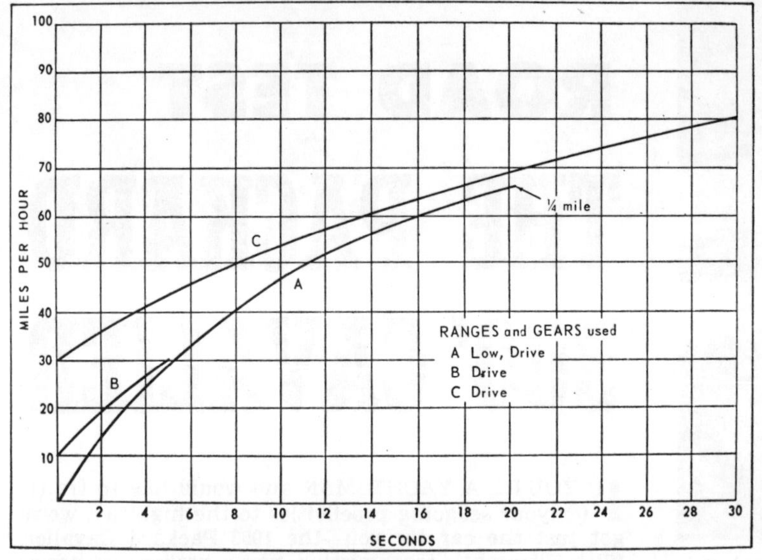

ACCELERATION

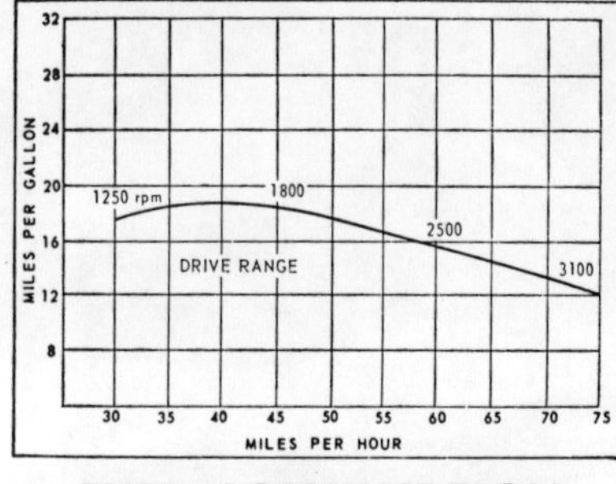

FUEL CONSUMPTION

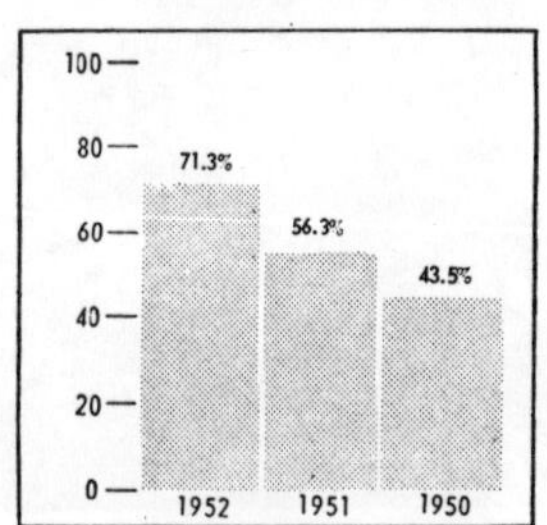

DEPRECIATION

PERFORMANCE

CHASSIS DYNAMOMETER TEST
(Checked on Clayton Mfg. Co.'s chassis dynamometer; all tests are made under full load)

RPM	MPH	ROAD HP
1200	31	47
2000	49	78
2500	64	98
2900 (maximum)	77	102

ACCELERATION
(In seconds; checked with fifth wheel and electric speedometer)

Standing start ¼ mile (67 mph; LOW and DRIVE range)	20.0
0-30 mph (0-32, car speedometer; LOW and DRIVE range)	5.0
0-60 mph (0-65, car speedometer; LOW and DRIVE range)	16.7
10-20 mph (DRIVE range)	2.3
20-30 mph (DRIVE range)	2.7
30-40 mph (DRIVE range)	3.5
40-50 mph (DRIVE range)	4.5
50-60 mph (DRIVE range)	5.5
60-70 mph (DRIVE range)	6.4
70-80 mph (DRIVE range)	9.7

TOP SPEED
(In miles per hour; clocked speeds over surveyed ¼ mile)

Fastest one-way run	102.73
Slowest one-way run	99.33
Average of four runs	100.93

FUEL CONSUMPTION
(In miles per gallon; checked with fuel flowmeter, fifth wheel, and electric speedometer)

Steady 30 mph	17.4
Steady 45 mph	18.2
Steady 60 mph	14.8
Steady 75 mph	12.0
Traffic	10.8

BRAKE STOPPING DISTANCE
(At speeds shown; checked with electrically actuated detonator)

30 mph	49 ft.
45 mph	103 ft.
60 mph	208 ft.

GENERAL SPECIFICATIONS

ENGINE

Type	L-head, straight 8
Bore & stroke	3.5 x 4.25
Stroke/bore ratio	1.22:1
Compression ratio	8:1
Displacement	327 cu. in.
Advertised bhp	180 @ 4000 rpm
Piston travel @ max. bhp	2833 ft. per min.
Bhp per cu. in.	.550
Maximum torque	300 @ 2000 rpm
Maximum bmep	138.34 psi

DRIVE SYSTEM

Standard transmission	Three-speed, synchromesh, using helical gears for first and second and spur gear for reverse
Ratios	1st 3.43, 2nd 1.53, 3rd 1.00, reverse 3.16
Automatic transmission	Ultramatic, torque converter with planetary gears for LOW and REVERSE ranges
Ratios	DRIVE: converter ratio (2.55 maximum at stall); LOW, 1.82 x converter ratio; REVERSE, 1.64 x converter ratio
Overdrive transmission	Planetary type with manual lockout and accelerator downshift
Ratio	.722:1 (overall 2.96)
Rear axle ratios	Conventional 3.9, Ultramatic 3.54, overdrive 4.1

DIMENSIONS

Wheelbase	127 in.
Tread	Front 60 in., rear 61¼ in.
Wheelbase/tread ratio	2.1:1
Overall width	77⅞ in.
Overall length	218⁵⁄₃₂ in.
Overall height	62²⁹⁄₃₂ in.
Turning diameter	44 ft.
Turns lock to lock	4⅓
Weight (test car)	4370 lbs.
Weight/bhp ratio	24.3:1
Weight distribution	Front 54.7%, rear 45.3%
Weight/sq. in. brake lining	20.98 lbs.
Tire size	8.00 x 15
Tire loading (% of recommended maximum at curb weight)	Front 92%, rear 77%

SAFETY CHECK

	YES	NO
DRIVER SAFETY		
Blind spot at left windshield post at a minimum?	X	
Blind spot at rear vision mirror at a minimum?	X	
Vision to right rear satisfactory?	X	
Windshield free from objectionable reflections at night?	X	
Dash free of annoying reflections?	X	
Left side of dash free of low projections?		X
Cigarette lighter, ashtray and glove compartment convenient for driver?		X
DRIVER AND PASSENGER		
Front seat apparently locked securely at all adjustment points?	X	
Metal strip eliminated between front quarter window and main door window?		X
Rear view mirror free of sharp corners?	X	
Right side of dash free of projections?		X
Adequate shock-absorbing crash pad?		X
REAR SEAT PASSENGERS		
Back of front seat free of sharp edges and projections?	X	
Rear interior door handles inoperative when locked?	X	
Adequate partition to keep trunk contents out of passenger compartment on impact?		X

PRICES

(Including retail price at main factory, federal tax, and delivery and handling charges, but not freight.)

	Clipper	Clipper Deluxe	Cavalier	Patrician
Two-door sedan	$2534	$2681	$---	$---
Four-door sedan	2588	2735	3234	3735
Hardtop coupe	---	---	3268	---
Convertible	---	---	3476	---

ACCESSORIES

Ultramatic	$199.00
Overdrive	110.00
Power steering	195.00
Easamatic brakes	39.45
Radio:	
Pushbutton with manual antenna	97.00
With electrical antenna	109.00
Automatic station selector with manual antenna	118.00
With electrical antenna	132.00
Rear compartment speaker	16.00
Power windows and front seat	153.00
Windshield washer	9.40
Back-up lights	10.80
White sidewall tires (additional cost per set):	
7.60 x 15	30.00
8.00 x 15	33.50
Two-tone paint	20.00
Fresh air heater & defroster	79.50
Tinted glass	45.20

OPERATING COST PER MILE

(In this portion of the test table, MOTOR TREND includes those items that can be figured with reasonable accuracy on a comparative basis. The costs given here are not intended as an absolute guide to the cost of operating a particular make of car, or a particular car within that make. Depreciation is not included.)

Cost of gasoline	$173.07
Cost of insurance	140.60
Maintenance:	
Wheel alignment	6.80
Brake reline (front only)	20.44
Major tuneup	15.60

(Labor only; includes: clean and adjust or renew points and plugs, adjust spark timing, overhaul carburetor, adjust choke, clean fuel lines, tighten cylinder head and manifold, check compression and adjust valves.)

Automatic transmission (adjust, change lubricant)	14.10
First year operating cost per mile (based on 10,000-mile annual average)	3.7¢

MAINTENANCE AND REPAIR COST ANALYSIS
(These are prices for parts and labor required in various repairs and replacements. Your car may require all of them in a short time, or it may require none. However, a comparison of prices for these sample operations in various makes is often of pertinent interest to prospective owners.)

	MATERIAL	LABOR
Distributor	$ 21.55	$ 2.80
Battery	20.95	2.00
Fuel pump	15.00	4.80
Fan belt	2.14	2.00
Valve grind	4.58	33.60
One front fender	34.78	37.25
Two tires	61.72	
One bumper	35.00	3.50
TOTALS	$195.72	$85.95

ROAD TEST

THE PACKARD '300' CAVALIER

Dash is free of Space Patrol gadgetry but speedometer is hard to read at night and flasher lights replace oil gauge, ammeter.

Got any bodies you want to dispose of? Packard trunk has 30 cubic feet. Below—Brake, throttle are almost same level.

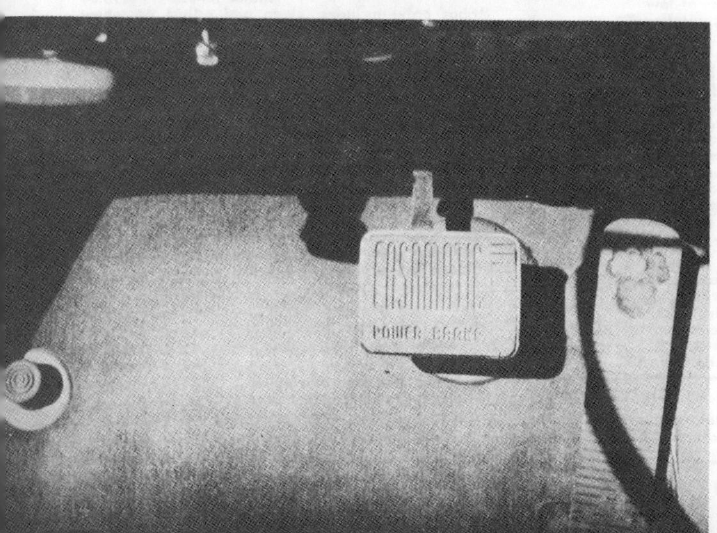

IF YOU'RE A YACHTSMAN and would like to transfer your seagoing proclivities to the highway, we've got just the car for you—the 1953 Packard Cavalier. With Ultramatic transmission, power brakes and power steering.

But before any Packard fans start hurling harpoons on the assumption we're calling their favorite a barge, let us explain: The seagoing simile comes naturally to mind after you've driven the Cavalier—with Packard's sweet power steering setup the wheel moves as easily as a rudder through water, with only that same slight feel of smooth resistance. The car is solid, but softly sprung, and almost as big as a cabin cruiser. And with Ultramatic it churns away from the stoplights with a very cruiser-like feel—and (alas) much the same acceleration.

Frankly, the ASR road test crew didn't expect to be rendered breathless by the changes in this '53 Packard—and they weren't. But, equally frankly, they were considerably impressed by the ease of handling, the reduction in driver fatigue and the excellence of vision. Like most men who deal professionally with automobiles, the test crew is inclined to automatically dislike automatic devices, but the Cavalier made some reluctant converts.

The merits of automatic transmissions—particularly torque converter transmissions—are still up for debate. But, after some days spent with the Cavalier "300," ASR has concluded that well-engineered power steering and power braking like Packard's can make the big American car something more than just endurable. For example, 360 miles of back country and secondary roads were packed into one day's test, with the same driver behind the wheel all the way. On roads like this it could have been an exhausting chore, one that would leave the pilot pooped and arm-weary. Actually, it was refreshing: the Packard's easy ride and low noise level got in their good work without being counteracted by the strain of wrestling its bulk by muscle alone. Incidentally, Packard's low hood line, and the fact the driver can see both front fenders, is a considerable aid in placing the car on narrow roads.

PACKARD'S POWER steering is the best ASR has tested yet. It is a doubleacting power cylinder attached directly to the steering linkage connecting rod, is in constant operation, and cuts the steering effort about 80 per cent—without losing road "feel." The number of turns from lock to lock are reduced from 5½ to 4, which, while not as direct as sports car steering, seems to be a good compromise. Because of the direct connection, the power cylinder also serves to damp out road shock, but without deadening the driver's sense of contact. Cost of this item is $195.

Even country roads can be traveled at an amazingly rapid clip due to better, faster control given by power steering.

Power brakes are a bargain at $39.45 and they do almost as much to ease the driver's task. Vacuum-operated and very light, they tend to batter passengers senseless until the driver gets used to just feathering them. Particularly good is Packard's arrangement of the broad pedal, which is almost at the level of the throttle. The company says this cuts application time 29 per cent and we'd be willing to go along with that, though the convenience of merely swiveling on your heel

Rear fender fins can be seen from driver's seat, simplify parking.

is the big thing. Even if the motor should conk out on a hill there are about three applications left in the reserve vacuum—and the brakes do work (though hard) without any vacuum.

The Ultramatic transmission is a pretty familiar story by now though Packard has added a new first turbine that supposedly increases the starting torque to 2.55-to-1. The operation is smooth enough, but in High range you don't exactly sprint away from the stoplights. More than most automatic transmissions Ultramatic benefits, performance-wise, from starting in Low range and then shifting full throttle to High at about 42 miles per hour. This really drinks up the gasoline, but the ASR crew found themselves resorting to it frequently under the pressure of city driving.

PERHAPS the best feature of Ultramatic is the direct drive clutch that locks out the torque converter down to about 11 m.p.h., eliminating that irritating revving up and down under varying load. Of course, you can get the torque converter any time you want it—up to about 60 m.p.h.—by kicking the throttle into the floor.

The foregoing concentration on gadgets may seem excessive, but that's the real news as far as the Cavalier is concerned. The basic design is an old story, though Packard has beefed the engine up to 180 horsepower with 8-to-1 compression and four-barrel carburetion and added such details as improved rubber bushings on the front suspension, a sturdier rear axle, and a new range of chrome spears, darts and lightning flashes along the body sides.

It would seem that Packard has squeezed just about as much out of its well-seasoned L-head straight-eight as can be obtained. But the engine is as smooth and quiet as anything you can get. The quiet motor, plus the Cavalier's substantial body and husky X-type frame, make 80-mile-an-hour conversations easy—providing you close the front vent windows firmly. Otherwise the wind roar is pretty obtrusive.

Interior furnishings of the test car—a pastel green four-door sedan from Earle C. Anthony, Inc., San Francisco—were substantial and quiet no Space Patrol gadgetry. Seats were chair height and the huge curved windshield was not too excessively tall. The rear view mirror did not interfere with normal forward vision and the windshield corner posts were moderately narrow. The chrome fins on the rear fenders do serve one functional purpose: the driver can see them both and mark the rear corners of the car for parking.

The instrument group is simple: three dials in front of the driver that contain on the left, fuel and temperature gauges, oil and ammeter flasher lights; center, the speedometer, with trip recorder; and, right, the clock. The styling of these is tasteful but, at night it's damned hard to see the speedometer needle at a quick glance—it just seems to fade out.

There is a separate ashtray for both front seat passenger and driver, but Packard might just as well have saved the money on the driver's: you can't get to it without a real struggle. The glove compartment is the bin type, but placed high so that it's hard for the driver to get at its contents.

Packard claims the largest trunk in the industry (30 cubic feet) and you can believe it. Fact is, you could carry nine passengers if the last three didn't mind traveling horizontally.

PRICE OF the Cavalier four-door F.O.B. is $3204, with excise tax. But very few purchasers get out at this level. L. H. Johnson, sales manager for the Anthony firm, says 95 per cent of the "300" series are sold with power brakes, Ultramatic and, of course, radio and heater. And some 70 per cent of the customers take power steering.

Summing it up, Packard has made a pretty successful attempt to cope with the problems presented by the big land-going yacht that Americans seem to prefer. The steering has been made fast and light—and accurate—by power, and the work has been taken out of the brakes by the same method. The vision is excellent, with all four fenders visible, the ride is cushiony (but not too horribly cushiony) and the general feeling of the car is satisfyingly substantial.

Body roll on the corners is not marked (particularly if you run the 8.00 x 15 tires about five or six pounds over the recommended pressure) and traction is good. The Cavalier does not feel tail-light.

There appears to be very little play in the steering wheel by U.S. standards and high cruising speeds feel safe—and are certainly easy to attain and hold, despite the moderate acceleration.

It is, in fact, a real land yacht —but with more virtues and far fewer vices than were shown by equivalent cars only a couple of years back. ●●●

PACKARD CAVALIER "300" DATA

SPECIFICATIONS

TEST CAR: Packard Cavalier "300" four-door sedan, equipped with Ultramatic drive, power brakes, power steering. Furnished by Earle C. Anthony, Inc., San Francisco.

ENGINE: *Type*, L-head straight eight. *Displacement*, 327 cu. in. *Compression ratio*, 8-to-1. *Bore and stroke*, 3¼ x 4½ in. *Brake horsepower*, 180 at 4000 r.p.m.

CHASSIS: *Frame*, box-section X-type. *Front suspension*, independent coil spring. *Rear suspension*, semi-elliptic leaf spring.

TRANSMISSION: torque converter, with direct drive clutch. Rear axle ratio, 3.54 to 1.

DIMENSIONS: *Wheelbase*, 127 in. *Weight*, 4125 lb. *Length*, 218 5/32 in *Width*, 78 in.

STEERING: Power steering, direct-acting hydraulic type with rotor pump, acting on worm and three-tooth roller. *Over-all ratio*, 22.5 to 1.

PERFORMANCE

Acceleration from stand start (Low-High column includes a full-throttle shift):

	Low-Hi	Hi-Range only
0-30 m.p.h.	6.3 sec.	8.1 sec
0-50 m.p.h.	12.6 sec.	15.4 sec.
0-60 m.p.h.	18.2 sec.	20.3 sec.
0-70 m.p.h.	25.1 sec.	27.9 sec.
0-80 m.p.h.	33.6 sec.	33.8 sec.

Standing ¼-mile: 21 sec. flat.

Top gear acceleration (full-throttle from steady speeds, allowing car to down-shift):

10-30 m.p.h.—5.8 sec.; 30-50 m.p.h.—9.5 sec.; 50-70 m.p.h.—13.6 sec.

Speedometer correction:

Car speedometer, m.p.h.	10	20	30	40	50	60	70	80	90
Fifth wheel m.p.h.	10	18	27.5	37	46	55	63.5	73	81

Packard Offers New Sportster with Italian Look, 180 Horsepower

PACKARD's bid for the super-duper sportster trade is the custom-built Caribbean above. It costs $5,200 and was developed from the hand-built Pan American which won styling and engineering awards at two motor shows. The car has a 180-horsepower engine and a 122-inch wheelbase. The Italian school of design is reflected in the wire-spoke wheels and cut-out rear fender. There is a real air scoop on the bonnet.

Traditional Packard lines take on new appearance in Clipper styling. High tail lights, new body molding are '54 changes

'54 PACKARD CLIPPER

A favorite family car, the Clipper still offers the Packard look—and at well under $3000, too

AN MT RESEARCH ROAD TEST REPORT by Walt Woron

TO MOST PEOPLE it comes as somewhat of a surprise that they can buy a Packard for under $3000. In the past, Packard and prestige have been synonymous. And with this generally comes price. The fact that Packard is now producing lower-priced cars may detract from this belief that the manufacturer has tried so hard to instill in the minds of the American car-buying public.

If I were to write an open letter to Packard, I would be tempted to recommend a divorcing of the lower-priced Clipper line from the Cavalier and Patrician, even to the extent of leaving off the Packard nameplate. Let the Clippers stand on their own merits; they have enough of them to make them highly interesting to many people. Of course, it appears that Packard is already anticipating such a move: the Packard crest on the grille and "Packard" in script on the trunk are the only written indications of the Clipper being a Packard; the Clippers have new rear fenders that are unlike those of the other models. There are other indications that this may be the last year when you can get a middle-priced car so much like one of America's most expensive ones.

The car we selected from among the three in the Clipper series for road test is the top Clipper mechanically. Performance is better than the less-powered Special (165 hp instead of 150), while its trim is not as plush as the Super. It's my opinion that the Deluxe will be the most popular of the three. And to me, its popularity will lie in the fact that it's a satisfying car to drive, one that you can head for mountains or desert early in the morning, and arrive fresh that night. In this respect, it's the equal of any car in its price class (which includes the DeSoto V8, Hudson Hornet, Olds 98, and the middle-sized Buicks).

It will cruise hour after hour at high speeds, riding you along in chair-height comfort, not causing you any mental or physical strain in keeping it on course.

Because of the extreme smoothness of the Packard ride (a point on which its makers justly pride themselves in their advertising) some people questioned MT about the test car's behavior on bad roads. Here's the answer: It's as much at home on a cow track as it is on the boulevard. After extremely rough bumps or dips, it

TEST CAR AT A GLANCE

REAR WHEEL HORSEPOWER

(Determined on Clayton chassis dynamometer; all tests are made under full load, which is similar to climbing a hill at full throttle. Observed hp figures are not corrected to standard atmospheric conditions)

47 road hp @ 1200 rpm and 31.5 mph
76 road hp @ 2000 rpm and 53 mph
92 road hp @ 2500 rpm and 68 mph
Maximum: 98 road hp @ 2850 rpm and 76 mph

SPEEDOMETER ERROR

Car speedometer read 34 @ true 30 mph, 50 @ true 45 mph, 68 @ true 60 mph

ACCELERATION

(In seconds; checked with fifth wheel and electric speedometer)

Standing start ¼-mile (reached 70 mph) 19.7, 0-30 mph 4.9, 0-60 mph 14.8, 10-30 mph (High) 3.8, 30-50 mph (High) 7.1, 50-80 mph (High) 18.3

RATING: GOOD

TOP SPEED

(In miles per hour; clocked over surveyed ¼-mile)

Fastest run, 102.4; Slowest run, 94.0; Average, 97.7

RATING: AVERAGE

FUEL CONSUMPTION

(In miles per gallon; checked with fuel flowmeter, fifth wheel, and electric speedometer. Mobilgas Special used)

22.7 mpg @ steady 30 mph, 19.6 mpg @ steady 45, 16.9 mpg @ steady 60, 13.0 mpg @ steady 75, 14.2 mpg in simulated traffic over measured course, 14.4 mpg tank overall average for 1885 miles

RATING: FAIR

BRAKE STOPPING DISTANCE

(To the nearest foot; checked with electrically actuated detonator)

46 ft. @ 30 mph, 96 ft. @ 45, 165 ft. @ 60

RATING: EXCELLENT

just stays serenely on course, not wandering or bounding around. Never once did it bottom, even over the ruttiest of roads. This gentle but controlled ride remains one of Packard's top cards.

The car does heel over at low speeds, so that when rounding a city corner you might think that you wouldn't relish driving it at high speeds; but, surprisingly enough, body lean is not at all extreme at high speeds. We found it worst at 20 mph.

Perhaps you, like the rest of us, do most of your driving under conditions altogether too tame to suit you but like to let it out occasionally when the road is clear. Then you'll be glad to know that the tail end of a Packard meekly follows the front around even a too-tight turn without trying to live a life of its own. We pushed the Clipper up to 70 on a mean curve we know and were unable to make the rear break away. Tire squeal was too loud, and out of character with the car's other behavior. No-squeal treads are optional, though, at no extra cost.

Starting with the wheel, which sits low in your lap where it won't obstruct anyone's vision, the whole steering system also seems designed for peace of mind.

In addition to the Clipper Deluxe on which we ran all our regular tests and which did not have power steering, a Super Clipper that did have the increasingly popular booster was mine for a long week-end. So I had an unusual opportunity to compare what was essentially the same car, both with the option and without.

With standard steering, the Clipper is not a strain to drive. It takes 4⅜ turns of the wheel to get from lock to lock (half a turn less with the power setup). Tugging is necessary only if you try to turn the wheels when the car is completely motionless. Packard's power steering is very much like its manual counterpart on the highway: the car moves solidly along, even at high speeds, with very little correction. If you do a lot of driving in close quarters, the linkage-booster power setup will give you finger-touch control of this hefty car. Another advantage: the turning circle is 43 feet on the standard car, two feet less with power. Otherwise, you may be surprised at the Clipper's easy control in standard trim. It's superior in this respect to many of its competitors.

Not the least of the factors that make the Clipper so comfortable a car to drive or ride in is the seating position. Whether you're behind the wheel or just looking at the scenery, you're at ease. High seats support your legs; low-silled, high windows let you see where you're going and where you've been; and vision for close maneuvering, with the Packard-pioneered low hood and high fenders, is something so pleasant to drive with that the industry seems to be adopting it wholesale.

By hitching up a little in the seat, you can see the big new Clipper tail lights that make a parking problem disappear almost completely. Of course, parking is one aspect of driving that definitely benefits from power steering. The no-fuss-no-muss smoothness of Ultramatic's takeoff is also responsible for a desirable feeling of being in complete control.

A Clipper with Ultramatic doesn't have particularly scintillating performance, but if you learn how to take full advantage of the straight-eight engine by using the transmission in the right way, you'll get acceleration similar to competitive V8s.

Using the Low range, wind up till you're at 50 mph; then drop into High (it corresponds to Drive in other automatics).

Packard's 165-horsepower, L-head engine has high accessibility rating. Although valves are hard to get at, most components are well-positioned for ready servicing

Photos by Tom Medley

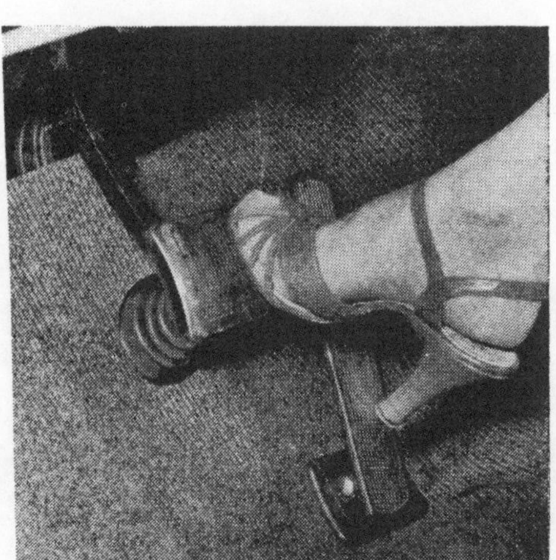

"Easamatic" power brake pedal requires only soft touch to bring Clipper to a halt

High seats, low hood, raised fenders add up to good view of the road through Clipper's wide windshield. Panel has drawer-type glove compartment mounted at right

You'll have skipped the torque converter part of the range—it no longer adds much push to the engine's own thrust at that speed—and you're in direct drive, the other part of the High range. This 1 to 1 setup gives you quite a high gear (the rear axle is 3.23 to 1 with Ultramatic) and it will take you on up as high as you're likely to go. On the test car, top was an average of 97.7 mph, with a top run of 102.4.

If you start out in Drive range, you'll make a pure torque converter start unaided by gears (as you would in a pre-'53 Chevy with Powerglide). Ultramatic seems slower than it is, because of a buttery smoothness. If you're not in a hurry, direct drive may cut in as low as 15 mph; if you really put your foot in it, it will wait till as high as 50. The time difference in Drive alone and Low-plus-Drive is about 3.5 seconds for acceleration over the standing quarter-mile.

If it goes, will it stop? It will indeed, in less space than it took any of MT's '53 test cars. The Packard's brakes deserve top rating on two other points as well: (1) Though the test car's power brakes were the popular low-pedal type, letting the driver pivot comfortably (and quickly) on his heel from throttle to brake, they offered no particular problem (as do some others of their ilk) when we switched off the ignition to test them with the vacuum tank depleted. Pedal pressure was only slightly harder with no booster than with a conventional braking system, an emergency advantage that other users of the handy low-pedal brake would do well to study. (2) The other striking advantage of the Packard's brakes was their total lack of fade, even when very hot in MT's severe tests. As a car for a family vacation, the Clipper passed this last all-important test to rate as a good choice for near-complete physical and mental comfort.

It is a good 40 years since Packard's looks became almost universally recognized. Today's Packard Clipper doesn't look much like the famed Model 48s and Twin Sixes, but it's very much in the same tradition. Back in 1951, Packard revamped its whole line. The change, everyone agreed, was for the better; though in no sense startling, the cars were modern and clean of line. What's more, they were built for people to ride in and to get in and out of with extreme ease (doors, for instance, are huge, and open almost at right angles to the body).

In looks, the test Clipper wasn't much different from those 1951 models, yet it's anything but old-fashioned. And it will remain good-looking. How do we know? Well, we've had a look at one of Packard's big body changes, the one to come in the company's all-new '55 cars. They ought to bring new enthusiasm both to buyers who have been intrigued by Packard's aggressive expansion program and to those in charge of that program in Detroit. But there is no question that they are related, not only to the '54 line, but to all Packards for many years back. They are a real credit to Dick Teague, Packard's youthful Styling Director (we'll tell you more about him next month).

Packard is still bucking the trend to the universal V8, but as you can see from our performance figures, the car is no laggard, even with soft-spoken Ultramatic. (For more spectacular dashes, there's overdrive; the Clipper is one of the few cars at its price with this high-performance option.) MT Research has yet to see a less cluttered engine compartment. With the exception of valves (always hard to reach on an L-head) and a power brake mechanism hiding under the steering gear, everything was easy to get at. With its 8 to 1 compression ratio, the Clipper Deluxe is content only with premium fuel (we used Mobilgas Special throughout our tests).

So it's still possible for car lovers who appreciate the traditional qualities of comfort, all-around room, and smoothness to get them, and in a medium-priced car that hasn't yet changed much from the big Packards. What changes the next several years will bring are still a matter for the crystal-ball crowd. Will Packard merge with another independent, possibly the Nash-Hudson combine now known as American Motors Corp.? Detroit sages say that it will have to; that an independent, especially one aiming for higher sales in the low-volume, high-quality field, hasn't a chance of lasting much longer against the staggering combined might of GM, Chrysler and Ford (it's interesting to note that the only real U.S. luxury cars, with the single exception of the senior Packards, are built by the Big Three).

But we'll bet that when it does combine, or reorganize, or whatever it has to do, that it will retain the Packard look, and that the '54 Clipper will still look proud many years from today's date on the calendar. —*Walt Woron*

GENERAL SPECIFICATIONS

ENGINE: L-head straight 8. Bore 3½ in. Stroke 4¼ in. Stroke/bore ratio 1.214. Compression ratio 8.0 to 1. Displacement 327 cu. in. Advertised bhp 165 @ 3600 rpm. Bhp per cu. in. 0.505. Piston travel @ max bhp 2550 ft. per min. Max torque 295 @ 2200 rpm. Max bmep 136.0 psi.

DRIVE SYSTEM: STANDARD transmission is three-speed synchromesh using helical gears. Ratios: 1st 2.43, 2nd 1.53, 3rd 1.0, reverse 3.16.

OVERDRIVE is planetary with standard gears, minimum cut-in speed 22 mph. Ratio: 0.72 (overall 2.95).

AUTOMATIC transmission is Ultramatic, torque converter with direct drive above 15 mph. Ratios: High: torque converter (max ratio @ stall 2.55 @ 1400 rpm) and direct drive (1.0); Low, 1.82 x converter ratio; Reverse, 1.64 x converter ratio.

REAR AXLE RATIOS: Conventional 3.9, Overdrive 4.1, Ultramatic 3.23.

DIMENSIONS Wheelbase 122 in. Tread 60 front and rear. Wheelbase/tread ratio 2.03. Overall width 78 in. Overall length 215.5 in. Overall height 62.4 in. Turning diameter 43 ft. (41 ft. with power steering). Turns lock to lock 4⅜ (3⅞ with power steering). Test car weight 4030 lbs. Test car weight/bhp ratio 24.4 to 1. Weight distribution 55% front, 45% rear. Tire size 7.60 x 15.

PRICES

(Including retail price at main factory, federal tax, and delivery and handling charges, but not freight)

CLIPPER SPECIAL, two-door sedan $2544. CLIPPER DELUXE, two-door sedan $2645, four-door sedan $2695, hardtop $2830. CLIPPER SUPER, two-door sedan $2765, four-door sedan $2815, Panama hardtop $3125.

ACCESSORIES. Automatic transmission $199, overdrive $110, power steering $178, power brakes $43, radio $102, heater $80, power-operated windows and four-way front seat $198, air-conditioning $647, whitewalls (exchange) $33.

DEPRECIATION

These figures will be given in a future issue. In the interest of accuracy, MT Research is re-evaluating the method of figuring depreciation.

ESTIMATED COST PER MILE

These figures will be given in a future issue. In the interest of accuracy, MT Research is re-evaluating the method of figuring estimated cost per mile.

PARTS AND LABOR COST

(These are prices for parts and labor required in various repairs and replacements. Your car may require all of them in a short time, or it may require none. However, a comparison of prices for these sample operations in various makes is often of interest to prospective owners. First price is for parts, second for labor.)

Distributor $19.03, $2.80; battery $19.95, $2.00; fuel pump $18.38, $4.80; valve grind $5.44, $34.20; one front fender $53.50, $14.00; bumper $37.45, $3.60; two tires $57.50. Total parts $211.25, labor $62.40.

King of the L-Heads:

Packard Hikes Passing Power

THAT'S NO SPOOK following me as I take a luxurious Caribbean for a workout. Instead, it's a '27 sedan that Packard has converted to a towing dynamometer, to give new cars extra work to do. Believe me, it was really quite a pull.

This is rough on a car, but I wanted to see if the Patrician bogs down easily. It doesn't.

That die-cast aluminum head is velvet-smooth inside and out, stopping carbon build-up.

New aluminum head and the highest compression yet give this big straight-eight brute a whopping torque.

By Wilbur Shaw
President, Indianapolis Motor Speedway

MAXIMUM torque when you need it plus some of the fanciest interiors I've yet seen in any car—that's what Packard has wrapped up for 1954 in its traditionally classic package. The grille is still *the* grille, Packard's familiar radiator shape dating (hold onto your bonnet and goggles) from 1904.

Behind the familiar Packard prows are cars put together after painstaking research into everything from bearskin carpeting to acoustic characteristics of big, flat body panels.

Not long ago I took a new 212-horsepower Patrician around Packard's test track and over their endurance roads to see what they had done to it. They told me that at 8.7 to 1, it had the highest compression ratio in the industry. At more than 4,000 pounds, that Patrician is Packard's biggest stock model and a lot of automobile. When they get that big, you tend to drive sedately—even though the Patrician will easily top a hundred. It's an extremely roomy car with five inches more leg room in the back seat than any other American six-passenger sedan.

It handles smoothly, the way a big boat should. Its power steering is easy but retains a natural feel. Company engineers told me they feel Packard, which was first with the frame-anchored, direct-acting unit, is on the right track. They're confident other firms will be going to the direct-acting setup before long. Clippers also have this system. Their manual ratio of 22.03 compares to a power ratio of 18.2.

Packard's power brakes retain that normal touch, too, with the aid of a reaction diaphragm. I liked the action of

THE BIG LEVER I'm pushing is the throttle of a Packard laboratory dynamometer. The scale at right shows that this big baby is putting out about 330 pound-feet of torque.

DEEP IN SOUND ROOM, an electronic shaker jiggles a hood assembly at various frequencies. Packard test engineer Roy Frailing adjusts oscilloscope that measures the response.

FASTEN YOUR UPPERS for this one. I took that plushy Patrician through once, which was all I wanted. I don't know how the bolts and welds manage to take it, but they do.

the brakes—they're not the touchy kind that slam you into the dash if you forget to gentle them.

With its 1954 cars, Packard is now going full throttle on its drive to recapture the luxury market's first place in sales. Packard lost this position in 1936 to Cadillac. Probably the clearest sign of this race can be seen in the 1954 Packard body. It's about the same as the 1953 body.

In other words, Packard once again will operate on the luxury-car formula: when a man invests in a big car he doesn't want one that will scream "last year" within a few months after his last bank draft has been cleared.

More Models Than Ever Before

Packard is putting a big team into the field. It's the biggest array of models in the company's history. There are three Clippers (Special, De Luxe and Super); two Packards (Cavalier and Patrician), and a Custom line, including the Caribbean sports convertible and some eight-passenger sedans and limousines priced to nearly $7,000.

While the Patrician's engine, a bronze-colored L-head brute, is a remake of Packard's well-known straight-eight, the other three eights for '54 haven't been changed much. Three engines power the remaining Clippers and Packards: 150 and 165 horsepower in the Clippers; 185 horsepower in the Cavalier, smaller of the Packards. Engine 5406, the 212-horsepower job, fires the Patrician and the big Custom cars.

They tell me that Packard edged over the 200-horsepower mark only as a kind of by-product. For the present, at least, they disclaim any part in the horsepower race. But they wanted to drop an engine into their heaviest cars that would give a powerful push on the rear wheels at speeds where it's needed most—between 40 and 70 miles per hour.

They succeeded in getting 17 percent more passing power and 10 percent more horses. The 359-cubic-inch engine now delivers 330 pound-feet of torque at 2,200 r.p.m. That's with Ultramatic transmission, Packard's torque converter, and represents a road speed of about 51 miles per hour.

I DON'T KNOW whose grandma embroidered the escutcheon on Balboa's cream-and-scarlet upholstery, but it sure is pretty. Like hex hub, it dates from Packard's early days.

PEEKING UNDER this way is inevitable the first time you see a Balboa hardtop. The bonnet shields the back window, which can be cranked down. It will be powered later.

The Patrician's new power mainly comes from an amazingly smooth, die-cast aluminum head, shaved down to eliminate breathing dams and topped with a four-barrel carburetor. Intake ports and the camshaft have also been reworked.

Packard has always been engineering-minded. If some recent models have seemed a bit noisier than they should have, you can bet your decibels they'll find out why. One approach to quietness is through proper body-metal design, and another is handled by good insulation. This year Packard is going hard after both.

Current body designs with their great expanses of near-flat metal mean lots of headaches for the people responsible for keeping out the flutters, rattles and buckles. That continental-styled hood, for instance, has only two "draws," the fluting at each side, to give rigidity to the hood panel. Without these it would flap around and bong like your grandmother's cookie sheets or a J. Arthur Rank trademark.

Dash Panel Thickened

Attacking the problem from an insulating standpoint this year, Packard engineers put together certain interior panels with special sound dampers. I saw one dash panel that's a real Dagwood sandwich. It was six layers thick, consisting of 3/32" indented felt, ⅜" jute felt, Kraft paper, .125" to .140" mastic, .090" embossed paper board, and dash-lining carpet. It didn't rattle. END

FACTS ON '54 PACKARD

Model: Packard Patrician 4-door sedan.

Engine: 8-cyl. L-head; 212 hp. at 4,000 r.p.m.; compression ratio, 8.7:1; piston displacement, 359 cu. in.; bore and stroke, 3 9/16" by 4½"; torque, 330 lb.-ft. at 2,200 r.p.m.

Weight: 4,142 lb.; per hp., 19.05.

Transmission: Ultramatic (torque converter, standard equipment), overdrive or standard shift; rear-axle ratio, 3.5:1 with Ultramatic, 4.55:1 with overdrive, 4.1:1 with standard transmission.

Steering ratio: manual 30.9:1, power 22.5:1; radius of turning circle, manual 22.5', power 21.5'.

Effective brake-lining area: 208.25 sq. in.

Springs: front, coil; rear, 5 semi-elliptic leaves, 2½" by 54⅝".

Outside dimensions: height, 62⅞"; over-all length with bumpers and guards, 216½"; width, 77⅞"; wheelbase, 127"; overhang, front 35¼", rear 54 3/16"; tread, front 60", rear 60 53/64".

Inside dimensions: seat-cushion width, front 62¾", rear 62"; leg room, front 43½", rear 48¾"; headroom, front 36", rear 35¼"; seat height, front 14", rear 14 13/32"; vertical distance, steering wheel to seat cushion, with seat in rear position, 5 1/32"; front-seat adjustment, horizontal 5", vertical 1½".

Tire size: 8.00 by 15.

Testing the 212 HP Packard Patrician

THE imposing Packard Patrician is its usual aristocratic self again this year, but it's been given an infusion of new power in the form of a larger straight-8 engine (around the Packard plant they call it "the *Big* Engine") which takes the palm for the highest compression ratio (8.7 to 1) and greatest displacement (359 cu. in.) in the industry.

The Patrician takes a plebeian mudhole. In rough going like this, and over bumpy roads, this Packard provided an excellent ride and was easy to control.

Patrician took curves nicely up to 45 *mph*, but above that speed there was noticeable body roll. In lateral sway test it showed a side tilt of 5.5° in going around 285-ft.-radius circle at 40 *mph*.

Power plant aside for the moment, however, the first thing you're likely to notice when you take this car out of the penthouse garage is that despite its size (overall length 216.4 in., curb weight 4,825 lbs.) it handles easily and responds swiftly and surely to the wheel. The ease of handling—a predominant characteristic—probably results from the combination of Packard's full-time but not overly touchy power steering and the four-way powered front seat which adjusts to exactly the driving position that fits you best. On the road, the car is outstanding in its directional stability; there's no noticeable wander and it holds a straight course with a minimum of help from the driver. At high speeds it settles into the road more securely than many cars with hotter performance ratings. In a word, the Packard Patrician is a good car for a long trip; it's less likely than many other cars to fatigue the driver and passengers.

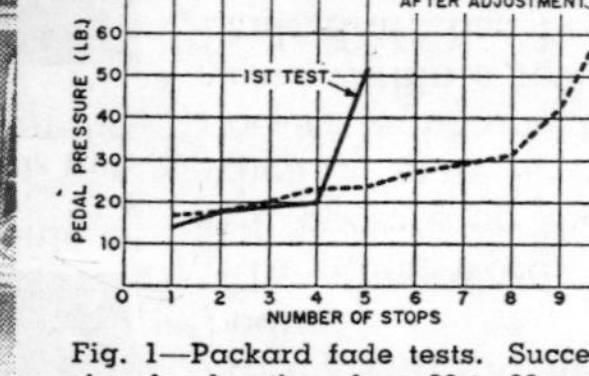

Four-way powered front seat adds much to driving comfort, permits relaxing change of position during long drives. Seat control buttons are at A. Note also window power controls (B) and wiper control on steering post (C). Some drivers may bump leg on parking brake handle (D) when it's pulled out.

Fig. 1—Packard fade tests. Successive decelerations from 60 to 30 *mph* at rate of 7 ft. per sec/per sec. Note improvement on second test after adjustment.

Among the other aids (in our test car) to the harassed motorist were power brakes, power windows, a motorized radio aerial, an air conditioning system and separate heaters for the front and back seats. And then a question follows, as the night the day: With all this attention to driver-passenger comfort, safety and convenience, who let the chrome-happy designer into Packard's interior design department? He should be sentenced to an 8-hour drive on a sunny day facing the changing glare from that broad-beamed, highly reflective chrome molding all around the inner edge of the windshield, the chrome around the gages, the chrome strip along the length of the dashboard and the large chrome controls for the heater and radio.

Here's a suggestion: why don't car manufacturers find out whether interior chrome is really what the public wants by designing their chrome trim and knobs so they can be snapped on as optional equipment if the customer wishes to have them? They might be surprised.

Mounted on a test stand, the Patrician's big 212 *hp* straight-8 engine would appear as in photo above. Placed under the hood (right), engine must share space with such extra equipment as power brake booster (A), power steering pump (B).

With its 212 *hp* motor the Patrician can get out and ramble. In the maximum speed run, our test driver took it up to the limit of the speedometer—110 *mph*—which was 105.5 *mph* true. Our test car had a 3.9 rear axle ratio (instead of the 3.54 ratio specified as standard for the Patrician) which helped acceleration but inhibited its top speed to some extent. By the way, the Packard's speedometer error was quite low at all speeds, in comparison to other cars tested this year. And the odometer error was on the minus side, meaning that the odometer isn't giving full credit for the total distance traveled.

Hardly anyone would wish the dignified Packard Patrician to be a hot rod, nor is it one. Yet our test car, handicapped by the extra weight of the 325-lb air conditioner and a two-speed automatic transmission which wasn't built for fast acceleration in the first place, went from 0 to 60 in the true time of 16.2 seconds. Of the six other cars tested this year, three were faster and three were slower.

Packard engineers point out that this big engine provides the greatest torque where it's needed most—that is, in the 40 to 70 *mph* range (where most highway driving is done), and especially between 50 and 60 *mph* where passing ability is most important. Although our traffic range acceleration tests don't correspond exactly with those two sets of figures, they show that the Patrician's performance in going from 20 to 40, 20 to 60, 20 to 70 and 20 to 80 *mph* is all right, but not outstanding in relation to other power-packed heavyweights tested. Moving from 20 to 80 *mph* in 27.7 seconds, it was about 7.6 seconds slower than the fastest car tested this year, and its 20 to 70 time of 20.4 was about 5

Drivers' Observations

ROADABILITY: Heavy, stable feel under virtually any kind of road condition. Very few small, multi-frequency vibrations. Minimum road shock. Tracking excellent, and it would take a lot of wind to push this car around much. Cornering ability satisfactory, but body roll is noticeable on the sharper curves. Power steering makes handling easy without taking away the wheels-to-road orientation that is important to so many drivers. Good weight distribution of 55% on front wheels, 45% on rear wheels contributes to smooth, non-pitch ride. There's a pronounced lurch when transmission upshifts from Lo to Drive; no forward creep in Hi, but some in Lo and Reverse when stopped.

RIDING COMFORT: Apparently designed around the concept that people who buy this car deserve top riding comfort and convenience; and the only fly in the ointment is the excessive interior chrome which throws glares and reflections all over the place. Seats are comfortably firm and amply wide, with plenty of headroom and legroom in both front and back seats. Special non-attached foot rests are provided in the rear compartment. Rear seat has wide, comfortable fold-down center arm rest. Side-mounted arm rests are well placed for comfort and are padded on the sides as well as the top. Front seat heater under dash and rear seat heater located under front seat do beautiful job of keeping car warm. For summer riding comfort this car had an air conditioning unit (optional equipment). Vertical adjustability of front seat (which also will fit wife-size leg lengths) will let you sit higher in order to reduce the sky glare area when making a long drive. Hope that 4-way seat adjustment becomes standard safety equipment on all cars.

INSTRUMENTS AND CONTROLS: Gages well grouped for good visibility; numerals and tolerances are quite readable. Silver dial letters on black background may not be as easy to read as white letters because of reflective characteristics. Words "Oil" and "Gen." light up to indicate lack of pressure or battery discharge. Directional signal arrows flash green with fast multiple clicking. Gear selector quadrant lighted for night driving—hallelujah. That's another feature that should be made standard on all automatic shift cars. Wiper control is coyly located on left side of steering post—a convenient position once you get used to reaching for it there. Wipers themselves are quiet, have good speed control; they're vacuum-operated, with a booster. Heater-blower controls call for a little reaching around the steering wheel to operate. Those controls are a mite complicated to figure out, requiring a reading of the instructions rather than a casual twiddling. Small ashtrays at left and right sides of dashboard are a shade narrow. Left one is directly above wife's left nylon. Headlight control button is real versatile: Pull it out to turn on the headlights; turn it to the right to get dash gage lights; turn it to the left to turn on the under-dash courtesy light. In addition to dash lighter there's another lighter mounted in rear seat ashtray. Pull-out glove drawer is lighted.

SPECIAL COMMENTS: Visibility all around very good, including good driver's-eye-to-road vision considering length of the hood. Non-glare rear-view mirror of adequate size to take good advantage of wrap-around rear window, but why the distracting chrome strip around the mirror? Left-to-right arrangement of positions on shift quadrant: P, N, H, L, R. You can shift directly from Lo to Reverse without going through other gears—a good feature for rocking out of mud-holes, but it's too easy to shift accidentally into reverse when you don't want to. Engine won't start unless gears are in neutral. Power steering pump gurgles a little—but not obnoxiously—on sharp turns. Large-sized parking lights look vulnerable and unprotected, might be subject to breakage. Bottom side of hood insulated with Fiberglas blanket. Accessibility for service of oil dip stick, oil filler, oil filter, battery, hydraulic pump, windshield washer, distributor and air conditioner parts all good. Accessibility of fuel pump and valve adjustment fair. Key operation of door locks a bit fussy. Sun and light reflections from hood ornament and headlight moldings can be annoying. Top of dash is shiny, too. Bumper jack works okay; interior of trunk is nicely finished, and low lip means convenient access. Patrician's floor insulation consists of a layer of sprayed-on insulation, a layer of asphalt-impregnated felt, a double-thickness layer of jute felt and deep-pile carpeting.

seconds slower than the fastest car.

The Ultramatic transmission, though not intended to produce fireball acceleration, helps pay its way by going a little easier on fuel consumption at the usual constant-speed highway driving conditions than do other hydraulic torque converters, which tend to penalize a car's mileage record. In the Packard Ultramatic, however, the converter automatically locks out at constant driving speeds (roughly, above 20 *mph*) and the car is in direct drive, which is more efficient in terms of gasoline consumption. The converter operates only during acceleration from a standstill or when the driver depresses the gas pedal to the floor to get extra speed for passing.

In our level road, constant speed tests the Patrician got a high of 16.5 *mph* at 30 *mph*. Taking the weight of the car into account, the ton-miles-per-gallon rate at 30 *mph* was 45.4—the second best such figure recorded in our tests this year. But in the five-gallon economy fuel consumption test, including typical city traffic and open road driving in about a 40-60 proportion, the mileage dropped off to an average of 12.5 over a distance of 62.6 miles. The effect of the torque converter on mileage in start-stop traffic driving is apparent.

Let's take a little closer look at the engine itself. Its reciprocating load factor at 60 *mph* (an index of stress and strain) was 1956, which is roughly equivalent to the force in pounds exerted by the piston on the connecting rod at the end of the exhaust stroke. This value, again the second highest encountered this year, generally has tended to be twice as large in L-head engines as in V-8s. However, the Packard engine was smooth and quiet—powerful enough so that it isn't overworked in pushing this big car around. Also, our engineers' calculations show 72% of the Patrician's 212 brake *hp* is delivered to the rear wheels, and this (once more) is the second-best such percentage among 1954 cars tested.

The Patrician's brakes have their work cut out for them in keeping a leash on this heavy car, and for the most part they do the job well. In panic stops from speeds up to 60 *mph*, this Packard's stopping distances conformed closely to National Safety Council standards for good brakes, and there was no swerving or slewing to mar the pattern. (The extra weight of the air conditioner in the rear end may have helped here.) Our fade tests, though, showed that the brakes may fade badly if the shoes are not kept in close adjustment to the drum. In the initial test it took only four decelerations from 60 to 30 *mph* to double the amount of pedal effort required, and serious fading occurred on the fifth stop. After the brakes were adjusted to minimum clearance (this was a brand new car and they hadn't been burnished in) the test was rerun, with marked improvement (Fig. 1). Eight decelerations were needed to double the initial pedal effort of 17 lbs., and serious fade took place on the ninth cycle. Remember that this test is rough, particularly on heavier cars, and imposes punishment far more severe than almost any ordinary driver is likely to give his brakes.

Wipers follow pattern that can be accepted as standard for most cars and which includes usual blind spots at lower left and right corners and top center of the windshield. The rear-view mirror has a four-way adjustment.

Air conditioner duct openings are located in rear window shelf.

Air conditioning unit itself nestles in rear of trunk, leaving ample space available to store luggage.

Water penetration tests showed the Patrician to have the tightest body of any of the '54 cars we've examined. In two 15-minute drenchings—one simulating a heavy rain and the other a reduced, directed stream—no bad leakage was detected, and there were only slight to moderate leaks around the vent windows and trunk seam. The engine started readily after both tests, but there was some misfiring from the idling motor when water was sprayed downward through the grille and at probable exposure angles from the bottom. This engine design doesn't block splash from below like a V-8 does, and there were no guard pans to keep water from coming up into it.

Factory-suggested retail price for this four-door Packard Patrician is $3,890, including federal taxes and delivery and handling charges but not transportation costs, state and local taxes or optional equipment. Ultramatic is standard in the Patrician. Power steering costs an extra $178, power brakes $43, combination power seat and windows $198, and air conditioning $647.

Packard Patrician Performance

MAKE OF CAR: Packard Patrician

START OF TESTS: February 8, 1954

GENERAL ROAD CONDITIONS (for gas mileage and acceleration tests): Portland concrete, smooth, dry and level

MILEAGE AT START OF TESTS: 60 **MILES COVERED IN TESTS:** 1040

GAS USED: Premium **OIL USED:** SAE 20W

CURB WEIGHT: 4825 lbs. 55% on front wheels, 45% on rear wheels

TIRE PRESSURES: 24 lbs. front; 24 lbs. rear for all tests.

SPARK SETTING: TDC

TEST DATA

GASOLINE MILEAGE (checked with fuel volume flow meter and 5th wheel. Temperature 61° F. Relative humidity 60%. Barometer 29.1 in. Hg. Carried weight 682 lbs. Two runs made in opposite directions on same road):

True Speed (5th Wheel)	True Miles per Gallon	Odometer Miles per Gallon	Ton Miles per Gallon (true)
20	15.3	15.3	42.2
30	16.5	16.4	45.4
40	15.7	15.6	43.2
50	14.3	14.2	39.4
60	12.2	12.1	33.6
70	10.2	10.1	28.1

TRAFFIC FUEL CONSUMPTION (simulated traffic pattern of city driving—stops, acceleration, braking. Carried weight 705 lbs.): True mpg 8.05. Odometer mpg 8.02. True ton mpg 22.2. Maximum claim that can reasonably be made for the car—slow acceleration and coasting): Odometer mpg 18.5.

ACCELERATION (timed with 5th wheel. Carried weight 689 lbs. Temperature 50° F. Relative humidity 50%. Barometer 29.7 in. Hg. Spark TDC. Figures are average of two runs in opposite directions):

True MPH	Gear Range	Average True Time (sec.)	True MPH	Gear Range	Average True Time (sec.)
0-20	Lo	4.02	0-70	Lo & Dr. Shift at 43	21.5
0-30	Lo	6.24	0-80	Lo & Dr. Shift at 43	29.0
0-40	Lo	8.76	20-40	Dr.	6.24
0-50	Lo & Dr. Shift at 43	12.0	20-60	Dr.	14.9
0-60	Lo & Dr. Shift at 43	16.2	20-70	Dr.	20.4
			20-80	Dr.	27.7

Minimum time for 0-60 mph (true) over level road with no wind, premium fuel and driver alone: 13.0 seconds.

ACCELERATION FACTORS (Temperature 50° F. Relative humidity 50%. Barometer 29.7 in. Hg. Carried weight 689 lbs. Spark TDC. Figures are calculated from average of two runs in opposite directions):

True Speed	Gear	MPH per Sec.	Ft. per Sec. per Sec.
10	Lo	4.9	7.2
20	Lo	4.5	6.6
30	Lo	4.1	6.0
40	Lo	3.5	5.1
50	Dr.	2.8	4.1
60	Dr.	2.1	3.1
70	Dr.	1.6	2.3
80	Dr.	1.1	1.6

HILL CLIMBING (calculated from accelerometer readings with allowances for rotational inertia. Data same as preceding test):

True MPH	Gear	Approx. Grade in %	Approx. Pull in lbs.
15	Lo	29	1510
40	Dr.	14	770

TOP SPEED AND SPEEDOMETER-ODOMETER CORRECTION: Odometer distance 10.0 miles; true distance 10.024 miles; odometer error at 35 mph 0.2% (minus):

MPH Speedometer	True Speed	% Error Speedometer	Engine RPM	MPH Speedometer	True Speed	% Error Speedometer	Engine RPM
				60	57.7	4	2710
Top Speed 110	105.5	4	4670	50	48.1	4	2270
90	86.5	4	3990	40	38.7	3	1830
80	76.7	4	3560	30	29.4	2	1390
70	67.1	4	3130	20	19.9	0.5	950

STOPPING ABILITY (Surface, Portland concrete, smooth and dry. Grade level. Surface temperature 50° F. Tires 8.20 x 15, 4-ply. Drag factor of road [average coefficient of friction between tires and road] 0.68. Pedal pressure 100 lbs. on all stops):

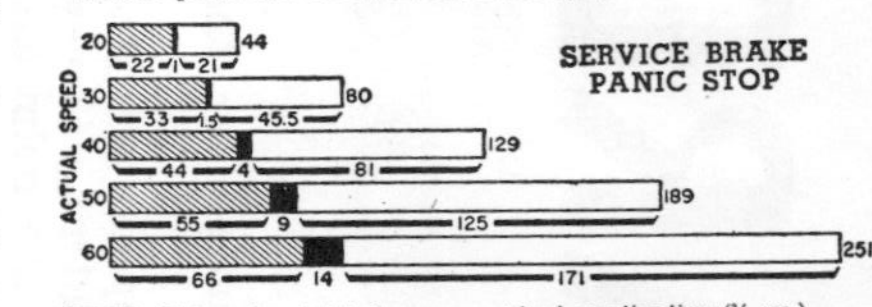

Distance traveled during average driver's reaction time (¾ sec.)

Brake lag: Distance covered between time brake pedal is depressed and wheels grip pavement and lock.

Braking distance: Distance covered between time wheels grip pavement until car comes to stop. Figures at ends of bars indicate total stopping distances in ft. (sum of reaction, brake lag and braking distances).

PARKING BRAKE TEST: Brake applied hard and suddenly from 20 mph actual speed

Braking Distance	Did Rear Wheels Lock? Right	Left
42 ft.	Yes	Yes

HORSEPOWER AT REAR AXLE (values calculated from accelerometer readings with allowances made for efficiencies and rotational inertia):

MPH True	RPM Engine	Equiv. Engine Torque (lb. ft.)	Axle Horsepower
86	3800	210	152 (max.)
67	3000	218	124
44	2000	200	76

Per cent of advertised engine horsepower supplied to rear wheels: 72%

CHASSIS DYNAMOMETER CHECK (Tests supervised by Glen Kunz, regional representative, Clayton Dynamometer Co. Temperature 65°. Relative humidity 50%. Barometer 29.1 in. Hg):

Speedometer	Engine RPM	Axle Horsepower
27	1250	40
36	1625	56
52	2300	90
68	3000	114
74	3400	120 (max.)

PERFORMANCE FACTORS (Calculated)

MPH (true) at maximum advertised horsepower 90.2 and torque 48.5. Engine rpm at 60 mph (also revolutions per mile) 2710 rpm. Average piston speed at 60 mph (also, ft./mile) 2040 ft./min. Cu. ft. per minute of mixture at 60 mph (also, cu. ft./mile) 282. Maximum engine horsepower (adv.) per ton of car (curb weight without air conditioner) 94. Reciprocating load factor (piston weight, bore, stroke, connecting rod) 26.6. Reciprocating load factor at 60 mph 1956. Maximum engine horsepower (adv.) per cubic inch displacement 0.59.

SPECIFICATIONS

ENGINE: L-head, in-line; bore 3.56; stroke 4.5; advertised maximum brake horsepower rated 212 at 4000 rpm; advertised maximum torque 330 ft. lbs. at 2000 rpm, corrected to 60° F. and 29.92 in Hg.; compression ratio 8.7 to 1; piston displacement 359 cu. in.; fuel specified premium.

TRANSMISSION: Ultramatic, torque converter, 2-speed; rear axle ratio 3.9.

STEERING: Turning circle 43 ft., curb to curb. No. wheel turns, lock to lock 4.75.

EXTERIOR: Wheelbase 127.5 in.; overall length 217 in.; overall width 77.75 in.; overall height 64 in.; curb weight 4825 lbs. (10 gal. fuel, oil and water); minimum road clearance 7 in. at rear shock absorber.

INTERIOR: Headroom, front seat 36.75 in., rear seat 35.5; legroom, front seat 39.5 in., rear seat 16.75 in.; hiproom, front seat 63 in., rear seat 61.25 in.; total front seat adjustment at floor 4 in.

VISIBILITY: Windshield area 989 sq. in.; rear window area 927 sq. in.; driver's eye to road over left front fender 42 ft., over hood center 47.3 ft., over right front fender 50.3 ft.

EQUIPMENT: Battery 6 volt, 17 plate, 120 amp. hours, located left front under hood; tires 8.20 x 15, 4-ply; recommended pressure 24 lbs. front, 24 lbs. rear, cold; springing, front coil, rear semi-elliptic; frame, box.

CAPACITIES: Fuel tank 20 gals.; crankcase 7 qts.; cooling system 19.9 qts. with heater; differential 4.25 pts.; luggage 30.5 cu. ft. usable (approx.).

CERTIFICATION

I certify that the test results in this report are the true and accurate findings in tests conducted on the automobile named under the conditions specified.

Edw F. Obert

Edward F. Obert, Member, SAE,
Chicago Section Chairman, TSME
Director, Automotive Research Laboratories
Professional Engineering Consultants
1204 Noyes Street, Evanston, Illinois

Nance of PACKARD

TWENTY years or more have passed into automotive history since the days when Packard was a name that ranked high on the select list of cars comprising the "prestige market," and now this quality automobile is hitting the comeback trail.

Before the 1930's, almost everyone who dealt in automobiles knew the story about the beautiful and glamorous young lady who, while driving her Packard through town, pulled up alongside the street curb and asked a handsome young man if he would like to go for a ride.

He wasn't backward and the day was as beautiful as she was, and out in the country she stopped the car, threw her arms up into the air and sighed: "You can have anything in the world you want."

The young man looked at her for a moment, then made his decision: "I think I'll take the Packard."

Not all Packard admirers were quite as fanatical, but you only have to "ask the man who owned one" to learn that quality and craftsmanship were terms the car wore gracefully and well.

In pre-depression days, Packard controlled an estimated 60 per cent of the fine car market in the U.S.A. Then came a kind of blackout in extensive sales operations. But the curtain has been lifted, and some of the most talked-about cars among the new 1954 models are Packards. Those who have seen these new Packards have already pushed a tremendous "word-of-mouth" advertising campaign for the big comeback.

Moving spirit behind these developments is Packard Motor Car Company's new president, 52-year-old James J. Nance who recently took the helm after 30 years of outstanding success as a business executive in other industrial fields.

A native of Ohio, Nance's administrative experience includes positions with the National Cash Register Company, General Motors and General Electric. As an executive, he has the reputation of doing "impossible" tasks quickly—and he is carrying this faculty into his new job of bringing Packard rapidly again to the forefront.

GREAT things for Packard can result from the administrative direction of a man who, as president of Hotpoint, Inc., an affiliate of General Electric, brought Hotpoint from ninth place to third place in the elecric appliance field even while GE—the parent company—was one of his competitors. Nance goes on the theory that the company which produces the

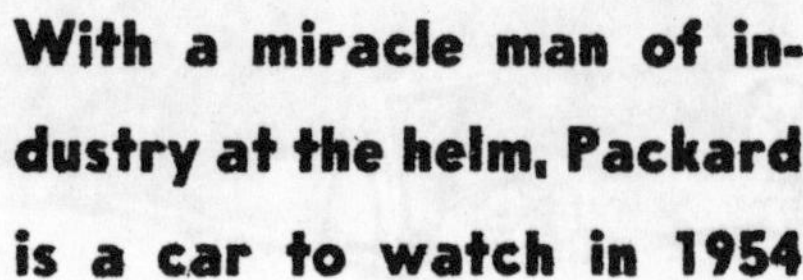

With a miracle man of industry at the helm, Packard is a car to watch in 1954

best product at the lowest price will not only succeed but will also accomplish a public service.

A man of broad outlook, he is actively interested in educational and medical problems and correlates these studies with his work as an industrial executive. Nance believes that commerce, health and learning are integral parts of progress, and that if all three forces work together the world will be a much better place in which to live.

Putting Packard back into the automotive swim is making heavy demands on President Nance's time and, for awhile at least, his wife and two children won't have him around their home as much as they would like.

If re-establishing Packard as a top-flight automobile will require executive direction that combines good business judgment and plain hard work, tempered with sympathy and good humor, then the job is as good as accomplished. Ask the man who knows Nance. ●●●

Above: James J. Nance, President of the Packard Motor Co., hopes to guide Packard back to its old role of leader in the class field. Left: The Packard Panther, an all-plastic sports car, was shown at the International Motor Show in New York. The engine is 275 hp.

The Convertible

Clipper Panama Sport Coupe

Clipper Deluxe Club Sedan

Clipper Special Club Sedan

PACKARD has added a new series of cars—in the Clipper line—to its 1954 models.

There is a new, more powerful engine in the 200 horsepower class for Packard cars in the luxury field, and all models have advanced styling, comfort and performance features.

The two lines—Clippers and Packards—now bracket the price range from the lower medium price class to the most luxurious custom-built models, with both family sedans and sports-type cars included in the various price classes.

In announcing the 1954 line, Packard pointed out that following a year "marked by the re-establishment of the company in the luxury car field," the company will move toward "the pattern of auto making which once gave it dominance in the top price group."

The luxury line of Packards will include seven models, ranging from a new deluxe hardtop, the "Pacific", a convertible coupe, two family sedans, and an eight passenger executive sedan, to the top of the line—custom built Caribbean sports car and a chauffeur-driven model priced up to $7,250.

Packard's medium priced Clippers, starting at $2,544, will be built in three series as the company moves further toward complete representation in its price classes. The company has added a Super series at the top of the Clipper line, which includes the Panama, a hardtop new to the line, the Super Club Sedan and the Super four-door sedan. Other Clippers are in the DeLuxe and Special series. The DeLuxe series includes a four-door sedan, a club sedan, and The Sportster; a club sedan is designated as a Clipper Special.

Leading mechanical innovation for the company in 1954 is the introduction of a new engine for its Packard line claimed the greatest capacity engine in any American passenger car, the new straight-eight delivers greater passing ability at the critical driving speeds of 40 to 70 miles per hour than any engine the firm has built in its 55 year history. It has a horsepower rating of 212 and is in all models except the Cavalier sedan.

Although the new Packard engine has greater top speed than its predecessor, its greatest characteristic is its ability to deliver power where needed, without undue engine strain and with maximum economy. An indication of its performance is seen in the results of tests conducted against the 1953 engine it replaces. In an acceleration test from a standing start, the car with the new engine had a lead of 11 car lengths (230 feet) before reaching 60 miles an hour, and a lead of 37 car lengths (750 feet) when it reached 80 miles an hour. The new engine has 359 cubic inches of piston displacement, and a compression ratio of 8.7 to 1, the highest in the industry.

Ultramatic, Packard's automatic transmission, is standard equipment throughout the Packard line on all models except the Cavalier and 8-pass. cars.

The wide selection of mechanical and styling features in the 1954 lines gives purchasers of both Packards and Clippers the opportunity of choosing the features they desire in their individual cars. There will be four basic engines: A Clipper special, with 150 horsepower; a Clipper DeLuxe, with 165 horsepower; the Cavalier engine, with 185 horsepower; and the Packard engine, 212 horsepower. One definite advantage of the engines is the fact that the maximum horsepower is reached at relatively low engine speeds; i.e., At 3,600 r.p.m. on the Clipper DeLuxe, and at 4,000 r.p.m. on the Cavalier and the Clipper Special.

To go with these power plants, buyers may order standard transmission, overdrive, or Ultramatic, Packard's automatic transmission. Completing the selectivity of power combinations, the company offers four different axle ratios. By combinations of engine, transmission, and axle ratio, owners may obtain maximum economy of operation, or at the other extreme, top performance. Special combinations are available for rough terrain, mountainous driving, city driving, highway, or any unusual driving condition.

Among the new features introduced are tires with squeal-resistant treads. These tires, available as standard equipment on all models, provide better traction and eliminate the irritating squeal most tires make on corners. The tread design also adds to the response of the tire to movements of the steering wheel and results in a stable tire at all speeds.

For the first time on any American passenger cars, tubeless tires are offered as special equipment. Advantages of the tubeless tires are their lightness, and cooler operation, a safety factor.

Throughout the line, the company is offering a choice of 23 exterior color schemes, five of them new for 1954. There are nine two-tone color arrangements. To blend with external colors, there is a wide selection of interior trims and upholsteries. In a new fashion approach, Packard makes available a line of linen upholsteries of top quality, done in smart contemporary designs. Advantages of the linen are long wear, a smooth surface that won't cling to coats or rough up furs, and comfort in both summer and winter. Upholstery fabrics include the new nylon matelasse, broadcloth, cord, nylon, and top grain genuine leather.

Caribbean Sports Convertible

Both lines have as optional equipment a new four-way power seat, adjustable with a touch of the finger to the most comfortable position for the driver. Other recent Packard contributions to easier, more luxurious motoring are continued in the cars. These include Ultramatic, Packard's automatic gearshift, power brakes, power steering, power windows, air conditioning, dual heaters with underseat outlets, and a selection of four different radios, which may be equipped with manual or electric antennas and front and rear seat speakers.

Another move toward customizing the cars provides additional riding comfort. For motorists who prefer a firmer ride, extra seat cushion springs may be added to any section of the seat, or throughout the entire seat. Seats of all models are located in the center area, cradled in the smooth riding section between the front and rear wheels. The seats are of normal chair height, an aid to both comfort and visibility, as passengers may see in all directions from natural sitting positions. The high crowned fenders and low hood allow the driver to see more of the road, and the windshield, although curved, is distortion-free. Windshields are available in clear plate glass or of the Solex heat absorption type, with or without the light filter area. ★

Cavalier 4-Door Sedan

Patrician 4-Door Sedan

Mayfair Sport Coupe

Caribbean Sport Convertible

Patrician 4-Door Sedan

Studebaker-Packard Corporation...

The New Packard V-8 Engine

The high efficiency valve-in-head Packard V-8 engine that develops 260 brake horsepower.

Horsepower on the new Packards ranges from 225 on Clipper models to 260 on other engines

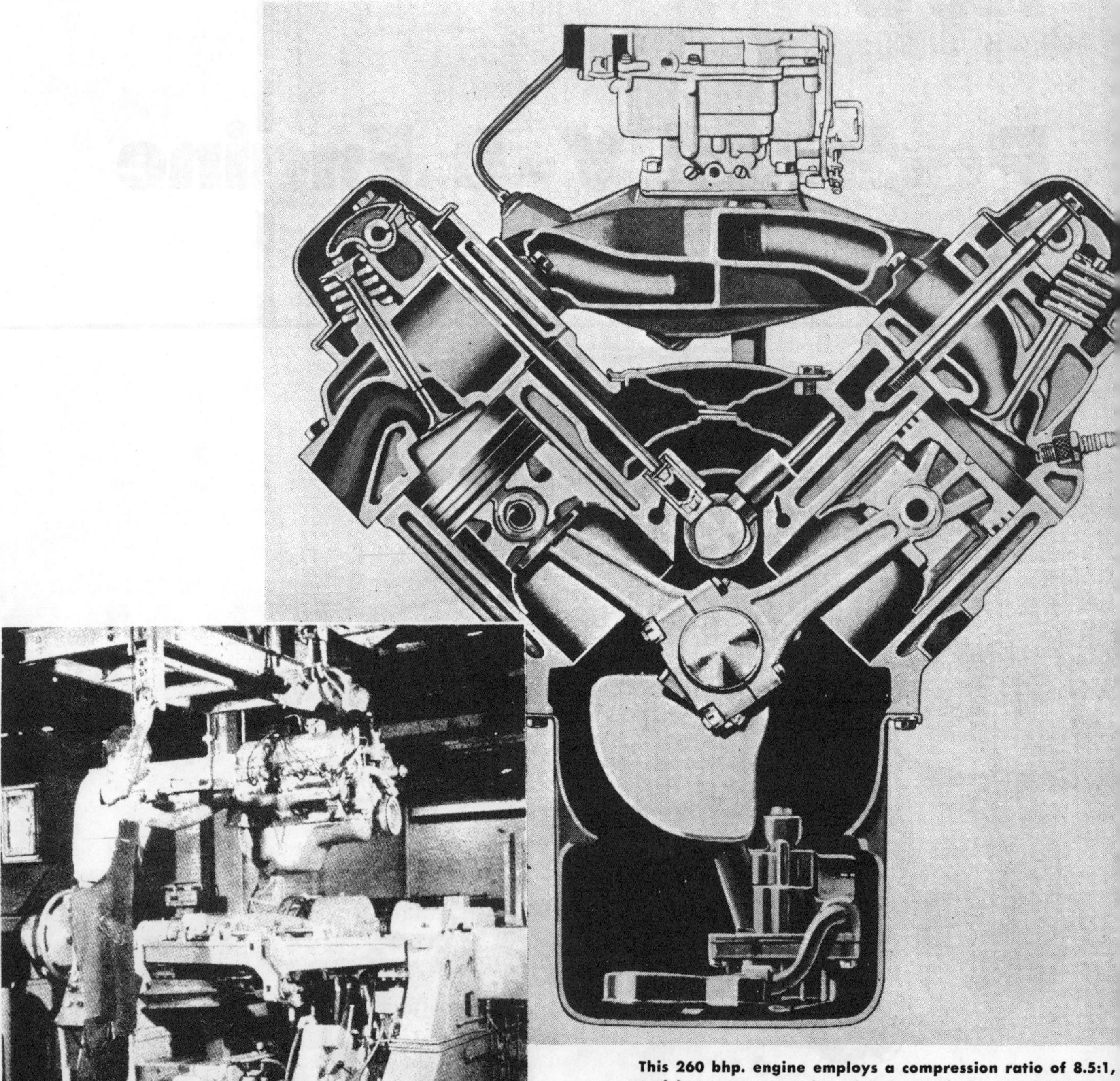

This 260 bhp. engine employs a compression ratio of 8.5:1, and has a torque rating of 355 pounds foot at 2,800 rpm.

Assembling the new 1955 Packard engine at the factory.

Before being introduced to the public a 1955 V-8 engined sedan was driven 25,000 miles at an average speed of 105 mph.

THE old faithful L-head straight 8 Packard engine has been superseded this year by a new valve-in-head V-8, an accomplishment preceded by nine years of planning.

The new engine is a half-inch lower, eight-and-a-half inches shorter and approximately eight per cent lighter than the old model. This permits a more favorable weight distribution which improves steering and handling.

The high turbulence, wedge-type combustion chamber is designed to provide a lower burning rate of the charge and to avoid a high rate of pressure rise resulting in freedom from objectionable combustion roughness.

The Packard engineers selected an 8.5 to 1 compression ratio, a decision based on the octane rating of the premium grade fuels most generally available. Octane requirements were established after extensive tests at the Packard Proving Grounds under a variety of driving conditions.

The decision apparently paid off as evidenced by a test run made under AAA sanction. A 1955 Packard traveled 25,000 miles in a total elapsed time of 238 hours, 41 minutes, 44.3 seconds, an amazing average of 104.737 miles per hour!

The induction system of the new Packard contains many improvements and innovations. For instance, the carburetor choke stove is located in the center exhaust cross over passage of the intake manifold. The flow of the exhaust gases through this passage is controlled by the action of the heat valve located at the junction of the left hand exhaust manifold and the exhaust pipe.

The cylinder heads are conservatively designed, being slightly larger than competitive makes and the cylinder block is exceptionally rugged and durable, which is characteristic of the entire engine.

Generally, the new power plant is exceptionally free breathing. Overhead valves are larger in head space in an attempt to provide maximum volumetric efficiency. Short stroke, low friction operation is aimed at increasing mechanical and thermal efficiency.

In short, the people at Packard believe they have achieved not only higher performance and greater economy but longer life as well. ☆☆

1955 PACKARD V-8 ENGINE SPECIFICATIONS

General

Type	90° V, 8 Cylinders
Valve Arrangement	Overhead Valves
Bore and Stroke (Inches)	4 x 3.5 Inches
Piston Displacement (Cubic Inches)	352
Firing Order	1-8-4-3-6-5-7-2
Compression Ratio	
Standard Head	8.5:1
Optional Head	Yes
Taxable Horsepower	51.2
Advertised Max. Brake Horsepower at Engine Rpm.	
Standard Head	260 at 4,600
Optional Twin Carbs.	N.A.
With Fuel (Octane and Method)	
Standard Head	93 (Research)
Optional Head	N.A.
Max. Torque (Lb. Ft. at Rpm.)	
Standard Head	355 at 2,400
Optional Twin Carbs.	N.A.

Pistons

Description and Finish	Cam Ground, Autothermic Flat Head, Slipper Type Skirt, Tin Plated
Weight (Pistons Only—Ozs.)	24.763

Rings

Type	
No. 1	Taper Face Compression
No. 2	Taper Face Compression
No. 3	Ventilated Oil Ring (Wide Slot)
No. 4 Oil or Compression	—
No. of Rings Above Piston Pin	3

Piston Pins

Length	3.250 Inches
Diameter	.9803 Inch
Type	
Locked in Rod, in Piston, Floating	Floating
Bushing	
In Rod or Piston	In Rod

Connecting Rods

Weight (Ozs.)	1 Lb. 10.688 Ozs.
Length (Center to Center)	6.7182 Inches
Bearing	
Type	Removable
Effective Length	.939 Inch
Clearance	.0005 to .0025 Inch
End Play	.003 to .011 Inch (Two Rods)

Crankshaft

Weight (Lbs.)	55 Lbs.
Vibration Damper Type	Rubber Floated
End Thrust Taken by Bearing (No.)	No. 5—Rear Main
Crankshaft End Play	.0035 to .0085 Inch
Main Bearing	
Type	Removable Steel Backed
Clearance	.0005 to .0025 Inch

Camshaft

Bearings (Number)	5
Type of Drive	Chain

Valve System

Hydraulic Lifters (Yes or No)	Yes
Special Provision for Valve Rotation (Intake, Exhaust)	None
Rocker Ratio	1.6 to 1
Tappet Clearance for Timing	
Intake	Not Used
Exhaust	Not Used
Timing Marks on Flywheel, Damper, Other	On Vibration Damper and Camshaft Chain Cover
Timing	
Intake	
Opens (°BTC)	14°
Closes (°ABC)	56°
Exhaust	
Opens (°BBC)	52°
Closes (°ATC)	18°
Intake	
Overall Length	5.712 Inches
Actual Overall Head Dia.	1.937 Inches
Angle of Seat	30° (Nominal)
Stem Diameter	.3725 Inch
Lift	.374 Inch
Outer Spring Pressure and Length	
Valve Closed (Lb. at In.)	78 to 86 Lbs. at 1.750 In.
Valve Open (Lb. at In.)	158 to 172 Lbs. at 1.375 In.
Inner Spring Pressure and Length	
Valve Closed (Lb. at In.)	None—Not Used
Valve Open (Lb. at In.)	None—Not Used
Exhaust	
Overall Length	5.690 Inches
Actual Overall Head Dia.	1.687 Inches
Angle of Seat	45° (Nominal)
Stem Diameter	.3715 Inch
Lift	.374 Inch
Outer Spring Press and Length	
Valve Closed (Lb. at In.)	78 to 86 Lbs. at 1.750 In.
Valve Open (Lb. at In.)	158 to 172 Lbs. at 1.375 In.
Inner Spring Press and Length	
Valve Closed (Lb. at In.)	None—Not Used
Valve Open (Lb. at In.)	None—Not Used

Lubrication System

Type of Lubrication (Splash, Pressure, Nozzle)	
Main Bearings	Pressure
Connecting Rods	Pressure
Piston Pins	Oil Mist
Camshaft Bearings	Pressure
Tappets	Pressure
Timing Gear or Chain	Pressure Jet
Cylinder Walls	Pressure Jet
Oil Pump Type	Gear
Normal Oil Pressure (Lb. at Rpm.)	45-50 Psi at 2,800 RPM
Type Oil Intake (Floating, Stationary)	Floating
Oil Filter Type (Full Flow, Partial Flow)	Partial Flow
Capacity of Crankcase, Less Filter-Refill (Qt.)	5 Quarts
Oil Grade Recommended (SAE Viscosity and Temperature Range)	Not Lower than Plus 32° F.....SAE 20 or 20W As Low as Minus 10° F. ....SAE 10W Below Minus 10° F.... SAE 5W
Oil Type Recommended	ML, MM, or MS Depending on Vehicle Operation

Fuel System

Fuel Filter (Type)	Ceramic
Fuel Pump	
Type (Elec. or Mech.)	Mechanical
Pressure Range	3.5 to 5.5 Psi
Vacuum Booster (Std., Optl., None)	Standard
Carburetor	
Number Used	One
Type	
Downdraft, Side Inlet, Other	Downdraft
Single or Dual	4 Barrel
Intake Manifold Heat Control (Manual, Auto., None)	Automatic
Automatic Choke Type (Integral, Other)	Integral

Exhaust System

Type (Single, Single with Cross-over, Dual, Other)	Dual

Cooling System

Type (Pressure, System, Atmospheric, Other)	Pressure System
Circulation Thermostat	
Starts to Open at	167°-173° F.
Water Pump	
Type (Centrifugal, Other)	Centrifugal
Number of Pumps	1
Bearing Type	Double Row Ball
Water Jackets Full Length of Cylinder (Yes, No.)	Yes
Water All Around Cylinder (Yes, No)	Yes

Electrical—Supply System

Battery	
Voltage and Plates/Cell	12-Volt
Terminal Grounded	Positive
Generator (Type)	Shunt
Regulator (Type)	Current and Voltage Control
Min. Gen. Rpm. Required	2,300

Electrical—Starting System

Starting Motor	
Engine Cranking Speed	40 Rpm.
Motor Control	
Switch (Solenoid, Manual)	Solenoid
Motor Drive (Engagement Type)	Solenoid Actuated Shift

Electrical—Ignition System

Distributor	
Spark Advance Data (at Distributor Shaft)	
Centr. Advance Start (Rpm.) C/S	300
Centr. Advance Max. Deg. at Rpm.	16° at 2,100 Rpm.
Vacuum Advance Start (In. Hg.)	6 In. Hg.
Vacuum Advance (Max. Deg. at In. Hg.)	10° at 12.5 In. Hg.
Breaker Gap (In.)	.016 Inch
Timing	
C/S Deg. at Rpm.	6° BTDC
Mark Location	Vibration Damper
Spark Plug	
Make and Model	Champion H-10
Gap	.033 to .037 Inch

Majestic new Clipper Constellation hardtop still retains one "classic" Packard feature—the inward scoop at the sides of the hood. Photo on right shows flashy two-tone upholstery.

PHOTOS BY DAN RUBIN

Complete Road Test:

Packard's Clipper "Constellation"

New chassis and engine make this the greatest road car in America.

AN AUTO AGE STAFF REPORT

WHEN PACKARD first announced, late last year, that they were coming out with an automobile featuring not only a new engine but a radical torsion-bar suspension, auto editors and car fans all over the country went into ecstasies just speculating about what the car would be like. Advance technical stories began to pop up all over the place describing the principles of torsion bar operation, giving the inside dope on how the engine was designed, etc., and we all became more and more fascinated.

But we have found from experience that any machine can look great on paper and still turn out to be, if not a dud, nothing too unusual either. So we decided to hold fast and reserve judgment and all comment until we could actually get

Front grille is slanted in towards bottom as are headlight shields, giving added feeling of speed.

Torsion-bar suspension makes this the finest cornering car to roll off an American production line in many a year. Note lack of lean.

Car can be steered through a tight circle with one hand off wheel, above. And it doesn't dip much under severe braking, either, as shown.

Interior of the Clipper is its weakest point; most upholstery is rather gaudy. Seating position is good, however, and vision excellent.

one of the new Packards to test. This was no simple task by itself, because a minor production tie-up earlier in the year held up deliveries and when the cars were finally made available to dealers they were snatched up by anxious buyers almost before they hit the showroom floors. But we kept after the harried Packard people and finally were given clearance to put a brand new two-door Clipper "Constellation" through its paces. Here's what we found:

Let's say it right away—here is a car that must be driven to be fully appreciated . . . not that it isn't good looking, because it is, but because it doesn't really shine in the beauty department. It's a great improvement over the bloated monsters that Packard brought out right after World War II and the over-all workmanship is top-notch, but its styling is just average for 1955 and we doubt that too many people will buy it on the strength of its eye-appeal alone. But just sit behind that wheel for 20 minutes and get the feel of the road and you're gone for good!

The first thing we did when we got the car was to test its riding qualities over the roughest roads we could find. We raced this machine over miles of rut-filled, rocky, twisty dirt roads and were amazed to find that the faster we went, the smoother the ride became. At 30 mph over a really bad road, in the new Packard you will feel the bumps to some extent, but go 50 or 60 mph on the same road and you will swear that you are riding on smooth concrete! This is no exaggeration, and the thing that impressed us even more was the com-

New V-8 engine at right is largest in the industry, displaces 352 cu. in., pushes car up over 110 mph. It is shown below reaching 100.

plete stability that went with the ride. It is a simple matter to make a car ride softly; just put big, soft coil springs in it. The only problem is that you may find yourself wafted comfortably but surely into a ditch one day when the going gets a bit too rough. Not with the Packard. You ride in comfort and safety too! That's something that even the Packard advertisements fail to mention, by the way. They speak of the softest ride in America, but any sports-car fan has known for years that torsion-bar suspension can give you a ride that has all the softness of coil springs and all the stability of stiff leaf springs. What's more, torsion bars are adjustable so that you can make the Packard ride even firmer if you so desire, for even more stability.

From the dirt road we went on to an open field with the same results, only more so. We did manage to get hung up on a huge log that was hidden in some tall grass, but jacking up the rear end got us out of that one in a jiffy. And here we learned something else. You may have heard about Packard's "load equalizer" that combines an electric motor with two extra torsion bars at the rear of the chassis to compensate for any additional weight in the rear, as when the trunk is loaded. The way this works is simple. Put a heavy weight on the rear end and hold it there for approximately seven seconds and the motor will start into action, twisting the extra torsion bars to make them, in effect, stiffer. The rear end of the car will then rise up until it is higher than the front, wait seven more seconds, and then lower itself until the car is dead level. Thus, the car will not sag at the rear end no matter how heavy a load you are carrying. All this can be controlled by a switch on the dashboard, so that you can hold the car, if you wish, with the rear deck up in the air. That is exactly what we did when we got hung up on the log, and we found it to be a great little helper for the ordinary jacking system. Should make tire-changing a lot easier. If you should buy a new Packard, we suggest you switch the equalizer off when you park the car; otherwise the neighborhood kids will wear your battery out in no time making the rear end of the car go up and down.

Just as the new suspension improves the Packard's ride, it makes the cornering something to behold. Packard has the best power steering unit in the country, anyway (it is anchored to the chassis more firmly, giving "feel" and ease of operation at the same time), and this, combined with the torsion bars, make the car corner almost like a small sports car. This has been said of many of the 1955 American cars by one writer or another, but what they usually mean is that the car can be *maneuvered* in close as well as a small car—not that it will stick to corners with the same tenacity. The new Packard will.

Turning CONTINUED ON PAGE 141

PACKARD NAME is reserved for the big prestige cars like one at left. Clippers come in three series on shorter (122 in.) wheelbase. Torsion bars and big V-8 are optional on the top Clipper.

'55 Packard Glides on Torsion-Bar Suspension

By Frank Rowsome Jr.
PHOTOS BY HUBERT LUCKETT

THERE'S plenty of solid news this year from Packard, enough to make up for the lean years. Highlights:

- A radically different suspension that does away with coil and leaf springs, and that combines two hitherto irreconcilables—soft riding and stable handling.
- A slick mechanism that automatically levels the car fore-and-aft, and that largely eliminates "bottoming."
- A pair of brand-new V-8s, brimming with torque and power.
- A redesigned automatic transmission, to provide gear-assisted starts for gee-whillickers getaway.
- And a sheaf of such other developments as a 12-volt electrical system, wrap-around glass, fancy styling, and interiors of sufficient lushness for the transport of a 24-carat maharajah.

The new suspension, which can be best described by the seat of the pants, is a fascinating mechanism. For compar-

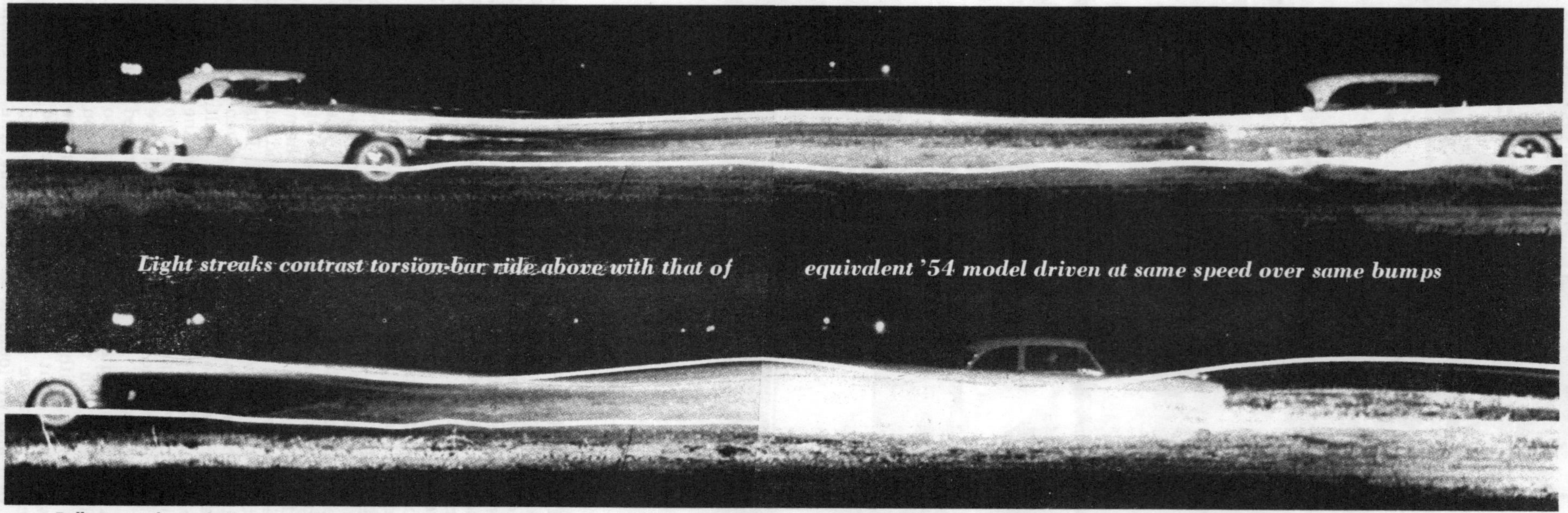

Light streaks contrast torsion-bar ride above with that of equivalent '54 model driven at same speed over same bumps

Bulb mounted on wheel nut gives lower light trace on each car. Second bulb mounted on fender charts behavior of body. This is a long W-shaped bump, taken at 35 m.p.h.

LOAD COMPENSATOR is demonstrated by having two people stand on back bumper (below left). For six seconds, car sags almost to limit. Then a geared electric motor winds up the leveling torsion bars and back of car comes up to design height (center) despite load. Back rises up extra high, right, when load is removed but after six seconds car returns to exact level.

LEVELER AT WORK

HEAVY BRAKING makes any car droop its snoot, but new suspension tames the tendency, as the sequence pictures below reveal. Both of the cars were going at same speed, with last year's model a half-length ahead, when brakes were jammed on hard. Older car shows a pronounced dive. New one lowers in front but does not rise as high in back, thanks to torque arms.

DIVE COMPARISON

New suspension gives far less squat on getaway

Sequence camera reveals how old and new compare on full-throttle acceleration. In the third frame, '54 car is almost dragging its rear bumper.

1955

1954

ison, PSM photographer Hubert Luckett and I first tooled a '54 Clipper over the mean back roads at the Packard proving ground. Like all Packards, the '54 gave a smooth, rather soft ride. But even though it was only moderately loaded, it proved willing to hit bottom when mildly provoked.

If you drove roughly, the '54 also showed a marked tendency toward diving when you belted the brake, and squatting when you tromped on the gas. Like the rest of the breed it still behaved in a gentlemanly fashion—who but a cad is going to flail a Packard?—but you were aware of the penalty paid for the softness of the ride.

Then Lucky and I tried the same roads, at the same speeds, in a '55 Clipper with the new torsion-bar suspension. The ride was fully as soft, maybe even softer. The car simply swallowed up bumps, the way a foam-rubber pad would swallow up surface inequalities of a piece of sandpaper.

Remarkably, however, there was no penalty for the absorbent-cotton ride. The car did *not* bottom on entering deep dips taken fast, and it did *not* rebound like a frightened gazelle on leaving them. On washboard surfaces, there was no balletlike wheel skitter. Best of all, the body showed a fine indifference to how you played the pedals; dive and squat could still be detected, but were tamed to insignificance. With torsion bars, the Packard personality changes from a dowager's to that of an able road car.

The problem. In quality cars these days the big thing is a "boulevard ride." It has been classically achieved by softening the springs, letting chassis and body weight creep upward and searching for shock-absorber valving that will tolerate such soft springs.

If you want to be shown, walk along a row of parked cars until you come to any expensive sedan built in the last few years. Put one foot on the bumper, in the manner of a small-town philosopher, and press lightly. The big boat will sink under your foot like a little canoe, revealing by its sponginess the degree of recent spring softening.

This hurts in some ways, of course. Such a car is a slave to its shock absorbers, and leaps like an antelope when the shocks grow weary. Loaded, it tends to bottom repeatedly on the rear-axle housing. It has a wide height range, riding high like a barely ballasted tanker when only the driver is aboard, but running almost awash with a full load. Worst of all, it can display soggy or ill-tempered handling characteristics at high speed or on turns.

The treatment. Packard's torsion-bar

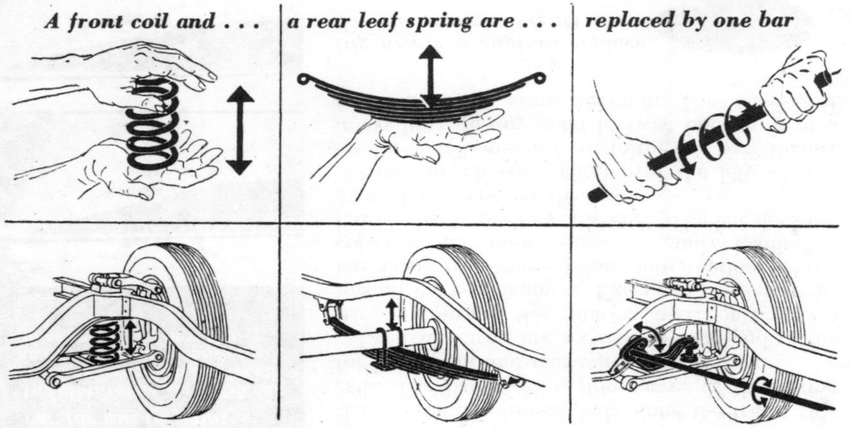

A front coil and . . . a rear leaf spring are . . . replaced by one bar

FAVORITE U.S. SUSPENSION has been coil springs in front, leaf springs in back, with rear ones also transmitting torque loads to frame. In new Packard, where a single torsion bar per side replaces both springs, front-end design is roughly the same but lever arm substitutes for the coil. In rear, another lever presses against stirrup in torque arm running from axle to frame. The

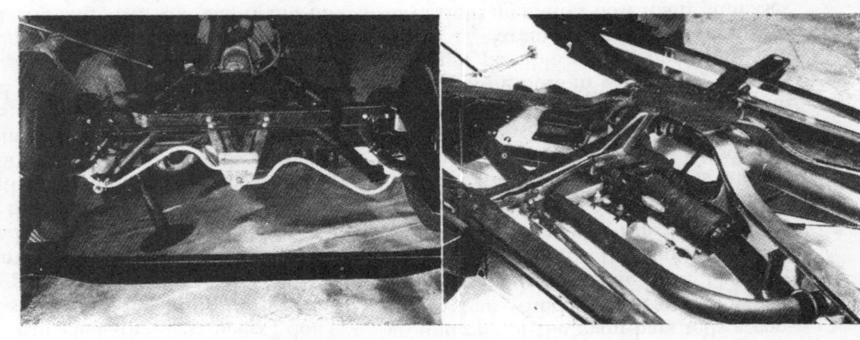

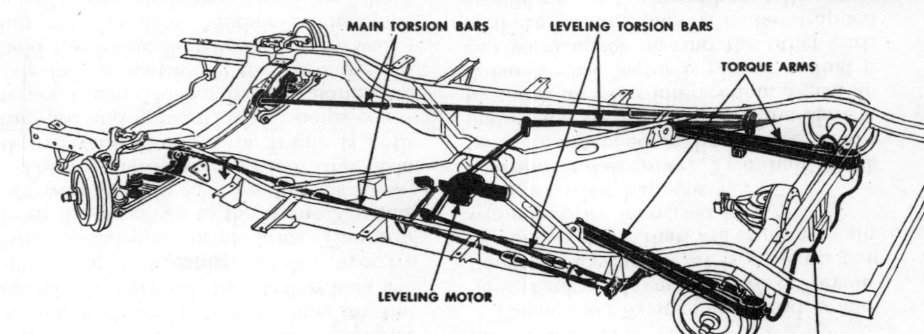

two torque arms take over the job of delivering rear-axle thrust, as well as brake torque and drag, to chassis. Pretzel-shaped bar in left photo above is stabilizer that ties axle against sideways movement. Heavily geared-down motor that winds up the ends of the leveling bars is shown in the right photograph above. It runs only when the car load changes.

Getaway race puts new car far out in front

In full-throttle start, '55 car leads by more than one length in three seconds. Gear-start automatic box aids new V-8.

suspension tries a fresh approach. In place of coil and leaf springs the car uses two alloy-steel bars, about nine feet long and one inch in diameter, that lie roughly fore-and-aft along the frame side rails. The bar at each side serves as the spring for both front and rear wheels on that side.

Cranklike arms are secured to each end of the bar, to transmit the rotation that constitutes a torsion bar's springiness. Except at the ends, the bar floats free—there is an antivibration rubber collar in the middle—and the only loading it has is what is put in at the ends. The bar does *not* expend its twist on the frame.

How can chassis weight over the left wheels, say, provide *opposed* twist to the left bar? Plainly it wouldn't do any good to twist both ends of a free bar in the same direction. The answer, of course, is that the arms at the ends are fitted to the bar in opposite directions, roughly 180 degrees apart.

Big new V-8 engines replace the old straight eights

Rated at 260 hp., this brute has bigger displacement than any current U.S. passenger-car mill. It has oversquare proportions, "parabolic" combustion chamber, overhead valves, and four-barrel carb. In the de luxe Caribbean, hp. is boosted to 275.

This means, among other things, that a force exerted on one end of the bar, as when the front wheel is deflected upward by a bump, does not get telegraphed to the frame as torsion. The force that whangs the front wheel up is simply spent in loading the rear wheel down. (More precisely, it is spent in winding up the torsion bar, but the reaction is mainly against the road in back.) The chassis and body just come along for the ride.

One way to visualize this is to imagine that you are a bulgy-muscled giant. Tilt a Packard so that the weight rests on the two wheels on one side. Then extend your arms out to touch both uplifted wheels and watch how, when you push the front wheel up, the back one goes down, and vice versa. (Incidentally, if you *are* a giant, and try this, you'll find that the torsion bar is preloaded—that it is "wound up" on installation, to balance out the chassis and body load at design height.)

Thrust, dive, squat. This ugly trio constantly bedevils suspension engineers. The rear springs in a conventional Hotchkiss drive have the extra job of sending engine and brake forces along to the chassis. In Packard, the torsion bars are spared this task, which is taken over by two pressed-steel torque arms. They run from the rear axle to the frame X member, and they do a lot for the car.

During hard acceleration, the axle thrust transmitted to the frame is both forward and *upward*, which helps counteract squat. During hard braking, the axle torque sent along the arms tries to hold the frame *downward*, partly washing out the dive. Neither tendency is wholly canceled—the engineers don't think it should be—but in both traits the car has gone from poor to fine.

A particular advantage of coupling front and rear wheels to a single bar per side is that the frame doesn't have to cope with twisting forces and local spring loads. Body and chassis simply float on four points, the four arms at the ends of the bars; and the body itself doesn't get wracked when the supporting surface is uneven. As a stunt, Packard people like to slam a sedan across a rough diagonal railroad crossing with the car doors on the "ajar" latch. That there is practically no rattling shows, they claim, that body twist doesn't occur. We made crossings of such ferocity as would, on my own car, have popped open the glove compartment and unlatched the hood, and the most the Packard did was utter a few muted clicks.

Leveler. So far, the suspension would give a soft ride and improved handling but it wouldn't do much—except with one specific load—for such other headaches as bottoming, changing height drastically, and having the headlight aim messed up by a load of luggage in the trunk. (A car must cope adequately with anything from one 100-pound lady driver to maybe 1,200 pounds of portly passengers and luggage.) Hitting bottom—which happens when the springs run out of jounce space and the axle housing blips rubber bumpers—naturally occurs much more readily when a large static load has already consumed much of the jounce space.

The answer is ingenious and brand-new (Packard favors the word "revolutionary"). Essentially, it is an extra pair of torsion bars that are automatically wound up by increased load.

Here's what happens:

Motor takes over. Two half-length bars are attached in back close to the main bars. In the middle of the chassis, by the X-member intersection, a geared-down electric motor is placed so that it can wind up or unwind the other ends of these leveling bars. A collar strapped around one of the main bars tells a control system whether the car is down in the stern or down in the bow. Then the control system tells the motor to start up, and which way to run. Levers twist the half-length bars just enough to raise or lower the rear until the car is level.

This mechanism, which is almost inaudible, keeps the body within a fraction of an inch of design height with full load. Hitting bottom while fully loaded, although possible on a jehosaphat of a bump, is extremely rare. Headlight aim stays right no matter how many suitcases you pile in the trunk. Caster angle in the front suspension is correct all the time, not just for one specific load. And the car looks better, resembling the slinky vehicles in advertisements.

Because it isn't practical to have the leveler working like crazy every time the car hits a bump—it wouldn't react in time, but it'd wear itself out trying—the control system has a six-second time delay built in. If you take plump Aunt Eppie for a ride, the car sags noticeably when she clambers in back. But she scarcely settles herself comfortably before the leveler gives a faint hum and the car comes back to normal height. This also works in reverse: If six people pile rapidly out of the car, it rises momentarily above normal, the faint hum occurs, and down it goes.

Automatic exceptions. Packard engineers built two other restrictions into the gadget besides the time delay. They didn't want it to work during braking—which may easily continue for more than six seconds—because the forward weight shift can improve stopping characteristics. So they wired the leveler through a special stop-light switch so that it doesn't get juice when your foot is on the pedal. And if you get a flat tire, using a bumper jack with the leveler at work is wildly exasperating, because the thing tries valiantly to make the other end of the car come up, too. So there is a "flat-tire switch" under the dash that cuts out the leveler and allows you to jack with only normal annoyances.

Prospects. Torsion bars aren't new, of course; several European passenger cars and most U.S. racing cars have gone to them. (Ordinarily, though, they are frame-anchored at one end.) The leveler does seem to be wholly new. It neatly solves problems that, while troublesome, are perhaps more vexing on spare-no-expense vehicles than on the heaps that most of us drive. The improvement in handling is notable, though perhaps enhanced by Packard's past problems in this department. The company admits to a slight weight penalty (less than a hundred pounds) and slightly higher costs.

Transmission. Until this year, Ultramatic drive has been noted more for smoothness than for zip. It combined a two-stage torque converter with a lock-up clutch that gave direct drive once the car got rolling. In the '55 version, the selector quadrant has two Drive positions, and in one you get the same sedate behavior you got before. In the other, it really lays back its ears.

At moderate throttle in the new setting, you get away by converter plus low-range planetary gearing, with a discreet upshift occurring in the 20s or 30s. At full throttle the box dishes out a maximum torque multiplication of 5.22 to 1, which gives theatrical getaway. If you hold full throttle, there's a forced upshift to high around 40 m.p.h. But if you give *more* than full throttle (by keeping the gas in the kick-down spot) this upshift will be "inhibited," and you can wind the poor thing up to a hysterical 5,000 revs or so, then ease back to plain full throttle for the automatic upshift.

New V-8s. Despite their long fondness for L-head straight eights, Packard people are old hands at V-type engines;

The easiest way to find out what's on your wife's mind is to sit yourself down in a comfortable chair.
—THE SIDEWALK SUPERINTENDENT

there were the famous Twin Sixes of 1915-23 and the Twelves of 1932-39. So it isn't surprising that they get into the act like veterans:

- Though there are three power ratings, there are two blocks, differing only in bore, that have displacements of 320 and 352 cubic inches ('55 comparisons: Cadillac and Chrysler have 331, Lincoln 341).
- Both engines have the same 3.5-inch stroke, and use the same con rods and bearings. Although one has a bore of 3 13/16 inches and the other four inches, the cylinder heads and camshafts are interchangeable, and the former will fit on *either* bank.
- Obviously planned with one eye on modern torque demands, the engines are husky enough to loaf most of the time. Ratings: 225 hp. at 4,600 r.p.m. and 325 pounds-feet of torque at 2,600 for the 320-incher in the Clipper Super and Deluxe series; and 245 hp. and 355 pounds-feet for the 352-incher in the Clipper Custom. Installed in the Packard series, the big baby is rated at 260 hp. and 355 pounds-feet. END

NEW CARS DESCRIBED

Completely restyled, the Packard 400 is the newest hard-top addition in the luxury field for 1955.

Torsion Bars for PACKARD

1955 PACKARDS AND CLIPPERS HAVE O.H.V. V-EIGHT ENGINES

LONG-AWAITED details of the 1955 Packard models from America's relatively conservative manufacturer have been filtering across the Atlantic for some time. This year's announcement was expected to prove particularly interesting following Packard's merger with Studebaker and the necessity for America's independents to answer the heavyweight challenge of the big three in a year of some sales difficulty. The surprise packet from the Studebaker-Packard corporation proves to be the adoption of torsion bar springing front and rear by a single 9ft torsion bar on each side. A secondary change lies in the adoption of V-eight power units to replace the eight-cylinder in-line engines used in previous years.

These V-eights are typical of contemporary U.S. practice, ingeniously compact and with a specially shaped sump to accommodate the massive transverse front chassis member necessitated by independent front suspension. A four-choke downdraught carburettor, topped by a large flat air-cleaner, nestles conveniently in the V and the Packard Twin-Ultramatic torque converter hydraulic transmission protrudes aft in place of the conventional gear box, though the conventional gear box is available on all models except the Patrician and the 400, with or without overdrive.

Over-square

The engine is very much "over-square," having a bore of 101.6 mm (4in) and a stroke of 77.47 mm (3½in), giving a capacity of no less than 5,768.25 c.c. (532 cu in). This is the unit for the Packard Patrician and 400 models and its power output on a compression ratio of 8.5 to 1 is quoted as 260 b.h.p. at 4,600 r.p.m. The torque rating is 355 lb ft at 2,400 to 2,800 r.p.m. An engine of similar dimensions powers the Clipper Custom series, but in this the power output is 245 b.h.p. at 4,600 r.p.m., though the torque figure is the same.

For the other two Clipper models—Super and De Luxe—a smaller-bored version of the V-eight is employed, 96.52mm (3$\frac{13}{16}$in) with a capacity of 5,243.87 c.c. (320 cu in). On a compression ratio of 8 to 1, this unit produces 225 b.h.p. at 4,600 r.p.m. and the torque rating is 325 lb ft at 2,400 to 2,800 r.p.m.

Use of single long torsion bars to serve both front and rear wheels is unusual practice; the front torsion opposes the rear. The Packard bars run in an elongated V, the point of the V facing forward, where radial links transmit the motion of the wishbone suspension to the springing medium. At the rear, outriggers support the fulcrums of radial links to trailing suspension arms, which are also disposed at an angle to the longitudinal line of the chassis. There are rear stabilizing links and a front anti-roll bar. Level riding of the car regardless of load variation is assured by a compensating torsion bar mechanism operated by an electric motor.

Automatic Transmission

Hydraulic transmission, known as Twin-Ultramatic, is standard equipment on all Packard models, but is optional on the Clippers. The torque multiplication ratio of the converter is 2.9 to 1, the highest of any torque converter in the industry, and with this goes a rear axle ratio of 3.54 to 1 for the Patrician and the 400 Packards, 3.23 to 1 for Clipper Customs and Supers, and 3.07 to 1 for the Clipper De Luxe. The Twin-Ultramatic transmission is one of

Originally planned as fa[r] back as 1946, the rang[e] of o.h.v. V-eight Packar[d] engines produces fro[m] 225 to 245 b.h.p. for th[e] Clipper models and 26[0] on Packard cars. A modi[-]fied version produce[s] 275 b.h.p.

Left: The Clipper Custom is the Packard company's new entry in the medium price field. The Packard Caribbean (right) caters for the high-performance market

those with an automatic clutch which locks the torque converter out of action at the requisite moment, thus eliminating any inherent slip in the fluid coupling.

Body styles are fairly conservative by American standards, however striking to English eyes. A horizontal-slat motif with a central V characterizes the front of the Packards, while a vertical-slatted grille of similar shape distinguishes the Clippers. Heavily hooded head lamps attract the eye, as does the massive wrap-round front bumper with its bomb-like projections, replacing normal overriders. Side treatment is singularly successful, slab-sidedness having been avoided both by breaking up the panels with chromium strips and colour treatment and by retaining a vestigial rear wing pressing, the leading edge of which incorporates courtesy lighting on the larger Packards. Both screen and rear window wrap round extensively. Wheel treatment is in complete harmony with the rest of the car and retains one long-standing Packard characteristic in the central hexagon of the Patrician and 400.

Special

A special addition to the normal range is the Packard Caribbean model, a sports convertible for limited production. This is powered by a modified version of the V-eight engine which is claimed to develop 275 b.h.p. and which drives through the automatic transmission. All the normal extras such as power-assisted brakes and steering, hydraulically operated windows and suchlike are standard on this model. The wheelbase is 10ft 7in. There are thus, in all, eight models available in the range: three Packards—Caribbean, Patrician, 400; two Clipper Customs—Constellation and four-door saloon; two Clipper Supers—Panama and four-door saloon, and a four-door Clipper de luxe. Overall lengths of the Packards are 18ft $1\frac{7}{16}$in and of the Clippers 17ft $10\frac{13}{16}$in. Overall width of all models is 6ft 6in and heights vary from 5ft $1\frac{1}{2}$in to 5ft 2.3in.

Field Tests

Planning of the new models is claimed to have started in 1946, and prolonged testing both in the laboratory and on the road has proved the new engines. Under the supervision of the American Automobile Association contest board, a four-door saloon with a prototype V-eight engine covered 25,000 miles in 238 hours 41 min 44.3 sec, giving an average speed of 104.737 m.p.h. Pit stops averaged only 49 seconds. This is certainly a remarkable performance over such a length of time and is likely to make a considerable impression on America's spring car purchasers. The company shows a canny outlook on America's matriarchal society. According to the head of Packard product planning, over 100 improvements have been incorporated in the new models as a result of feminine recommendations and market research in the motoring desires of women. "Our studies indicate that women will have the principal influence in an estimated 70 per cent of family car purchases during 1955," he said. "We believe that the automobile manufacturer must give women what they want in a car, not what we think they ought to have."

As an aid to this end the company set up a "choice panel" in 1953, composed of 400 women car owners, stylists, fashion authorities, editors, school teachers, interior decorators and housewives.

Packards will be available on the British market in accordance with the agreement signed during the latter half of 1954, whereby normal imports of American cars are resumed, but English list prices are not yet available. The sole concessionaires in England are Leonard Williams and Co., Ltd., Great West Road, Brentford, Middlesex.

An exterior courtesy light, styled into the outside of the door panel, operates when the doors are opened and when the head lights are dipped, to improve passing and parking vision

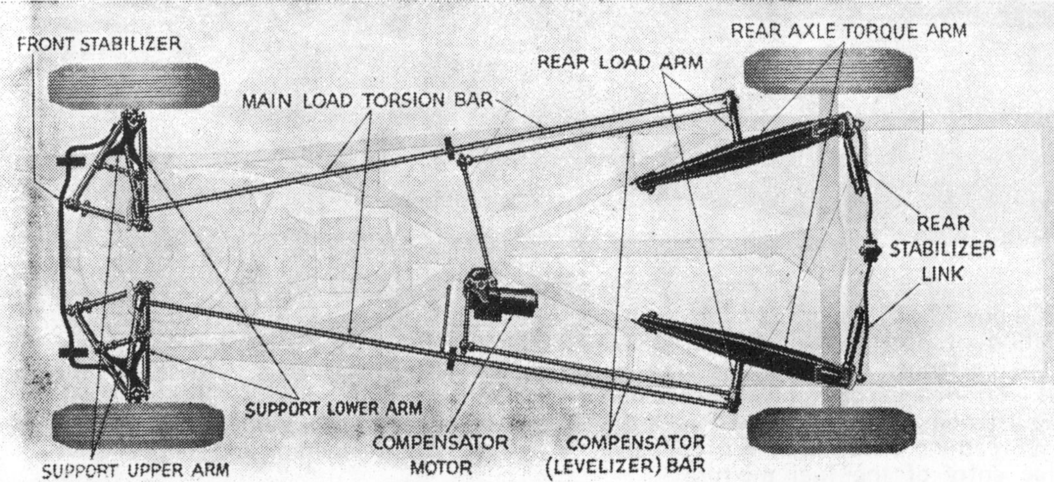

One of the new mechanical features of the Packard and Clipper range for 1955 is Torsion-Level suspension. Torsion bars serving both front and rear wheels at once replace coil springs at the front and half-elliptics at the rear

Auto Review

This completely restyled Packard 400 is the newest hardtop entry in the luxury field for 1955. In addition to its new exterior styling, a suspension system known as 'Torsion-Level' is featured. The system eliminates the customary coil-and-leaf springs, but instead uses long torsion bars interconnecting the wheels.

1955 Packard

The Packard Patrician is powered by a big 352 cubic-inch displacement V-8 engine of 260 horsepower. Boasting a torque rating of 355 foot pounds at 2,400-2,800 rpm., this is the largest displacement engine available in the passenger car field. Its size, according to Packard engineers, is based on the fact that high torque performance can only be obtained from an engine of adequate displacement. Free-breathing is an outstanding feature of the Packard V-8 engines. Among the major elements contributing to maximum breathing efficiency are large valves with big head diameters and larger valve ports that permit free entry of the fuel mixture.

In the medium and upper-medium price field, Packard offers the Clipper Custom four-door with Twin Ultramatic transmission which ensures maximum get-away performance from standing starts and safe passing ability in all speed ranges. While a family resemblance has been retained, Packard and Clipper models portray distinctively different styling concepts. The all-new frontal look on Clipper models gains added distinction from headlights hooded by long fender forms and a lower and wider grille. Both lines have sweep-around winshields and are available in seventeen single tone exterior color schemes and thirty-six two-tone combinations. Tubeless tires are furnished as standard equipment.

Auto Review

1955 Clipper

Since it was planned back in 1946, the designers of the high torque, high efficiency, valve-in-head Packard V-8 engines for 1955 have had the benefit of a long-range look at the course of modern engine development. In addition, the engine has been proof-tested in the laboratory and on the road.

The Studebaker - Packard's star in the Clipper class is its sleek Constellation. This powerful hardtop model has a 245-horsepower V-8 engine and also incorporates the 'Torsion-Level' ride. Both the Packard and Clipper lines, according to a company official, have been engineered with the recommendations of women drivers recognized and kept in mind.

PACKARD

Has V-8 Engine and New Suspension

Torsion bar four-wheel suspension is the biggest news about the 1955 Packard.

PACKARD, the first American manufacturer since the war to use anything but coil springs and wishbones at the front and semi-elliptic springs at the rear as a suspension medium, is selling their torsion bar system on all cars except the lowest-priced Clipper.

The new V-8 engines are standard on all cars and automatic transmission, power brakes, steering, window lifts and seat adjustments are available on all models.

Packard make two series of cars —the Clippers, in the medium price field, and the Packard, a high-priced competitor of Cadillac and Lincoln.

The new suspension is fitted on Packard and the higher-priced Clipper models.

Two long torsion bars run from each front wheel to the corresponding back wheel. Control arms link the wheel to each end of the torsion bar.

Thus bump action from the front wheel is transmitted to the corresponding back wheel and not absorbed directly by the chassis.

In addition there are two compensating torsion bars, the tension of which is varied by an automatic electric motor. No matter what load is placed in the car, the springs automatically level themselves with a second lag.

Thus the car stays level even when fully loaded, the rear axle does not bottom even if the boot is full and the headlights stay level.

Coil springs and wishbones at the front and semi-elliptic springs at the rear are retained on the low-priced Clipper model which will be imported to Australia.

But we will see the V-8 engine, and all imported models have automatic transmission as standard.

Two sizes of engine are installed —one in the Packard and high-priced Clipper models and a smaller displacement in the lower-priced Clippers.

One of Packard's luxury cars—the "400" hardtop two-door saloon.

A new twist: courtesy lights on the outside.

The 1955 Clipper four-door saloon.

The large engine has a bore of 102 mm. and stroke of 89 mm. Capacity is 5,886 c.c. and S.A.E. horsepower 260 at 4,600 r.p.m. (S.A.E. horsepower includes the amount required to drive the various engine accessories. It is correspondingly higher than the equivalent British brake horsepower.) Compression ratio is 8 to 1.

Torque is 355 lb./ft. at 2,400 r.p.m.

In the higher-priced Clipper the power is 245 b.h.p. One change is a compression ratio of 8 to 1 instead of the Packard's 8.5 to 1.

The smaller engine has a bore of 97 mm. and stroke of 89 mm. Capacity is 5,733 c.c. and output 225 b.h.p. at 4,600 r.p.m. Compression ratio is 8 to 1.

Torque is 325 lb./ft. at 2,400 r.p.m.

All models have a four-barrel down-draught carburettor.

The transmission now has an extra ratio in the automatic gearbox. It gives a wider range of acceleration for passing or starting.

Dimensions of the Packard are: Wheelbase, 10' 7"; length, 18' 1"; height, 5' 2"; width, 6' 6".

On the Clipper they are: Wheelbase, 10' 2"; length, 17' 10"; height 5' 2"; width, 6' 6".

Rear axle ratios vary from 3.54 to 3.07 to 1.

Shock absorbers are telescopic, steering is by worm and toothed roller and 8.00" x 15" tubeless tyres are fitted on the Packard. 7.60" x 15" tubeless tyres are standard on other models, but tubes are optional.

Styling is changed as well. The car has the now-popular vertical windscreen pillar, with the glass sloping forward from it.

There are courtesy lights on the outside of the car and 33 color combinations are offered. More than 60 different interior treatments are available with any of the exterior colors. END

A chassis diagram shows the new torsion bar suspension. Two long torsion bars support two wheels each, assisted by compensating bars of shorter length. An automatic electric motor adjusts the compensating bars according to the load in the car.

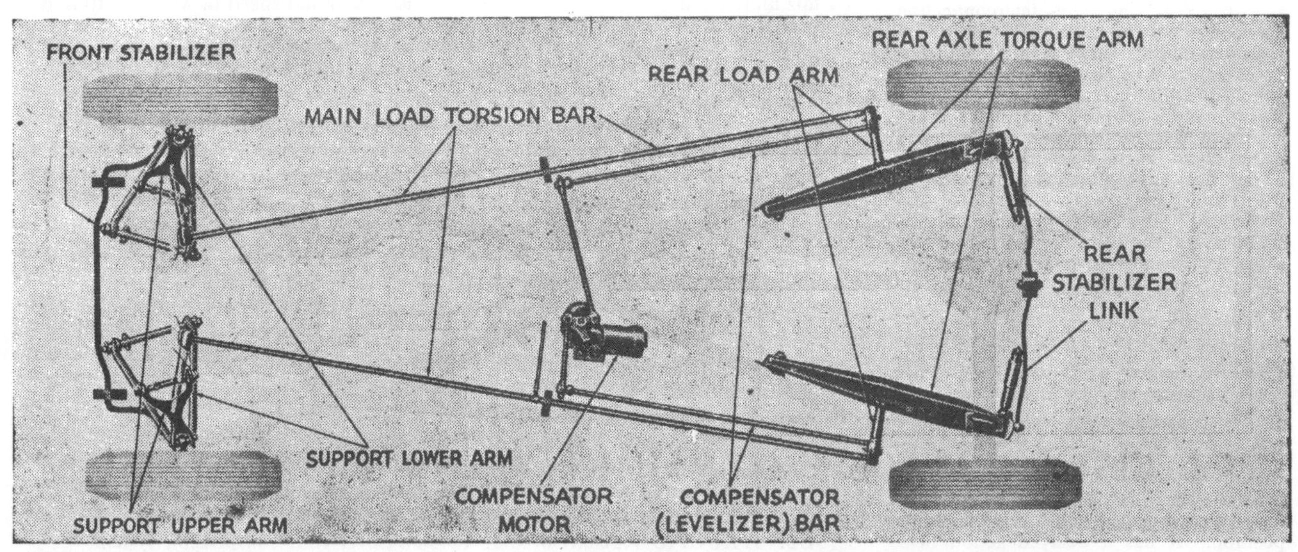

CHROMIUM is not excessive, and the lines are less flamboyant than expected, in this newcomer from America, photographed beside the Thames.

JOHN BOLSTER TESTS THE

Packard Clipper with "Torsion-Level Ride"

. . . and finds it a remarkable car, shining with bright ideas

THE work of a road test driver is always interesting, but just occasionally it becomes really dramatic. That is when a new car arrives with some feature which is obviously a great step forward over all that has gone before. Such a feature is the Packard Torsion-Level Ride.

During the last few years it has become generally known that the front and rear suspension of a car cannot be considered separately. Leaving out the higher mathematics, it's obvious that when a front wheel passes over a bump, the rear wheel on the same side will suffer a similar deflection a moment later. If the car is to remain completely level throughout, the wheel that isn't going over the bump should hang on a bit tighter, and then quickly hand the load over to its mate while it, too, vaults the obstacle. That is an over-simplification of a very complicated problem, but it explains why no conventional suspension system gives an absolutely flat ride.

This general idea has been current for some time, and a small Continental car already exists which has interconnection between the front and rear suspension. It has fallen to the Packard engineers, however, to take the thing to its logical conclusion, and like all really great ideas, it's extremely simple. They have taken a pair of 9 ft. torsion bars, and installed them down each side of the chassis. Then they have attached either end to the front and rear suspension, and "balanced" the car on the fulcrum points. As the illustration shows, the arms are connected so as to "wind up" the two ends of the bars in an opposite sense. Thus, they are enabled to carry the weight.

In order to accommodate changes of load (passengers and luggage), it has been necessary to design an automatic device to keep the balance constant. This consists of an electric motor, coupled to a pair of auxiliary torsion bars. A sensitive switch cuts in the motor if the rear of the car is higher or lower than normal, and levels the riding position. It has a delayed action of 5 to 7 seconds, so that it responds only to changes of load and not to bumps

Introducing this revolutionary suspension system in their new car, Packards also came across with a new engine. This is a V-eight of some 5.8-litres capacity, with four carburetters combined in one unit, and the extremely high compression ratio of 8.5 to 1. It is very much over-square, the dimensions (101.6 mm. x 75.5 mm.) being of the same order as those of the Grand Prix Ferrari. As installed in the Packard Clipper, it develops 245 b.h.p. at 4,600 r.p.m.

The Packard automatic transmission also has some novel features. For normal use, the car moves off on a two-stage hydraulic torque converter, which progressively "changes up" without any steps until a clutch locks it solid for direct drive. However, for really savage acceleration, the lever can be moved to the "dart" position. This brings an extra epicyclic reduction into play, which is also subject to automatic selection. Of this more anon. . . .

When I went to the works of Leonard Williams & Co., Ltd., on the Great West Road, I was agreeably surprised to find that "my" car was quietly painted in a dark shade of blue. It had far less chromium decoration than the average American car, and the instrument panel, with proper round, separate dials, was slightly reminiscent of some of the best Continental sports cars. Of course, the Packard seemed *enormous* at first, and I could just about have laid full length on either of the bench-type seats. The upholstery and general finish was superb.

On moving off in the ordinary "drive" range, I was at once struck by the smoothness of the transmission. It approaches, in fact, very close to perfection, and the simplicity of driving in heavy traffic has to be experienced to be believed. I plunged straight into London during the strike chaos, and the ease with which the big machine glided forward, either inch by inch or in a sudden rush, was a revelation.

Speaking of sudden rushes, let us come to the "dart" position on the quadrant. This need only be used when you want to beat a 100 m.p.h. sports car away from the lights. The acceleration on this lower gear is simply electric, and a change up to the higher range can be secured by lifting the accelerator for a momentary pause. Down changes are automatic.

The use of this gear is very seldom required, the "drive" position sufficing to deal with all normal opposition. There is no reason why one cannot use the "dart" all day, except that the running then becomes less effortless. The big engine runs at higher revs., and the change down can be felt Ultimately, the same high top gear is engaged, and it is only at the lower speeds that the extra epicyclic reduction comes into play.

The acceleration figures of this 37 cwt. luxury car give one furiously to think. It flings itself from a standstill to 60 m.p.h. in 10 seconds dead, without a trace of wheelspin and extraordinarily little dipping of the tail. Furthermore, its maximum speed of around 110 m.p.h. (120 on the "clock") is fully in keeping with its acceleration performance. It means that you and I, who drive sports cars, are probably in danger of being passed by a Packard, which is a pretty sobering thought!

The suspension is quite phenomenally

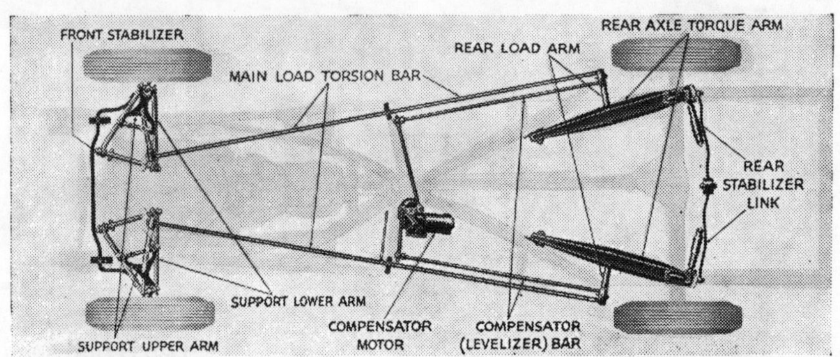

CONSTRUCTION details of the "Torsion-Level Ride" suspension system.

"soft", and at first the floating sensation is a little uncanny. There are no quick movements at all, and a marked absence of pitching, which is emphasized by the absolute steadiness of the headlight beams. It was, however, a very small thing that convinced me that this new ride really is something different. I have a daughter who is a martyr to that distressing malady, car sickness. Normally, she suffers most in cars with soft suspension. Yet, a long run in the Packard completely failed to produce the slightest symptom, and Annabelle is now a fervent admirer of the Torsion-Level Ride!

Naturally, the Packard is not at its best on sharp corners. This is simply because they are relatively so much sharper for this enormous automobile. Nevertheless, it is surprisingly controllable on faster bends, and will sweep through typical main road curves at around 85 m.p.h. One does not expect it to corner like a light sports car, of course, but it puts up a very competent performance and shows no pronounced tendency to under- or over-steer.

My test car was fitted with power steering, and this I really loved. It gives incredibly light control at all speeds, the servo doing 80 per cent. of the work, and the driver only 20 per cent. Yet, there is no loss of sensitivity or "feel", and there is some caster return action. I felt entirely at home with it at once, even at the highest speeds. I dislike heavy steering intensely, and this 5.8-litre car was lighter to handle than an "eight" or ten.

Any very fast and heavy car must give the brakes a man-sized job. The servo brakes on the Clipper are powerful, and need only very light pedal pressure. I employed them frequently at three-figure speeds and did not suffer from fading or increased pedal travel. Nevertheless, there was a smell of hot linings after this treatment, and I think it is unreasonable to use these brakes as one would those of a light sports car, in spite of their obvious potency.

The all-round visibility, driving position, and location of the instruments and controls, get full marks. The deeply hooded headlamps are powerful, too, a far cry from the feeble 6-volt lights of earlier American cars. The heating and demisting system is more than adequate for the coldest transatlantic winter, and the superb radio which, by some electronic magic, can even tune itself in, is just one of the many "extras" one may specify.

To some extent, all this luxury is paid for in terms of fuel consumption. I feel, though, that the figure I obtained is not excessive when one considers the size and speed of the car. A driver who was content to make less use of the performance could probably register about 15 m.p.g.

There remains the question of sheer size, and it is certainly often suggested that American cars are too big for British roads. I would rather say that British roads are too small for American cars, and too small for most British cars, too. It is true that one cannot nip through gaps in the traffic as one can with the smaller European cars. Nevertheless, the sheer power often makes up for that, and one can pass four or five cars at a time instead of taking them one by one.

When this new Packard was introduced, it was driven, under official A.A.A. observation, for 25,000 miles at the makers' test track. The average speed, including all pit stops, was 104.7 m.p.h. This is the finest performance ever put up by a production car, and proves that the high maximum speed and rapid acceleration are certainly not bought at the expense of reliability and long life.

ACCELERATION GRAPH

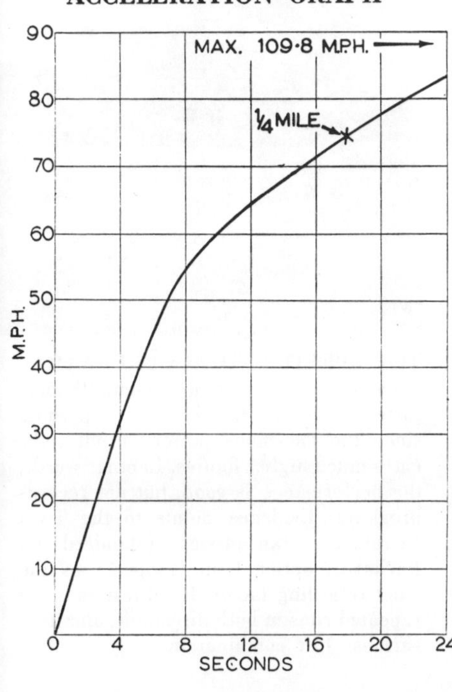

Specification and Performance Data

Car Tested: Packard Clipper Custom 4-door saloon. Price £1,870 (£2,650 5*s*. 10*d*. including P.T.). Extras on test car: Twin ultramatic transmission, £156 15*s*. 1*d*.; Power steering, £83 7*s*. 5*d*.: Power brakes, £28 16*s*. 7*d*.; Heater and defroster, £59 10*s*. 0*d*.; Signal seeking radio with electric antenna and rear speaker, £95 16*s*. 9*d*., all including P.T. Total, £3,074 11*s*. 8*d*.

Engine: Eight cylinders in Vee, 101.6 mm. x 75.5 mm. (5,768 c.c.). Pushrod operated overhead valves. 245 b.h.p. at 4,600 r.p.m. 8.5 to 1 compression ratio. Four-barrel downdraught carburetter with automatic choke and idling control, oil bath air cleaner, silencer, and flame arrester. Coil and distributor ignition with automatic advance.

Transmission: Two-stage torque converter with direct drive clutch and auxiliary two-speed epicyclic reduction gear, automatically controlled. Open propeller shaft. Hypoid bevel rear axle, ratio 3.23 to 1.

Chassis: Box and channel-section cruciform braced frame. Independent front suspension by wishbones, normal rear axle, with telescopic dampers all round. Front and rear suspension coupled by a single 9 ft. torsion bar on each side. Rear suspension has auxiliary compensator torsion bars to give automatic levelling by electric motor. Front anti-roll torsion bar. Rear trailing arms and stabilizer link. Power steering by engine-driven hydraulic pump. Hydraulic brakes with servo. 7.60-15 ins. tyres on bolt-on disc wheels.

Equipment: 12-volt lighting and starting. Speedometer, ammeter, oil, fuel, and temperature gauges, and clock. Flashing direction indicators. Heating, demisting, and ventilation system. 3-speed wipers and screen washers. Radio.

Dimensions: Wheelbase, 10 ft. 2 ins.; track, front 4 ft. 11¼ ins., rear 5 ft.; overall length, 17 ft. 10¼ ins.; width, 6 ft. 6 ins.; height, 5 ft. 2 ins. Weight 37 cwt.

Performance: Maximum speed 109.8 m.p.h. Standing ¼-mile 17.8 secs. Acceleration, 0-30 m.p.h. 3.8 secs., 0-40 m.p.h. 5.2 secs., 0-50 m.p.h. 7 secs., 0-60 m.p.h. 10 secs., 0-70 m.p.h. 15.4 secs., 0-80 m.p.h. 21.6 secs.

Fuel Consumption: Driven hard, 12.2 m.p.g.

SEQUENCE of operation (above, right) of the levelling system. With increased load the tail dips, then levels automatically. With load removed, the tail rises, then again levels itself.

★

INSTRUMENT layout (right) is easy to survey. Two pedals indicate the automatic transmission.

Clipper hits a sharp corner hard. Although wheels dig in deep, the body holds an even keel—a benefit from new torsion bars.

Packard Road Test

New engine and new suspension— that's the Clipper Custom

SPECIFICATIONS

Engine type	OHV V-8
Displacement	352 cubic inches
BHP	245 @ 4600 rpm
Compression ratio	8.5-TO-1
Bore	4"
Stroke	3½"
Torque	355 ft.-lbs. @ 2400 rpm
Transmission	TWIN ULTRAMATIC
Rear axle ratio	3.23-TO-1
Wheelbase	122 inches
Dry weight	3915 lbs.
Turning circle	43 feet
Steering lock-to-lock	4 3/4 turns

PRICES

Car	$2925
Transmission	$199
Radio	$92-132
Heater	$82
Power Steering	$115
Power Brakes	$40
Air Conditioning	$627

ENGINE of the Clipper Custom comes from a new V-8 family that holds top spot for '55 in torque and hp ratings and displacement. Although pre-introduction rumors were wild, the V-8 is conventional in design, is also noted for its physical size. The four-inch bore is equalled by only one other make and, when engineers are so inclined, overboring will make it easy to achieve 300 hp. Accessibility for regular servicing is good, except for fuel pump, distributor and spark plugs.

TOP SPEED AND ACCELERATION place the car in the upper-middle performance bracket. This is surprising, since the enormous power output indicates much higher figures. In other words, the performance is *good*, but not record-breaking. Evidence points to the Twin Ultramatic transmission (standard on Packards, optional on Clippers) as the chief retarding factor. Road testers made repeated runs in both directions, and used various shift combinations.

RIDE calls for a flat and unequivocal statement: it is the best among current American cars. Example: when going through a deep road dip at speed, the wheels follow the pavement down and up, but the subsequent bouncing is gone. The car bottoms, rises and then the rear settles gently into position.

HANDLING QUALITIES are definitely superior and the car is obviously easier to control, as the torsion bars wind and unwind. Through sharp bends, steering is sure and steady. Body heel is so slight that a new feeling of flat cornering is present. When traveling at speed on a straight and level road, there is a sensation of "snaking" along. After some experience at the wheel, the feeling disappears. Packard servicemen say torsion bar system is trouble-free. The load-compensator, which contributes to good handling, allowed exhaust pipe on test car to scrape ground when coming out of driveways, but adjustment is easy.

INTERIOR is in keeping with Packard tradition of luxury and quality. Cranking up windows is almost effortless, but rear-view mirror does not provide adequate vision, either horizontally or vertically. And the black upholstery and floor mats show dirt and lint easily. Polished dash top is in horizontal plane to eliminate annoying reflections.

STYLING of the Packard-Clipper lines, like the engine, was basis for inaccurate speculation before 1955 models were introduced. Instead of radical changes, appearance is characteristic of the manufacturer, with wrap-around windshields (free of distortion), chrome trim and paint used to keep pace with the times. Most drastic alterations came in the front end treatment, which many observers comment favorably upon. Although front doors do not open wide, entrance is easy, while all four fenders are visible from the driver's seat. The 1955 bodies are the first in recent years that have been built by Packard itself (they had been supplied by a vendor) and the changeover has not affected the make's excellent finish.

BRAKING TESTS, conducted on dry pavement, produced stopping distances of 52-78-156 feet from 30-45-60 mph. This is about par. The brake pedal is located on the same plane as the accelerator pedal, but apparently is not designed for left-foot use. Interesting point: of all '55 cars tested, Clipper engine was only one that did not stall in panic stops from all speeds. When brakes were locked and car came to a screeching halt, engine continued to run smoothly and quietly.

FUEL CONSUMPTION brought a surprise. The Clipper Custom, with its 245 hp, gets really superior mileage out of a gallon of gasoline. The top gear of the twin-drive Ultramatic will really pay off in the long run, and the performance with overdrive could very well be astonishing. Good example of how high horsepower does not have to be expensive when it comes to operating costs. Unusual fact: the Clipper got better mileage at 45 mph, than it did at a steady 30!

CAR TESTED: 1955 PACKARD CLIPPER CUSTOM V-8

TEST CONDITIONS

Altitude 2800 feet
Temperature 72 degrees
Wind GUSTY – 17 mph
Gasoline TEXACO PREMIUM

ACCELERATION AND TOP SPEED

MPH	0-30	0-45	0-60	30-50	40-60
Seconds	4.4	8	12	5	6.6

Standing ¼ mile 19.5 seconds
Fastest one-way run 106 mph
Top speed avg. 4 runs 104 mph

SPEEDOMETER CORRECTIONS

Car Speed-ometer	Actual Speeds
20	17
30	25
40	35
50	44
60	52
70	60
80	68
90	78
100	87

BRAKING DISTANCE

MPH	Stopping Distance
30	52 feet
45	78 feet
60	156 feet

FUEL CONSUMPTION

MPH	Average
30	18 mpg
45	20 mpg
60	16 mpg

The Packard Clipper

Packard is among the best-cornering American cars of '55, Tom found on his test course.

Torsion-bar suspension and a 245-hp V8 engine make the Clipper Custom a great car to drive, says Tom.

By Tom McCahill

IN a major effort to maintain its place in the automotive sun, Packard for 1955 has made a double-barreled switch from former models. Changing over to V8 engines after 30 years with the straight 8's was like Harry Truman voting Republican. But the really big change was in tossing out the old coil-and-leaf springs for the more advanced torsion bar suspension.

This is a terrific step forward and required a lot more industrial guts than has been displayed in the fair state of Michigan since Governor Soapy Williams was just a bubble. Torsion bars are not exactly a brand-new method of keeping the fanny off the ground, as this type of suspension reached its development height in Germany many years ago and Dr. Porsche brought it to its peak with the Auto-Union Grand Prix cars during the days of Hitler. It is a great system, however, far superior to anything else ever used on American cars, and Packard showed plenty of courage in bringing it over here.

For those unfamiliar with torsion bars and how they work, here is a rough explanation. Actually there are several types of torsion bar springs but basically a torsion bar is a steel bar. It is connected by load arms to the rear axle and the front wheel assembly. Torsion means twisting and a torsion bar, which replaces the ordinary spring, will twist and absorb shock in addition to supporting the frame and body. In this respect its work closely simulates coil or leaf springing as we have known it.

Packard, however, is the first car in automotive history to use what they call full-length torsion bars. Approximately nine feet long, they run the entire length of the car from front to rear on each side of the chassis frame. Attached to forged steel arms at both ends, they transform the rotary motion of the arms into the twisting action of the bars. Up front the arms extend outward toward the front wheels and in the rear they point inward to the rear axle, where they are anchored.

With the unique Packard system, when a front wheel hits a bump the wheel naturally shoots upward. But since it is connected to the rear wheel on the same side by a torsion bar, this upward movement twists the shaft and exerts pressure to keep the rear wheel from shooting upward too. This compensation from front to rear is a major feature of this unit and is responsible for the new Packard's excellent roadability and cornering properties. The Packard system can be designed to provide a softer or firmer ride by varying the thickness and length of the torsion bars, as well as by altering the strength of the front and rear stabilizers.

In addition to torsion bars Packard has a so-called Load Levelizer which is operated by a little electric motor. This means that if you visit your cousin, the doorman at Fort Knox, and he loads up your trunk with gold bricks, this electrical genii will square things so that the car will stay just as level as when it was unloaded.

This gadget will also make dandy fun for the kiddies if you park outside the local marijuana-and-tonic house and forget to turn off the compensator switch, which is so well hidden under

Uncle Tom liked the across-the-hood view of the good-looking new Packard Clipper.

Huge trunk, here accommodating 240-pound Jim McMichael, is mammoth for a big sedan.

Clipper features hooded chrome-lined headlights, also seen on many other 1955 cars.

Racy Clipper's powerful new V8 engine pushes it along at top speed of about 105 mph.

the dashboard that I never did discover it until my tests were almost over. As long as the switch is on, the Levelizer never quits. So if three or four kids jump on the back bumper, the rear end will

Packard's novel Load Levelizer makes car sink down under load (top picture), lifts it high when load is removed (center) and then restores it to level—automatically.

sink down almost to the ground. After a five or seven second delay, whirring noises will pierce the atmosphere and your car's tail will go Otis-elevating skyward with the kids aboard for a free ride. A pack of determined urchins could keep this up until your battery was dead as last Fourth of July's champagne. So remember to flick off the toggle switch when you park.

The car I tested was the Clipper Custom and on this job I definitely felt that the ride should have been firmer. This can be done as explained earlier. But don't get the impression that I think the Packard suspension system is a poor example of torsion bar springing. It is a good one but I like a firm ride, perhaps a firmer ride than do Sunday drivers. It is possible, with torsion bar suspension, to build a car that will outcorner and outmaneuver any other American car. In my standard test corners I found that the Clipper was faster than most American cars in getting around before breaking away and is among the best-cornering Detroit cars for 1955.

When driving this car at high speeds, meaning 90 and above, you get the feeling that the rear wheels turn with the front wheels, undoubtedly due to the fact that, in this design, the front torsion bars are connected with the rear wheel bars. Actually, this car feels as flexible as a warm snake on twisty roads. But it is a great ride and once you get the hang of it, after more than 500 miles of driving,

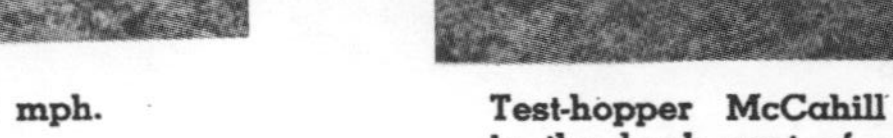

Test-hopper McCahill doesn't often ride in the back seat of any car but he tried Packard's and found it very comfortable.

it becomes very restful and pleasant.

The Packard Motor Car Company supplied my test car which I kept for some time before returning. Before I had driven this car ten miles, I was ready to trade it in on a used pogo stick. Fortunately, I analyzed the trouble, though it was my first whack at the new Packard V8. Somewhere in Packard service, before I got the car, enough water got in the gas tank to hold the National Water Skiing Championships on. This does not encourage good motoring. Several pints of alcohol later—alky I had dumped into the tank to pick up the water—the big V8 was running as smoothly and as easily as a con man proposing to the farmer's daughter. Though this is not the biggest engine in the super-thyroid Packard camp from a horsepower standpoint, it displaces 352 inches, which is much larger than any other American engine today. The Custom Clipper claims 355 foot-pounds of torque and 245 brake horsepower. The biggest Packard engine, with the same displacement and torque, develops 275 hp.

This 4,000-pound, four-door sedan is a brilliant performer, though not record-breaking or sensational. It'll do a corrected speedometer 0-60 in 11.9 seconds when using the right-hand triangle of the Drive range, which is similar to third in a dual-range HydraMatic. Zero to 30 averages 4.2 seconds and 0-50 takes between 7.8 and 8 seconds flat. It'll get to

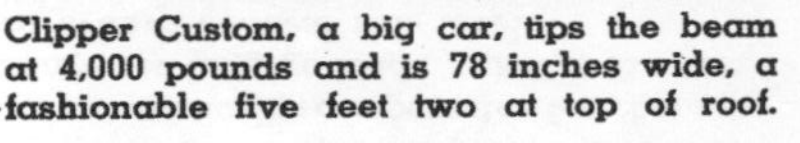

Clipper Custom, a big car, tips the beam at 4,000 pounds and is 78 inches wide, a fashionable five feet two at top of roof.

70 mph from a standstill in 16.9, which is hardly slow, but from here on up the guided missile action retards considerably until it reaches absolute top of between 105-108 mph.

Before summing up, I have one or two small beefs about this car, or the particular model I drove, which I must point out. First, this [*Continued on page* 194]

SPECIFICATIONS

MODEL TESTED:

1955 Packard four-door Clipper Custom sedan

ENGINE:

8 cylinder, V-type; bore 4 inches, stroke 3.5 inches; maximum torque 355 foot pounds @ 2400-2800 rpm: brake horsepower 245 @ 4600 rpm; compression ratio 8.5 to 1

DIMENSIONS:

Wheelbase 122 inches; overall length 214¼ inches; tread 59.7 inches front, 60 rear; width 78 inches; height 61.9 inches; weight 4,000 pounds; standard tire size 7.60x15; gas tank 20 gals

PERFORMANCE:

0 to 30 mph, 4.2 seconds
0 to 50 mph, 7.8-8.0 seconds
0 to 60 mph, 11.9 seconds
0 to 70 mph, 16.9 seconds
Top speed, 105-108 mph

SPEEDOMETER ERROR:

At 60 mph on speedometer, actual speed 55.3 mph

McCahill Tests Packard

car was equipped with a green sunglass band that extended down from the top of the windshield more than three inches. Tie this up with the fact that the electric seat's up-and-down movement appeared to be no more than one inch, and any guy over six feet tall, who sits any straighter than a pretzel, is practically forced to look through this green goldfish bowl whether he wants to or not. Once, just at twilight, I was forced to drive more than 20 miles with my neck cocked in heron fashion so that I could see under the damned thing. The ground clearance is on the low side, I figure under six inches, and I shaved a number of high-crowned farmer's roads. The low point appears to be the levelizer unit.

Now for the goodies. This is an extremely comfortable car and the view across the hood is pleasing. Even the radiator ornament (and I seldom like them) is designed not to be annoying in any way. The rear seat is real lush, with a truly soft pull-down arm rest. The instrument panel is as fine-looking as I have seen on an American car and the two ashtrays, one for the driver and another for the front seat passenger, are a good feature. The glove compartment is large enough to store a Welsh Corgi and a stuffed bonefish but it could stand more pitch toward the back. The upholstery is of excellent quality.

This is an extremely soothing car to drive, in or out of traffic, and it has a trunk large enough to store the Pittsburgh Pirates and a framed picture of Leo Durocher. Seriously, this trunk is gigantic in size, especially for a four-door sedan. The torsion bar suspension gives you a great ride and Packard deserves a lot of credit for introducing it on these shores. I believe the best I can say for the car is that if I had to make a coast-to-coast trip starting tomorrow, I don't know of any full-size American car I would rather drive than this Packard. •

ATOM-BOMB SHELTER

Combine practicality and security by engaging in this two-in-one project which includes a double garage and a sturdy concrete shelter built into one corner. Shelter may be used for storage or as tool room. For your copy of the complete plans which include diagrams and full instructions, remit $1.00 to *Mechanix Illustrated* Plans Service, Fawcett Building, Greenwich, Conn. Plan No. HJ-18.

Packard V-8 starts 25,000-mile test run in which it set amazing average speed record of 104.7 miles per hour. Conducted under the eyes of the American Automobile Association Contest Board, the drive shattered a total of 146 other records.

Far and Fast!

A Packard V-8 engine marked a new milestone in speed by covering 25,000 miles at the amazing average of 104.7 mph. under Triple A supervision

By M. E. STUART

DURING the cold days and nights at the end of October last year, certain events took place at Utica, Mich., which are of vital importance to the automobile world in general and the American motorist in particular. These results have not received the publicity and acclaim which they deserve, for they are momentous and highly significant. No automobile manufacturer in the world can disregard what took place at Utica between the 22d and 31st of October, 1954, when an American-built domestic sedan with a 1955 engine, and incorporating an unconventional (for the U. S. manufacturer) suspension system, was driven a distance equivalent to the circumference of the earth at an average speed of 104.7 mph.

The average motorist looks upon the figure of 100 mph. as fantastic, and it is doubtful whether it is possible to find many persons capable of visualizing the maintainance of this velocity for nearly 25,000 miles. Those who cannot appreciate the significance of this feat may well doubt its value, but value it certainly has. If a car is capable of travelling this great distance at such a high speed, and without any serious mechanical attention, it can be logically assumed that it is capable of travelling twice that distance at half the speed. The fact that the car covered this distance at the claimed speed cannot be refuted, for although the test took place in secret, it was carefully observed by an impartial group representing an internationally-recognized automotive organization. These observers can, if called upon, verify the quoted figures.

We can assume that the owner of one of these cars has before him 75,000 miles of carefree motoring, provided that he averages 30 mph. over this distance. It must be admitted that to the motorist this is quite a degree of reliability, not to be expected from every car manufactured today. This claim to reliability can be statistically proved. There is no need for the manufacturers of this car to rely on fancy advertising cliches

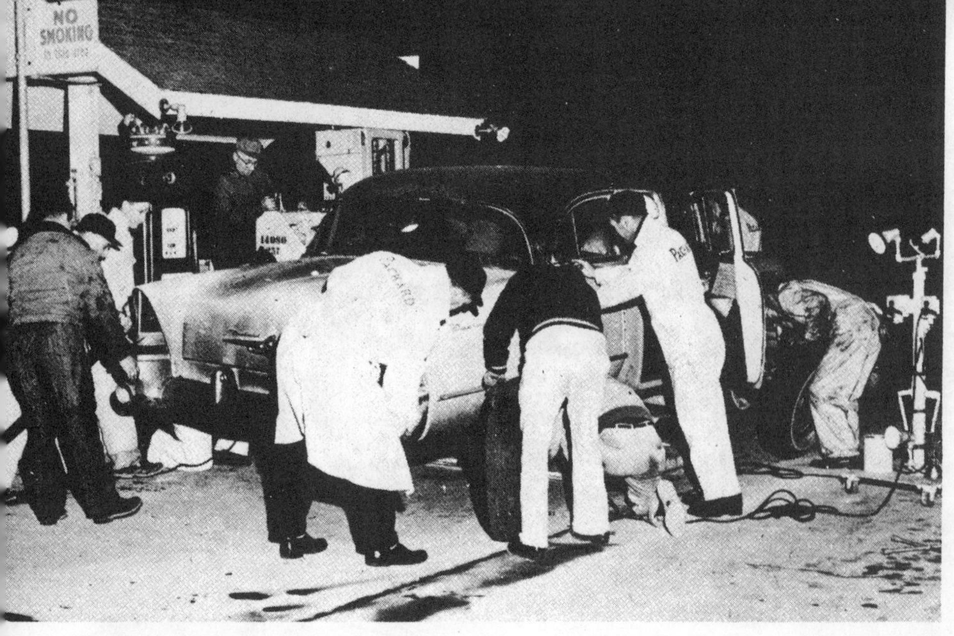

Packard racked up 147 records in making the run

Pit stops were fast and infrequent. They averaged only 49 seconds each.

Packard proving ground test track at Utica compares with Indianapolis oval.

to extoll the virtues of their wares, the figures speak for themselves.

The significance of this high performance and reliability is not confined to the United States, for the achievement is comparable to those accomplished by the European manufacturers and measurable according to internationally-recognized standards. The last time a manufacturer went out to establish long distance production car records, the record for 10,000 miles was raised to 100.65 mph. Now an American firm has taken the limit for 25,000 miles to nearly 105 mph. This rather eclipses the European effort, but, not for long, for the European manufacturer believes in testing his wares by collecting records and challenging others to do better, unbiasedly informing the potential purchaser of the results.

The only regrettable fact about the October test conducted by the Studebaker-Packard Corporation, with one of their 1955 Packards with the new torsion-bar suspension, and observed by the American Automobile Association, is that it is not given official international recognition—then neither was the case of the European sports coupe which was driven 10,000 miles at 101 mph.

The reason why these figures do not qualify for the international, or national, record book is because the tests were carried out on an unrecognized circuit, that is, a circuit recognized by neither the AAA or the Federation International

Plenty of racing experts were on hand for the spectacular performance. Here, Tommy Milton, Roscoe Turner, Ralph De Palma check times with an AAA official.

During the Packard run drivers were changed every 50 laps, or about every 70 minutes. But most of them couldn't wait to get back under that wheel again.

de l'Automobile, as it does not comply with their record-breaking requirements. Although the European car ran on a recognized track, it did not abide by the rules, as it was halted for the replacement of a vital part of the car—the 10,000 miles at 101 mph. is as unofficial as the 25,000 miles at 105 mph. The makers of the sports coupe that covered the 10,000 miles at over 100 mph. considered, and rightly so, that the achievement was worthy of world-wide publicity; the American achievement is worthy of greater praise and attention.

There can be no doubt that the new Packard is a "world" beater, as it has already proved itself. But to what extent? The list of records which were bettered by the V-8 engined car may surprise those that still doubt the full capabilities of the American vehicle, and induce the European constructor to make another attempt on the 10,000 mile record and also tackle the 25,000 mile target. The 1955 Packard bettered the following: ten World Unlimited records; eight International Class B records; twelve U. S. National Unlimited records; fourteen U. S. National Class B records; fifty-five U. S. National Unlimited records for Closed Cars, and forty-eight U. S. National Class B—Closed Car records.

Making a grand total of 147 individual records! The AAA-checked times showed that the car exceeded the National records by as much as 36 mph., the World Unlimited records for all distances from 10,000 to 25,000, as well as bettering all the daily records from three to seven days. Truly a series of achievements that rightly deserve to be voiced abroad, for they are achievements that can be appreciated by those who are uninfluenced by advertising boasts that are glowingly phrased, but fail to stand up to detailed evaluation.

The Studebaker-Packard Corporation can be considered the most promising concern in an industry that is becoming bogged-down by its own line of sales-talk, actually beginning to believe that the customer wants what he or she is being forced to buy. The Studebaker-Packard Corporation does not follow the line of their competitors, but an interestingly individual policy that shows initiative, a practical appreciation of future trends, and, above all, courage.

It is sincerely hoped that this company, which has not relied upon the comic-strip dream car to gain mass attention, has started a trend which will make its competitors publish facts and figures, with logical conclusions, when describing their wares. Far too long has the slick copywriter been telling the motorist what is good for him, couching his glamorous sounding sentences in terms of horsepower, "Y" blocks, power accessories, etc., but, rarely emphasizing the vital facts about reliability, good all-round performance, fine roadability, positive steering and economical running costs. ☆☆

Late on ninth day, the Packard V-8 had completed the distance around the world—24,902 miles. A few minutes later the last turn was made on lap number 9,851. The 1955 model had successfully passed toughest test in the annals of motoring.

Distinguished Company

The Packard Patrician for 1955 is a combination of luxury and high performance

By G. M. LIGHTOWLER

IN PRESENTING this road report on the 1955 Packard Patrician, we move into the distinguished automobile class and review a car that appeals to the owner who requires a combination of luxury and high performance.

From a technical point of view the Packard is outstanding among 1955 cars, as it incorporates two great engineering achievements, one of them a complete departure from convention and contemporary American thought on automobile construction.

Any deviation from the stereotyped pattern and the following of a new idea is to be applauded. Only through adoption of new ideas can a manufacturer hope to progress in a world that is becoming more and more competitive. The U. S. automobile manufacturer must consider world trends along with domestic demands. Competition among overseas manufacturers is as intense as it is here and with more makes of cars (and consequently more models) the motorist of the world can choose one to suit his pocket and personal idiosyncracies. It must be admitted that since the end of World War II the U. S. domestic automobile manufacturer has shown little initiative in the production of his commodity, apart from outward design, and has not made any startling contribution to the advancement of automobile engineering. The stylist and salesman have dominated the production line.

Exceptions to these generalizations are cars bearing the emblems of the Houses of Studebaker and Packard; now the Studebaker-Packard Corporation. Cars of these two marques incorporate features that are decidedly individual, features that are not confined to their styling and coachwork. In previous issues of CAR LIFE (February and May) we dealt with the latest Studebakers; now we turn to the Packard.

Engineering should be the prime concern of all who make automobiles for the present-day motorist, for with speeds rising and the density of traffic increasing, every effort should be made to obviate the possibility of the vehicle misbehaving in an emergency. This important duty of the manufacturer is too often ignored in his desire to market a car that delivers a high horsepower and carries a large comfortable body.

One of the important features of a car that aids safety best is the suspension design. Just because one car is heavier than another does not mean that the weightier vehicle has better suspension and better roadability. This, as we have stated in other articles, is one of the fallacies of the day. One of the finest cars for roadability is an Italian make, much lighter than the majority of cars produced here. Has a truck better roadability than the domestic sedan? It is all a matter of suspension geometry and the scientific distribution of weight that guarantees correct dissipation of forces acting on the chassis and body when a car is cornering or traversing rough surfaces.

The Packard Division of the Studebaker-Packard Corporation has made a great contribution to the world's motor industry in evolving a torsion bar suspension system that works successfully on a large sedan. This demonstrates, for the first time, that at least one manufacturer realizes that the conventional leaf and coil springs leave much to be desired in cars that now have a top speed of over 100 mph. Not only is the 1955 Packard safer than many of its contemporaries, but it is much more comfortable. There is nothing very new about torsion bar suspension systems, as the principle has been used for years in some of the fastest cars made by overseas manufacturers, but it is strange it has taken so long for American makers to realize its great advantages and reliability.

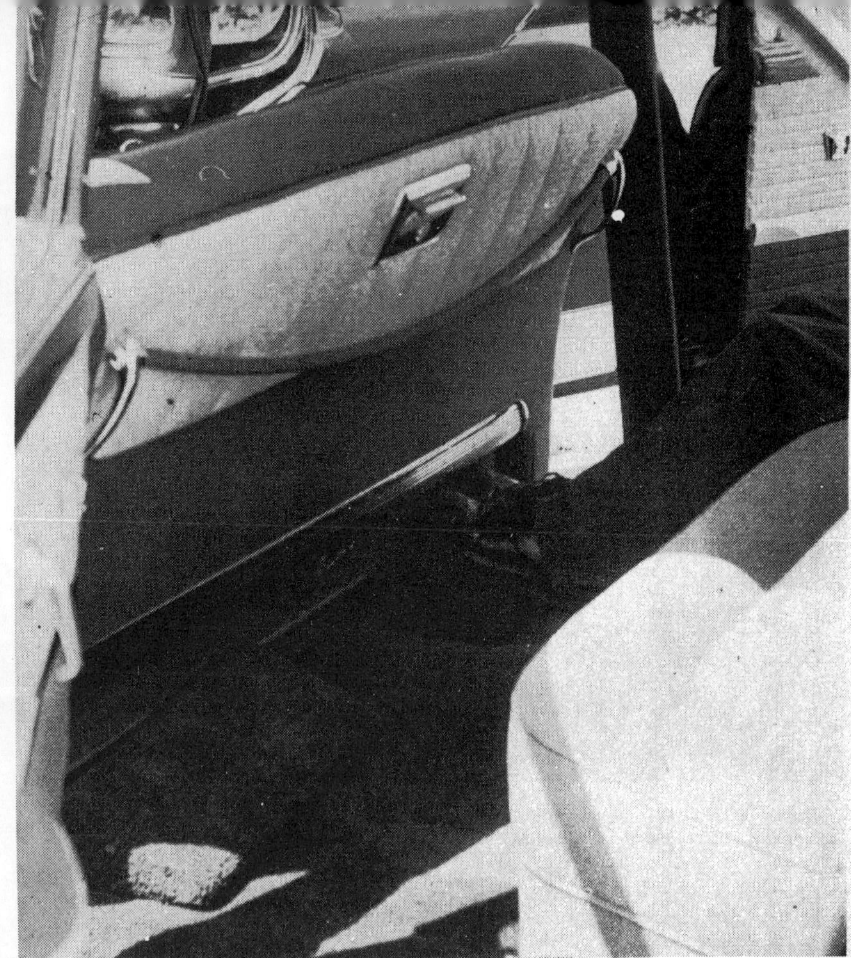

Spacious rear-seating arrangement is made even more comfortable through use of movable foot rests. Despite ample room, one doesn't feel like a pea in a pod.

Influence of fighter plane cockpit is seen in Patrician's instrument panel.

Coupled with this innovation of the torsion bar suspension, which calls for nothing but praise, is utilization of a new V-8 engine that develops 260 bhp. Before being brought onto the market this engine was subjected to the toughest sort of test. Incorporated in a four-door Packard Patrician sedan, the engine ran for nine days, taking the car over a distance of 25,000 miles at an average speed of 104.7 mph.! After such a test the engine, and the Patrician, were considered suitable to be sold to the motorist.

One cannot say that the Patrician is the most delightful car to behold among the glamorized chariots of 1955, but (and this is of far more importance to us who are worried about advancement of the gadget at the expense of engineering) it is the most interesting vehicle of the 1955 brood from the aspect of progress and development. It is an indicator of future trends that will be followed by other manufacturers.

The model made available to us through the courtesy of Bernie Thomas, public relations, the Studebaker-Packard Corporation, Detroit, and Jay H. Thomas, Jr., zone manger of the Washington office of the corporation, was equipped with all the available accessories. These extras included fresh air heating, defroster and front underseat heater; radio with three-way tuning, electrically operated antenna and rear compartment speaker; power brakes; Packard power steering; electrically operated window lifts; four-way power-operated front seat; solex glass with shaded plastic windshield and white sidewall tires. With these extras the car sells for slightly over $5,000, dependent upon cost of transport to point of sale and local taxes.

The first thing that strikes the reviewer of the Patrician is its size. It is a big car and must be treated as such, for one expects certain characteristics not associated with cheaper and smaller cars. This car is produced for a very definite individual buyer and certain aspects of the vehicle would not be commented upon if they appeared on a smaller car.

Outward appearance of the Patrician, apart from its apparent size, does not at first demand attention, but further inspection will reveal it is designed with a functional slant. The utilization of chrome has not been too abused and shows an appreciation of proportion. We do not, however, like the adoption of the large bullet-like protrusions in-

Glimpse of the 260 bhp. engine which averaged 104.7 mph. in nine-day test.

The V-8 engine was subjected to one of the toughest tests on record

corporated in the front bumper assembly; they are offensive equipment rather than defensive, and it is thought that their use might have been better left to the company that first introduced them. The wraparound windshield, which from the point of view of distortion is the best we have been forced to look through, has less violent curve in it, and, in fact, curves from the center. We haven't been sold on the wraparound windshield, as yet, and can see little advantage in its incorporation, other than from a selling angle. Packard in this instance has done a good job in blending in an awkward piece of equipment without bringing back the side supports to such a position that they obstruct entrance and exit from the front compartment.

Designed with a functional slant, the Patrician's use of chrome is in keeping with its place as a luxury car. Wraparound windshield affords good vision.

One of the newest features on the outside of the car is the fitting of a courtesy light in the leading edge of the rear fender bulge, an integral portion of the rear door. This courtesy light, connected with the exterior lighting system, automatically lights up with opening of the front doors. The treatment of the rear light, traffic indicator and back-up light fixture is massive, but in proportion to the car as a whole.

The rear luggage trunk is immense and could be adequately used as a sleeping compartment, should the sleeper be of average stature. (We have slept in more cramped surroundings.) The rear radio speaker is attached to the fixed portion of the roof of the trunk and it is felt that careless insertion of a trunk or heavy bag could easily disconnect the speaker wiring or knock the speaker itself from its seating.

The rear compartment of the Patrician is spacious and comfortable. Unlike many large cars, it does not make one feel like a solitary pea in a pod when sitting in the rear. The provision of loose footrests could only be found in a car of this type.

There are two interior lights, one in front above the instrument panel (which operates upon opening either of the front doors) and one in the roof to the rear of the back seat that lights up when the rear door is opened. This rear light can be turned on by a manual switch on the left central door post.

If the decoration of the instrument panel and facia is too gaudy, the color scheme and appointments of the interior of the Patrician are conservative and restrained, befitting a car of this nature. Upholstery is of good quality fabric with floor mats of a heavy pile.

The instrument panel reflects the influence of the fighter aircraft cockpit, and one wonders if production of Rolls Royce engines by the Packard concern during the last war might not have had an effect on the Patrician in more ways than just in the engine department and the instrument panel. Although dials on the instrument panel are grouped in a sensible and pleasing manner, they are not too easy to read. The simulated gold background with the silver dials and gold figures does not make for easy reading, and dials should be read in an instant. At first, the mass of knobs and levers may confuse the driver, but he need not worry for all are well placed and after a few minutes of familiarization can be operated easily. One thing we applauded as soon as we sat in the car (and although it is a small item, it is the small items that make or mar a particular model) was an ash receiver near the driver, but in practice we found that this tray was badly placed.

From the driving seat we were surprised to find that we had a most re-

CAR LIFE'S test driver hasn't had one too many for the road; he's demonstrating amount of space in the Patrician's luggage compartment. Although a Packard owner probably wouldn't have to, our driver says he's slept in smaller quarters.

markable field of vision, bearing in mind that this is a big car. It is not often we have the opportunity to praise a driving position, but this is one of the best. The right hand fender is clearly visible and after a short time of driving one loses the sense of frontal expanse. The front seat is adjustable for upward and lateral movement, but (and once again we came up against this bench seat), if the seat is adjusted for the short-legged driver the long-legged passenger objects because he, or she, cannot stretch out his, or her legs. The bench seat was a boon to the American car as long as cars were constructed with plenty of room to the fore, but nowadays with the reduction of height of the engine compartment and a general backward movement of the power plant and accessories the long-legged passenger is in trouble. Mr. Packard, may we please be offered individual bucket seats; some of us are short-legged drivers with long-legged girl friends!

We found that the steering wheel was well placed and that pedals of the accelerator and brake were in a position that might well be copied by all other manufacturers. For the first time this year we found ourselves braking a car with automatic transmission without any exaggerated lifting of the right leg. The position of the brake in relation to the accelerator is perfect.

The Patrician has, as standard equipment, the dual range Ultramatic transmission, a system that takes a lot of work out of driving but at the same time leaves the driver a sense of security. The dual range, signified by two small triangles on the shift selector panel, gives a choice for fast open highway driving or tight town driving where rapid acceleration is needed. It is simple after driving through a town to move the lever over to the left and obtain the right ratios for continued country travel.

We did not feel it necessary to test this car for speed; we already knew it could do better than 100 mph., far more than the ordinary driver is ever going to demand, and the amount of torque was obvious from the moment we pulled away from the first red light we encountered. Frankly, performance leaves nothing to be desired.

The ride needs comment, for it is on this subject that the Packard people have hung their reputation this year. This is a big and luxurious car and one automatically expects an ultra-soft and easy ride, but with the Patrician such is not the case. The ride is soft, but

CONTINUED ON PAGE 153

Commendable feature is courtesy light in leading edge of rear fender bulge.

Bullet-like protrusions on front bumper don't appeal to CAR LIFE'S tester.

Traffic indicator, back-up and rear light assembly is well-proportioned.

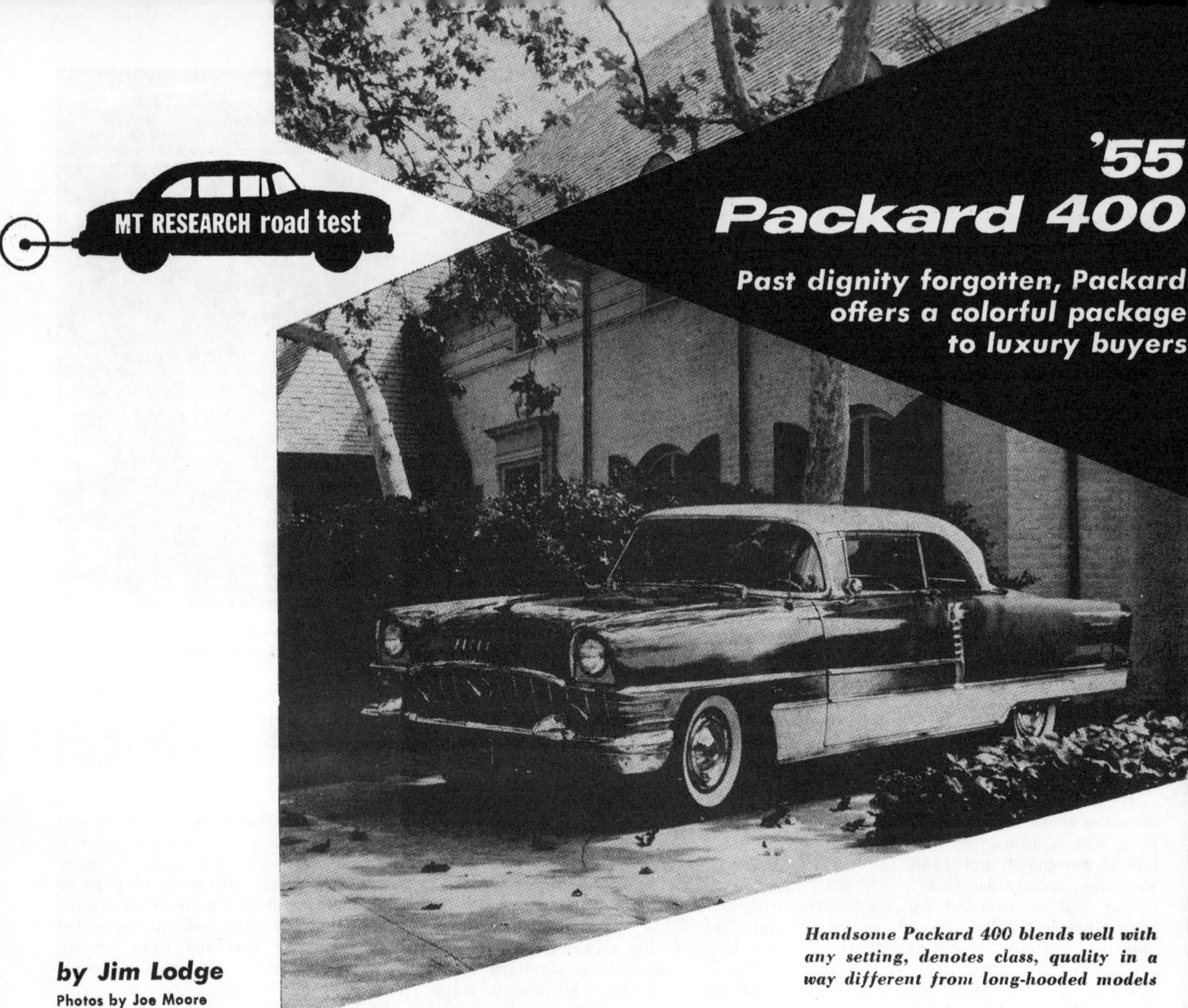

'55 Packard 400

Past dignity forgotten, Packard offers a colorful package to luxury buyers

Handsome Packard 400 blends well with any setting, denotes class, quality in a way different from long-hooded models

by Jim Lodge

Photos by Joe Moore

DISCUSSING PACKARD as a prestige car, we're often inclined to dismiss the newness of the '55 and think only of this top model in the light of Dietrich 12s. The '55 Packard is something really different in the high-price class, so let's forget the cormorants perched atop long, high hoods, and take a look at the things MT learned about this new Packard.

Test car: Packard 400 hardtop, Ultramatic (standard equipment), optional power steering, power brakes, pushbutton windows and seat, radio, heater.

Engine: Differs from 245-hp Clipper Custom engine described in June MT only in exhaust system. Packard's system, optional on Clipper Custom, is true dual system (no crossover pipe). Uses same 4-barrel Rochester carburetor, Clipper's hydraulic valve setup, 8.5 to 1 compression ratio for 260 horsepower.

Other options: All conceivable extras, including air conditioning. Engine option limited to buying another model—superb "limited edition" Caribbean convertible with 275 horsepower.

While smaller than '54's 359-cubic-inch straight 8 in displacement, lighter by 54 pounds (64 counting radiators), and 8 inches shorter, 352-cubic-inch short-stroke V8 has 22 per cent more horsepower, 7 per cent greater torque, 25 per cent more valve head area, 29 per cent decrease in friction-horsepower loss. According to Packard, this V8 is ". . . potentially capable of being enlarged beyond the displacement obtainable with any other 1955 automotive engine, indicating extremely conservative design in anticipation of possible future requirements for still greater power and torque."

WHAT THE CAR IS LIKE TO DRIVE

Driving position: As comfortable as any car tested this year. Except for pulled-on emergency brake being in way when getting in or out, plenty of room to move around. Wheel position good, slightly higher than in Clipper due to lower seat. Controls handy, well marked, easy to use with no need to stretch.

Vision: Top-notch forward vision over low hood; high fenderline. No windshield distortion thru normal line-of-sight area. If possible, dictate to dealer proper positioning of outside mirror if you're buying a Packard (or any other car). We've seen many different installations of Packard's glamorous side mirrors, some very good, some extra-bad.

Ease of handling: As flexible as smaller (by 3½ inches overall) Clipper in town, on curving roads, on the open highway. Good all-around vision helps here, as does Packard's linkage-type power steering (just over 3¾ turns lock to lock), which maintains nearly constant feel, or resistance.

Acceleration: Good in all ranges, won't give you that "sitting duck" feeling out in the passing lane. Ultramatic's 2-position DRIVE setup offers smoothness or acceleration—but rarely both at low speeds. In lower of 2 ranges (right-hand dot on quadrant), you'll gain 1½ seconds in standing ¼-mile, 1½-mph boost in speed crossing the line. To 60, you'll have 3-second advantage. Having kickdown to low gear in this range moves you from 10 to 30 mph 1½ seconds faster than in smoother DRIVE range, which has kickdown only to torque converter from direct-drive hookup.

Braking: Preliminary tests showed braking ability equal to lighter (by 440 pounds) Clipper Custom. Packard's brakes reluctant to lock at instant pedal was hit —a nice feature when, as in this case, car comes to rapid, non-skid halt. Packard has larger drums, larger lining segments than Clipper series.

Roadability: Surprisingly good; often felt like true stiffly sprung car, never slipshod during MT's tests. More rear-wheel hop over washboard roads than Clipper Custom. Fine high-speed car. Stable, sensitive to touch on steering wheel at cruising speeds, no wind wander.

Ride: Don't let that mass of bars and links on the chassis displayed at your dealer's showroom be misconstrued as rugged in ride as well as construction. It's solid all right, but those "trapeze bars" can float you thru severest of dips with greatest of ease.

Initial lunge common to all cars coming out of dip or over bump is followed by eerie sensation of not coming back to earth with jarring rebound. Packard "hangs up" (actually, rear wheels brace themselves downward after front has lifted), comes down softly, with no oscillation. Smooth, strange, refreshing reaction unique with Packard, T-bar Clippers.

WHAT THE CAR IS LIKE TO LIVE WITH

Riding in the front seat: Roomy, comfortable seats, plenty of legroom. Dashboard deep, wide, handsome, but can be uncomfortably near knees with seat in forward position.

Riding in the rear seat: Nothing drab here; luxurious hardtop test car quite spacious for 2-door model, denoted quality, livability. (Figures in General Specification table are for 4-door sedan.) In back, more than in front, you realize advantage of level ride, for effect is greater when you're not looking for bumps.

ECONOMY AND EASE OF MAINTENANCE

Fuel economy: Ultramatic can serve you well if you choose correct axle option for your needs. Choices are 3.07, 3.23, 3.54. Test car's 3.23 fared well, considering powerhouse up front. Higher 3.07 (lower-ratio) gear should do even better, won't cause lugging feeling with largest-displacement '55 V8 backing it up.

Is the car well put together? We can answer that question with some authority. Test car's noticeable file marks around headlight, tail light "eyelids," and around door posts led to survey of many other Packards at showrooms, parked along street. Others were well finished, had better paint jobs, indicating ours was early production model, or just poorly detailed. Interiors of all cars checked looked good.

How did it hold up? Everything worked right, felt, looked as if it would hold together for a long time to come. Good shape at end of trying test.

Servicing: Falls about mid-range in accessibility ratings of '55 V8s. Service station attendants said only, "Which one's crankcase and which one's transmission dipstick?" (Packard's 2 dipsticks fairly close together.) Engine's design features, including engineered compensation for carbon buildup problems and longer-range problems like piston slap, cylinder scoring, indicate long engine life.

GENERAL SPECIFICATIONS

ENGINE: Ohv V8. Bore 4.0 in. Stroke 3.5 in. Stroke/bore ratio 0.875. Compression ratio 8.5:1. Displacement 352 cu. in. Advertised bhp 260 @ 4600 rpm. Bhp per cu. in. 0.74. Piston travel @ max. bhp 2683 ft. per min. Max. bmep 152.1 psi. Max. torque 355 lbs.-ft. @ 2400-2800 rpm.

DRIVE SYSTEM: AUTOMATIC transmission is Ultramatic, 4-element torque converter with planetary gears and direct drive above 15-55 mph, depending on throttle position. RATIOS: Drive, torque converter only and 1.00 (direct drive) or, at separate quadrant position, 1.82 x converter ratio, torque converter only and 1.00. Low, 1.82 x converter ratio. Reverse 1.63 x converter ratio. Maximum, converter ratio at stall 2.9. Other transmissions not available.

REAR-AXLE RATIOS: Ultramatic, 3.54 standard, 3.07, 3.28 optional.

DIMENSIONS: Wheelbase 127 in. Tread 60 in. front, 60.9 in. rear. Wheelbase/tread ratio 2.10:1. Overall width 78 in. Overall length 218.5 in. Overall height 62.3 in. Turning diameter 45 ft. (43 with power steering). Turns lock to lock 4¾ (3⅞ with power steering). Test car weight 4660 lbs. Test car weight/bhp ratio 17.9:1. Weight distribution 54% front, 46% rear. Tire size 8.00 x 15.

PRICES: Patrician 4-door sedan $4040, 400 hardtop $4080, Caribbean convertible $5932.

ACCESSORIES: Radios $109, $132, heater $128, power steering $115, power brakes $40, power seat $70, power windows $108, air conditioning $652.

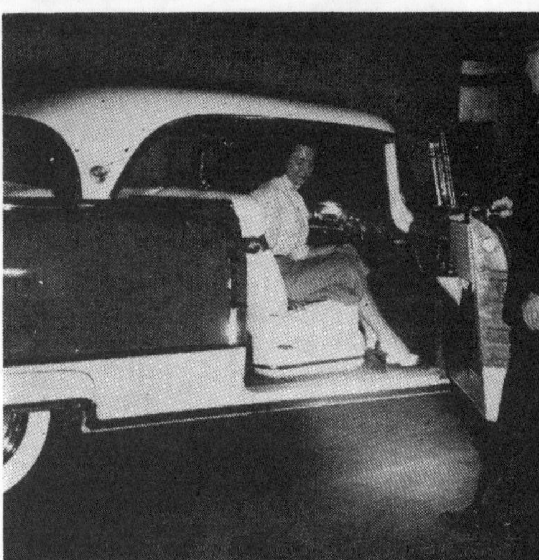

Side-mounted courtesy light proves really worthwhile, stays on (with less glare) as "running light" with headlights on

TEST CAR AT A GLANCE

'55 Packard 400 with Ultramatic

REAR-WHEEL HORSEPOWER
(Determined on Palmini Engineering's Clayton chassis dynamometer. All tests are made under full load, which is similar to climbing a hill at full throttle. Observed hp figures not corrected to standard atmospheric conditions.)

103 road hp @ 2000 rpm	
147 road hp @ 2500 rpm	
Max. 158 road hp @ 3200 rpm	

TOP SPEED
(In miles per hour over surveyed ¼-mile.)

Fastest 1-way run	111.0
Slowest 1-way run	109.3
Average of 4 runs	110.1

ACCELERATION
(In seconds; checked with 5th wheel and electric speedometer.)

Standing start ¼-mile (76.3 mph)	18.6
0-30 mph	3.9
0-60 mph	11.4
10-30 mph	3.0
30-50 mph	4.5
50-80 mph	13.3

SPEEDOMETER ERROR
(Checked with 5th wheel and electric speedometer.)

Car speedometer read 33	@ true 30 mph
50	@ true 45 mph
68	@ true 60 mph
82	@ true 75 mph
120	@ top speed

FUEL CONSUMPTION
(In miles per gallon; checked with fuel flowmeter, 5th wheel, and electric speedometer. Mobilgas Special used.)

Steady 30 mph	18.4
Steady 45 mph	16.3
Steady 60 mph	14.6
Steady 75 mph	12.5
Stop-and-go driving over measured course	11.3
Tank average for 688 miles	10.5

STOPPING DISTANCE
(To the nearest foot; checked with electrically actuated detonator.)

30 mph	44
45 mph	89
60 mph	151

Safety Rating
(Percentage)

Packard Patrician 72

Four-Door Sedan

THE PATRICIAN has the same engine as the Clipper, but is slightly more tuned. This engine has already been publicly proved reliable by taking a Patrician 25,000 miles at an average speed of 104.7 mph.

Had they possessed a slightly better steering mechanism and a more positive response to the wheel, the Packard products might have had the edge on the Lincoln. Both Packards investigated had a high quality of construction.

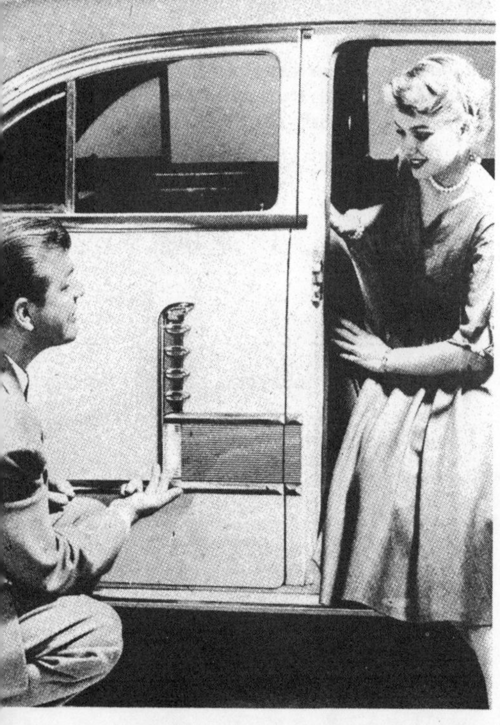

Safety Rating
(Percentage)

Packard Clipper Custom 72

Four-Door Sedan

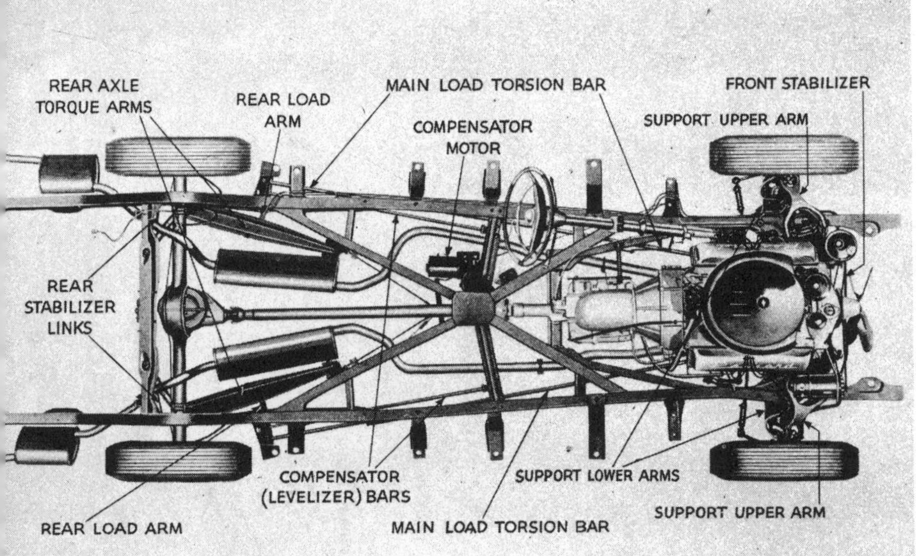

THE PACKARD CLIPPER CUSTOM incorporates the new torsion bar suspension, which rates the greatest safety factor in any of today's U. S. automobiles. The weight distribution of the car is excellent, compensation even being made for the shifting of weight. It will be noted that the Clipper and Patrician run very close to the Lincoln for the top safety honors.

Packard uses torsion bar suspension in place of the old coil and leaf springs.

Packard's Big Engine Spurs New Power Race

374-cubic-inch job is out in front with a mighty 310 hp. You control it with automatic push buttons on a keyboard.

By EDWARD D. FALES JR.

YOU are about to drive the new Packard Patrician around the 2½-mile test track at Utica, Mich. You're a little excited because this isn't just billed as a 290-310 hp. engine: it's the *biggest* U.S. production-car engine (374 cubic inches). And you're going to control it by playing Packard's new "driver's piano."

This is a little console of six push buttons sticking out from the steering post and nerved electrically to the transmission system. Push D and you work up through a two-stage torque converter into direct drive. Push H and you have plush torque conversion throughout—from zero up.

They hand you the '56 Patrician—a slick piece of class. Nothing gaudy. It's got a long-low-wide look. The tail beacons flare like northern lights when you toe the wider '56 brake pedal.

There are three men with you in this four-door family packet on a 127-inch wheelbase. You stop at the track gate while three other '56 Packard products go by at 100 m.p.h.: first a "400" hardtop convertible, then the '56 Clipper (the medium-price "hot car" with a 270-hp. V-8), and finally up around 115 comes the $6,200 Caribbean.

Now the track's clear. You punch D on the piano and gun the engine. A servo-motor shifts you into drive. You plan to ease into the first turn at 60-65. But, whoa! What are you doing at 90?

Now you see why Packard's bright young men are grinning over their planning boards this year. They claim:

- *Fastest getaway* (still to be proved).
- *Horsepower* in the highest brackets (290 plus, and the Packard Caribbean is billed at 310).
- *Torque* that soars to a potent 405 foot-pounds in the Caribbean, Patrician and "400."
- *Highest compression ratio*—10 to 1.
- *Biggest cylinders*—4⅛-inch bore (up from four inches in 1955) and a shorter, 3½-inch stroke.
- A new "self-locking" differential that automatically throws torque to the slow wheel when one wheel spins madly. Re-

THAT HOOD HIDES what Packard calls the biggest engine in the industry. The four-door Patrician's lights have longer eaves. Grille and ornament are new; bombs are farther apart for that wide, low look.

THIS MAN-SIZED V-8 has been given the job. Outwardly it looks much the same as the '55, but inwardly it's got bigger cylinders, elliptical firing chambers, a shorter stroke and longer spark plugs. The valves are quieter.

COMING ROUND A HARD TURN in soft, deep ruts, the author let the front wheels get untracked, got ready to wrestle back to the road but found no loss of balance or control.

sult: you now get 50-50 drive instead of 90-10 when one wheel is in the snow.

With all this scat, why didn't you *know* you were taking off? Here, frankly, is something that pains the engineers. They want you to get a *jolt* when you gun it.

But this car gets away like an arrow from a bow. In the 50-75 passing range, where acceleration counts most, it just lifts its tail and goes. You're arrow level.

This is due to the 26 feet of torsion bars that Packard put in for 1955 and has now made available all through the line.

If you use the new 2.87 rear axle, you'll get overdrive economy and still have a terrific kickdown and a torque curve that has backbone right up to 80.

What a test shows. You've been scatting around this track for an hour. And you've noted: no tire squeal on sharp turns . . . no wandering . . . a rear mirror that (like some others) gives you a hopelessly inadequate 300-foot view . . . a steering handgrip that's *really* comfortable.

With three passengers, 100 m.p.h. is enough for you—though a "400" with a test pilot at the wheel scoots past you on the high wall with three gents aboard.

"She's doing 105 and only loafing," says a test driver in your car.

And in that remark lies the real '56 Packard story.

A while back, shirt-sleeved Packard brain-trusters found themselves on a spot.

Other designers were trimming weight. Engines would be small but oh so strong. They'd go right up to 250 hp.

Then and there, the engineers made up their minds:

- The hp. race wouldn't stop at 250.
- It would take BIG engines to stand the gaff.
- Then they made a third decision: "We'll make block and crank big so that when the time comes, we'll be ready."

Buzzing curves at 95 you realize the time is here and the big block and crank are taking it in stride. There's hardly a sound. You're chatting with the boys in the back seat. The dial goes on up to 120. But what do you want with two miles a minute? You hold her down and get that "just loafing" feel.

How did they get the extra Wheaties into the same engine that in 1955 was rated 260 hp. with 352 displacement?

The big block, says Packard, lets the bore go up from 4 to 4⅛-inches and still leaves room for plenty of water. (It's this, Packard says, that's kept it from having a single cracked V-8 block.)

The new engine keeps the same rods, cylinder heads, bearings and four-barrel carburetor. Crank's a little huskier but basically the same. Only inside the block do changes show, and in the rings and carb. Pistons are sturdier, valve stems wider (⅜ inch). Valves lift .024 inch higher. Manifold passages are wide and husky, and valves are two inches.

Packard says it gets away with 10-to-1 compression by going to an elliptical fire chamber and a "long reach spark." Business end of each plug is up on a pedestal where it gets a real scouring.

Packard also sent its four-barrel carb into surgery. A couple years ago drivers who didn't start in low beefed about a "flat spot." Even though they mashed their feet right down into the carburetor, they strangled their starts. To fix this asthma, the venturis have been changed. And a nerve from the throttle now refuses to let the secondary throttle open and spoil everything until your engine has enough speed to accept it! END

FOUR-WAY TOGGLE SWITCH replaces seat-control buttons. Just flip the lever the way you want the seat to go.

TOUGHER, THICKER new crash pad tops a rich gold dash panel. Glove box has a new lip to keep things from tumbling out.

FLICK OF THE WRIST changes Caribbean's "sofa" from daytime leather to plush brocade fabric for evening elegance.

Elegance and push-button ease mark new Packard line

"TURN THE MEDALLION" latch is easy to turn when you want to snap the trunk lid open. It's a new feature in '56.

HEADLIGHTS are sinking in deeper and deeper. Eaves or hoods have been extended another five inches forward in '56.

SWEEP-SECOND HAND on the electric clock serves no practical purpose beyond helping time your starts and passes.

$6,200 two-masted Caribbean has even Detroit whistling

'56 CARIBBEAN: This is the luxury car in which the V-8 breaks through the 300-hp. barrier with 10 to spare stashed under its gleaming bonnet. There are twin radio masts aft. Besides the convertible shown, there'll be a hardtop. New automatic push-button drive control will be standard.

Clipper will be sold as a separate line, not as a Packard

352-CUBIC-INCH V-8 powers the "hot" Clipper line, which is to Packard what Oldsmobile is to GM. Test pilots say Clipper's top speed this year is up 10 m.p.h. to 116. Frame has been beefed up like Packard's '55. Result: there are fewer body noises. Fishmouth tail lights are new.

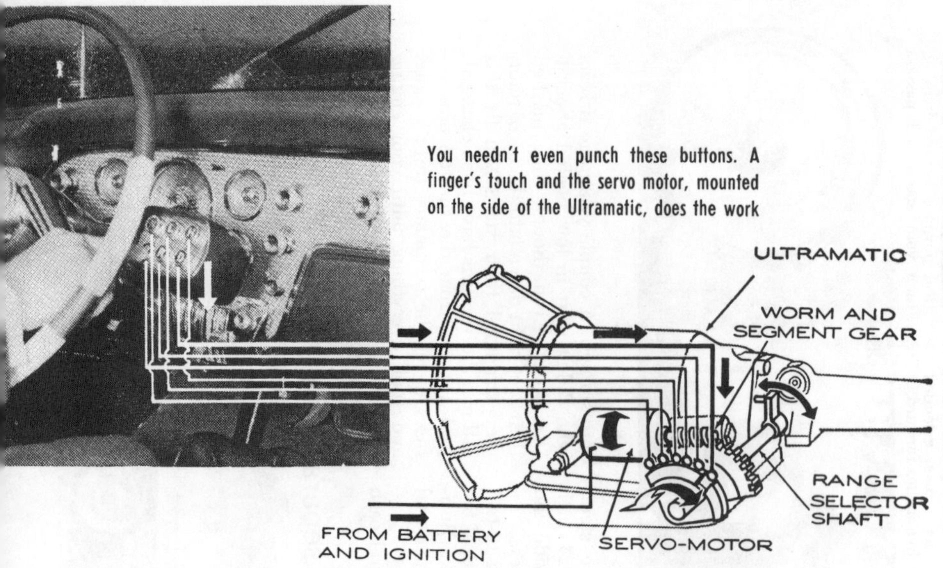

You needn't even punch these buttons. A finger's touch and the servo motor, mounted on the side of the Ultramatic, does the work

New this year is a Caribbean hardtop, styled like the convertible with twin rear antennas

New grille and headlights repeat wraparound's curve. This is the Patrician, largest 4-door

PACKARD and

PACKARD was 55 years old on Oct. 2, 1955. Executives of the current, rejuvenated company are the 1st to admit that all has not been placid down thru the years. This was especially true during the late '30s and early '40s when Packard lost its grip on the high-price field. Once lost, one's reputation takes a long time to re-establish in *any* field, but the new Nance management has convinced the public that the company now produces a truly fine car, even tho they may not sell in quantities comparable with Cadillac.

A separate car from the Packard is the new '56 Clipper, which will be registered as such from here on in. This is more than just a legal technicality; the name Packard appears nowhere on the car. The move pretty much justifies Nance's claim that Studebaker-Packard is the country's 4th largest producer of a *full line* of cars. Between the Champion and the Caribbean, every price class is bracketed.

Biggest mechanical change is the new electrically operated pushbutton Ultramatic transmission. It is standard on the Caribbean, optional on Clippers and Packards. Unlike Chrysler's version, which is actuated by cable controls, the pushbuttons on this one signal a servo motor located on the side of the transmission. Incidentally, the transmission itself is 95 pounds lighter than before, due to extensive use of aluminum castings. It worked real fine when Walt Woron and I drove the car at the Packard Proving Grounds, but let him tell it in his own words:

The transmission controls are on an arm extending from the steering column on the right-hand side. It has 6 buttons in sequence; along the top N, L, and H, along the bottom P, R, and D. You can reach any one of these without even taking your hands off the steering wheel, around the wheel rim or thru it over the spoke. The latter method seems most convenient.

The controls are well thought out, safety-wise. I deliberately switched from DRIVE to PARK at about 70 mph.

Price leader, but blend-of-old-and-new style leader as well, Clipper Deluxe 4-door shows off huge and jetlike yet pleasing lights-bumper combination

Clipper Super's Panama hardtop looks much longer with 2nd-color sash around midriff, has suitably better performance to match its deftly remodeled looks

There was a loud racheting noise emanating from somewhere in the transmission, but the engineer riding with me said that it was only a built-in warning. The transmission was not being damaged, and shifted like a "pre-selector" to PARK as soon as I came to a standstill. Much the same happens if you push REVERSE while moving forward at any speed above a walking pace. There is no warning noise, but the car won't shift until you have slowed down to approximately 5 mph.

It takes about one second for the electric motor to go from PARK to REVERSE, which are at opposite ends of the sector in the actuator. The unit is, of course, wired so that you can start the car only when in PARK or NEUTRAL, and the buttons will not work at all with the ignition off. Your youngster can punch the buttons all he wants should the car be standing unattended in the driveway, but it will stay in PARK or whatever gear you may have left it in.

Surprisingly enough, there is no safety feature to prevent an inadvertent switch to LOW while driving at high speeds. We questioned Packard engineers on this and they point out that altho you will experience pretty violent deceleration if, say, you do this at 80 mph, no damage will be done to the transmission, and this capability makes an execellent extra emergency brake. NEUTRAL, on the other hand, is safetied because Ultramatic (like most other automatics) can be seriously harmed by prolonged coasting.

An electric power failure could pose a problem on a Packard or Clipper equipped with the new controls. Whatever gear it is in should this happen, you stay in. The only solution would be to call a service truck and attach a booster battery. If the unit itself fails, as with a blown fuse, it must be replaced on the spot or the car towed rear wheels up to the nearest Packard garage.

I found the instrument panel basically unchanged except that the gauges now have gold numerals, letters, and indicators on a silver background. A sweep-second clock is standard on all Packards and most Clippers. The panel is very rich looking but not the most legible in the industry.

A slightly refined torsion bar suspension system is standard on all Packards as well as Super and Custom Clippers, and altho not specified, we presume it is optional on the Clipper Deluxe. The front and rear torque arm links have been lowered, introducing a tendency toward understeer new for this system. Steering is considerably faster in all models, the number of turns from lock to lock being decreased from 4.2 to 3.8. The column has a flexible coupling to dampen road shock, but should this diaphragm arrangement be damaged, a metal-to-metal contact takes over to prevent loss of control.

A much publicized option for Packards will be a non-slip (power-dividing) differential. Many varieties of these have been on the accessory market, but this one was developed by Packard in conjunction with their gear supplier. For a detailed report on a similar differential (Hi-Tork) see the August MT. *Continued*

Unsnap your Caribbean's tough leather seats, turn them over, and you have a party-going car with seats of brocade to impress anyone at all

CLIPPER

At the very top of the line is the impressive Caribbean convertible, with twin airscoops atop its clean hood. Rear reflectors are Packard hexagons

continued from page 29

'56 Packard and Clipper

Altho I didn't get a chance to drive a Packard equipped with one of these new differentials, I have had experience with Don MacDonald's car, which has a similar setup. A unit like this is admittedly non-essential (except, perhaps, for rural mail carriers), but at least once a year most of us get stuck in mud or snow, and that is where it pays off. In normal driving, it adds that little extra in satisfactory performance which makes it more than worth its additional cost (neighborhood of $100).

Packard demonstrated this dramatically on their proving ground by slipping a pan of ice under the right rear wheel of a Caribbean not equipped with the new differential. A man stood behind it holding onto a rope attached to the car. The driver got nowhere, despite the whine of the slipping right rear wheel. Then this Caribbean was replaced by another equipped with the new differential. The pan of ice was put in place, the car was hooked chain-gang fashion to 5 other Packards (with engines off), and the driver easily towed the whole entourage off the cake of ice and down the road.

Good transmission of power is coupled to plenty of it under the hood thruout the whole Packard and Clipper line for '56. Deluxe and Super Clippers offer 240 horsepower (at 4600 rpm) and 350 pounds-feet torque (2800 rpm), while the Custom ups this to 275 and 380, respectively, at the same rpms. Packard tops the industry with 290 horsepower and, more important, 405 pounds-feet of torque available within the vital passing speed range. If you want a powerpack on top of this, you can have it; Caribbeans come equipped with a dual (4-barrel) carburetored V8 claiming 310 horsepower, a convenient 5 above Cadillac's current peak. Much of this increase can be credited to a 10 to 1 compression, an all-time publicly available high.

About the only change in body models is the addition to the Caribbean line of a 2-door hardtop, complete with a Derham-like fabric-covered steel top. Neither Packard nor Clipper offers a 4-door hardtop as yet, a fact which will probably adversely affect some sales but can't economically be remedied until 1957's new tooling.

Clippers offer you a choice of 3-speed, overdrive, or Ultramatic transmissions, whereas Packard uses the automatic as standard equipment. Every power assist in the book can be had at extra cost, except on the Caribbeans where everything except air-conditioning is standard. It would seem as tho Packard and its newly divorced mate, Clipper, are out to solidify their substantial 1955 inroads into Cadillac's previously private bailiwick. One can't help but applaud such an endeavor.

—Don MacDonald

the 1956 packard

HIGHLIGHTS: 374 cubic inches with 310 hp top, pushbutton gear selector, non-slip differential, safety features, reversible seats, double kick-down transmission with aluminum housing

IN A DETERMINED effort to regain some of its past share of the automotive market Packard last year introduced a line of cars featuring new engines, much-revised styling and the advanced torsion bar suspension system. It just takes a look and a ride to prove there will be no coasting in 1956. Major engineering innovations, bigger and more powerful engines, important changes and improvements in the transmission and numerous detail styling changes have been introduced in new models.

In addition, greater distinction is being made between Packards and Clippers—they're now two separate lines and styling differences are more emphatic than in the past—in order to establish the Packard line as a group of true luxury automobiles.

Big and solid in appearance, the '56 Packards feel powerful, yet smooth and comfortable. A ride around the company's 2½-mile test track proved that. The car in which we rode was a Packard 400 hardtop.

It cruised effortlessly at 70 and 80, just loafing. It went from there on up to 110 and 115 on the speedometer with no trouble and held that pace with no trace of fuss or bother. This silky-smooth power is due, of course, to Packard's having introduced the biggest, most powerful engines in the industry in its 1956 line. All the new Packard engines have a displacement of 374 cubic inches! Engines offered in Caribbean models are rated at 310 horsepower and those for the Patrician and 400 models are rated at 290. Torque of both is 405 foot pounds at 2800 rpm and each have a 10 to 1 compression ratio.

Packard has not aimed at higher top speeds, however. Its engineers report that the emphasis was on economy and improving low and mid-range acceleration for better passing ability. They claim they have increased fuel economy up to 20 per cent over previous models, despite the fact that engines are bigger. They point out that axle ratios can be lowered (numerically) due to high torque. (Ratios as high as 2.87 are available this year with Ultramatic transmissions.) This improves economy, extends engine life.

Handling, excellent in 1955, has been improved with no sacrifice in comfort. The torsion bar suspension has been changed slightly to increase stability. The two-piece rear roll bar has been lowered about two inches and the pivot point of the rear torque arms has been lowered about an inch.

In addition, weight distribution has been improved; it's 52 per cent front, 48

Dual radio aerials on some top luxury models are acceptance of an idea which long has been custom car feature.

Deeper hooded headlights and rearrangement of grille-bumper layout alter front. Note lowered bumper section.

Caribbean hardtop takes a banked turn at speed. As companion to Caribbean convertible, car is new to Packard line in '56.

per cent rear. One of the most important factors here was use of aluminum in several key applications.

The entire automatic transmission housing is made of aluminum, for example. This cut about 95 pounds off this unit, making it the lightest automatic transmission in this country by 20 lbs.

Two of the innovations for which Packard is becoming noted to be introduced this year are the push-button transmission control (see page 14) and non-slip differential. The new "locking" or power-dividing differential transmits extra power to the rear wheels in the proportion it's needed, sending more to the wheel which is getting the most traction. This not only makes it a snap to pull out of mud or snow when cars with conventional differentials are merely spinning their wheels, but improves cornering greatly. For details, see Special Reports.

Packard interiors are truly lush, in keeping with the luxury car theme. Fine fabrics and carpeting are used in all models. The Caribbean's reversible seats are an interesting innovation.

The instrument panel, changed only slightly from last year, seems to be well set up. The speedometer dial, for example, is large enough so that numbers have been spaced well apart, making it easy to read. Seating position is comfortable

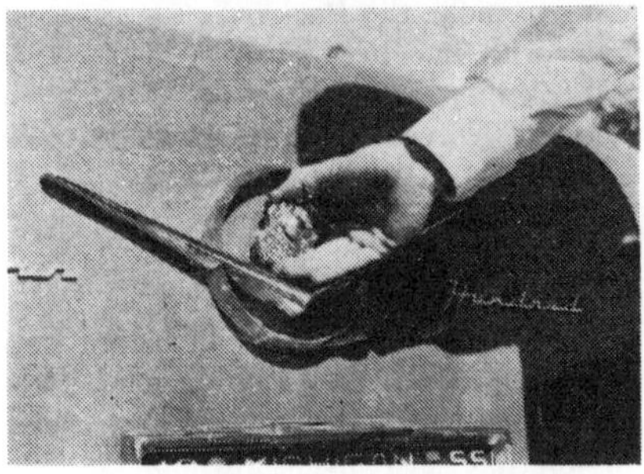

Trunk of 400 is opened by turning emblem in center of deck lid (above), although snow and ice might complicate matters. Tail (below) is more massive.

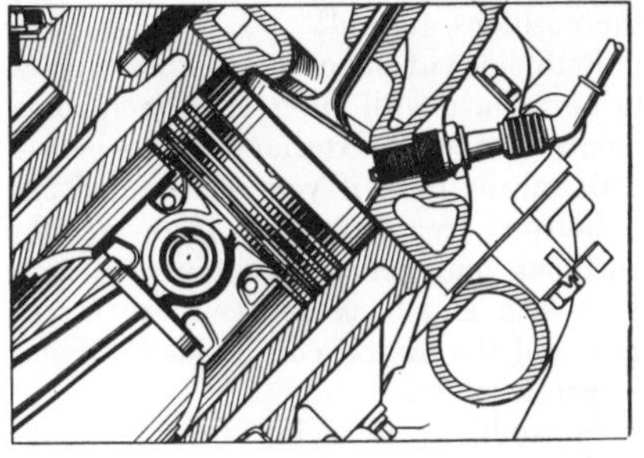

Packard's V-8 has 10-to-1 compression (above) with long-reach plugs for highest ratio out of Detroit. Below is overall view of the whopper that has 4⅛ bore.

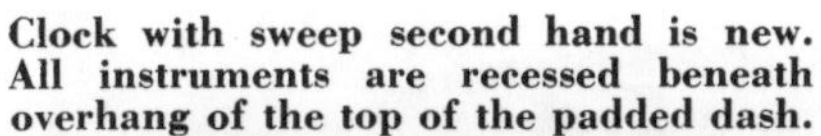

Clock with sweep second hand is new. All instruments are recessed beneath overhang of the top of the padded dash.

Seat cushions on the Caribbeans are both reversible and removable, with zippers for separating from foam rubber.

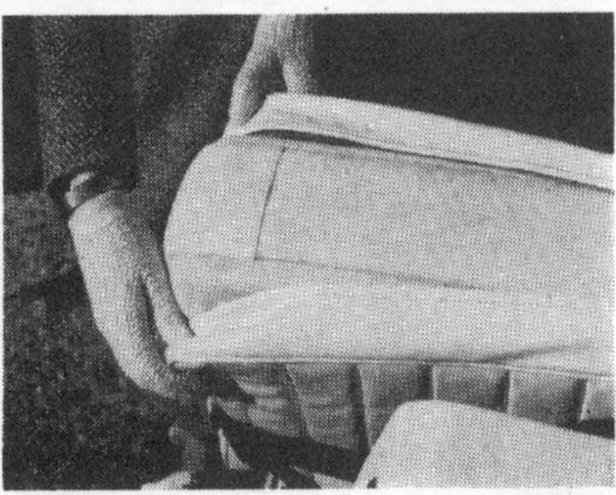

Detroit Editor Ken Fermoyle takes notes on Packard's huge engine of 374 inches. In some versions it's rated at 310 hp!

for both driver and passengers. Even in air conditioned Packards which have the evaporator assembly mounted in the passenger compartment, there is no serious loss of legroom for the right front seat passenger. The evaporator would make it uncomfortable for the middle passenger if three were riding in the front seat for any great distance.

Safety features include padded instrument panels, safety door latches, optional safety belts and a system whereby the driver can lock all doors by pressing a push-button.

A fresh, new interior styling feature has been originated by Packard for its 1956 Caribbean models. By using reversible foam rubber cushions with different upholstery on each side, Packard has made it possible to change the interior appearance of the new Caribbeans simply by unfastening a few snaps and turning the cushions around!

Both sides of the cushions are designed to harmonize with other interior appointments and with exterior color schemes. This means that, if you get tired of one upholstery treatment you can reverse the cushions and get an entirely new look. Both seat and back cushions are reversible and the switch can be made in just a couple of minutes.

In addition to being reversible, the cushions have zippers so the upholstery can be removed from the foam rubber cores for easy cleaning.

The idea is a simple one, yet extremely practical. It's not hard to foresee this idea setting a new trend in automotive interiors.

It's almost certain that the idea will be a hit with the ladies. They would be able to select the side of the cushion which looks best with the outfit they happen to be wearing at the moment.

It looks very much like Packard has stolen a march on its competitors as far as interior styling is concerned. It will be interesting to see if other manufacturers pick up the idea in the future.

Packard's Ultramatic transmission has been improved in several ways other than the aluminum housing, which lightens it and gives better cooling. It is the only transmission with double "kick-down." By pressing the accelerator half-way down you drop into the next lower ratio; flooring it puts you into a still lower gear. This gives a driver more positive control over his shift points, helps him use his acceleration as he needs it.

The power steering system has been redesigned to cut steering effort about 10 per cent, at the same time making steering faster by cutting number of turns needed lock to lock.

Thus, while the new Packards don't look tremendously different at first glance, you can see that this is deceiving. Packard isn't relaxing its efforts to win back its former glory. •

the 1956 clipper

HIGHLIGHTS: becomes a separate make, 275 hp top, new frame, restyled front end, pushbutton gear selector, transmission with aluminum housing and double kickdown

CLIPPERS are going to have to stand on their own four wheels from now on. In line with President James Nance's plans to make the Packard name synonymous with fine luxury cars, the Packard and Clipper lines have now been completely divorced. Nowhere on the new Clippers for 1956 does the name "Packard" appear.

More than ever before, however, the Clipper is capable of carrying on by itself in the medium and upper-medium price field. Noticeable styling changes, a big engine with lots of torque and power, torsion bar suspension thruout the line and a general beefing up of the whole car to increase quality and durability put the Clippers in an excellent position to strike out on their own with the 1956 models.

Displacement of all Clipper engines is now 352 cubic inches. Deluxe and Super models are rated at 240 horsepower and deliver 350 foot pounds of torque at 2800 rpm. They use two-barrel carburetors. Custom Clippers, equipped with four-barrel carburetors, are rated at 275 horsepower and 380 foot pounds of torque at 2800 rpm. All Clipper engines have 9.5 to 1 compression ratios.

Torsion bar suspension contributes to a ride that is as comfortable and stable as offered by any of its competition—and that can't be touched by most. Clippers have benefitted by detail refinements to this suspension system which have resulted in improved handling and stability over 1955 models. A new, heavier gage frame also helps in this respect by increasing torsional rigidity. The redesigned frame has also reduced the road noise level.

Styling changes have obviously been made with the idea of giving Clippers a distinct identity, an appearance that's all their own and is as different as possible from Packards. Most of the changes for 1956 have been concentrated at the front and rear of the cars. Headlights are more

Clipper Custom four-door. Note how the body molding treatment lends itself to the two-tone paint job. This is the year that the car emerges as a distinct make and restyling has been aimed at making it look as different as possible from Packard.

deeply hooded. The grille is now made up of a series of finely textured, horizontal chrome strips which wrap right around the front fenders to the front wheel wells. The "Dagmars" or bullet-shaped bumper guards have been moved outboard to a point directly under the headlights to give an illusion of greater width.

At the rear, the most obvious change is the notched, vee-like rear fender treatment. Deck lid height has been raised slightly by means of a slight hump at the rear of the lid—this is true of Packards, too—to increase trunk area.

Side body moldings have been redesigned also. On Custom and Super models bright metal trim creates a wide horizontal swath from front to rear which lends itself very nicely to two-tone color treatment. More sparing use of chrome is made on the lower-priced Deluxe series.

Comparison rides in the new Packards and Clippers won't turn up any noticeable difference to the casual observer. Although the Clippers at 122 inches are five inches shorter in wheelbase than Packards, there isn't much to choose between the two cars as far as a comfortable ride is concerned. The small margin the Packard holds in this department will be cancelled out for many by the slightly better agility and cornering prowess the shorter wheelbase gives the Clippers. Actually, however, it will take a knowing judge to detect much difference in either area.

The push-button gear selector introduced for Packards are also available as optional equipment on Clippers. The improved Ultramatic, lightened by use of an aluminum housing and featuring the double kick-down gear system, is used on Clippers too.

Interiors in the Custom and Super Clippers are only slightly less plush than those in the Packards. A wide choice of upholstery and trim combinations is being offered buyers. Seating position for both driver and passengers is very good with all controls readily available to the driver. The center glove compartment is handy and addition of a small map pocket and embossed circles in which cups or glasses can be placed on the drop-down compartment door increases its utility.

President Nance remarked to a group of newsmen before the new cars were introduced that his company is trying to make the Clipper a quality car that offers a little more than other cars in its field.

Market research, he added, has indicated there is a good segment of customers in this field who want a car that meets these standards, one that has some individualistic appeal. This is the group Clippers are aimed at. And, judging from 1956 efforts, they are on target. These cars have a lot to recommend them. •

Rear end of Clippers has been changed by deeply notched tail and integral bumper. General shape is something like '55, but lights have different position.

Bumper guards have been moved outboard to lend wider look, while lowered bumper segment makes car look closer to road. Parking lights mounted far out indicate width of car at night.

CAR LIFE CONSUMER ANALYSIS:

1956 PACKARD

CLEARLY a luxury car, Packard makes no attempt to aim at any other section of the market.

This year Packard is in a better overall position than at any time in more than 20 years as far as sales percentage in the high-priced field is concerned. Packard's engineering has been conservative until recently—so much so that this traditionally fine car came very close to becoming automotive history.

Now, with the success of the torsional suspension system fairly well established (it's long been popular in Europe on cars where roadability and handling ease is of paramount importance), Packard has seen fit to let go two more bombshells! This time it's a new differential that the makers term *non-slip,* and an electrically operated push-button transmission control.

The new differential prevents one wheel spinning uselessly while the other refuses to move, as when one side or the other is bogged down in snow or mud. Standard on all Packards is this first major rear end improvement in three decades, while the electrical push button transmission control is optional on the regular line of passenger cars and standard on the swank Caribbean hardtops and convertibles.

All engines are now of 374 cu. in. displacement, the result of increasing the bore of last year's block by an extra ½ inch (stroke is 3⅛ inch, bore 4⅛). Most powerful engine as well as largest announced to date, this power brute delivers 290 bhp at 4600 rpm with one 4-barrel carburetor in the sedans and hardtops in the "400" and "Patrician" lines.

Use of two 4-barrel pots and special manifolding increase this advertised output to 310 bhp in the Caribbean series. These latter rigs, incidentally, offer the only standard three-tone color schemes available on the first production '56 Packards. On all series the compression ratio is 10 to 1, or enough to put the double whammy on the majority of more plebian transport. Rated torque is 405 ft. lbs. at 2800 rpm.

This biggest engine in the industry requires premium grade fuel, can deliver up to about 17 miles per gallon on long trips while cruising at 60 mph in the second element of the dual range Ultramatic. Torque and weight/power ratio being the important factors they are, this big heavy car will go to an honest 60 mph from a dead start in 10½ seconds, which is moving even in Big Three language.

The dual range automatic box locks up mechanically, begins at 24 mph and continues in this favorable condition up to about 70. The low ratio rear axle permits speeds in excess of a true 112 mph.

Cruising along at highway speeds—say 50 mph—you can mash the accelerator pedal and surge through either of two step-down detents to boost you to 80 mph in about 8½ seconds.

Stylewise the '56 is a facelift job—a new hood, new rear deck, and far better use of chrome and color, but with the same luxurious quality brought up to date that has always made Packard a distinguished car. ●

YOUR CHECK LIST

☑ ☑ ☑ ☑ ☑ means top rating

PERFORMANCE ☑ ☑ ☑ ☑ ☑

All any sane person could logically want or need. With the biggest number of torque-producing inches of any domestic production car, those who enjoy driving will be well advised to keep an eye on the speedometer—this engine is very quiet.

STYLING ☑ ☑ ☑ ☐ ☐

Like its slightly smaller brother, the Clipper, more or less uninspired but eminently adequate and certainly functional. The vertical trim along the leading edge of the rear fender bulges has a practical purpose: exterior frosted lights that double as courtesy and side marker lamps.

RIDING COMFORT ☑ ☑ ☑ ☑ ☑

Probably the most comfortable ride ever engineered into an American car. If you can't stand the thought of even the slightest dips, try the torsion ride that Packard has had the guts to pull out of the hat before the big boys.

INTERIOR DESIGN ☑ ☑ ☑ ☑ ☐

Restraint has been the watchword of Packard's interior decorators who, thus far, have not gone whole hog on quite as much brightness to scramble the vision.

ROADABILITY ☑ ☑ ☑ ☑ ☑

Tops in its class and nearly as agile as several smaller roadworthy cars whose size gives them their only advantage over this car. The revolutionary suspension system can spell the difference between leaving the road and sticking; it's better still this year with the non-slip differential.

EASE OF CONTROL ☑ ☑ ☑ ☑ ☐

In its size class, the Packard is probably the easiest handling car—would be even easier to maneuver with 3 turns lock-to-lock steering instead of almost 4 turns.

ECONOMY ☑ ☑ ☑ ☐ ☐

Big cubic displacement means a lot of space to fill up each time an exhaust valve opens. Around town Packard owners can expect little more than 12 miles per gallon—in fact 12 mpg would be good. But economy covers more ground than fuel consumption, and on this score Packard repairs can be expected to be few and far between.

SERVICEABILITY ☑ ☑ ☑ ☐ ☐

Requires periodic attention to the electrical load levelizer; those equipped with the electrical push button transmission control will be potentially liable to occasional trouble that solenoids can suffer.

WORKMANSHIP ☑ ☑ ☑ ☑ ☑

The equal of its high-priced competitors in every way. Body panels fit nicely; the chassis reflects a high degree of attention and is finished with great care;

DURABILITY ☑ ☑ ☑ ☑ ☑

Since this is the second year for the new suspension system and the third year since a major body redesign, it seems safe to conclude that serious bugs have been ironed out.

VALUE PER DOLLAR ☑ ☑ ☑ ☑ ☐

Packard has suffered from depreciation trouble ever since the war; in some regions this is more likely than others. However, with prosperity still high, and with a vigorous sales campaign geared to again resuming the old Packard position in the automotive sun, dollar value is on the increase.

THE PACKARD IS THE CAR FOR YOU

If . . . you want the car with the most torque produced in any domestic car.

If . . . you want a big car that stands out from the peas-in-the-pod-type of styling that has gripped Detroit designers.

If . . . you want the most bump-free ride in American production cars.

If . . . you want a car that's easy to control, especially when you consider the size and weight of this big vehicle.

If . . . you want a car that has many styling firsts that will be picked up by other manufacturers in the next year or two.

CAR LIFE CONSUMER ANALYSIS:

1956 CLIPPER

LAST YEAR saw the attempted launching of Packard's medium-priced CLIPPER as a separate make in its own right.

Torsional suspension, as on Packard, was an industry first; elegant interiors and a restrained though plentiful use of chrome on the exterior marked this rather squarish 122-inch wheelbase, two-ton car that somehow still was unmistakably Packard.

New styling gives the '56 Clipper a new hood line and better forward vision than last year's good driver view. The rear deck has been redesigned; gone is the center bulge in the deck lid, and new larger tail lights have a cathedral window appearance. In overall shape the grille is unchanged but the lines within the frame are horizontal.

Safety door latches withstanding three times the impact stresses of previous latches are standard, and an ingenious under-dash system of solenoids inside each door allow the driver to instantly lock all doors in one easy motion.

The brake pedal has been enlarged on models equipped with Ultramatic (as most will no doubt be), and the optional power brake is much improved and not nearly as touchy as was last year's. Hard drivers will also be pleased to know that fins have been incorporated onto the brake drums and that repeated hard usage during a test drive failed to induce any fade after more than a dozen hard panic-type stops. Unfortunately, the steering wheel has not come in for any safety modification.

Curb weight of the '56 Clipper hardtop and sedan (no convertible as yet) is around 4,000 pounds, but two variants of the rugged 352 cu. in. V8 engine introduced in '55 allow very favorable weight to power ratios of from about 16½ to 14 pounds per brake horsepower which explains acceleration to a true 60 mph from a standing start in 11 seconds.

The most costly Clipper, the *Custom,* has a 4-barrel carburetor on the big engine and turns out 275 bhp at 4600 rpm. The *Super* and *Deluxe* models have the same engine but with two-barrel carburetors which deliver a potent 240 bhp at the same rpm. Torque is the greatest yet on any medium priced line: 380 and 350 foot pounds at 2800 rpm respectively. All engines have 9.5 to 1 compression ratios—and so they require premium gas.

Clipper still offers a choice of standard 3-speed transmissions with or without overdrive. Worth noting is the fact these high torque engines permit the use of a very low rear axle ratios of either 3.07 or 2.87, permitting fairly resonable fuel economy with automatic shifting.

We drove a Clipper with dual range Ultramatic and the 3.07 rear axle, and it was capable of giving from 14 to 18 miles per gallon depending on driving speeds.

The excellent torsional suspension with the electrically actuated load levelizer (which can be switched *off* if desired) has been improved to eliminate the small amount of rear end sway that was noted in '55.

Handling is fine, the best of any car in its class, but we would prefer to see fewer than nearly four turns lock-to-lock steering for quicker recovery. A baby-buggy ride with cornering close to that expected in sports-type cars is what makes this car an attractive package to the medium money buyer who loves to drive. ●

YOUR CHECK LIST

☑ ☑ ☑ ☑ ☑ means top rating

PERFORMANCE ☑ ☑ ☑ ☑ ☑

In its class, and with a competent driver at the wheel, there will be few cars whose stock equipment will enable them to threaten this car. This over-110-mph car has superb *go.*

STYLE ☑ ☑ ☑ ☐ ☐

This is a matter of opinion, but we believe the Clipper has a certain squarish bulk and lack of definite theme on the exterior. There is little coordination between front and rear where the bumpers are concerned.

RIDING COMFORT ☑ ☑ ☑ ☑ ☑

This car rides at the top of its class. Torsional suspension is the first really new suspension idea on domestic cars since the war, and we predict you'll like it if you try it.

INTERIOR DESIGN ☑ ☑ ☑ ☑ ☐

Much original thought (considering Clipper's relationship to Packard) with all instruments well placed. It has an easily reached glove case and a safety padded dash. The back of the front seat is padded to protect rear seat occupants—the only one of its kind thus far.

ROADABILITY ☑ ☑ ☑ ☑ ☑

Torsional suspension, unlike last year, is now standard across the line on all Clipper series. Ease of handling and exceptional stability regardless of road conditions, and smoothness of ride make this feature well worth the additional cost Clipper may require above a few class competitors.

EASE OF CONTROL ☑ ☑ ☑ ☑ ☐

The car stands near the top in this category. Only negative aspect is the somewhat slow steering which is unnecessary on a car normally equipped with power steering. Improved brakes that resist fade almost magically, good road view, and happy throttle response make this car easy to drive.

ECONOMY ☑ ☑ ☑ ☐ ☐

Moderately good mileage as cars go and good engineering make Clipper as easy on the pocketbook as any two-ton high-powered car. Highway cruising at a steady 55-60 mph should produce at least 16 mpg even with automatic transmission.

SERVICEABILITY ☑ ☑ ☑ ☐ ☐

The same problems as in most overhead valve V8 engines will be the lot of Clipper owners. Changing the spark plugs will not be as frequent with the

WORKMANSHIP ☑ ☑ ☑ ☑ ☑

Equal in this category to any but the most expensive low production and hand-built cars. Early production units examined show careful assembling and finishing worthy of a great tradition.

DURABILITY ☑ ☑ ☑ ☑ ☑

Close study of engineering specifications indicate that this Packard variant will be as durable as its forebears. The majority of Packard built cars are still in everyday service as a matter of record.

VALUE PER DOLLAR ☑ ☑ ☑ ☐ ☐

Though resale has not been an outstanding Packard (or Clipper) feature in recent years, it is slowly on the rise. One must consider other factors —unique engineering features not available elsewhere on this side of the Atlantic, superb ride and excellent roadability.

THE CLIPPER IS THE CAR FOR YOU

If . . . you want a car that's easy to control and has excellent brake design.

If . . . you want a car that you will not have to wait months to buy, yet will give you years of service and pleasure.

If . . . you want a big-car performance with a good weight to power ratio.

If . . . you want a car with the latest advancement in riding comfort, the torsion bar ride.

Biggest in the business, both in size and output, is the V-8. Yet accessibility is good. Oil filter and neck are up front.

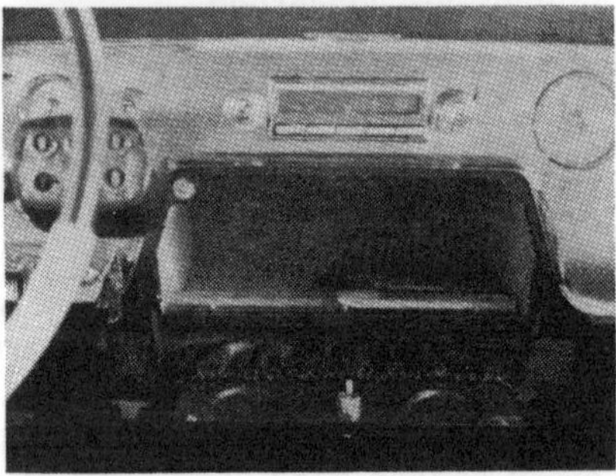

Even glove compartment is big as well as being handily located in center. Note table-like lid for holding drinking cups.

Fermoyle found seat cushions softest of all makes, yet good support for long drives. In some series they're reversible.

Driver's Report—THE BIG NEW PACKARD

BY KEN FERMOYLE

They call it "the greatest Packard of them all." Fans of the classic era may not agree—they rarely do—but the makers of the car have plenty of good arguments on their side

THE FIRST thing I noticed about the Patrician four-door used for this report was the way I sank into the super-soft seat cushions. The old saw about "ankle-deep rugs" popped into my mind—and you can draw your own comparison! I wondered if they would give you enough support to be comfortable on a long drive. After putting in the better part of the day behind the wheel, however, I can assure you that they do. Tho soft, they're well-designed and, with four-way power controls, can be adjusted to position which suits you best.

The Packard is noteworthy for the careful detail touches which make for comfortable riding and driving. For example, dual ash-trays are mounted at extreme ends of the instrument panel, are easy to get at for either driver or passengers.

Other unique features are the outside courtesy lights

mounted in the trim strips on each side of the body; they light up the ground around the doors to prevent stepping into holes or puddles and also serve as side running lights at night.

The performance of the new Packard is excellent for a car of its size and weight. The huge 374-cubic-inch V8, largest in the industry, is responsible for this, of course. We made a series of acceleration runs at the company's Utica proving ground after first calibrating speedometer error (it proved to be about seven per cent fast).

Times for a number of 0 to 60 runs averaged about 11.5 seconds. From 0 to 30 took about four seconds flat, not exceptionally fast but more than adequate for a car of this size. From 0 to 45 took 7 seconds. Good mid-range passing ability was reflected in 50 to 80 times of about 12.5 seconds. Surprisingly fast was the 17.7 seconds in which the Packard turned the standing quarter-mile. These figures show just about what was expected; due to its weight (nearly 5,000 lbs. during these runs) it takes a little time to get underway and overcome initial inertia. Once it's rolling, however, the 405 lbs.-ft. of torque turned out by the big engine make it move! These acceleration figures can't be regarded as the ultimate that can be expected from the new Packard performancewise. The car usd was handicapped by the fact that it wasn't broken in; it had less than 200 miles on it at the time. Also, there was a driver and two passengers in the car. A driver alone would probably be able to shave the times quoted. Certainly a car with several thousand miles on it would do better.

Since the car was so new no effort was made to check top speed. A Packard test engineer did report that drivers were getting up to 115-116 on the 2½-mile proving ground track. That means that the car is capable of more, since you can't get up to the same speeds on the track as would be possible on a straight stretch of similar length. Although the turns are steeply banked they still cut speed at the top end a minimum of 5 mph.

The Packard *feels* very powerful all thru the speed range. Punching the throttle brings instantaneous response and the speedo needle swings across the dial with no hesitation. The big V8 pulls the car along without the slightest feeling of strain or fuss. The Ultramatic transmission, not one of the best of the automatic gearboxes for acceleration, is extremely smooth and shiftpoints are just barely felt even when you really push the car.

After a lengthy session on the track, we headed for the back roads to check out the ride and handling qualities of the Patrician. A lot has been said and written about the torsion bar suspension, so there isn't much to be added. The ease with which it floats you over rough washboard gravel roads and the way it levels out chuckholes and beat-up railroad crossings is amazing. The front end dips somewhat over the worst potholes, but is extremely difficult to bottom. It's next to impossible to make the back end approach the bottoming point.

Corners can be taken at speeds you wouldn't think possible in a car of this size—and the suspension keeps it on an even keel unless you do your darndest to make it lean. I did feel, however, that the Clipper handles a bit better than its bigger brother. This is probably due to the longer wheelbase and greater weight. The Packard seemed to break loose on tight turns a little quicker than did the Clipper reported on in last month's MOTOR LIFE. It didn't stick as tightly in hard turns, I felt. Probably very few Packard owers will attempt to push their cars thru corners the way we did with this car, however.

The car used for this report was, as mentioned earlier, a four-door Patrician sedan. It was loaded with just about every option offered except the limited-slip differential and air conditioning. It had power brakes, power steering, power seat and windows, push-button gear selector, deluxe signal-seeking radio with rear speaker and push-button antenna control etc. All functioned perfectly and added a lot to driving ease and comfort. (The radio was excellent, incidentally. The speaker system was the type which permits either front or rear speaker to be used alone, or lets you balance the volume of each to any degree you desire by turning a single knob.) It had the 3.54 rear axle ratio (you can get as high as 2.87).

Styling of the car is hard to assess. It achieves the desired effect of massiveness and, while basic lines are not too different from some of the other cars in its class, several distinctive touches keep it from being taken for anything but a Packard. Bright metal side trim is restricted to the textured strip running horizontally the full length of the body; this treatment gives it a less gaudy appearance than many current models. However, since styling and appearance reaction depends to so great an extent on personal likes and dislikes perhaps it's best just to say that current Packards are a big improvement over the upside-down bathtubs of the earlier postwar years! It's doubtful that many will argue with that!

It's interesting to note that Packard is not making an attempt to get into the volume production act that is causing so much discussion today. Rather, it has initiated a program of "old-fashioned quality selling" and improved customer service. A system of quality controls and individual road testing of each car will be used to make sure the cars are in top condition before shipment to dealers. An elaborate customer relations program is being instituted. Packard hopes that these innovations and a continuing policy of incorporating engineering advancements will help win back the enviable reputation it enjoyed in the past. It's a sound idea and the 1956 is a sound car. The combined appeal of these factors should be a big factor in winning Packard its share of buyers in the luxury car market. •

Probably the ultimate in Frenched headlights on current production models, with the under surface fully chromed.

Grille appears to be too gaudy for a car of Packard's quietly luxurious characteristics. Layout should be simpler.

More restraint has been exercised on side trim. Massive exhaust and taillights suit styling of car that's really big.

Tight fast turn produces little lean, although right front tire shows terrific "squash." Feel of the road, good control were always present.

We continue our regular monthly series of road tests by Bill Holland, Indianapolis winner and member of the Champion Sparkplug 100-Mile-an-Hour Club, with the Clipper. Coming up in the next issue: Chevrolet and Rambler tests.

Bill Holland Tests.....

▶ Out at the Studebaker-Packard Proving Grounds, Utica, Michigan, I recently had the chance to try the new Clipper on their two and a half mile track. The car I drove —a 1956 Clipper Custom four-door sedan —had the full power treatment; power windows, seat, brakes, steering, aerial, plus 270 horses of power under the hood.

The ride given by the 1956 model is amazing. The torsion bars that are now standard on all Clippers make a remarkable improvement and give this car the smoothest ride I have so far experienced. I drove through the grass in the center of the proving grounds track at 70 mph, with no difficulty in handling the car or staying in the seat. The torsion bars completely eliminate coil and leaf springs. New Monroe shock absorbers are used. In spite of the comparatively soft ride of the Clipper I found a minimum of body roll when cornering hard, and also very little dive in the front end when making an emergency stop. Road shock in the front end, quite noticeable in the '55 models, has been very much improved.

Next to the smoothness I was impressed by the very low noise level and the lack of any rattles or thumps. This has been accomplished by many unseen changes, the main one being a much heavier frame under the car, which takes most of the strain off the body and eliminates the possibility of its developing rattles after a few thousand miles. The dash and floorboards have three times the amount of insulation used last year, eliminating all engine noises from the inside of

Left: Holland shows how push-button drive control is activated without lifting hand from wheel. Single switch now operates power-seat control.

Below: Schematic diagram of the electric push-button Ultramatic transmission operation, the only system offering a "safe-parking" feature.

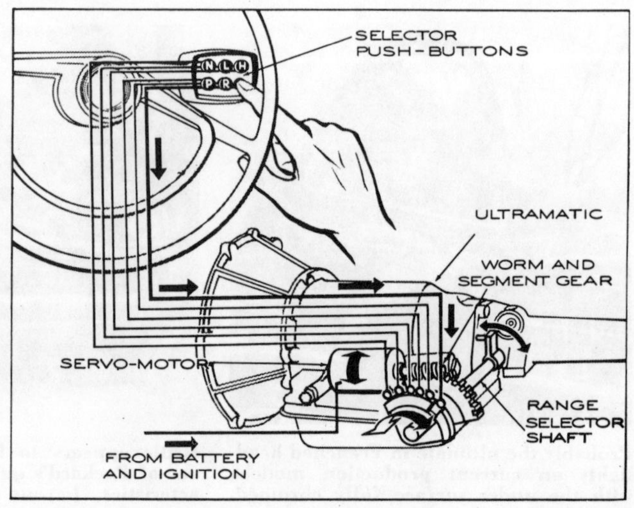

After his test drive, Bill Holland inspects the Clipper engine with Bob Alexander, proving grounds' engineer, who indicates the many changes.

The Clipper Custom

By Bill Holland

Two-door hardtop in the Custom series. Clipper torsion-bar suspension gave Bill what he calls "smoothest ride I have so far experienced."

the car. The body mounts are bigger and thicker, too.

The Clipper offers all the usual safety features: seat belts, padded dash (and it is really padded, about one inch of sponge rubber); oversize brakes; and the safety door latches are a little heavier than most I have seen. The power steering ratio is faster, too: 16.4.

The new push-button transmission is available on all Clippers at extra cost, and works like a charm. The buttons are located on the right side of the steering post, just under the wheel, and can be operated with one finger without removing the hand from the steering wheel. The system is electrically operated and requires only a light touch. Two of the important safety features of this system are: when the car is moving five mph or faster, you can push the reverse or park buttons and nothing happens; and, when you stop the car and turn the key off it automatically goes into park, so the car will not roll either forward or backward.

The transmission is much smoother when shifting and when, in the D or drive position, the accelerator is depressed to the floor under 55 mph, it will drop down two gears for extremely fast acceleration; when it is in the H or high drive position it will drop back very smoothly to the highway passing gear. This position is the best to use on ice or snow too, as the take-off is very smooth. When the transmission is in high gear it is a direct drive just like a straight clutch, with no loss of horse-power due to slippage, and results in better gas mileage. The transmission case, by the way, is made of aluminum this year, and is about 85 pounds lighter.

The engine looks just like last year's from the outside, but as soon as you stand on it you know it's been changed to get all that extra go. It is 270 hp and 352 cubic inches, and puts out 380 foot pounds of torque at 2800 rpm.

The two most needed changes in the '55 have been taken care of very nicely by increasing the secondary venturis in the pot or carburetor from 1-1/16" to 1-3/16" and the intake valves from 1-15/16" to 2", giving the engine much better breathing; and by using new hydraulic valve lifters that let the engine turn about 5200 rpm before pumping up. This is a decided advance over last year's 4700 rpm.

I was told by the chief experimental engineer for Clipper that the leak-down condition that caused the clatter under the hood for several seconds when first starting up in the morning, has been corrected with the new lifters. The shape of the combustion chambers has been changed and is now cast instead of being machined. Compression is raised from 8.3:1 to 9.5:1. There are new long-reach spark plugs and a new cam, with more overlap and a redesigned ramp to give quieter valve operation. All these changes add up to more horsepower and an amazing three and a half mpg increase in gas mileage, bringing it up to 19 mpg with automatic transmission.

The Clipper for 1956 is a real pleasure to drive—smooth and yet so responsive. I drove all through downtown Detroit and then headed for the winding roads out near the proving grounds. The car is easy to drive in traffic and handles well on the turns.

At the proving grounds we made our top speed and acceleration tests. We clocked it at 115 mph, with only the driver in the car, and using the uncorrected speedometer. Acceleration figures and specifications are below. They add up to a powerful car with major improvements in two areas of automobile design where there was plenty of room for improvement —driving comfort and safety.

SPECIFICATIONS & PERFORMANCE

ENGINE
Type: V8 valve-in-head
Displacement: 352 cu. in.
Compression ratio: 9.5 to 1
Bore & stroke: 4" x 3½"
Brake horsepower: 270 at 4600 rpm
Torque: 380 ft. lbs. at 2800 rpm
Carburetor: four-barrel

BODY & CHASSIS
Wheelbase: 122"
Length: 214-13/16"
Height & width overall: 62", 78"
Drive: Rear axle torque arm
Transmission: Ultramatic, overdrive, or standard
Tires: 7.60" x 15"

PERFORMANCE:
Acceleration with uncorrected speedometer
0 to 30 mph: 3.8 sec.
0 to 60 mph: 10.3 sec.
30 to 60 mph: 7.0 sec.
50 to 80 mph: 12.1 sec.

Packard

FOR YEARS Packard coasted on its reputation which was created during the Twenties and early Thirties when the firm produced a fine automobile which the classic fans now revere. Most of us will remember the famous Packard radiator and hood which was as much Packard as the tail fins are Cadillac today. However, the strenuous competition Packard was receiving from Cadillac and other factories in the mid-Thirties forced them to produce an inexpensive car, a fact which saved the company from bankruptcy but cost Packard its tremendous lead in the luxury-car field.

In 1956 the company management is conscious of this mistake of the past, and they've wisely set out to correct it by completely separating their cheaper cars, the Clippers, from the Packard nameplate. Whether they'll regain a fair share of the fine-car market is anybody's guess, but we do know that their 1956 product is a real contender and a true luxury automobile comparable to any of the cars discussed here.

Base price of the Packard Patrician four-door sedan at the factory is $4160, making it one of the lowest-priced sedans in this field. However, when we went over the car with a fine-toothed comb we found that it doesn't lack much from providing the buyer with plenty of luxury items. The '56 Packard is big and solid in appearance and has the biggest and most powerful engine in the industry, developing 310 horsepower and 405 foot-pounds torque. Riding in the car proved to be silky-smooth with Packard's torsion-level suspension system, giving positive car control even on rough roads. Interior of the Patrician is lush; sitting position is high and comfortable; instrumentation is attractively set in a foam-rubber padded dash panel. Yes, the detailing is there and quality workmanship, too. Packard may again be on the way to re-establish its name in the fine-car market.

Boldness of line adds distinction to the Clipper, although to some tastes the use of chromium plating may seem lavish. Front and rear windows wrap well round to provide good visibility. The wheel discs are standard fittings

The Autocar
ROAD TESTS

No. 1598

PACKARD CLIPPER
Custom Saloon

INTEREST in Packard cars increased last year when a new form of suspension was introduced. However, until recent provision of a Clipper Custom saloon by the British concessionaires (Leonard Williams and Co., Ltd., Packard Buildings, Great West Road, Brentford, Middlesex) it had not been possible to conduct a full test. The car has proved worth waiting for, and the technical innovations have come well up to expectations.

In conformity with American practice, the model has very recently undergone a face-lift, emerging as the Executive touring saloon, in which form it is currently available. However, differences between the cars are virtually confined to the frontal appearance, and for test purposes the models can be regarded as almost exactly similar.

The 5,768 c.c. capacity of the V-eight engine in itself indicates something of the character of the performance, for, with 275 b.h.p. available at 4,600 r.p.m., it will be realized that even though the car has a spacious six-seater body, the Clipper is very fast indeed. Also it has an abundance of those things desirable in a fast touring family saloon, with the exception that the brakes are not consistently up to European average standards.

As the highlight of general interest in this model focuses on the suspension, it is worth summarizing briefly the arrangement of the basic components. Torsion bars, more than 9ft long, connect the front and rear wheel on each side, with short torsion bars connecting the rear wheels to the frame. As a front wheel rises on a bump, a reaction is carried to the rear wheel, which, in effect, prepares that wheel for the bump to come. The reaction points are situated near the fore and aft centre of gravity and as a result the car tends to rise and fall without pitching. Additionally there is an anti-roll bar at each end.

Another feature of the suspension is a mechanism which keeps the car at a constant level regardless of the weight of occupants or luggage. A two-way motor is fitted centrally, from which additional, shorter, torsion bars run to the suspension at the rear. When the car settles under the weight of loading, the motor operates through these smaller bars to raise the car to the predetermined level. There is a seven seconds delay in the switch controlling the motor, so that the levelling mechanism does not react to changes in loading resulting from bumps, braking or acceleration. Thus the springing is adjusted automatically to the load for any particular journey, and the characteristics of the car when lightly or heavily laden are very similar. The mechanism can be switched off for jacking or parking purposes. The cost of manufacturing and fitting this suspension is high, and it may well be that in the future Packards will have to find a less expensive alternative that will provide similarly successful results.

On thc road the performance of the suspension is excellent. First impressions suggest that the car is characteristic of the majority of large, softly sprung American models, but after a few miles of open road motoring these feelings change to the conviction that here is something unusual. The ride remains soft, in the boulevard tradition, perhaps softer even than other cars of similar size and type. Yet there is no pitching, no yawing, or any of that soft but

With automatic transmission there are, of course, only two pedals. The selector for the transmission protrudes from the steering column. The driver can see all the instruments through the upper half of the steering wheel, and a padded roll at the top of the facia prevents reflections in the screen. Pull-out ash trays are fitted in the facia

The massive 5.7-litre V-eight engine is compactly housed. The water and oil fillers, battery vent plugs and engine and transmissio.. dip sticks can all be reached easily. The bonnet is lined with sound-deadening material, and is spring loaded to remain open without the use of a supporting strut

The motif on the Clipper is a ship's wheel, which appears on various parts of the car; here it can be seen centrally on the radiator grille. The Marchal head lamps are recessed in chromium-plated cowls. The plated bulges below the head lamps are decorative

pronounced rising and falling that tends to induce travel sickness. And of particular importance on British roads is the almost complete absence of roll on corners.

It was found that on sinuous roads astonishingly high speeds could be maintained with complete stability and, providing the braking limitations were borne in mind, with confidence. Full appreciation of the merit of this suspension occurs only when the car is driven over roads known by the driver to be indifferently surfaced, and on which he knows the maximum safe and comfortable speeds at which other softly sprung large cars can be driven. So deceptive is this Packard that in these conditions, and before the speedometer had been checked, it was thought that the optimism in the instrument was much greater than subsequently it proved to be.

With more sensitive steering the cornering capability could be used to greater advantage, for with 4½ turns from lock to lock, the speed on winding roads was limited by the dexterity of the driver with the steering wheel. Although not equipped with power assistance, the steering was not heavy even for parking manœuvres, and the action, if low geared, was positive. There was no appreciable kick back at the wheel, yet there was "feel". On slippery surfaces the steering was sufficiently sensitive to indicate the nature of the surface. This is important—and rarely found—on cars with a low-geared mechanism as a skid cannot be corrected very quickly. Tyre noise was slight even on corners taken fast, and the thumping noise that usually results from running over "cats' eyes" was unobtrusive.

The Clipper (and Executive) is produced by the Studebaker-Packard Corporation, and to judge it in perspective it must be remembered that it is not a cheap family saloon even by American values. Thus, if the car is to sell it must be something rather special, and this it certainly is. In the car tested, a number of optional extras were fitted, but the standard equipment itself is lavish for it includes Ultramatic transmission, power-assisted brakes, radio, heater, windscreen washer, reversing lights, and smaller items. Power steering is also available, but not on cars converted to right-hand drive, as was the one tested.

The automatic transmission is a two-stage torque converter coupled to a two-speed epicyclic gear train; the overall transmission ratio varies according to load up to a maximum speed of 70 m.p.h. in the indirect gears. Called Twin-Ultramatic, this transmission was introduced last year, before which there was only one epicyclic train. When accelerating at full throttle in the Drive selector position the car gets under way in the lower indirect gear, a single gear change being felt as the second epicyclic train comes into operation.

The torque converter ratio continues to diminish until direct top is brought into operation by the automatic engage-

The fin rear wings house tail, indicator and reversing lights; the prominent fin tops make good sighting points for the driver and, in conjunction with the wide rear window, additionally aid reversing. Overriders are standard ment of a clutch which locks out the torque converter. Under light throttle openings direct drive is achieved similarly but at a much lower speed, and for those who drive quietly there is a high range position on the selector which eliminates the lower range completely. Another position of the selector locks the transmission in the low range, primarily for use on long descents on which the car would otherwise remain in top.

Because of the amount of horsepower available most of the driving is accomplished in direct drive with occasional use of the higher indirect gear. Up and down changes are smooth and snatch is rarely experienced even with hard acceleration. That a car weighing more than two tons laden as tested can cover a standing quarter mile in 18.5sec, and reach 90 m.ph. in well under half a minute, is distinctly exhilarating. There are few cars of such size that can produce a performance of this calibre. The engine is not merely responsive to light pressure on the throttle but additionally it delivers its power smoothly. There is never any trace of snatch, never a jerk when the throttle is opened—just a smooth but vigorous push in the back.

On roads largely free from other traffic this Packard covers the ground at very high speed without effort, almost regardless of road surface. Wind noise with the windows closed is not distracting. A long journey is a joy. It is accomplished without fatigue, quietly, effortlessly and comfortably.

In Britain the Clipper cannot be driven at or near the limit of its performance because the brakes, particularly at the rear, overheat. With a slight following breeze the car reached a genuine 110 m.p.h., and the needle of the electric test speedometer was still rising gently when the driver decided to slow down, knowing that there was the possibility of fade. Towards the end of an admittedly arduous day spent collecting test information, the brake linings failed before all items of data could be completed. Initially the braking power is good, and those who drive fast might, with advantage, change to a more heat-resistant lining.

Cruising speed is limited only by traffic conditions, and its maintenance is aided on narrow roads by visibility so good that, for its size, the car is remarkably easy to position accurately. Both front wings are visible to a driver of average height, and even in crowded city conditions the car can be driven confidently without its driver getting that "tender elbows" feeling.

The windscreen wraps well round, aiding vision in spite of some distortion at the sides. The mirror takes advantage of the wide rear window, and the high, finned shape of the rear wings further helps reversing. Manœuvring is simplified by both the visibility and light steering. At extra cost a seat mechanism can be provided which power-operates in four directions, but on the car tested the seat was moved manually. The driving position provides armchair comfort, with the steering wheel conveniently placed—although telescopic adjustment would enable it to suit the precise requirements of more drivers. The armrest on the driver's door does not interfere with his control of the car.

The speedometer is mounted directly in front of the driver, with the other important instruments grouped round it where they are all easy to see. They include temperature gauge, oil pressure indicator, ammeter and fuel gauge. There is also a tell-tale for the head lamps' main beam.

All the minor controls are well sited. Only the clock is fitted on the passenger side, and the radio controls are, appropriately, central, above a good sized lockable glove compartment.

The radio is one of the best yet encountered. Setting a knob determines the degree of selectivity, after which at a touch on a bar the set seeks out stations automatically, stopping, perfectly tuned, at each station until the bar is touched again. When the indicator reaches the end of the scale it jumps back to the beginning again. Tone and selectivity are excellent. The aerial mast is operated electrically, but on the test car the mechanism short circuited,

The car seats six in complete comfort, and access to the front and rear is easy. All the doors hinge at their forward edges. Orthodox window mechanisms were fitted to the car tested but power operation is available at extra cost. There are armrests on all the doors. The aerial mast at the left is raised or lowered electrically

The fore and aft length of the luggage locker is deceptive. The locker itself will accommodate an enormous quantity of luggage. Luggage does not have to be lifted over a high step. The locker lid is released by turning the central spokes of the ship's wheel motif

albeit without affecting reception although the aerial was lowered. The volume remained steady in the narrowest of city sidestreets, and even under bridges. No appreciable interference was picked up from trolley buses.

The facia lighting is particularly good, instrument markings growing softly but clearly. A scientifically designed safety roll capping the facia prevents reflections in the screen. The wipers cover good arcs but leave an inverted, V-shaped, unswept portion in the centre of the screen which tends to reduce the visibility of the front wing farthest from the driver.

Luggage space is of a size to which the illustration fails to do justice. The locker extends forward so far that it would be easily possible for an adult to climb inside and, with a pillow, curl up comfortably for the night. When loading up, hard luggage may be placed over the shallow step, and soft bags more conveniently tossed into than placed in the far corners. The 7.60-15in spare wheel lies in an inclined position on the right, where it takes up but a small proportion of the total space available.

The head lamps, small compared with their European counterparts because of U.S. laws, are effective for fast night travel. They are of French Marchal manufacture, linked to an orthodox foot dipper. The interior light operates automatically when a door is opened. Fuel consumption at 13 to 18.6 m.p.g. is not unreasonable for a car of this size and power. The $16\frac{1}{2}$ gallon (20 U.S. gallon) tank is sufficient for comfortably more than 200 miles even with hard driving. Only in out-of-the-way places are Packard owners likely to do their own routine maintenance, but for those who do, there are 24 grease or oil nipples requiring attention every 1,000 miles. The handbook is of average standards, but includes unusually comprehensive information on oil viscosity grades for various temperatures, specifications and part numbers for the light bulbs (numbering more than 20), the same for fuses, and a list of methods for removing everything from chewing gum to lipstick from the upholstery.

The Packard Clipper may be summarized as an unusually comfortable big car, with a suspension system of special merit. It is soft without being sloppy, and the car has a formidable reserve of power that will take it into three-figure speeds without apparent effort.

Having set a particularly good example in matters of performance and comfort, it is to be hoped that this good car will be made even better by a revision of the braking system, so that it will prove just as desirable on tortuous, crowded roads as it must be to drivers whose motoring is largely conducted on great motorways.

PACKARD CLIPPER

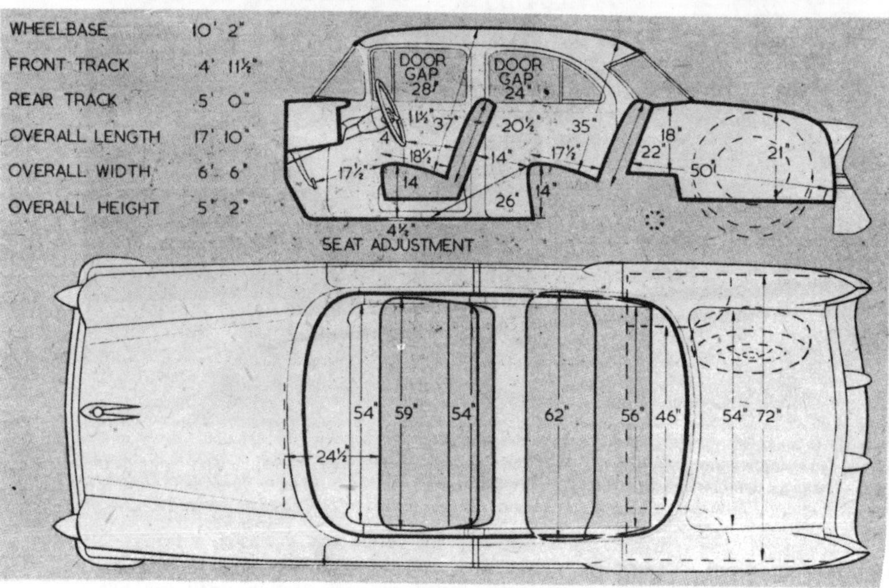

Measurements in these ¼in to 1ft scale body diagrams are taken with the driving seat in the central position of fore and aft adjustment and with the seat cushions uncompressed

PERFORMANCE

ACCELERATION: from constant speeds.

Speed Range, Gear Ratios* and Time in sec.

M.P.H.	Drive Range
10—30	3.8 sec.
20—40	4.6
30—50	5.8
40—60	7.2
50—70	9.1

*Gear ratio in top 3.31 to 1.

From rest through gears to:

M.P.H.	sec.
30	4.05
50	8.4
60	11.3
70	15.2
80	21.3
90	28.8

Standing quarter mile, 18.5 sec.

SPEEDS ON GEARS:

Gear	M.P.H. (normal and max.)		K.P.H. (normal and max.)
Top	106	(mean)	170.6
*	110	(best)	177.02

* Needle still rising gently.

BRAKES: See text.

FUEL CONSUMPTION:
14.6 m.p.g. overall for 560 miles. (19.4 litres per 100 km).
Approximate normal range 13–18.6 m.p.g (21.73–15.1 litres per 100 km).
Fuel, first grade.

WEATHER: Dry, sunny, slight breeze.
Air temperature 56 deg F.
Acceleration figures are the means of several runs in opposite directions.

SPEEDOMETER CORRECTION: M.P.H.

Car speedometer:	10	20	30	40	50	60	70	80	90	100	110	116
True speed:	11	20	29	39	47	56	66	75	85	92	103	110

DATA

PRICE (basic), with saloon body, **£2,577.**
British purchase tax, **£1,289 17s.**
Total (in Great Britain), **£3,866 17s.**

ENGINE: Capacity: 5,768 c.c. (352 cu in).
Number of cylinders: **8.**
Bore and stroke: 101.6 × 88.9 mm (4 × 3.5 in).
Valve gear: o.h.v., pushrods.
Compression ratio: 9.5 to 1.
B.H.P.: 275 at 4,600 r.p.m. (B.H.P. per ton laden 131.7).
Torque: 380 lb ft at 2,800 r.p.m.

WEIGHT: (with 5 gals fuel), $38\frac{3}{4}$ cwt (4,340 lb).
Weight distribution (per cent): F, 54.8; R, 45.2.
Laden as tested: $41\frac{3}{4}$ cwt (4,676 lb).
Lb per c.c. (laden): 0.81.

BRAKES: Type: Two leading shoe.
Method of operation: hydraulic.
Drum dimensions: F, 11in diameter; $2\frac{1}{4}$in wide. R, 11in diameter; $2\frac{1}{4}$in wide.
Lining area: F, 95.9 sq in. R, 95.9 sq in. (92.5 sq in per ton laden).

TYRES: 7.60-15in.
Pressures (lb per sq in): F, 24; R, 24 (normal).

TANK CAPACITY: 17 Imperial gallons.
Oil sump, 10 pints.

TURNING CIRCLE: 43ft (L and R).
Steering wheel turns (lock to lock): $4\frac{1}{2}$.

DIMENSIONS: Wheelbase: 10ft 2in.
Track: F, 4ft $11\frac{1}{2}$in; R, 5ft.
Length (overall): 17ft 10in.
Height: 5ft 2in.
Width: 6ft 6in.
Ground clearance: 7in.

ELECTRICAL SYSTEM: 12-volt; 60 ampère-hour battery.
Head lights: Double dip; 40–50 watt bulbs.

SUSPENSION: Independent wishbone front, live axle rear, interconnected by torsion bars. Automatic levelling. Anti-roll bar at front and rear.

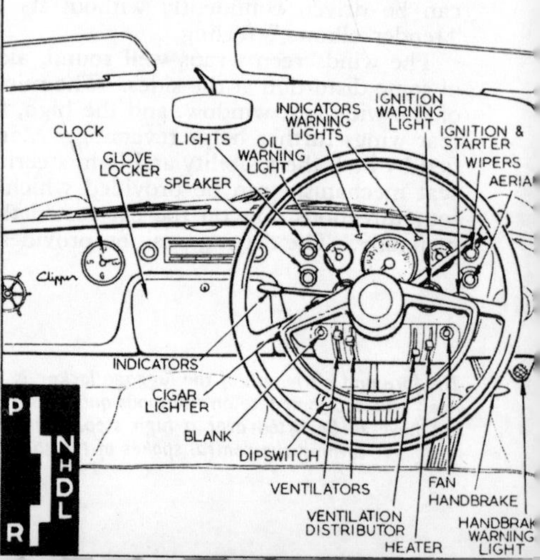

Packard's Clipper

CONTINUED FROM PAGE 91

to the engine, we find that Packard's new V-8 is the largest in the industry and it actually has been almost detuned for 1955. In other words, there is a lot of room for modifications. We feel that this engine is good for at least 350 horsepower—not that the car needs it—and we predict that it will be upped to that figure in the next year or so. It has amazing torque, and that is where real acceleration comes from. And speaking of torque, the Packard Twin Ultramatic transmission, with two "drive" positions, has the greatest torque multiplication in the industry—2.9 to one.

As for our own acceleration and speed runs, zero to 30 mph came to 4.2 seconds, 40 mph took 6.8 seconds, 60 was reached from a dead start in 11.6 seconds consistently. The Constellation engine puts out 245 hp as opposed to 260 hp on the "400" and Patrician models, and this particular car was completely untuned; the dealer had just received it. Just the same, we hit an average top speed of over 105 mph for three runs.

Later braking checks served only to confirm what we had thought the first moment we drove the Packard—here is the finest road car in America. ●

SPECIFICATIONS

ENGINE: V-8, overhead valves; bore, 4.00 in.; stroke, 3.50 in.; total displacement, 352 cu. in.; developed hp, 245 at 4,600 rpm; maximum torque, 355 ft. lbs. at 2,400 rpm; compression ratio, 8.5 to one; single four-barrel carburetor; ignition, 12 volt.

TRANSMISSION: Twin-Ultramatic torque converter; torque multiplication, 2.9 to one.

REAR AXLE RATIOS: 3.9 to one (manual); 3.23 to one (automatic).

SUSPENSION: main-load torsion bars of manganese steel running full length of chassis, attached to front and rear load arms; levelizer torsion bars also attached to rear load arms and to cross member at center of chassis; hydraulic shock absorbers.

BRAKES: four-wheel hydraulic; power booster.

DIMENSIONS: wheelbase, 122 in.; front tread, 59.7 in.; rear tread, 60 in.; width, 78 in.; height, 62 in.; over-all length, 214.8; turning circle, 43 ft.; steering, four turns, lock to lock; dry weight, 4,100 lbs. (approx.); tires, tubeless, 7.60 x 15.

PERFORMANCE

ACCELERATION:

Zero to 30 mph:	4.2 seconds
Zero to 40 mph:	6.8 seconds
Zero to 60 mph:	11.6 seconds
30 to 50 mph:	4.8 seconds
40 to 60 mph:	5.2 seconds
50 to 70 mph:	6.0 seconds

TOP SPEED: 105 mph plus.

Blend of Packard and Clipper features is new Executive series under test here.

DRIVER'S REPORT

Packard's NEW Executive

BY KEN FERMOYLE

PACKARD'S new Executive models, a blend of Packard and Clipper features, represent an attempt by the company to get broader coverage of the market. "They're for the buyer who wants a Packard, but can't afford or doesn't want to spend over $5,000 on an automobile," explains a company spokesman.

A two-door hardtop and four-door sedan are offered in the Executive series. Both are based on the 122-inch wheelbase chassis used for Clippers and have the same 352-cubic-inch, 275-hp V-8 engine used in Clipper Customs. Styling is a combination of Packard and Clipper—Clipper rear fender lines; Packard grille and interior appointments, and a few distinctive, but minor, trim touches that identify the cars as Executive models.

A pre-introduction driving trial in one of the new Executive four-doors revealed that it is closer in performance and handling to the Clipper Custom than to bigger Packard models.

Curb weight of the car was 4,438 lbs. and it had a 3.07 rear axle ratio. The car had only about 75 miles on the clock. With all this in mind it was felt that the average time of 11.7 seconds from 0-to-60 mph was very creditable—especially since there was a driver and two passengers in the car during the runs. The standing-quarter was turned in 19.1 seconds and indicated speed at the end of the stretch was 77 mph. From 0-to-80 took 20.4 seconds and from 50-to-80, 10.8 seconds. Time from 0-to-45 was 7.4 seconds. All runs were hand-timed with a pair of watches and allowance was made for an eight per cent speedo error.

The Executive offers a buyer everything he can get in the more expensive Packards; limited-slip differential, torsion bar suspension, push-button gear selection, a wide range of power assists—all are available. Interiors of cars in the series are handsomely finished and are easily on a par with all competitive makes.

Actually the car is more in the nature of an upper-crust Clipper Custom than a poor man's Packard Patrician, having more in common with the Clipper. This is no drawback, however, since the Clipper Custom in itself is a lot of mighty nice automobile. The dressed-up and more expensive looking Executives will undoubtedly win a lot of friends among those who like the idea of Packard prestige, but want to stay on the low side of the $5,000 mark. ●

The Motor Road Test No. 16/56 (Continental)

Make: Packard **Type:** Clipper

English Concessionaires: Leonard Williams, Ltd., Packard Buildings, Great West Road, Middlesex

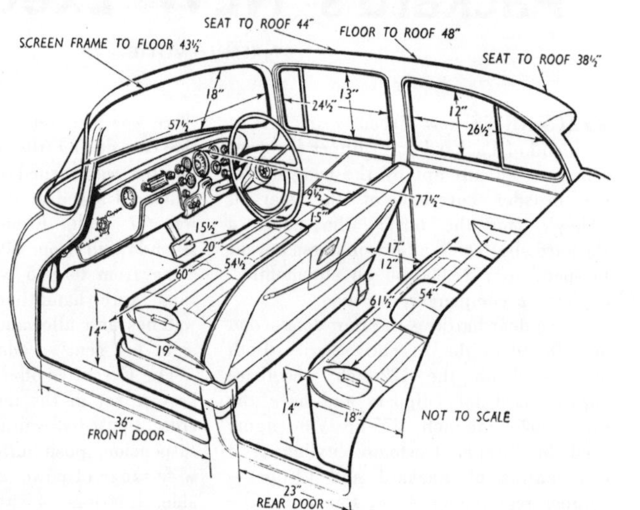

Test Data

CONDITIONS. *Ostend-Ghent Motor Road, barometer 29.97 to 30.12 in.; air temperature 60°-70°F.; wind variable 5-10 m.p.h.*

INSTRUMENTS

Speedometer at 30 m.p.h.	5% fast
Speedometer at 60 m.p.h.	5% fast
Speedometer at 90 m.p.h.	7% fast
Distance recorder	5% fast

MAXIMUM SPEEDS

Flying Quarter Mile

Mean of four opposite runs	113.4 m.p.h.
Best time equals	115.2 m.p.h.
"Maximile" equals	107.5 m.p.h.

Speed in gears

Maximum speed in Converter	70 m.p.h.
Maximum speed in 1st gear	60 m.p.h.

FUEL CONSUMPTION

26.0 m.p.g. at constant 30 m.p.h.
25.0 m.p.g. at constant 40 m.p.h.
22.5 m.p.g. at constant 50 m.p.h.
20.5 m.p.g. at constant 60 m.p.h.
18.5 m.p.g. at constant 70 m.p.h.
16.5 m.p.g. at constant 80 m.p.h.
14.0 m.p.g. at constant 90 m.p.h.
Overall consumption for 358 miles, 21.6 gallons =16.6 m.p.g. (18 litres/100 km.).
Fuel tank capacity 17 gallons.

ACCELERATION TIMES Through Gears

0-30 m.p.h.	4.3 sec.
0-40 m.p.h.	6.3 sec.
0-50 m.p.h.	8.4 sec.
0-60 m.p.h.	10.9 sec.
0-70 m.p.h.	15.2 sec.
0-80 m.p.h.	20.0 sec.
0-90 m.p.h.	26.7 sec.
0-100 m.p.h.	34.6 sec.
Standing Quarter Mile	18.2 sec.

ACCELERATION TIMES on Two Upper Ratios

	Converter High	Low
10-30 m.p.h.	4.2 sec.	3.2 sec.
20-40 m.p.h.	5.4 sec.	4.2 sec.
30-50 m.p.h.	5.4 sec.	4.0 sec.
40-60 m.p.h.	6.2 sec.	4.6 sec.
50-70 m.p.h.	7.5 sec.	—
60-80 m.p.h.	8.4 sec.	—
70-90 m.p.h.	11.4 sec.	—
80-100 m.p.h.	13.7 sec.	—

WEIGHT

Unladen kerb weight	38½ cwt.
Front/rear weight distribution	54½/44½
Weight laden as tested	42¼ cwt.

HILL CLIMBING (at steady speeds)

Max. top gear speed on 1 in 20	95 m.p.h.
Max. top gear speed on 1 in 15	85 m.p.h.
Max. top gear speed on 1 in 10	72 m.p.h.
Max. gradient on High	1 in 4.3 (Tapley 523 lb./ton)
Max. gradient on Low	1 in 3.3 (Tapley 667 lb./ton)

BRAKES at 30 m.p.h.

0.45g retardation	(= 67 ft. stopping distance) with 25 lb. pedal pressure
0.65g retardation	(= 46½ ft. stopping distance) with 50 lb. pedal pressure
0.70g retardation	(= 43 ft. stopping distance) with 75 lb. pedal pressure
0.85g retardation	(= 35.4 ft. stopping distance) with 125 lb. pedal pressure

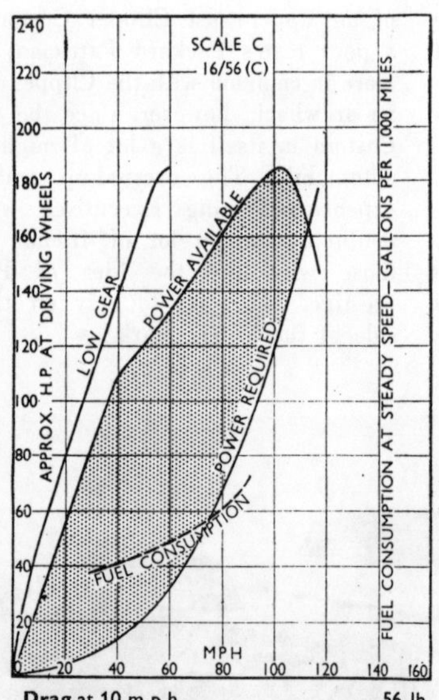

Drag at 10 m.p.h.	56 lb.
Drag at 60 m.p.h.	203 lb.

Specific Fuel Consumption when cruising at 80% of maximum speed (i.e., 90 m.p.h.) on level road, based on power delivered to rear wheels .. .. .. 0.58 pints/b.h.p./hr.

SCALE C 16/56 (C)
HIGH GEAR
RATE OF ACCELERATION (AVERAGE OVER 10 M.P.H. SPEED RANGE) M.P.H. PER SECOND
FT. / SEC./SEC.
APPROXIMATE EQUIVALENT GRADIENT CLIMBABLE AT STEADY SPEED AND TAPLEY LB/TON.
1 IN 3 · 1 IN 4 · 1 IN 5 · 1 IN 6 · 1 IN 8 · 1 IN 10 · 1 IN 20 · 1 IN 50
SPEED IN MILES PER HOUR

Maintenance

Sump: 8 pints, S.A.E. 20 S. W. **Gearbox:** 9 pints, S.A.E. **Rear axle:** 3½ pints, S.A.E. 90. **Steering gear:** S.A.E. 90. **Radiator:** 42 pints (3 drain taps). **Chassis lubrication:** By grease gun every 1,000 miles to 28 points. **Ignition timing:** 5° B.T.D.C. **Spark plug gap:** 0.035. **Contact breaker gap:** 0.016 in. **Valve timing:** I.O., 14° B.T.D.C.; I.C., 62° A.B.D.C.; E.O., 54° B.B.D.C.; E.C., 18° A.T.D.C. **Tappet clearances:** Hydraulic Zero Lash. **Front wheel toe-in:** 0-1/16 in. **Camber angle:** 5° 50". **Castor angle:** Minus 0.5° to minus 1.5°. **Tyre pressures:** Front 26 lb., rear 24 lb. **Brake fluid:** Lockheed. **Battery:** 12v. 60 amp.-hr. **Lamp bulbs:** Head, sealed beam 40/50 w.; side and tail, 18/3 w.; reversing light, 18 w.; rear number plate, boot, interior, 6 w.

Ref. A/S.2/56.

THE PACKARD CLIPPER

An Exceedingly High Performance American Family Car With a Number of Interesting Technical Features

In Brief

Price: £2,475 plus purchase tax £1,238 17s. equals £3,713 17s. (with various optional extras).

Capacity	...5,243 c.c.
Unladen kerb weight ...	... 38¾ cwt.
Fuel consumption ...	... 16.6 m.p.g.
Maximum speed ...	... 113.4 m.p.h.
Maximum speed on 1 in 20 gradient	95 m.p.h.
Maximum high gear gradient	1 in 4.3
Acceleration:	
10-30 m.p.h. in high ...	4.25 sec.
0-50 m.p.h. through gears	8.4 sec.

Gearing: 27.5 m.p.h. in top at 1,000 r.p.m.; 117.5 m.p.h. at 2,500 ft. per min. piston speed.

A GLANCE at the data page for performance quoted for the Clipper model built by the Packard Co., shows that this is a car with altogether outstanding performance by European standards. The mean maximum speed of 113.4 m.p.h. is faster than any car built on this side of the Atlantic which is capable of carrying five people, and a run in each direction was made at 115.2 m.p.h. That these very high speeds were not achieved at the sacrifice of the quality of acceleration is shown by the fact that only 4¼ seconds are required to go between 10 and 30 m.p.h. (even when in the "high" section of the transmission) and only 9.4 seconds to accelerate to 80 m.p.h. from 60 m.p.h.; correspondingly, the car will sustain 95 m.p.h. on a 1 in 20 gradient and 72 m.p.h. on a 1 in 10 gradient.

Full use of the transmission will provide 60 m.p.h. from rest in less than 11 seconds, 80 m.p.h. in less than 20 seconds, and here again one may search in vain the statistics of English and Continental cars for similar figures outside of the sports car class.

As the Clipper is emphatically not a sports car, but an exceedingly quiet saloon, capable of carrying six persons and their luggage in complete comfort, one might assume that at the least there would be a severe penalty in fuel consumption. It is all the more notable to find that the overall figure turns out to be 16-17 m.p.g. as a reflection of the remarkable specific consumption of 0.58 pints per b.h.p./hr. when the car is travelling at a cruising 90 m.p.h.

So much for the figures.

Exceptional Representative?

One has only to drive the car for a short distance to realize that the American car has made great strides in the past five years, not only in sheer performance but also in handling. But there are nevertheless some grounds for believing that the Clipper may be in some degree exceptional in this respect for it combines a weight distribution more closely allied to European practice than American with a suspension system found rarely in principle and of unique detail design.

Reference to the side view silhouette of the car will show that the front seat is almost in the centre of the wheelbase and both this and the engine are therefore farther back in the frame than is now common. A considerable effort has been made to offset the weight of a V.8 power unit which has a capacity of 5.2 litres and a nominal output of 225 b.h.p. and of a transmission which embodies a lock-up clutch, a four element torque converter, a multi-plate clutch, and a two-train epicyclic gear. The latter elements are enclosed in a light alloy casing which reduces weight by 95 lb. and in consequence the front wheels support a comparatively modest 54% of the unladen weight of the car, the laden weight being supported about equally fore and aft.

The car submitted for test by the British concessionaires Leonard Williams and Co., Ltd., had been converted by them to right-hand drive, a change which excludes power steering. This notwithstanding very little effort is needed on the wheel, and response to the helm is consistent and reasonably rapid since the five turns from lock to lock move the front wheels through a very big angle in order to achieve a turning circle of 41 ft. with a wheelbase of over 10 ft.

The driving position also calls for favourable comment, for the front seats are high and although having only a

NO DECEPTION: The powerful-looking front view of the Packard is no deception as it has a maximum speed substantially over 110 m.p.h. and corresponding hill climbing ability.

LENGTH AND PROPORTION: Despite an overall length of 18 ft. the Clipper is a well proportioned car due partly to a low build well demonstrated by this picture.

simple fore and aft adjustment the driving position was found equally comfortable by large males and small females. This is indeed an altogether exceptionally easy car to drive, and bears a hallmark of quality in that after a few hundred yards the driver ceases to be conscious of the size, in spite of the somewhat formidable width of 6½ ft. and a length of 18 ft.

As is normal on modern American cars outside the lowest price range, there is no clutch pedal on the Clipper, but unlike most of them there is a solid and direct drive from the flywheel to the back axle in all conditions at over 70 m.p.h. and, with progressively reduced throttle opening, down to 24 m.p.h.

What happens below 70 m.p.h. can be determined by the driver. If he puts the gear selector lever in "H" the car will accelerate from rest to 70 m.p.h. using a fluid converter which offers an increase in torque of 2.9 times with the engine running at 1,650 r.p.m. On full throttle this will be the minimum speed of the engine, and the torque increase will diminish above 45 m.p.h. to zero just before the lock-up point of 70 m.p.h. or 2,500 r.p.m.

If the gear lever be put into "drive" the car will start from rest in an epicyclic gear having a reduction of 1.82:1 with a corresponding increase in starting torque. On full throttle this gear will be held in engagement up to 60 m.p.h. at which point it will be automatically disengaged

SPACE & GRACE: An exceedingly large luggage locker has its capacity but little reduced by the carriage of the spare wheel. It is flanked on each side by the striking tail fins which as shown (*right*) are blended into the tail lights and the rear bumper.

plicity itself, and the converter solely may be relied upon for all ordinary driving. Only when exceptional acceleration is required in traffic or when climbing a steep hill need there be any resort to the low range of the transmission in either of its manifestations. In either case, it is pertinent to comment that the engine is so quiet, and the change from one ratio to another so smoothly effected, that from the passenger's point of view this Packard might well be powered by a fixed gear steam plant, and with wind noise also at low level the car gives astonishingly relaxed transport at cruising speeds which can range between 80 and 100 m.p.h. on suitable roads. As one might suppose, there is some increase in noise at over 110 m.p.h., and on the car tested it was impossible to sustain speeds of this order until the engine had been fitted with Bosch Type 225 sparking plugs.

Successful Suspension

At all speeds, and over all road surfaces, the combination of steadiness and comfort shows that the new Packard concept of torsion bar suspension fully repays the great experimental effort which it represents. The car is unique in that there are only two 9-ft. long torsion bars each of which runs from one end of the car to the other, being wound up anti-clockwise by the front to the wishbones and clockwise by links to the rear axle. Thus, when the front wheel goes over a bump the reaction is transmitted to the rear wheel (cross racking of the frame being thus avoided) and by reason of the exceptional length of the torsion bars a very low rate suspension can readily be provided. But the front and rear suspensions have an equal rate although, unavoidably, the weight on the front wheels is fixed and the weight on the rear wheels variable. To meet the liability of the rear to sink when laden there are stiffening torsion bars linked to the rear axle through an electric motor which is sensitive to trim and, after a delay of 5 or 7 seconds, will put the car on an even keel.

WELL FURNISHED: The handsome facia panel of the car is shown left, also the common level for the throttle and brake pedals. Below can be seen the striking interior effects made possible by modern upholstery fabrics.

and followed by the lock into direct drive at 70 m.p.h. However, in this position of the gear lever, releasing the throttle will cut out the epicyclic gear at lower speeds; similarly, pressing the accelerator pedal to the floor will re-engage the epicyclic gear at any speed below 60 m.p.h. Lastly, if the lever be put in "LO" the second sequence of events will be followed except that the epicyclic gear is permanently engaged below 60 m.p.h. irrespective of throttle opening. In this condition therefore a measure of engine braking is obtainable although it is less than might be expected owing to the high slip factor in the torque converter when it is being driven by the back axle.

Although this description may seem complicated, in fact driving the car is sim-

- - - - - - - Contd.

It is sufficiently sensitive to react to the introduction of a few gallons of fuel.

The car has a reasonably low roof-line and although the ground clearance on occasions proved inadequate the low centre of gravity made it possible to take fast corners in considerable confidence with no noise from the tyres. On sharp corners in mountainous districts the behaviour was somewhat less happy but it was only in this somewhat extreme condition that the size and soft suspension of the car were found to be of disadvantage.

In more ordinary long distance runs the 6-ft. width of the front compartment, a wraparound windscreen nearly 6 ft. wide and 18 inches deep, and the 4 ft. provided between the floor and the roof, gave an air of spaciousness which was particularly agreeable. Moreover although the car tested was the cheapest in the whole range, the level of the appointments, the design and finish of the instruments and facia panel, the Lurex upholstery and the well executed design of the interior hardware, must all be considered exceptional even when the car bears the burden of British import duty and purchase tax.

A fitting of particular interest was a radio set in which one could blend front and rear speakers to choice with sound from stations which the set selected electronically after pressing a button. The antenna could be raised and lowered at the turn of a switch, which was characteristic of the lavish standard of fittings which included a clock, although regrettably the locker space was limited, and there was no alternative accommodation for small parcels except behind the back seat ahead of the wraparound rear window. An illustration displays the enormous luggage space available, and a test of the rear seat showed that the ride here was as good as it was in front.

Braking Problems

In view of the many admirable qualities of the Clipper it is to be regetted that a serious criticism must be made when we come to the important question of brakes. With less than 100 sq. in. per laden ton these are on the small side for a car capable of running steadily at 100 m.p.h., but unfortunately, their limitations are not caused only by restricted lining area. The shoes themselves are designed to give a substantial self-servo effect (thus multiplying overall braking differences caused by changes in friction coefficient) and a very small pedal travel is compensated by a vacuum servo. These features make it easy to transfer the toe of the shoe from the throttle to the brake pedal, and little more than toe pressure will bring the car to rest from moderate speeds at a normal rate of stopping. Unfortunately, when combined with very poorly ventilated drums this system also results in the rate of retardation falling to virtually nil after one emergency stop from 100 m.p.h., or a half-dozen quick stops from 60 m.p.h. Even more discouraging, within half an hour of not very fast driving on winding roads it is impossible to stop without pumping on the pedal and when on the fourth or fifth pump the shoes catch up with the expanded drums the overall servo action can produce an effect of considerable violence.

It must be emphasized that these unfortunate symptoms do not make themselves felt in the case of main-road motoring at ordinary speeds, or at high speeds on auto routes, but unfortunately in Europe these are not the sole conditions in which a car is used, and upon which criticism of behaviour is based.

Mechanical Specification

Engine

Cylinders ...	V.8
Bore ...	96.8 mm.
Stroke ...	88.9 mm.
Cubic capacity ...	5,243 c.c.
Piston area ...	91.3 sq. in.
Valves ...	Pushrod o.h.v.
Compression ratio ...	8.5/1
Max. power ...	225 b.h.p.
at ...	4,600 r.p.m.
Piston speed at max. b.h.p.	2,700 ft. per min.
Carburetter ...	Carter double choke
Ignition ...	Auto Lite coil
Sparking plugs ...	Champion N18
Fuel pump...	Mechanical
Oil filter ...	By-pass

Transmission

Clutch ...	Nil
Top gear ...	1 : 1
Converter...	2 : 9 : 1 at 1,650 r.p.m. of flywheel
Low gear ...	1.82 : 1
Propeller shaft ...	Open
Final drive...	Hypoid bevel 3.07 : 1
Top gear m.p.h. at 1,000 r.p.m.	27.5
Top gear m.p.h. at 1,000 ft./min. piston speed ...	49

Chassis

Brakes ...	Hydraulic
Brake drum diameter ...	11 in.
Friction lining area ...	192 sq. in.
Suspension, front and rear:	Common torsion bar with leveler.
Shock absorbers:	
Front ...	Monroe telescopic
Rear ...	Monroe telescopic
Tyres ...	7.60 x 15 Tubeless

Steering

Steering gear ...	Gemmer
Turning circle (between kerbs):	
Left ...	41½ feet
Right ...	41 feet
Turns of steering wheel, lock to lock ...	5

Performance factors (at laden weight as tested):

Piston area, sq. in. per ton ...	43.3
Brake lining area, sq. in. per ton ...	93
Specific displacement, litres per ton mile...	5,420

Coachwork and Equipment

Bumper height with car unladen:
Front (max.) 20 in., (min.) 9¼ in.
Rear (max.) 18 in., (min.) 13 in.

Starting handle ...	No
Battery mounting ...	Below bonnet
Jack ...	Ratchet
Jacking points ...	Beneath bumpers

Standard tool kit: Jack; combined brace and jack handle; grease gun; tyre pump; hammer; 2 screwdrivers; pliers, plug spanner; adjustable spanner; set of 6 spanners.

Exterior lights: Two head, two parking, two tail.

Direction indicators: Two front flashing, two tail ditto, with rear lights.

Windscreen wipers ...	Two by vacuum pump
Sun vizors ...	2

Instruments: Clock, speedometer, water temperature, fuel level, oil pressure.

Warning lights: Indicators, dynamo charge, main beam, hand-brake on.

Locks:

With ignition key ...	Front doors glove locker
With other keys ...	Rear boot
Glove lockers ...	One
Map pockets ...	Nil
Parcel shelves ...	Behind rear seat
Ashtrays ...	Three
Cigar lighters ...	One
Interior lights ...	Roof, glove box, luggage locker
Interior heater ...	Yes
Car radio ...	Yes

Extras available: Push-button gear control, front underseat heater, electric window lifts, power front seat, white wall tyres, Solex glass, wheel trim rings.

Upholstery material: Lurex, Vinyl and leather

Floor covering ...	Carpet

Exterior colours standardized: Various in single, double and triple-tone combinations.

Alternative body styles ...	Hardtop coupe

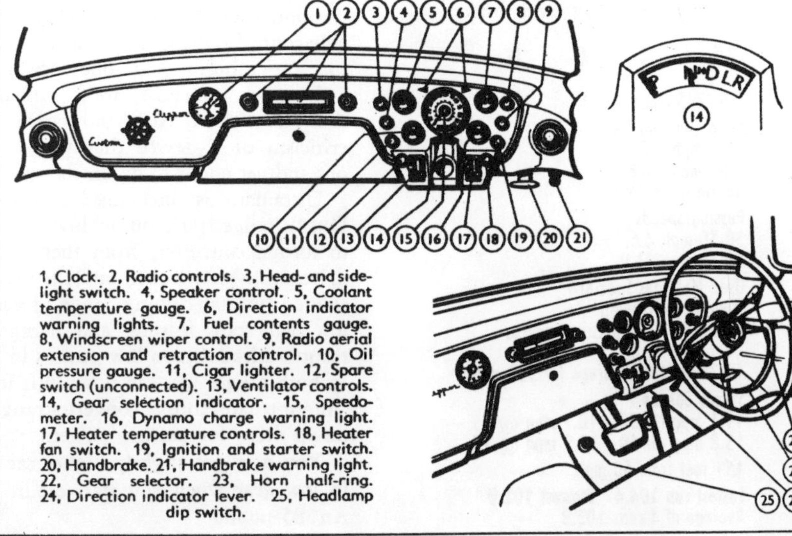

1, Clock. 2, Radio controls. 3, Head- and side-light switch. 4, Speaker control. 5, Coolant temperature gauge. 6, Direction indicator warning lights. 7, Fuel contents gauge. 8, Windscreen wiper control. 9, Radio aerial extension and retraction control. 10, Oil pressure gauge. 11, Cigar lighter. 12, Spare switch (unconnected). 13, Ventilator controls. 14, Gear selection indicator. 15, Speedometer. 16, Dynamo charge warning light. 17, Heater temperature controls. 18, Heater fan switch. 19, Ignition and starter switch. 20, Handbrake. 21, Handbrake warning light. 22, Gear selector. 23, Horn half-ring. 24, Direction indicator lever. 25, Headlamp dip switch.

JIM LODGE AND AL KIDD

drivescription '56 Clipper

A GADGETEER'S DELIGHT was our Clipper Custom sedan, with pushbutton Ultramatic control (optional), self-leveling torsion bar suspension (standard on all Clippers this year), and limited-slip differential. A couple of hidden switches under the dashboard worked the automatic car levelizer and electric door-locking device (see last month's MT). The car also had power steering and brakes.

PERFORMANCE

	'56 (275-bhp engine)	'55 (245-bhp engine)
ACCELERATION	From Standing Start 0-30 mph 4.1 0-45 mph 7.2 0-60 mph 11.3 Quarter-mile 18.3 and 77 mph	From Standing Start 0-30 mph 4.0 0-60 mph 11.9 Quarter-mile 18.7
	Passing Speeds 30-50 mph 4.5 40-60 mph 5.2 50-80 mph 12.1	Passing Speeds 30-50 mph 4.6 50-80 mph 13.9
FUEL CONSUMPTION	Used Mobilgas Special Stop-and-Go Driving 13.0 mpg highway trip average 9.9 mpg city driving average 11.4 mpg tank average for 455 miles	Used Mobilgas Special Stop-and-Go Driving 11.8 mpg over measured course 13.2 mpg tank average for 938 miles
	Steady Speeds 19.7 mpg @ 30 17.6 mpg @ 45 14.9 mpg @ 60 12.4 mpg @ 75	Steady Speeds 19.1 mpg @ 30 18.7 mpg @ 45 15.8 mpg @ 60 12.9 mpg @ 75
STOPPING DISTANCE	158 feet from 60 mph	151 feet from 60 mph
TOP SPEED	Fastest run 109.2 Slowest 105.3 Average of 4 runs 107.1	Fastest run 104.4 Slowest 102.9 Average of 4 runs 103.3

Its recontoured combustion chambers give a 9.5 to 1 compression ratio. Long-reach sparkplugs are new, as is a revamped 4-barrel carburetor (Clipper Super and Deluxe have 2-barrel carbs) which keeps the secondary throttle from opening until the engine is revving high enough to accept the added fuel mixture.

Clipper's electrical transmission control lived up to its claims: It was easy to shift as touching a typewriter key, refused to engage REVERSE or PARK over 5 mph, automatically went into PARK position when ignition was turned off regardless of gear engaged; but it also echoed some fears we voiced when it was introduced. With the car parked on a grade we suddenly found ourselves lacking all gears. We pushed button after button, regained gears mysteriously after about 5 minutes of waiting.

Our troubles, say Packard engineers, could have been due to a wide combination of ills. It was a wet, slushy day, and it's possible that the underside wiring had shorted out; or it could have been just a loose wire at one of the many junctions between the buttons and transmission. Whenever there's a short circuit, a heat-sensitive circuit breaker will separate. When the condition clears itself, the coupling returns to normal.

Did you ever feel that you were about to break off the shift lever trying to pry an automatic transmission out of PARK on a steep hill? Ultramatic's electrical system now takes this battle off your hands, and the energy required to pop the parking pawl can overload the electrical system. If this was our trouble, the circuit breaker may have blown, then rejuvenated itself for a successful shift.

Compared with Chrysler Corp.'s cable-operated, left-hand, mechanical pushbuttons, Ultramatic's setup is in a more natural position for this generation of right-hand shifters. But its size and its position also obstruct part of the dashboard. Chances are this 1st-year location will be changed, or the instrument panel will undergo restyling. With any change in position should come a mechanical override control outside the transmission housing, providing at least one forward gear.

In years to come, we'll probably be the 1st to look back and laugh at our criticism of a device that you can't get out and get under to fix on the spot!

Ultramatic is unchanged in operation: DRIVE range starts off in low gear, shifts to torque converter, from there to direct drive (converter locked out); HIGH is considered normal driving range, doesn't use low-gear start feature, and doesn't have throttle kickdown to low gear as in DRIVE. In both ranges you can downshift into the "intermediate" torque converter range from direct drive for passing power.

You now get slightly higher car speeds in low gear when you start off in DRIVE. An 85-pound

CLIPPER

weight reduction with the new aluminum Ultramatic transmission housing also gives better weight distribution.

Test car's "split-traction" rear axle, despite rumors, is *not* the Hi-Tork unit described in August '55 MT. Clipper's differential uses cam, not spring, action to engage cone clutches, is referred to as an "unlocking" unit. Further explanation: wheels are "locked" when traveling straight ahead; wheel which loses traction is unlocked from drive action to keep it from spinning. Packard and Clipper differentials are now made by Spicer.

On the road, value of this axle was readily apparent when roads became icy; we could put the right rear wheel on the gravel shoulder for traction and the left wheel wouldn't spin helplessly on pavement as in conventional setups. Differential can cause slight snake-dance on glare ice when both wheels are able to spin; wheels take turns seeking (and getting) traction, can make rear end move from one side to the other. We couldn't feel advantage of having full traction at outside wheel in curves—but it's there, and with a standard-shift car you might be aware of this, possibly notice what seems like oversteer until you got used to it. Ultramatic, with its slippage and smoothness, doesn't have as close a relationship between throttle pressure and wheels.

Driving the Clipper, you find little changed from the '55. Seat is still high, vision excellent. Power brake pedal, low to floorboard, has no-grab action; accelerator pedal is still uncomfortably high for long-trip driving.

At the base of the 56's steering column is a rubber cushion which isolates road shock from the steering wheel (steel discs take over to form rigid coupling should cushion become torn or damaged). New, too, is 10 per cent reduction of steering wheel turns. Clipper power steering, again noticeably accurate, retains creditable amount of road feel. There's little play or looseness in system, no unexpected power boost as you start to turn the wheel, no binding or stiffness at any point. Wheel return after hard turns could be snappier. Altho the engine refinements upped output, Clipper did well to hold its own against the '55 car in acceleration tests, for rear axle is considerably higher-geared. Standard ratio in '55 was 3.23, this year's is 2.87 to 1; test car ran 3.07 axle, one of 5 ratios offered.

Standing-start acceleration times shown were made in DRIVE range; average times in HIGH range ran 5.8 (0-30), 9.9 (0-45), 15.5 (0-60) and 20.6 (quarter-mile, with speed of 71 mph).

Under fade tests, Clipper's brakes weren't impressive except in the light of recuperative power. Fading early (1st noticeable on 4th stop from 60 mph, complete from 5th thru 10th stops), brakes recovered effectiveness much faster than we've come to expect. Swerve was nearly non-existent at all times.

Roadability was generally good. There's no loss of roadworthiness over winding, bumpy roads. Washboard roads caused wheel hop, at times moved rear end completely out of lane. Clipper suspension is on soft side of average, has low spring rate at wheels; this causes wheels to rise further, come back down slower, can make car move more easily than a stiffer one.

Clipper has no peer—unless it's Packard—in ability to smooth out dips and humps. Front end comes up out of a rise in a normal enough manner, but it never bounds back down. Instead, it waits until the rear end has braced itself and leveled off, then it comes down in an almost imperceptible movement.

At normal highway speeds car was disturbed only slightly by uneven road surfaces; at high speeds it was exceptionally stable; there was no chassis or steering wheel vibration, no tendency to float or crab as crosswinds caught it—a claim none of our other test cars have been able to make this year.

In tight turns, where most cars will bear heavily on the outside front wheel, Clipper uses torsion bars to resist weight transfer; they act as they do when front end tries to go down in a dip. Result is less lean and tire squeal, more tendency to drift or slide before the wheels lose traction with the road.

The very actions that make hard maneuvers less violent tie right in with good riding qualities. Nothing in Clipper's class is more level; body floats over railroad crossings, takes detours without pitching. But chassis shock-absorbing ability is bettered by others in this class, for you can still hear and feel wheel bounce over ruts and tarstrips, even tho body remains absolutely level. Wind noise was blessedly lower than in most cars tested; engine and transmission noise were noticeably less than in '55 Clipper, due largely to higher axle gearing and lower rpms. —**Jim Lodge**

PACKARD EXECUTIVE	☑☑☑☑☑ MEANS TOP RATING
At 275 bhp the Executive ties for highest powered car in its price range. Push-button Ultramatic gives quick choice of acceleration or economy.	PERFORMANCE ☑☑☑☑☐
Typically Packard, but in our opinion the most pleasing style job of the entire Packard-Clipper family.	STYLING ☑☑☑☑☐
Equal to, it not definitely better than, any car in (or below) its price class. On some rough surfaces it offers the smoothest ride of any American car ever built.	RIDING COMFORT ☑☑☑☑☑
Generally well thought out with good vision and seating position adding to driver comfort. Instrument dials are over-decorated, not too easy to read.	INTERIOR DESIGN ☑☑☑☑☐
Torsion bar suspension gives a stable and balanced performance on most surfaces and a very good resistance to heel-over in sharp curves.	ROADABILITY ☑☑☑☑☐
With power steering and push-button Ultramatic transmission there is very little for the driver to do but exercise good judgment and regulate the accelerator.	EASE OF CONTROL ☑☑☑☑☑
Although engine is fairly accessible, there are a number of items throughout the car such as the torsion bar levelizer and the electric push-button control that will require service and periodic adjustment.	SERVICEABILITY ☑☑☑☐☐
The Executive gives every evidence of being able to stand up over the years. Body is solidly built and engine well-designed.	DURABILITY ☑☑☑☑☐
There are no conspicuous faults in Packard's trim and paint finish or assembly, it is about equal to others in its field, falling below average in respect to interior moldings and hardware.	WORKMANSHIP ☑☑☑☑☐
A well-built, good looking and beautifully riding and performing car, handicapped by high rate of depreciation. The car must be considered as a long term investment in good transportation.	VALUE PER DOLLAR ☑☑☑☐☐

PACKARD EXECUTIVE

Factory List Price: **$3560**

THE EXECUTIVE comes into being as a result of Studebaker-Packard's desire to fill the hole in the company's price line that lies between the $3200 Clipper Custom in the medium price class and the $4200-plus Packard in the highest price class. Selling at around $3600, the Executive will compete with Chrysler's New Yorker and Buick's Roadmaster.

The new Packard is more a product of production line sleight-of-hand than of the engineering laboratory or styling studio. The car is basically a 122"-wheelbase Clipper Custom with grille and front end components borrowed from Packard's parts bin.

Other minor details of interior trim and instrument styling are Packard's too. The only styling exclusive to the Executive is the 5-inch wide color band bordered with chrome strips which runs plumb-line straight from headlight hood to taillight trim. Although this styling idiom is typical of the Packard-Clipper family, it is in our opinion by far the most pleasing of the many variations on the color band theme.

From an engineering aspect the Executive is identical to the Clipper Custom, sharing the same chassis with torsion bar suspension and the same 352-cubic inch V8.

The engine is equipped with a four-barrel carburetor and develops 275 bhp at 4600 rpm and a whopping 380 ft. lbs of torque at 2800.

Torsion bar suspension gives a degree of riding comfort equal to any other car in Executive's price class. It is particularly good at smothering small surface irregularities like broken concrete or cobblestones. On some types of bumpy blacktop roads, at certain speeds, the torsion bar layout gives a gentle, bobbing motion that is unlike the action of conventional independent coil-spring suspensions. Roadability and handling are better than average, and power steering gives fairly quick control. Unassisted manual steering is not recommended on a car as heavy as 4200-plus lbs.

Teamed with Ultramatic the Packard V8 engine gives smooth performance at all speeds. The "H" and "D" positions on the electric transmission control permit the driver to switch from a direct (torque converter locked out) cruising ratio to a lower ratio for acceleration or hill climbing without the necessity of kicking accelerator to the floor.

Summing up: the Executive is a distinctive looking car, comparing favorably with the Chrysler New Yorker and Buick Roadmaster in price, performance and appearance. With this car Packard has gone a long way towards reviving the confidence that its name once inspired. ●

This beautifully-handling luxury car boasts push-button controls and many other excellent details

PACKARD 400

LAST YEAR, when formerly staid Packard introduced torsional suspension plus an automatic electrically-driven "levelizer" that keeps the car on an even keel under overloaded conditions, it was obvious that things were going to start popping around Detroit. The industry just couldn't be caught short with Packard uncorking "firsts" right and left. So, the push-button transmission control idea was born and this year Packard is only an "also ran" when it comes to push-buttons. However, Packard's new six-button keyboard is a bit different from what the Chrysler chaps have to offer—Packard's is electrically activated.

The styling studio has finally taken the bulge out of the rear deck and made an attempt to slenderize the lines. The tail-lights, called *cathedral* type by the stylists, have been accentuated, and a six-sided reflector reminiscent of Packard's ancient symbol has been added beneath the huge red lens. Up front the grille has been given the strength-through-heavier-chrome treatment both above and below the bumper, and the *Dagmars* on the latter have been moved outward even with the headlights while the parking lights (which double as turn signals) have been wrapped around the fenders so they can be seen from the sides. They've hung on to the very sensible courtesy light on the rear fender, but they've restyled the chrome trim along the sides. We thought that the '55 Packard had a broken look along the body sides and that the two-toning was less than esthetic, so we're happy to say that we honestly think that the '56 model is greatly improved as to line.

Size is almost identical with the previous model. Weight is not much less, but is much better distributed, partially due to the Ultramatic transmission case being re-engineered and built of aluminum. This results in a weight decrease of something like 95 pounds, making this, according to Packard, the lightest-weight automatic transmission currently on the

Packard's grille is still easily recognizable, although the chrome is heavier this year and the bumper guards have been moved far outward.

Packard engineers have made further improvements in the novel torsion-bar suspension they introduced last year, and handling is even better.

The cathedral-type tail-lights have been given prominence in styling, and the rear deck in general has been slenderized for more eye appeal.

Another "first" chalked up by Packard this year is the new "non-slip" differential, which directs tractive effort to the wheel needing it.

PACKARD: Other model: *Caribbean*: Dimensions same as Packard. Engine: same size, 310 h.p. @ 4600 rpm, 405 ft. lbs. torque @ 2800 rpm.

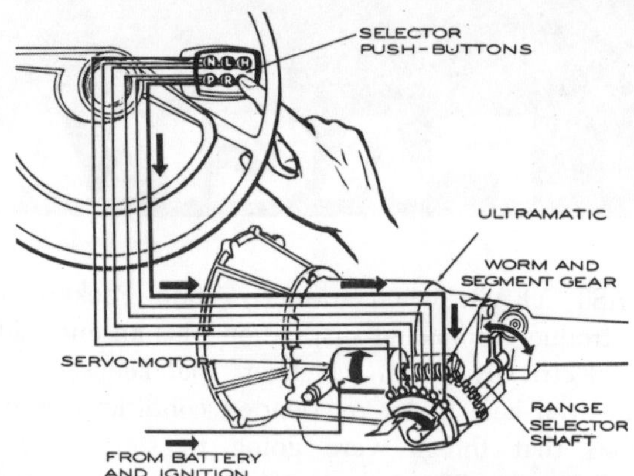

The new pushbutton driving system is absolutely effortless, since a servo-motor does all the work, as you see in this schematic diagram.

market. Thus, the weight in the front has been decreased, and the result is better distribution.

This brings us logically to the handling characteristics of this large car. Briefly, the new model handles better than last year's; on the hardest corners there's scarcely a trace of wheel hop or sideways lurch when one rear wheel overspeeds the other. The reason for this is that Packard has done it again: pulled another *first* out of the engineering hat. This new development is the "non-slip" differential which does something for which automotive engineers have striven for many years: it causes the tractive effort to be directed to the wheel which needs it. In other words, if a new Packard happens to be sitting against the curb or off the side of the road with the right pair of wheels on ice or in sand or mud, the left rear wheel will automatically do the work instead of refusing to budge while the bogged wheel spins merrily but ineffectively around.

Further improvements have been made to the torsion bar suspension; the rear end of the car has received attention, and the main torsion bars are slightly longer. A switch on the dashboard allows one to inactivate the "levelizer;" in use, this gimmick permits the overloading of the trunk if need be without the annoying tail end droop of conventionally-sprung cars.

Packard considers the torsion bars and "non-slip" differential definite safety features. To this contention we heartily agree, since both make driving safer and roadability much surer. Standard, also, is the padded top of the dash panel; safety belts capable of withstanding the specified CAA load are optional.

Also an extra, unfortunately, is the previously mentioned push-button drive control. With a total of six buttons (for neutral, low, high, park, reverse, and drive) arranged in two horizontal rows, this electric drive system is located in a position that corresponds to that of the conventional lever. Optionally available on all Packards, except on the plush and colorful Caribbean convertibles and hardtops on which it is standard equipment, this drive system has its own safety features; placed in "park," the system cannot be taken out of "park," even accidentally, until the key has been inserted and turned in the ignition. Switching off constitutes an automatic lock in "park." Also, one cannot, at speed of more than 10 m.p.h. place the reverse button in operation; an interlock takes care of this and thus prevents damage to the transmission.

The Ultramatic for '56 has undergone improvement, too; there are now two stepdowns for passing snap: depressing the accelerator half way at city traffic speeds produces a drop in ratio while fully depressing the pedal at highway speeds gives final stepdown up to around 70 m.p.h.

Packard is betting all its dough on cubic inches and torque, the latter being more important in the usual driving speed ranges than horsepower. This year's engines are the largest capacity to date, have the most torque and the greatest horsepower; if this isn't enough, consider the Caribbean with two four-barrel carburetors and other vitamins for a total of 310 horsepower. On the regular Packard line you'll get somewhere over 12 miles per gallon; on the Caribbean, better own an oil well. Seriously, though, this is a driver's car, the nation's best handling luxury vehicle, and one that's beautifully and carefully built.

PERFORMANCE:

ACCELERATION, corrected speeds (from standing start):
Zero to 30 mph: 3.6 seconds (speedometer read 32)
Zero to 45 mph: 6.4 seconds (speedometer read 46)
Zero to 60 mph: 10.2 seconds (speedometer read 65)
HIGHWAY ACCELERATION (with stepdown) 50 to 80 mph: 10.9 sec.
MAXIMUM SPEED: Approx. 115 mph
FORWARD VISIBILITY over hood: About 23 feet.

SPECIFICATIONS

(all in inches unless noted otherwise)

PACKARD 400

CHASSIS & BODY:

Wheelbase	127
Tread—(front, rear)	60, 60-9/10
Length overall	218½
Width overall	78
Height overall	62-3/10
Ground clearance	6
Turning circle diameter	45 feet
Steering wheel stop-to-stop	3⅞ turns with power; 5 mechanical
Tire size	8.00 x 15
Weight (shipping)	4355 lbs.
Overhang....(front, rear)	32-3/10, 55-4/10
Brake lining area	208¼ sq. in.
Weight to brake area ratio	20.9 lbs. per sq. in.
Weight to power ratio	11.23 lbs. per BHP

ENGINE & DRIVE TRAIN:

Cylinders, block, valves	8, 90° V, overhead
Bore and stroke	4.125 x 3.5
Displacement	374 cu. in
Compression ratio	10.0
Brake horsepower (maximum)	290 @ 4600 RPM
Torque	405 ft. lbs. @ 2800 RPM
Carburetor	4-barrel downdraft
Fuel pump	Mechanical
Fuel tank capacity	20 gallons
Exhaust system	Dual
Crankcase capacity	5 quarts (add 1 for filter)
Drive shaft type	Exposed
Rear axle ratio (and available transmissions)	3-speed Manual: None; Overdrive: None; Automatic: 3.54
Cooling system capacity	27 quarts with heater

INTERIOR DIMENSIONS:

Shoulder room	57 front, 55½ rear
Headroom	36-2/10 front, 34-9/10 rear
Legroom	43 front, 48-8/10 rear

CONDITION AND PERFORMANCE OF AN 'AUTOMATIC' PACKARD

The Packard looked particularly smart with the hood lowered, when the car appeared to be even wider than it actually was. During the test the luggage boot lock was out of order

The long, eight-cylinder, side-valve engine is partially obscured by the large air filter. The small six-volt battery on the right was a temporary expedient while one of the correct size was being purchased by the vendors

AFTER SIX YEARS

OCCASIONALLY a used car of unusual type is offered to us for test and evaluation. If it is unique or there is very little likelihood of similar models being available in this country, it is our practice not to include the assessment in the Used Car series of articles.

Recently a light blue, 1951 model Packard Convertible came our way, and we were glad of the opportunity to study not only the condition of an American car after five years' use in this country, but also the way in which the automatic transmission, with which it was fitted, had stood up to long use in British traffic conditions.

The first impression on taking over was one of mild alarm at the embarrassing size of the vehicle, for this was greatly exaggerated when viewed from the left-hand driving seat. For the first mile or two it was instinctive to pull almost into the gutter as oncoming traffic approached. But after further experience, when accustomed to gauging its width, it was remarkable how very easily and precisely the car could be controlled even in heavy traffic. This was helped considerably by the ability to see the offside wing from the driving position.

When familiar with the control of the car, it was possible to take stock of its characteristics, and they were quite different from what had been expected. The ultra-soft "boulevard" ride for which many American cars are noted was not to be found on the Packard. The suspension was soft by British standards, but the road surface could be clearly felt, and over really bad sections of road the car took quite a shaking.

A favourable result of this tendency to firmness was that the car was directionally stable at reasonable speeds, and the cornering and roadholding were much above the average for this type of vehicle. The degree of roll on cornering was not excessive and although the 7.50 × 15in tyres gave audible information of all that was going on, the car could be driven quite fast round most main road corners.

The steering, although not power-assisted, required commendably little effort, even when manœuvring. At normal speeds only the lightest touch on the wheel was required to control the car, and in spite of the extremely low gearing of the mechanism, there was no detectable lost movement at the wheel.

Heavy pedal pressure was required to overcome the initial movement of the brake pedal, but thereafter increased pressure produced efficient retardation. At low speeds the servo action was a little unpredictable, and a careless jab at the pedal could be quite exciting. At high speeds, the weight of the Packard, combined with the shrouded brake drums, made it advisable to start braking early.

In 1951, automatic transmission was

Instruments were well sited, and the driving position was comfortable; the drive selector was on the right of the steering column, and the control for the winking indicators on the left. Both feet could be used on the large brake pedal in emergency. There was no interior light

The hood movement took considerable current from the temporary battery so that it was essential to keep the dynamo charging when raising or lowering it. Although in good condition, when in the raised position it was a poor fit all round, particularly above the windscreen

very much more of a novelty in this country than it is now, but the system applied to the Packard must still be commended. There was no indication that the transmission had deteriorated any more than would be expected after five years' use.

The selector lever had the usual five positions (P, N, H, L and R), the selection being indicated in a little quadrant on the steering column, which was illuminated when the side lights were in use. Normally the H position (High range) was engaged.

To start the engine it was necessary simply to switch on the ignition with the drive selector in the Park or Neutral position and press the accelerator right down. Usually the engine needed about three or four turns before it would fire; the throttle could then be released and the necessary drive range selected. When the selector was in the Park position a positive transmission brake was in action; this was particularly useful since the handbrake was out of adjustment.

At about 25 m.p.h., with a small throttle opening, a slight change in the exhaust note and a slight surge could be detected, whereupon the driver knew that the engine was pulling through direct drive, with the torque converter not in operation. Unless full throttle was used, the take-off from a standing start was slow in H range, and in traffic it was preferable to make frequent use of the L (Low) range.

With this engaged, the drive is transmitted through—in addition to the torque converter—a low ratio planetary gear. This gear is held, irrespective of the throttle opening or the speed of the car, until the lever is moved back to H, which is the moment when the driver feels the only slight jolt which it seemed possible to achieve with this transmission.

There must be some power loss in the torque converter, but the only indication of the engine speed was provided by the exhaust note. With the hood down, this could be heard clearly and was rather pleasing, without being unnecessarily loud.

The big side-valve engine has eight cylinders in line, and a swept volume of $4\frac{3}{4}$ litres; it develops 135 b.h.p. at the low speed of 3,600 r.p.m. Never more than the slightest sound was heard from it during the whole test. When the throttle was depressed for maximum acceleration a kick-down switch re-engaged the torque converter; but even at the high revolutions which this permitted, the engine continued to remain commendably silent.

In the performance table below it will be noticed that the acceleration deteriorated considerably once 50 m.p.h. had been reached. The maximum speed of the car was not investigated, but is likely to be in the vicinity of 85 m.p.h. in High range and 50 m.p.h. in Low range.

PERFORMANCE FIGURES

Acceleration from rest		
to 30 m.p.h.	7.2 sec	(5.8 sec)
to 50 m.p.h.	15.4 sec	(13.7 sec)
to 60 m.p.h.	23.6 sec	(21.3 sec)
20 to 40 m.p.h.	6.3 sec	(5.5 sec)
30 to 50 m.p.h.	8.2 sec	(7.9 sec)
40 to 60 m.p.h.	12.7 sec	

The figures in parentheses were taken using both L and H ranges, the change being between 30 and 40 m.p.h. with sustained full throttle. All other acceleration figures were taken in H range alone.

At all speeds there was a noticeable tremble in the steering column which amounted to rather more than normal road shocks. Above 60 m.p.h. this rapidly increased; at 70 m.p.h. a marked vibration set in over the whole of the front of the car, and the movement of the steering column was disconcerting. It may be that this was due to nothing more than the wheels being out of balance or out of alignment, but it was a fault which needed rectification.

In some respects the car did tend to confirm the fact that American cars are constructed for use over a reasonably limited period. Knobs would come off in one's hand, and with the hood up the car was draughty and rattled to an excessive degree. The carpets had worn well but the seats and door trim were shabby. The general under-bonnet appearance was untidy, with rust and dirt in evidence. The heater and air conditioning ducts had deteriorated badly, which explained the inefficiency of this unit. The heater fan was not working, nor was the clock. On the other hand, the radio was excellent, and the fuel gauge and thermometer were accurate.

The Packard's light blue cellulose was in first-class condition, and the chromium was sound.

The car gave the strange impression that it would keep running indefinitely; certainly the mechanical condition was satisfactory apart from the faults mentioned. The engine was consuming oil at the rate of approximately 1,000 m.p.g. There was no oil pressure gauge.

The Packard's fuel consumption was more than usually dependent on the demands being made on it. Driving the car hard the consumption readily rose to 9 m.p.g., and during the unusual conditions when the performance figures were being taken, petrol fairly poured through the engine. However, for normal use in which rapid acceleration was avoided, 14 m.p.g. was obtainable.

There is no doubt that Packard had done well to obtain such ease of control on this big vehicle.

For attracting attention, there are not many cars to beat it. On parking it in a public place, the driver would return to find a little crowd had gathered to examine it. To operate the automatic hood in such places was to run some risk of a charge for obstruction.

For comfortable transport the Packard also had a lot to offer; it had more accommodation for eight people than most British cars have for six. The penalty for this was the great size and thus, the difficulty of manœuvring and parking in confined spaces or heavy traffic.

The mileometer of the car was not working and gave no help in assessing the distance that had been covered. However, the total is probably at least 50,000 miles. A close examination of the engine and transmission supported our impression that they had not been overhauled in any way. Hills Garages, Ltd., of High Road, Woodford Green, Essex, who provided the car, are offering it for sale at £850.

J. S. M. B.

CONTINUED FROM PAGE 115

far from easy. There is a certain amount of nose dive on hard braking, but nothing like that normally associated with cars of this caliber. There is a slight sensation of roll on the corners, but never that terrifying feeling that if the car had been going two miles an hour faster it might well be skating on the doors. The road-holding qualities of the Patrician can be directly attributed to the torsion bar suspension system, which uses neither coil nor leaf springs!

A diversion might well be in place here to explain the functioning of the torsion bar system, but before we do so let us state that although the system employed on the Patrician will iron out the regular bumps, like those experienced from street car tracks or normally rough roads, it can be caught unawares with big bump or dip; it is thought that the present system could be tightened up considerably without losing any of the "softness" of the ride.

A torsion bar suspension depends upon the twist or torque properties of a metal bar, which has the same, but more limited, qualities as an elastic band, which when twisted tends to revert to its original position. In the case of an automobile suspension system the principle relies upon two bars running approximately parallel to the chassis, fixed in the rear and swinging free at the front in accord with the movement of the front wheels. These bars are assembled under tension so that they tend to force the front wheels downwards; when the car hits a bump the bars are wound-up, but the amount of wind is usually less than that which can be dealt with by the elasticity of the metal, which means that the force actually gets back to the rear chassis shackles. If the force is quicker than the elasticity of the bar, definite jolting is felt. Such movement then is experienced in the rear of the car and not under the front wheels. This disposes of frontal disruptions. In the rear, torque arms relying on the same principle and working in conjunction with a stabilizer linked to a fixture below one of the transverse rear chassis members, transmit any large unwarranted forces to the central "X" member of the chassis.

A refinement is the torsion levelling system that automatically adjusts the level of the automobile should there be any irregular weighting. With this equipment weight distribution is uniform at all times even if there is overloading in the rear in comparison to the front, or vice versa. This leveller is coordinated so that it does not act when there is momentary redistribution of weight or force, such as upon fierce braking or acceleration. It operates in conjunction with a time switch, with a lag of six to seven seconds.

Summarizing, we would be bold enough to say that to date this is the car of the year in its class; it is not the most eye-catching, but is the most "automobilistic" U. S. car of its type. It has been a pleasure to road test the Patrician. ☆☆

Compromise car? Yes. To be lightly dismissed for that reason? Certainly not!

story and photos by Joe H. Wherry

PACKARD CLIPPER Drivescription

DRIVING ANY CAR on Studebaker-Packard's proving ground at South Bend, Ind., is highly interesting, for this track is capable of handing a car as terrific

STUDEBAKER? Yes, underneath you'll find a chassis like the Stude sedans'.

a beating as any in the industry. Even the big high-speed loop, said to be the oldest still in use in the industry, is rough with the repairs necessitated by age. While speeds in excess of 100 miles per hour are thus difficult to maintain, the track does show up the durability of a car.

So driving the new Packard Clipper in its newly adopted environment was an interesting assignment. A few months ago there were only about 1200 Packard dealers in the entire nation. Now, because many Studebaker dealers have taken on the new line, there are some 2000. What manner of car is this that is slated to perpetuate one of the industry's most historic names? Is it just a more luxurious Studebaker or is it a distinctive make in its own right? Before answering these two questions, let's drive the new Clipper models.

Beneath the hood is the same engine arrangement used in the Studebaker Golden Hawk—a 289-cubic-inch overhead-valve plant with solid lifters, a 7.8 to 1 compression ratio, and a two-barrel carburetor which takes the rammed air from a high-efficiency, belt-driven McCulloch supercharger. The power of this unit, as you no doubt already know, is 275 horsepower at 4800 rpm; torque is 333 pounds-feet at 3200 rpm.

The latest information shows the overdrive transmission to be standard, with a 4.27 to 1 rear axle. A three-element automatic transmission is optional but will be the most frequent installation; thus equipped, the rear-axle ratio is 3.31 to 1. I was fortunate in being able to drive Clippers with each gearbox. Of the two models offered, a four-door station wagon (called the "Country Sedan") and the four-door Town Sedan, the former is the more roadable because of better weight distribution. For this reason the best acceleration was obtained with the wagon, despite its curb weight of 3982 pounds against the sedan's 3825.

Fortunately there were few icy spots on the straightaways, and initial wheelspin was minimized by not holding the power brakes or revving the automatic-equipped engine. To a corrected 60 mph from a standstill took exactly 11 seconds in the station wagon equipped with Flightomatic. The sedan, with more weight on the front wheels and less on the rear wheels, made it to the 60 mark in 11.6 seconds with the overdrive transmission. The latter would undoubtedly trim the socks off the wagon, regardless of transmission, with a couple of hundred pounds of dead weight tossed into the trunk. Clutch action in the stick-shift sedan was light and the fast-revving blown engine sprang to life so quickly that the greatest problem was keeping the rear wheels from spinning. The heavier wagon, even when handicapped with the automatic transmission, consistently broke away faster to 60 mph.

BLEND of Packard's recent tail light design and high fenders with South Bend-inspired body shell is by no means a failure.

The automatic transmission quadrant is like that in the new Studebaker line with positions for PARK, NEUTRAL, DRIVE, LOW, and REVERSE. In DRIVE you have a passing step-down up to 60 mph with either the automatic or the overdrive transmission. Cruising along at 50 mph and suddenly mashing the accelerator pedal to the floor gave an immediate jump to 80 mph in 10.3 seconds in the automatic-equipped wagon; the sedan with the stick showed up better at higher speeds with 10.0 seconds.

Down in the city traffic speed ranges where Mr. and Mrs. John Q. Public vie with each other in the great traffic light grand prix, the new Clipper will hop to a true 30 mph in 4.1 seconds with an automatic transmission and to 45 in an even 7.0 seconds. Stick-shift artists will make the same marks in 3.9 and 6.8 seconds respectively if they refrain from popping the clutch too sprightly, especially in the sedan.

As for top speed, either the wagon or the sedan will exceed 100 mph with ease. Less than a mile of straight track is available between the two sweeping curves on the South Bend proving ground, but, by coming out of the big curves at 80 mph, it was relatively simple to gun up over the century zone and still have plenty of time left to slow down before entering the next turn.

The finned brake drums, introduced last year by Studebaker, incorporate a weather seal by means of a tongue and groove seal between the drum and backing plate. The effective lining area is a fraction over 195 square inches. These are not the largest brakes for a car of the Clipper's weight, but they are among the most effective. During more than an hour of acceleration tests on both Clippers tested, there was little noticeable fade even during the most severe and repeated braking from speeds up to 60 mph.

The cornering ability of the new Clipper is good, although not exciting. There is considerable lean on hard corners (see photo, page 27), but the driver is not as apt to notice this as are onlookers. Power steering, with 4¼ turns of the wheel from lock to lock, is standard and manual steering is not specified at all. The Saginaw power unit is used, so there is still a fair amount of road feel left to the driver and some resistance as well.

At this point we come to a suitable place to explain the "why" of the station wagon's superior handling as compared to that of the sedan. In the first place the wagon's wheelbase is 116.5 inches while that of the sedan is 120.5; maneuvering slowly, this difference is first evident in a shorter turning diameter: 39.5 feet as compared to the sedan's 41. The overall length of the wagon is 204.8 inches; the sedan is just seven inches longer. Both body styles use the same independent coil front suspension at first glance, but only the sedan is equipped with the variable rate springs. In the rear the semi-elliptic springs are the same length on each car, but the sedan uses five leaves while the wagon has four main and two helper leaves for a softer ride under all load conditions. Here we find one of the few wagons that rides as well as the corresponding sedan.

The shorter wheelbase of the wagon could account for slightly better handling, but the weight distribution really tells the tale. On the scales in the engineering shops at the proving ground the station wagon's front end weighed 2211 pounds and the rear 1771. In comparison the lighter-weight sedan equipped with stick shift weighed in at 2227 pounds for the front and just 1598 pounds in the rear. With a weight/power ratio of 14.48 pounds per bhp for the station wagon and 13.91 for the sedan (both at curb weight), it's not difficult to understand why it's so necessary to use the accelerator gingerly when taking off to prevent time-wasting wheel spin.

Inside, powered front seat and windows are available. The dashboard is distinctively Packard and features conventional push-pull and turn-type auxiliary controls in contrast to the Studebaker's toggle switches. The speedometer is of the horizontal type without trip odometer. The charge-discharge and oil pressure indicators are of the warning light variety and the fuel level indicator has the familiar needle marker.

Transmission control pushbuttons are no more; the accelerator pedal and brake pedal are positioned as in the Studebaker —that is, a little farther apart than is customary, with about 3½ inches space between. The windshield is, of course, wrapped around; distortion at the sides is less than average. A happy item is the electrically operated wiper system. Gold-colored plating graces most of the interior hardware and standard equipment items include such things as clock, lighter, armrests on all four doors, built-in foot rests in the sedan's rear compartment, dashboard padding, automatic trunk light and folding rear center armrest in the sedans, and a luxuriously thick floor carpet in both models.

Interior space parallels that in the Studebaker President Classic (the basic chassis of which is shared with the Clipper sedan) and the upholstery of metallic "matlace" material is over thick foam rubber seat foundations. This marks the first year since '50 for a station wagon under the Packard name.

Many will imagine themselves to be concerned because this car admittedly uses the same basic body shell as the less expensive Studebaker line. This should cause little concern, however, because the use of one body shell over two and even three different nameplates is an old Detroit habit, too. When the decision was made to bring Packard production to South Bend, the styling lads performed an arduous task in an incredibly short time— the Packard-like grille and rear quarter panels were styled in a fraction of the usual time, as were the new instrument panel and exterior trim. The net result is a car readily distinguishable from the Studebaker and, in fact, from two to five inches longer, station wagon and sedan respectively.

With the same rated power as previous Clippers, performance should be even better due to the weight decrease of some 300 pounds. The installation of the supercharger should be welcomed by power enthusiasts, for the additional 30 per cent boost in the fuel-air mixture thus provided offers one of the easiest and most economical means of increasing efficiency and output. (See Spotlight for more supercharger news.)

The continuation of one of the most honored names in the industry depends upon the success of this medium-priced Packard Clipper for '57. We cannot foresee the future, nor can we divine the public's reaction; we do, though, believe that the driver who wishes something off the beaten path in '57 at least owes it to himself to closely examine and drive the new Clipper. Our two check cars were early production models; each had too few miles on the odometer for the best indication of performance. As for craftsmanship, close examination disclosed each car to be well assembled in all respects. **—J. H. W.**

IDENTITY is perhaps best preserved in the front seat, where Packard dials and high-cost trim join Studebaker controls.

GOLDEN HAWK comes to mind in the new engine compartment, with its V8 using McCulloch blower, mechanical lifters.

1957 Packard Clipper, two inches lower, 300 lbs. lighter, offers best performance, handling, in marque's history. Low pressure supercharging, limited slip diff., revised springing, auto. transmission as standard equipment are features.

SLICK SUPER PACKARDS

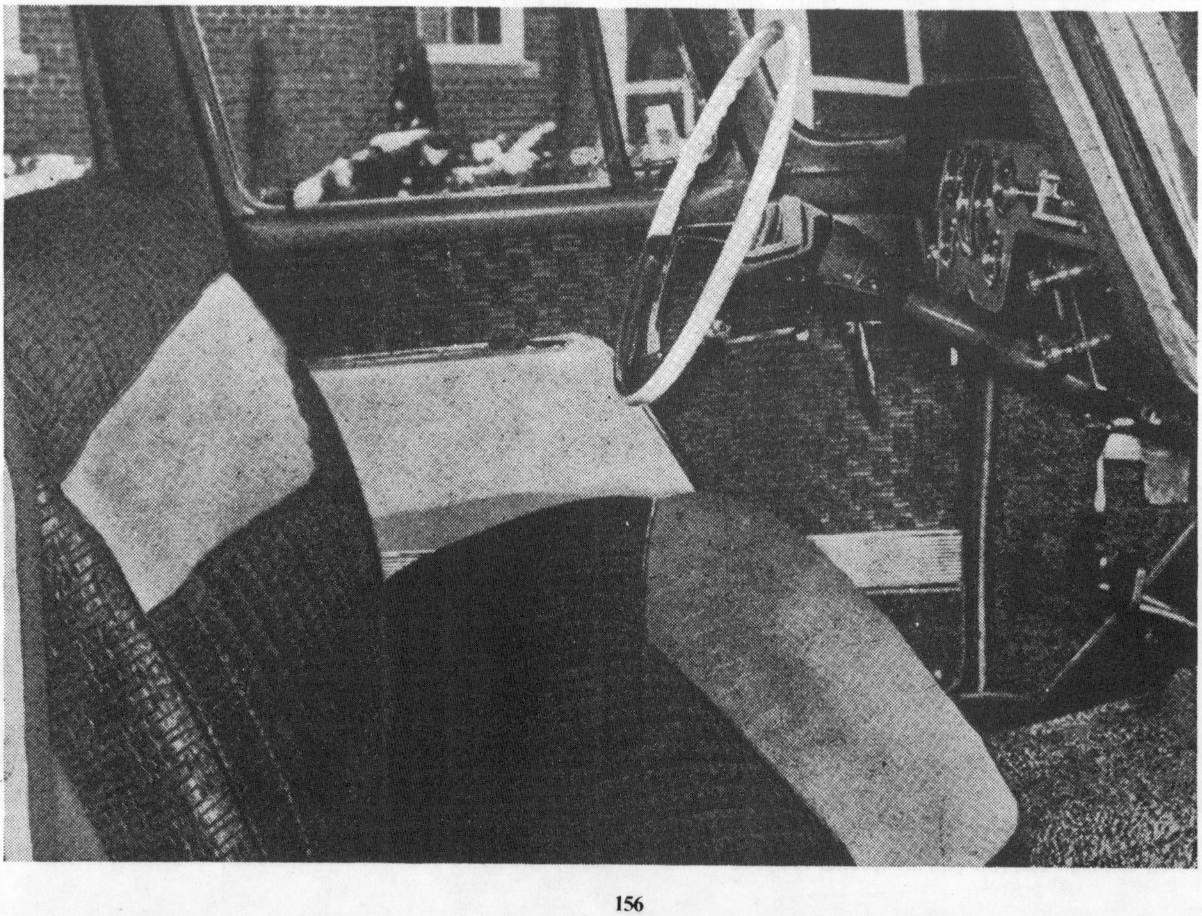

Clipper station waggon, first dual-purpose Packard since 1950, has 275 h.p. supercharged engine, limited slip diff. 65 cu. ft. load space is provided.

FOR 1957

New, lower lines, quality fitments, higher performance, supercharged engines combine to keep Packard saying . . . Ask the man who owns one!"

THE new 1957 Packard Clipper line with a low, modern silhouette and what is said to be the best performance and handling characteristics in company history was introduced only a month ago by Studebaker-Packard dealers throughout the United States.

The 1957 line including the four-door sedan and four-door station waggon will offer 15 per cent better performance and advanced engineering features which are exclusive in the medium priced field for 1957, among them a supercharger and automatic transmission as standard equipment, and the Twin-Traction limited slip differential as optional equipment.

The new sedan is two inches lower and 300 pounds lighter than last year's models, providing a lower centre of gravity and improved front-rear weight ratio. Wheelbase is 120½ inches.

The Packard Clipper station waggon, Packard's first station waggon since 1950, combines improved passenger car performance and luxury appointments, in keeping with Packard's fine car tradition, with a 65-cubic foot load carrying capacity.

◀ *Dashboards in Clipper series are fibreglass, heavily padded; looks more like a traditional dashboard than on most U.S. makes. Upholstery has garish motif, is most luxurious.*

The new cars represent a major move toward parts and body interchangeability, a two-year goal of the company. The automobiles are the first to be made in South Bend following consolidation of all company car and truck manufacturing there.

Greater engine performance in the Packard Clippers is provided by a completely new engine for this line. It is a 289-cubic inch overhead valve V/8 engine with a McCulloch type supercharger as standard equipment. The engine is rated at 275 horsepower.

The new Packard Clippers are said to have up to 15 per cent. better passing and acceleration performance than in 1956, due chiefly to the use of the supercharger, along with the Flightomatic transmission and a new 3.31-1 rear axle ratio.

The supercharger, a similar unit to that fitted to the Studebaker Hawk series, provides maximum power during acceleration while permitting of normal fuel economy at cruising speeds.

Increased performance in the 1957 Packard Clippers has been aimed at the passing speed ranges for additional safety. In pre-production tests at the Studebaker-Packard proving grounds near South Bend, the new Packard Clipper sedan equipped with automatic transmission accelerated from 30 to 60 miles per hour, the normal passing speed range, in 6.51 seconds. From a standing start to 60 miles per hour, the car clocked 10.45 seconds.

Studebaker-Packard Flightomatic transmission, standard on both the sedan and station waggon models, offers greater driving flexibility than in previous models. The Flightomatic torque converter automatic transmission incorporates a positive kick-down gear for improved passing ability, and constant second gear performance for negotiating steep grades and provides increased fuel economy.

A completely new suspension system for Packard utilises the variable rate control of front springing adopted by Studebaker-Packard for the first time this year. This new suspension combines the stiffer springing action needed for a smooth ride on rough roads and the softer springing necessary for a smooth ride on city boulevards.

The Twin-Traction safety differential, pioneered by Packard in 1956, will be optional on the new models. The differential automatically compensates for driving conditions on icy, muddy or slippery roads by transferring the major engine driving power to the rear wheel having the best traction. In conventional differentials, driving power is transmitted to the wheel having the least traction, causing spinning and slipping.

CONTINUED ON PAGE 159

NEW PACKARD PRESENTS A DIFFERENT APPEARANCE THAN STUDEBAKER EVEN THOUGH MOST OF THE COMPONENTS ARE DUPLICATED.

PACKARD ROAD TEST . . .

SINCE the 1957 Packard Clipper was first introduced a few months ago, there has been much comment as to whether or not it was wise to give a Studebaker-based car such a label. Many have wondered also just why it is being produced; "what does it offer that you can't get in a Studebaker?" they ask.

A road test can't answer the first question satisfactorily, but it did supply replies to the second.

But first of all, let's understand that current Clipper is not a high-luxury car priced 'way up in the upper-medium price class, as were its immediate forbears.

It is meant to compete with the DeSotos, Mercurys and Olds with a base price of just over $3000.

Now, what do you get that you can't get in a Studebaker for less dough? First, better performance than any Stude but the Golden Hawk offers. And you get the extra Hawk performance at the expense of a comfortable rear seat.

Second, more luxurious interior trim and distinctive exterior styling features. True, the Clipper uses the same basic body shell as Studebaker's President series cars, but this is common practice in the industry. All cars in the medium-priced class share shells with other makes built by the same corporation.

Third is the intangible prestige factor. It can't be measured, but goes like this: When anyone thinks of Studebaker, they inevitably think of cars in the low-priced field. The fact that the new line carries the Packard Clipper name immediately identifies it as something of a bit more value, a car with a higher price tag.

Do these factors warrant purchase of a Clipper in preference to a Stude President? Depends on the individual, but the reasons quoted are exactly the same as those which influence most buyers to go into the medium-priced field rather than the low-priced.

How about the car itself? It definitely is a good one. Its performance and fuel economy are equal to most direct competitors—and better than some. The same is true of roadability and handling. Overall quality is outstanding. Ride and general comfort is good, although it is this department the Clipper might suffer slightly by comparison with its competition.

The necessarily fast re-styling job done by Studebaker-Packard was done well, in spite of the haste. The Clipperized rear fenders and tail lights at rear and the grille at front look good on the basic Stude shell.

On the road, Clippers feel solid and controllable up to and over the 100 mph mark. They lean on corners and steering is too slow—but that's true of practically all current models. There isn't a great deal of sway and the tendency to wallow through tight turns found in cars with over-soft springing is absent. Ride is comfortable, although a shade on the firm side.

Interior appointments are in keeping with the price tag. Seats are comfortable, well-positioned. One point, however, that may sound minor but will be important to all smokers—except those who are left-handed—concerns ash trays.

There aren't any on the dash. Clipper front seat occupants have to use ash trays located in door-mounted arm rests. As mentioned, this may be no problem for left-handed drivers—but it's rough for right-handers. Could even be a safety hazard under certain conditions, because of the difficulty in locating and reaching the trays while driving.

Acceleration isn't blinding, but it's good. The 10.5 second average quoted for 0-60 mph runs includes those made using drive range only, plus some using low to start and shifting manually to drive range at 45 mph. Best times (around 10.2 seconds) can be obtained by shifting to drive momentarily at about 45 and then back into low. This holds the transmission in intermediate and makes a big difference in 0-75 runs.

Overdrive with the 4.27 axle—3.31 is standard with Flightomatic—would bring 0-60 times well under nine seconds.

Top speed wasn't checked, but 110 was seen on the unusually accurate speedometer and the Clipper was still

MC CULLOCH supercharger on Studebaker V-8 engine gives the Packard 275 horsepower with less total weight than that of last year's Packard engine, which was heaviest on market.

building up when it had to be backed off for a curve.

A word must be said about Studebaker-Packard quality in general for 1957. The company's public comments about new stress in this area isn't just talk. It's really doing a job. All S-P cars checked this year have been unusually good quality-wise. Extra emphasis, of course, is placed on Clippers.

Current Clippers have the tough job of bearing the proud and old Packard name. They definitely aren't cut from the traditional Packard cloth, but they have nothing to be ashamed of. They're sound cars with qualities that should recommend them to discerning buyers who want and appreciate what they offer. •

PACKARD CLIPPER TEST DATA

Test Car: 1957 Packard Clipper four-door sedan
Basic Price: $3212
Engine: 289-cubic-inch ohv V8 with supercharger
Compression ratio: 7.5-to-1
Horsepower: 275 @ 4800 rpm
Torque: 333 @ 3200
Dimensions: Length 212 inches, width 77, height 60, tread 57 front and 56 rear, wheelbase 120.5
Curb Weight: 3825 lbs.
Transmission: Flightomatic (Borg-Warner) three-speed automatic
Acceleration: 0-30 mph 4 seconds, 0-45 mph in 6.9, 0-60 mph in 10.5
Gas Mileage: 14 mpg average
Speedometer Correction: Indicated 30, 45 and 60 mph are actual 29, 44 and 58

FIFTH WHEEL is used during road tests to assure accurate results Factory "customizing" job on Studebaker shell makes Packard standout from lower priced Studebaker sedans.

SLICK, SUPER, PACKARDS FOR 1957

CONTINUED FROM PAGE 157

New and improved safey features on the Packard Clippers include these as standard equipment: directional signals, back-up lights, full-width safety padded instrument panel, safety-cone steering wheel, and the safety-finned brake drums.

The finned brake drums, offered for the first time on the Packard line this year, increase cooling area by 100 per cent., thus helping to combat brake fade due to heat. In addition, the new drum is said to increase brake life by as much as 30 per cent.

In the Packard fine car tradition, the new Clippers combine luxury interior fabrics and trim with a new dimension in silent driving. Heavy duty silencing pads applied to the floor, and deep-pile carpeting on interior kick-panels, dashboard liner, and lower door trim panel sections, are sound-deadening innovations.

In the station waggon the roomy cargo deck and convenient tail gate are as modern as the styling in the sedan, with deep-pile carpeting extending the length and width of the cargo deck.

In styling, the Packard Clippers retain the distinctive Packard trademarks including swept-back vee tail lamps, dashboard, massive grille and bumpers. The wide, wrap-around grille incorporates corner parking lights for side as well as forward illumination. A three-and-one-half inch wide chrome rub rail running the length of the car accents the long, low lines and serves as a colour separator for Packard's new two-tone paint combinations in 14 choices.

Standard luxury interior features include an electric clock, integral arm rests in all four doors, stow-away rear seat centre arm rest (in the sedan), snack tray glove compartment door, automatic trunk light, two inch foam rubber cushions for both front and rear seats, and a built-in foot rest for rear seat sedan passengers. Standard exterior features include dual exhausts and chrome wheel covers.

Optional equipment at extra cost includes tinted safety glass, power steering, power windows, power brakes, air conditioning, push button signal-seeking radio, dual rear electrically-operated radio antennae, rear speaker, safety belts, and safety-padded sun visors. ●

REPAIR COST GUIDE

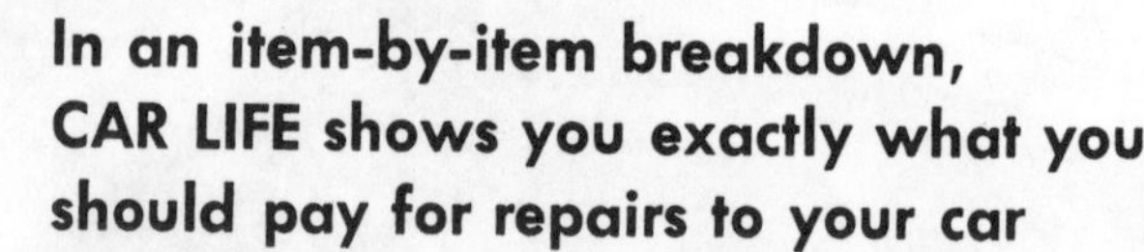

In an item-by-item breakdown, CAR LIFE shows you exactly what you should pay for repairs to your car

THIS GUIDE has been compiled to help you make an accurate estimate of the cost of any common repair that might have to be made to keep your car in top running condition. The prices quoted for labor costs are computed at the rate of $5.00 an hour. Costs may vary slightly in some sections of the country, but the figures presented are representative of those to be expected in most areas in the U.S.

PACKARD

	1949-1954 8		1955-1957 V-8	
	LABOR	PARTS	LABOR	PARTS
ENGINE				
GENERAL TUNEUP	$18.50	EXTRA	$27.50	EXTRA
REMOVE AND REPLACE REBUILT ENGINE	45.00	385.00	55.00	435.00
REPLACE RINGS	48.00	29.20	72.00	27.00
REPLACE BEARINGS (RODS & MAINS)	31.50	42.20	18.75	26.20
REPLACE CAMSHAFT	39.00	39.00	43.50	28.70
REPLACE LIFTERS	SOLID	SOLID	22.00	33.00
REPLACE CRANKSHAFT	97.00	185.00	65.00	89.00
VALVE OVERHAUL	45.00	EXTRA	55.00	EXTRA
VALVE ADJUSTMENT	8.00	1.00	HYDRAULIC	HYDRAULIC
REPLACE CYLINDER HEAD (ONE)	12.50	45.20	15.00	42.10
REPLACE PISTON (ONE)	22.25	15.25	29.50	13.75
OIL PUMP				
REMOVE & CLEAN OIL PAN	9.50	1.00	9.00	2.25
REPLACE OIL PUMP	6.75	16.85	8.75	13.75
REPLACE FILTER CARTRIDGE	1.75	2.35	2.00	2.45
CARBURETOR				
ADJUST CARBURETOR IDLE	1.50	NONE	3.00	NONE
OVERHAUL CARBURETOR	10.00	EXTRA	14.25	EXTRA
INSTALL REBUILT CARBURETOR	3.25	13.50	7.00	28.50
CLEAN & ADJUST AUTOMATIC CHOKE	2.00	NONE	2.50	NONE
CLEAN AIR FILTER (OIL BATH)	1.50	.50	1.50	.50
FUEL SYSTEM				
REPLACE FUEL & VACUUM PUMP	5.00	14.85	6.50	16.80
REPLACE GAS TANK	6.25	25.00	7.00	18.25
REPLACE GAS GAUGE (TANK UNIT)	6.50	5.25	3.00	3.40
REPLACE FLEXIBLE GAS LINE	1.00	1.85	2.00	2.25
EXHAUST SYSTEM				
REPLACE EXHAUST PIPES (LEAD & CROSSOVER)	8.00	9.25	10.00	13.10
REPLACE MUFFLER (ONE)	4.50	13.50	4.50	10.75
REPLACE TAILPIPE (ONE)	3.50	9.50	3.50	7.85
IGNITION				
SET TIMING	2.00	NONE	2.50	NONE
REPLACE POINTS AND CONDENSER	5.00	3.00	5.00	3.00
CLEAN & ADJUST POINTS (INCL. SET TIMING)	2.75	EXTRA	2.75	EXTRA
CLEAN & ADJUST SPARK PLUGS	2.25	NONE	4.50	NONE
REPLACE COIL	1.75	8.00	2.00	8.00
OVERHAUL STARTER	10.00	EXTRA	12.00	EXTRA
REPLACE STARTER	3.00	48.50	3.00	40.00
GENERATOR & BATTERY				
CLEAN & ADJUST VOLTAGE REGULATOR	3.00	NONE	3.00	NONE
REPLACE REGULATOR	2.50	14.50	2.00	13.25
OVERHAUL GENERATOR	8.00	EXTRA	8.50	EXTRA
REPLACE GENERATOR	2.50	51.00	3.00	42.20
COOLING SYSTEM				
REVERSE FLUSH RADIATOR & BLOCK	6.50	NONE	6.50	NONE
REPLACE RADIATOR	10.00	86.50	8.25	93.00
REPLACE WATER PUMP	5.00	25.00	9.50	28.75
REPLACE FAN BELT	1.75	4.00	2.50	2.75
REPLACE THERMOSTAT	1.75	3.50	1.75	3.25
REPLACE ALL HOSES (INCL. HEATER)	4.00	4.25	5.00	3.95
CLUTCH & TRANSMISSION				
ADJUST CLUTCH	2.00	NONE	2.00	NONE
REPLACE CLUTCH (COVER, DISC, & T.O. BEARING)	25.00	50.95	22.50	38.00
REPLACE TRANSMISSION (MANUAL)	15.00	208.65	15.00	168.00
OVERHAUL TRANSMISSION (AUTOMATIC)	68.00	EXTRA	68.00	EXTRA
ADJUST AND SERVICE TRANSMISSION (AUTO.)	11.00	EXTRA	12.50	EXTRA
BRAKE SYSTEM				
ADJUST BRAKES	2.50	NONE	2.50	NONE
RELINE BRAKES (INSTALL EXCHANGE SHOES)	13.75	22.50	19.25	12.75
REPLACE MASTER CYLINDER	6.50	12.00	9.00	10.85
REPLACE WHEEL CYLINDER (ONE FRONT)	4.00	4.50	4.00	3.85
FLUSH & REFILL HYDRAULIC SYSTEM	5.00	1.00	5.00	1.00
CHASSIS				
REPLACE FRONT SPRING (ONE)	5.20	11.10	7.25	9.25
REPLACE REAR SPRING (ONE)	8.50	21.00	6.85	21.50
REPLACE FRONT SHOCK (ONE)	7.00	6.25	3.50	7.10
REPLACE REAR SHOCK (ONE)	3.00	6.25	3.00	7.10
OVERHAUL FRONT END COMPLETE	42.00	EXTRA	53.00	EXTRA
TIGHTEN CHASSIS	5.00	NONE	5.00	NONE
COMPLETE LUBRICATION & OIL CHANGE	2.50	EXTRA	2.50	EXTRA

NEW CARS DESCRIBED

1957 Packards

4-7 LITRE ENGINE HAS McCULLOCH SUPERCHARGER

A station wagon, last available in 1950, is reintroduced. The platform of the two-piece rear door supplements the normal 65 cu ft load carrying capacity

A variable delivery McCulloch supercharger, similar to that of the Studebaker Golden Hawk, supplies pressurized air up to a maximum of 5 lb sq in above atmospheric through the carburettor

SIX months after most of the American manufacturers announced their 1957 models, Packard have released details of their new season's products. The recently formed Studebaker-Packard Corporation have been through a particularly lean period financially, and their losses over the past 2½ years have reached the staggering total of 69 million dollars.

Concentrating their efforts in the medium-priced field, they have obviously arranged for a great deal of interchangeability between the body components of the new Clipper and the Studebaker President and Champion. These new cars are the first to be produced at the South Bend factory of the Corporation following the consolidation of automobile manufacture there, arising out of the agreement with Curtiss Wright who came to the rescue with additional finance. The name of Daimler-Benz also has been linked recently with this group.

The engine of the new Clipper is identical with that of the Studebaker Golden Hawk (4,736 c.c. vee-8), and includes a supercharger which increases its performance by 15 per cent. In this form it produces 275 b.h.p. (gross) at 4,800 r.p.m., with a maximum torque of 333 lb ft at 3,200 r.p.m., corresponding to a b.m.e.p. of 175 lb sq in. The supercharger is a centrifugal McCulloch type, belt-driven from the front of the crankshaft. It features a clever variable-ratio pulley assembly which automatically holds the rated boost of 5 lb sq in in the speed range from 3,000 to 5,000 r.p.m. This gives a large increase in medium speed torque, as well as in peak power.

The engine is small in comparison with its competitors, and supercharging undoubtedly has been adopted to keep pace with the present American fashion for high acceleration. Performance figures issued for the new Clipper state that it can reach 60 m.p.h. from a standing start in 10.45sec and, in the more normal passing speed range, from 30-60 m.p.h. requires 6.51sec.

Another feature common to the 1957 Studebaker range is the variable rate front suspension, achieved by close-coiling the lower turns of the helical springs. On large deflections these become coil-bound, which increases the rate of the spring and, in effect, stiffens the suspension.

The Studebaker-Packard Flightomatic transmission is standard equipment on all models. It incorporates a positive kick-down, and constant second gear performance for negotiating steep gradients.

The twin traction, limited slip differential pioneered by Packard last year is again optional. This device automatically helps in driving on ice or mud, by transferring the driving power to the rear wheel which has the better traction, as distinct from an orthodox differential in which it is transmitted to the one having the lesser traction.

It is surprising—to observers in Britain, where it has been common for many years—to learn that for the first time finned brake drums are fitted by Packard. This increases the cooling area by 100 per cent and should improve braking. The manufacturers claim that it will eliminate fade, but experience of the braking of American cars would indicate that the causes are more deep-rooted and fundamental to design than can be fully met by this simple innovation.

In styling, the Clippers retain the distinctive Packard trade marks of swept-back vee tail fins and lamps, a massive grille extending round the side of the car, and bumpers which are outsize, even by American standards. The 1957 line consists of a four-door sedan and a station wagon, the latter reintroduced after an interval of seven years.

The 1957 Packard Clipper four-door sedan is 2in lower than last year's model. It is the only medium-priced American car to have automatic transmission as standard equipment. A controlled slip differential is optional as last year

The bold front end of the '58 Packard juts well forward of the headlights. A mesh grill is set into the body behind the heavy front bumper. A supercharged 289-cubic inch engine rests beneath the massive hood. Its output is 275 horsepower.

PACKARD

PACKARD HAWK	
ENGINE TYPE	V8 (supercharger)
BORE AND STROKE	$3\frac{9}{16}$ x $3\frac{5}{8}$
DISPLACEMENT	289
BRAKE HORSEPOWER	275
MAXIMUM TORQUE	333
COMPRESSION RATIO	7.8-1
OVERALL LENGTH	$205\frac{1}{16}$
OVERALL WIDTH	$72\frac{5}{8}$
OVERALL HEIGHT	$54\frac{3}{4}$
WHEELBASE	$120\frac{1}{2}$

Packard takes on the Hawk look for '58. The classic lines long associated with Packard have been seasoned with Continental verve and sports car flair. The long hood carries a functional air-scoop. The rear deck flows out and down, giving a long symmetrical appearance. The squared-off lines of the classic Packards are gone forever with these '58s.

Packard's tail fins are canted outward at a rakish angle so as not to impede the driver's vision when parking or driving on the open road. Top quality leather is used throughout the interior. The dash sports a full complement of dials including one for manifold pressure.

First Feel Behind the Wheel

studebaker

STUDEBAKER-PACKARD is entering the 1958 car season with reassured hopes that the recent slump—the worst in its 105-year history—is nearing an end.

In 1956, after the merger with Packard, the company hit an all-time low. To the rescue came Roy T. Hurley at the head of the Curtiss-Wright Corp. Excess production facilities were disposed of by S-P, and a blood transfusion in the form of hard cash shot new life into the ailing organization. To the helm as president went Harold Churchill, who had been chief engineer and who, with Mike De Blumenthahl, presently chief research engineer, has been largely responsible for many notable automotive developments—free wheeling, overdrive, hill-holder, etc.

A pruning of the brass took place; an economy model, the Scotsman, was successfully launched amid fancied obituaries suggested by a few well-meaning pessimists; and finally the announcement came as this was being written that current losses, while still too great, have been cut to one-fifth of their former size and that, if all continues as indications now suggest, the struggling firm could very well finish the year with a switch in bookkeeping ink—from red to black.

SMOOTH HOODS of Champion (top) and Commander wagon carry block letters only. Dual lights are option on Champion, standard on Commander and President.

Generally speaking, the current models will be continued with little change, and at least two new body models will be announced some time after initial on-sale dates for the Studebaker Scotsman, Champion, Commander and President. Packard will be in showrooms with some traditional lines early in November also. In our December issue we'll have more new Studebaker models to show and to discuss, but as things now stand, here are the new features for '58.

Starting at the ground and working up, we find that 14-inch wheels are standard on all Commander, President and V8 station wagon models. Due mainly to completely new floor pan and roof stampings, the overall height is now two inches lower in the sedans, about one inch lower in the already very low Hawk coupe models, and a shade lower in the wagons.

This lowering has been accomplished without any sacrifice in interior space—even in headroom—for a new one-piece driveshaft has permitted a lower transmission tunnel. The gearbox has an extended shaft, too, and for the first time in years only two U-joints are to be required on Studebaker cars.

Only the Scotsman continues to ride on the 15-inch wheels—the car has found favor in many rural areas—and the Champion, while being listed with the large wheels as standard equipment, will offer 14-inch wheels optionally.

With the exception of the roof and floor stampings, '58 Studebakers will use the same basic body structure as in recent years. New external sheet metal, however, will impart a modernized appearance although no radical changes have been made.

Dual headlights and tail fins—the latter patterned somewhat after those of the Hawk—are now featured across the board on all models, wagons as well as sedans, with the exception of the Scotsman and the Hawks. The Scotsman will be little changed

'58 and packard

by *Joe H. Wherry* Detroit Editor

THINNER ROOF (see Champion, top) and smaller wheels lower all models without cramping interiors. Luggage space is large. Commander has chromed tail lights.

EASILY READ Cyclops Eye speedometer is incorporated in new instrument grouping; telltale lights are for ammeter and oil pressure. Dash is efficient, simple.

"Studebaker-Packard improvements for '58 are not in vain...their cars show greater promise than at any time in past three years."

according to this writer's conversations with Duncan MacCrea, chief stylist, and others in South Bend. In the belief that a fairly substantial market exists for basic, though full-sized, family cars, the Scotsman will be cleaned up here and there in minor details while its identity will be even more pronounced from the rest of the line.

The Champion will have dual headlights as a factory-installed option—the prototype we drove at the proving ground had conventional single lights. When we asked why this exception to duals as standard equipment, we were reminded that S-P enjoys an unusually good export market; it seems that many of these overseas customers prefer the single lights. A few dollars are saved in this way for those who are price-conscious.

Other principal styling changes are confined to details: all sedan and wagon hoods are now smooth and lack the customary ornament—instead, chromed letters spell out the name across the hood just above the grille. The latter is of the same shape as in '57—only the vertical spacers have been changed in number.

The Champion and Commander models have new, thin, full-length stainless steel strips; the larger President (the prototype was unavailable during our visit) will have different trim. The tail fins have a pronounced flair; they are longer and thicker than those of the Hawks and tail lights are distinctive from the coupes'.

Little change has been made in any of the S-P engines from the L-head Champion unit shared with the Scotsman to the largest 289-inch ohv V8 unit which, combined with the "Jet Stream" McCulloch-made supercharger, powers the Golden Hawk Stude and the Packard running mate. Compression ratios have, in the V8s, been raised about one point. At this writing little else can be said other than that '58 will probably see the blower confined to the Studebaker and Packard high-performance Hawks.

Automatic transmissions will out-number mechanically shifted units. The dual ratio lever-operated Borg-Warner gearbox or the three-speed synchromesh stick-shifted box, with or without overdrive, will be available on all models except for the low-priced Scotsman, in which automatic is not available, and on the Hawks, where choice is overdrive or automatic.

Studebakers have always been good road cars but in recent years, in all frankness, they have not quite met the competition insofar as off-the-beaten-path roadability and preciseness of handling are concerned. Finned-type brake drums of about 195 square inches gave recent Golden Hawks exceptionally good braking with less than normal fade; in '58 the large President sedans will share this advantage. The Commander V8 and lesser six-cylinder models as well as most wagons will have conventional smooth drums.

The lower overall height has helped handling to some extent, but in the driveable Silver Hawk V8 (259.2-cubic-inch engine), in the Commander and the Champion, a better feel was evident. A look underneath the front end partially explained the improvement—a new anti-sway bar fitted between the lower control arms assists stability when cornering smartly. Nose-diving on fast stops seemed to be less, too, and there was not quite as much rear end squat when digging out from a standstill. The front end geometry and the steering are unchanged, but the variable rate front springs have been im-

BASICALLY ALIKE are chassis of 116.5-in. wheelbase sedans. Here, with Commander V8 engine, are new one-piece propeller shaft, longer transmission shaft housing which lowers front compartment tunnel, new anti-sway bar, small wheels.

proved with new rate calculations and the shock absorber valves have been altered to some extent.

The rear suspension has been considerably changed, though this will not readily be apparent at first glance beneath. New semi-elliptic leaf springs aft are asymmetrical throughout the line. The rear axle—still a rigid type despite many rumors stemming from the Mercedes-Benz link—is U-bolted to the springs in the usual manner, but the rear portion of the spring is approximately one-third longer than that forward of the axle. This has resulted in frame modifications and new and stronger trunion mountings for the springs. Greater rear end stability, less tendency to sway or to break away under extreme handling circumstances, decreased tail end dipping on acceleration or rising on severe braking are some of the advantages claimed for the car.

These claims are justified—to how large an extent it is impossible to say at this writing, for the cars driven were prototypes and maximum performance and roadability tests were impossible due to the cars being scheduled for advertising photography, dealer appraisal, and the like. Certainly the cars rode better, cornered better, and were generally improved on all counts, so far as roadability and handling ease are concerned.

Performance tests, as regards acceleration and fuel consumption, were out of the question. Several fairly fast laps of the proving ground high-speed oval were made in the Silver Hawk V8, however, and speeds over 90 mph (true) were accomplished without strain. On the back road we were able to snake through the handling and ride patterns with enough dispatch to feel assured that the '58 improvements have not been in vain—these cars show greater promise than previously.

Inside there are new instrument groupings in all sedan models. The Cyclops-Eye speedometer is retained—it should be—but it is now incorporated within the main instrument panel, requiring a downward glance. Toggle switches continue to be used for auxiliary controls; windshield wipers and air ventilation and heat controls are still operated by horizontally moved levers. The condition of the generating and oil pressure systems is indicated by warning lights. The foot controls have been slightly repositioned—the optional power brake pedal now sits lower, allowing much quicker shifting of the foot from accelerator to brake.

The Hawk models are the least changed in the entire line as far as styling is concerned. "Why change drastically when Hawk acceptance has proven we're on the right track for those who want a jaunty

STUDEBAKER HAWK

STUDEBAKER Golden Hawk retains sportive flavor; has new side grille mesh, center medallion.

STUDEBAKER SPECIFICATIONS

ENGINE:	Champion*	Commander	President
Type	L-head 6	Ohv V8	Ohv V8
Bore and Stroke	3.00 x 4.38	3.56 x 3.25	3.65 x 3.62
Displacement	185.6	259.2	289
Advertised bhp	101	180 or 195	225
Compression ratio	7.8:1	8.3:1	8.3:1
Torque @ max. rpm	152 lbs.-ft. @ 1800 rpm	260 lbs.-ft. @ 2800 rpm	305 lbs.-ft. @ 3000 rpm
DIMENSIONS:			
Wheelbase	116.5	116.5	120.5
Length	202.4	202.4	206.2
Width	75.8	75.8	75.8
Height	58.0	57.8	57.5
REAR AXLE:			
3-speed Synchromesh	4.10	3.54	3.54
Overdrive	4.56	3.73	4.09
Automatic	3.54	3.31	3.31

*All specifications for Scotsman are same as for Champion except overdrive axle ratio is 3.54, and no automatic transmission is available.

INTERIOR of Golden Hawk offers power window lifts, keeps full instrument panel; no leather upholstery.

"Studebaker-Packard chassis modifications offer improved roadability, handling, comfort."

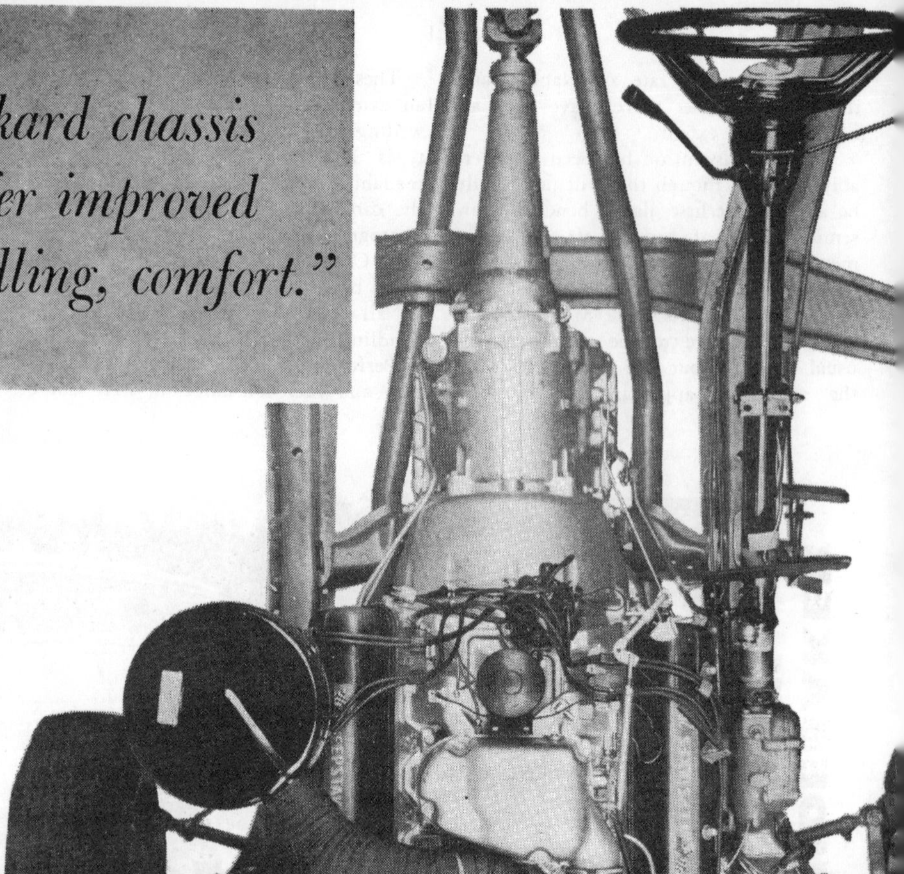

sports-like family car?" is the way De Blumenthahl countered our query as to the reasons behind no important styling changes.

That is a pretty good answer, it seems, since Hawk sales have been one of the main bright spots in the recent S-P picture. Most reports indicate that the average Hawk owner is a youngish family man with two or three youngsters—he can afford but one car, wants it to be something of a sports type with spirited performance as well.

In '58 the chief Hawk change is in the rear seat. The collapsible center armrest has been omitted so that three persons can now be accommodated where only two were carried formerly. Leather upholstery is no longer an option; in the sedans there's a wide range of long-wearing fabrics featuring metallic thread as well as attractive plastics. Foam rubber is used over the coil seat springs, of course, as it is in sedans and wagons.

GOLDEN HAWK shares 120.5-in. wheelbase chassis with President — supercharger on 289-cu.-in. engine is on Hawk only. There's more power with 8.3 compression.

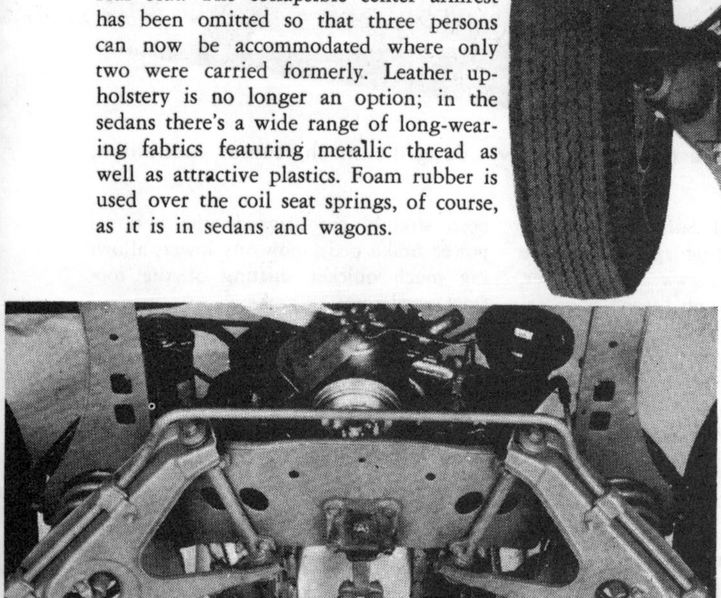

NEW ANTI-SWAY BAR with improved coil spring rate build-up improves Golden Hawk handling. Rear-swept control arms give some trailing link effect. Lack of frame crosspiece underneath crankcase facilitates servicing.

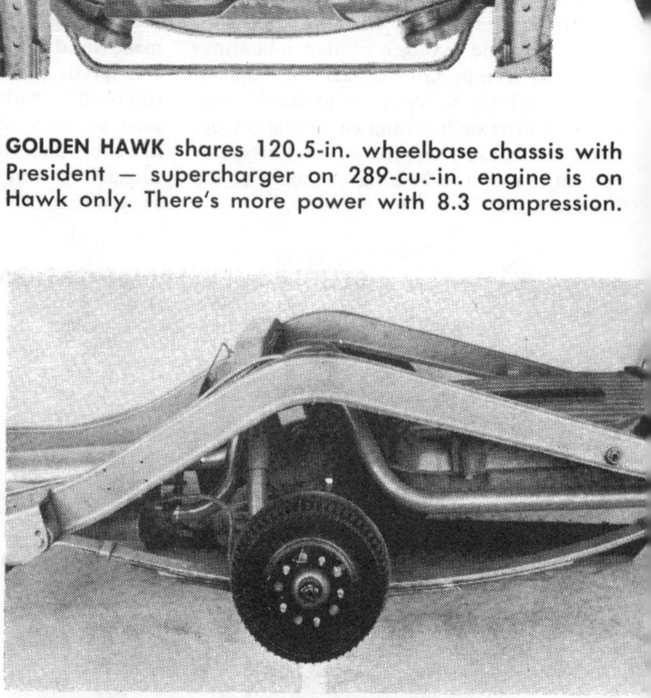

ASYMMETRICAL SPRING, shared with all other models, is principal rear suspension change on Golden Hawk. Big finned brake drums, for reduced fade, are standard on Golden Hawk, President, and new Packard Hawk.

PACKARD HAWK

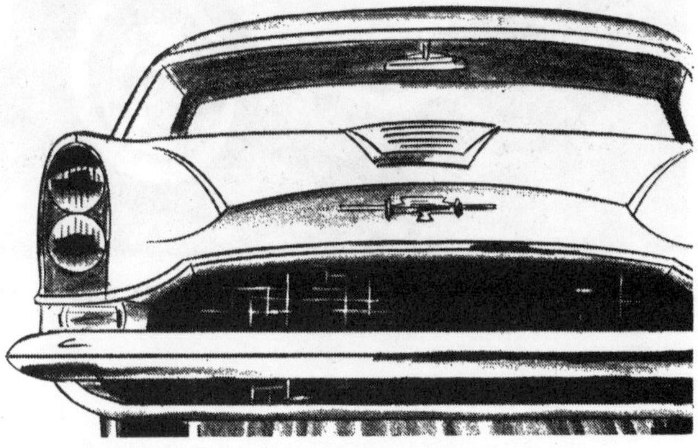

PACKARD HAWK interior has rich leather throughout. Folding center armrest makes it practical 4-seater. Covered spare lies flat; fins are like Golden Hawk's.

FRONT of Packard Hawk (top) suggests wide airscoop of Grand Prix competition models. Hood has traditional Packard lines. MT's Sept. conjecture erred on lights.

A LOW SLOPING HOOD characterizes the newest S-P model—the Packard Hawk. The sides of the long hood are longitudinally dished—a bit of Packard tradition returned. As we predicted some time back, the new Packard Hawk (why S-P didn't upgrade the bird's name commensurate with the marque's noble history no one seems to know) is basically like the Studebaker Golden Hawk. Front styling changes of drastic and distinctive nature point up S-P's contention that they are able to perform die changes with speed—one reason being that S-P has recently purchased the facilities of its former die supplier.

In the rear the Packard Hawk owns a deck lid much like that of the '53 Loewy coupe. To this has been added an imitation spare wheel imprint—shades of the Imperial which proved, it seems, that people like to be fooled and don't mind a 'phony' at all. Inside, the Packard Hawk is completely done in quality leather from seats to padded dashboard to door panelling. Beneath the sheet metal it's a Studebaker Golden Hawk, blown 289-cubic-inch mill and all. The Packard sedans are to be announced later.

Improved air-conditioning and its extension to the Hawks offers, for '58, the choice of either under-hood or trunk mounting. Tinted glass is optional, as are first-time power window lifts in the Hawks.

In 1958 S-P management hopes to prove its view that distinction and craftsmanship can forge success for a quality line of different cars. Time will tell.

PACKARD'S LUXURY COUPE proved above average in roadability with much scat; spare on deck is decorative only.

1958 PACKARD HAWKS

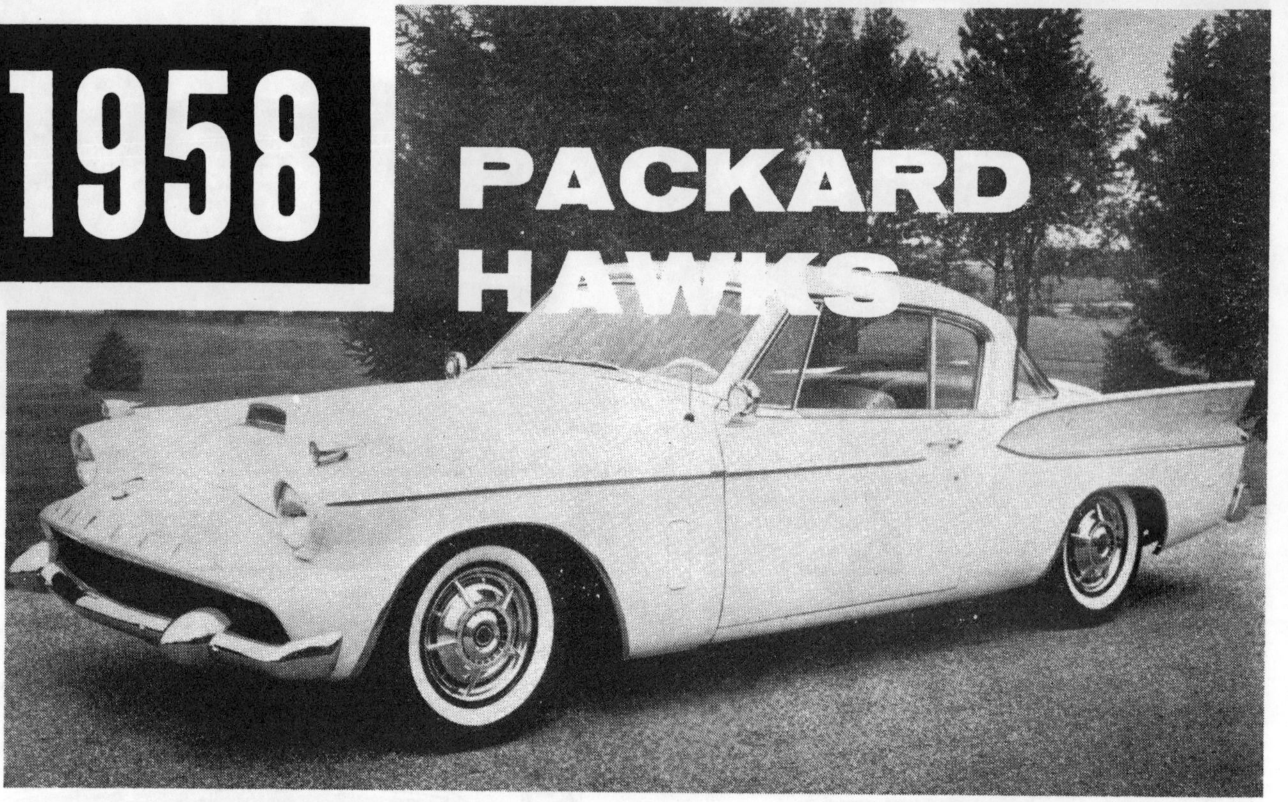

THE UNSUCCESSFUL "FISH-MOUTH" FRONT STUDEBAKER USED IN 1955 SEEMS TO HAVE BEEN REVIVED FOR THE PACKARD.

A new bid for the limited class of buyers who prefer substantial touring cars of the European type—that seems to be the objective of the ultra-luxury Hawk

PHONY MOUNT in deck lid has nothing to do with spare tire. The rear bumper bears no resemblance to one used at the front, which suggests failure to integrate design features.

NEWEST bird hatched in South Bend is the 1958 Packard Hawk. A low sloping hood with a wide air intake stretching across the entire front of the car, an embossed wheel design in the deck lid and classic leather trim are among its more distinctive styling features.

The hood is broad and flat, has an air scoop mounted on its leading edge. In combination with the very low nose section, this furnishes close-range forward visibility unexcelled by any full-size American car.

That this new Hawk shares the same body shell used by Studebaker Hawks is unmistakable when it is viewed in silhouette. It has the same flaring rear fender fins and jaunty roof line.

Leather upholstery is used in interiors—and, to some extent, on exteriors! Both the inside and outside of the window sills are covered with leather. The effect is interesting, but how the leather will react to constant exposure to the elements is dubious.

Powerplant of the new Hawk is the same 289-cubic-inch V-8 used in 1957 Packard Clippers and Golden Hawks. It is supercharged and develops 275 hp.

Chassis is the same 120.5-inch unit used in Golden Hawks and has the same suspension changes made in those models for 1958. These include longer rear springs mounted with only about one-third of their length extending forward of the axle and a link-type anti-sway bar fitted between front lower control arms.

Fourteen-inch wheels and ribbed or laterally finned brake drums are standard equipment. Studebaker-Packard's Twin Traction limited-slip differential is optional.

S-P officials report that premium quality construction will be emphasized in building Packard Hawks, in keeping with both the Studebaker and Packard tradition of fine craftsmanship.

"We're more interested in quality than quantity," said Harold Churchill, S-P head. The Packard Hawk obviously will not be a large-volume automobile, but if the quality promise can be kept it should appeal to those who want a well-built car that is different. •

First Feel Behind the Wheel

PACKARD

by Joe H. Wherry
Detroit Editor

DRIVING THE '58 PACKARD is surprisingly pleasant. The front suspension has undergone slight but important changes: the shock absorbers have been improved, and there is a new anti-sway bar in the front. The rear semi-elliptic leaf springs are asymmetrical so as to handle increased loads with less deflection. A new one-piece driveshaft enabled the engineers to lower the tunnel, which formerly was quite high, especially in the front seat.

Overall height is about two inches less than in '57. The wheels are now 14-inchers. Basically the Packard is a Studebaker, let's face it. However, S-P finds justification for using the same basic body shell as the Studebaker—this is the modern manner to save tooling and production costs.

Chief stylist Duncan McRae has accomplished much, and in little time too. Dual headlights, standard on all models, form the basis for rather extensive restyling that has been done with remarkably little in the way of new dies.

A facelift? Yes, but more than was to be expected. The four-door sedan and the station wagon appear less changed, although they share the new grille which is synonymous with that of the Packard *Hawk* (Nov. MT).The low and sloping hood is Fiberglas, as is the grille frame and the front body extensions which make the grille possible. The dual headlights result from a widening of the front fenders with separate metal. The hood air-scoop is non-functional.

Most attractive in the line is the thin-roofed two-door hardtop sedan. The prototype was stiff and hand-built, but we were able to step it up for a few moments. Driving with the automatic transmission in DRIVE-1, we clocked zero to 30 mph in 3.9 seconds; to 45, 7.2; to 60, 11.9; from 50 to 80, 12.8. The ride was good (there will be no air suspension for S-P in '58), cornering was much improved over past years, and the seating was comfortable. Rear legroom in the two-door hardtop is competitive with the industry, perhaps better than some of the higher priced prestige models.

Prestige? No, S-P brass candidly admit that the current Packard is not of that class. "We offer distinction and quality craftsmanship," they will tell you.

All of the usual options from air conditioning to powered windows are available. The engine, 289 cubic inches of reliable ohv-V8 design, is shared with the Studebaker President series, thrives well on regular grade fuel, will be above average in fuel economy. There will be no supercharger on the Packard passenger cars—that's left to the Hawk. /MT

PACKARD station wagon has air of distinction, if not prestige.

BUSY ENGINE area sees every bit of space taken up by the supercharged 289 cubic inch power plant. Sloping hood does not raise high enough for best access.

PHOTOS BY COLIN CREITZ

Gone forever are the marks of its greatest era — but Packard retains a name for styling, quality and mighty performance.

DISTINCTIVE styling, quality and excellent performance were among the attributes which distinguished Packard's sportier models back in the classic era. While they might never achieve classic status, 1958 Packard Hawks can boast of the same features.

Despite that, and their name, Packard Hawks have a closer kinship with the Studebaker Golden Hawk than any Packard car. Except for styling and a few dimension differences, the two are identical.

Ingenious Studebaker-Packard stylists, however, have made sure that Packard Hawks would have a distinct personality of their own.

They molded a completely different front end for new Hawks bearing the Packard nameplate — using fiberglass generously—and added a number of luxury touches calculated to help them live up to the Packard tradition.

From a functional standpoint it didn't take long behind the wheel of the test car to learn that the Packard Hawk has benefited greatly from the experience of S-P engineers with past models of the Golden Hawk.

This is especially true in the area of handling and roadability. When S-P began selling Golden Hawks during the 1956 model year, the company was offering a car which had gobs of performance and intriguing styling, but left a lot to be desired in the way of handling characteristics.

The first Golden Hawks were powered by the very heavy Packard-designed V-8. Weight distribution was very poor (about 59 per cent on the front wheels) and roadability suffered as a result. Overly slow steering didn't help the situation.

A switch to Studebaker's light V-8, a change to a better steering gear and several other engineering developments improved the situation in 1957.

Additional subtle, but important, improvements for 1958 have helped make the Packard Hawk a better road car than its predecessors.

It's capable of cornering faster, with less body lean and more security. It's still no sports car in the true sense of the phrase, but is much closer to the ideal than 1956 or 1957 Golden Hawks.

Major reasons for the improvement are a lower center of gravity and revisions to front and rear suspension. The Packard Hawk is almost one-half inch lower than 1956 and 1957 Golden Hawks, due to the change to a one-piece drive shaft and the use of 14-inch instead of 15-inch tires.

PACKARD HAWK ROAD TEST

FRONT END STYLING GIVES THE PACKARD A PERSONALITY DISTINCT FROM ITS HAWK COUSINS. FIBERGLASS IS USED HERE EXTENSIVELY.

... VIEW DEMONSTRATES THE INGENUITY OF S-P DESIGNERS WHO HAVE CALLED UPON EVERY VARIATION OF THEIR BASIC BODY.

HAWK DASH includes speedometer, tachometer, manifold pressure, fuel, ammeter, oil pressure, water temperature gauges.

ADEQUATE trunk space is highlighted by plaid interior lining and a tailored hat-box type cover for the spare tire.

REAR LIGHTS and tail fins are Packard's homage to current fads as is the dazzling gold accentuation stressing the fins.

Variable rate coil springs are still used in the independent front suspension, but a larger diameter stabilizer bar is now used.

Rear springs are four inches longer than in past Hawks and the rear axle is now mounted ahead of the springs' center point, reducing rear end squat during fast starts and front end dive when braking.

(Even better roadability would probably have resulted, in comparison to earlier Hawks, if spring rates had not been reduced to make for a softer ride.)

As might be expected, the Packard Hawk is an extremely capable performer. It's not any quicker than the original 1956 Golden Hawk—but it doesn't need to be! Acceleration in the automatic transmission-equipped test car was very good, would be even better with overdrive. (Flightomatic transmissions are standard in Packard Hawks and overdrive manual gearboxes are available as an extra-cost option. No conventional three-speed transmissions are offered.)

Acceleration times from 0-60 mph of under 10 seconds are more common now than when the first Hawks appeared some three years ago, but any car which can consistently get from a standstill to 60 mph in just a few tenths over nine seconds must still be regarded as a rapid vehicle.

Past experience has indicated that Golden Hawks with overdrive and the 4.09 rear axle are roughly one-half second faster from 0-60 than those with automatic transmissions. This would very likely hold true for Packard Hawks, too.

Interiors of these latest—and most expensive—Hawks are very lush. Top quality leather upholstery is used throughout. Top of the dash is padded and covered with leather.

Hawk instrument panels have become renowned for excellence and this Packard version is no exception. Current Hawks undoubtedly have the finest instrumentation setup now being used in an American-built car. It's elegantly simple, attractive and highly functional.

All gauges and dials are round, have easy-to-read white markings on a black

Test Data

Test Car: 1958 Packard Hawk
Body Type: two-door hardtop
Basic Price: $3995
Engine: supercharged ohv V-8
Carburetion: single two-barrel
Displacement: 289 cubic inches
Bore & Stroke: 3.56 x 3.63 inches
Compression Ratio: 7.8-to-1
Horsepower: 275 @ 4800 rpm
Horsepower per Cubic Inch: .95
Torque: 333 @ 3200 rpm
Test Weight: 3768 lbs.
Weight Distribution: Front 2110 lbs., rear 1658 lbs. (56% of weight on front wheels)
Transmission: Flightomatic, torque converter plus three-speed planetary gearset
Rear Axle Ratio: 3.31-to-1
Steering: 4.25 turns lock-to-lock
Dimensions: Wheelbase 120.5 inches, overall length 205.17, width 71.3, height 54.63, tread 57.3 front and 56.3 rear.
Suspension: Independent coil springs front, semi-elliptic leaf springs rear
Tires: 8.00 x 14 tubeless
Gas Mileage: 13.6 mpg average
Speedometer Error: Indicated 30, 45 and 60 mph were actual 29, 43.2 and 56.1 mph, respectively.
Acceleration: 0-30 in 3.6 seconds, 0-45 in 6.1 and 0-60 in 9.2

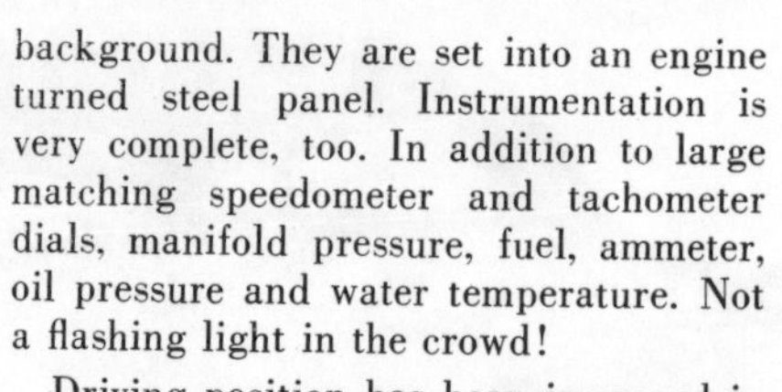

background. They are set into an engine turned steel panel. Instrumentation is very complete, too. In addition to large matching speedometer and tachometer dials, manifold pressure, fuel, ammeter, oil pressure and water temperature. Not a flashing light in the crowd!

Driving position has been improved in comparison to Golden Hawks. Distance from the steering wheel to the front seat back is one-half inch greater in the Packards, and that's just enough to clear up a problem noticed last year during the test of the 1957 Golden Hawk.

Since Hawk steering is not particularly fast, it is often necessary to twirl the wheel a good deal. Last year it was found the steering wheel was so close to the driver's lap that his hands would hit his thighs in situations requiring much wheel movement. This restriction to freedom of driver movement was a potentially serious hazard and it's good to find it has been eliminated.

Another annoying flaw has been carried over from past Golden Hawks, however. The brake pedal is in the same awkward position. The driver's foot is repeatedly impeded by the steering column as he attempts to shift his foot from accelerator to brake pedal. Nor is the pedal wide enough to permit easy left foot braking as can be done in most makes with automatic transmissions and no clutch pedals.

Equally annoying to cigaret-smoking drivers is the lack of a convenient ash tray. There is a small one mounted in the left door, but one must reach around or through the steering wheel to get at it.

The Packard Hawk has one-half inch more headroom in the front seat than Golden Hawks and 1.6 inches more rear headroom. The rear seat is divided, making the Packard Hawk definitely a five-passenger automobile.

The car's appearance is just as sporty as its performance. The low, sloping fiberglass hood and full width horizontal air intake gives it something of an imported car flavor.

S-P's use of fiberglass in reshaping of the basic Hawk front end design, incidentally, is a good indication of how valuable this material can be for cases where only limited production volume is expected.

Quality of the test car was high, as has been the case with most S-P products checked during the past year. All body parts, including those of fiberglass, were smooth and ripple-free, fit properly and were covered by an excellent paint job.

Packard Hawks are substantially higher than Golden Hawks ($3995 vs. $3282 basic price) and there are those who feel that their distinctive styling and minor dimensional advantages are worth the added cost. There are certain to be those who appreciate the unusual styling features and added luxury touches. •

PACKARD

Price range (Advertised delivered price)
$3,262

PACKARD has but one wagon as last year, a four-door model on the same 116.5 in. chassis as used by the Studebaker Commander. Although the Packard is a six-passenger vehicle, an optional folding third seat is available. This seat faces to the rear, holds two adults or three children and folds flat into the cargo deck much as the third seat on Chrysler Corporation wagons. However, entrance to the Packard third seat is more difficult because of the conventional swing-up transom which forces passengers into a deep crouch as they enter the wagon.

The Packard differs from last year's model in styling of the hood, grille, front and rear fenders as well as side trim. The engine is the same 289-cu. in. unit used in the '58 Studebaker President. In last year's Packard station wagon this engine was supercharged and had a rating of 275 bhp, 50 more than the current model. The reduction in engine output to 225 doesn't leave the Packard wagon under-powered as it weighs some 3800 pounds, the approximate weight of a Plymouth V-8 wagon of equal power. Packard fuel consumption should be reasonable in that it has an engine about 10% smaller than Plymouth's.

The Packard wagon's ride is better than last year due to new "two-stage" rear springs. These springs have four main leaves which support the wagon without undue stiffness when empty and two additional "helper" leaves which come into play when wagon is heavily loaded.

New for '58 is the Packard Hawk, family sports coupe that has distinctive grille extending to the full width of automobile.

PACKARD

AT PRESSTIME, the only 1958-model Packard announced by Studebaker-Packard Corp. was the Packard Hawk, a distinctively styled version of Studebaker's Golden and Silver Hawk sport coupes.

The Packard Hawk is powered with the 289 cu. in. Studebaker V-8 engine equipped with variable-rate McCulloch supercharger and developing 275 horsepower.

Styling differences between the '58 Packard and Studebaker Hawks include a low, sweeping full-width air scoop on the Packard in contrast to Studebaker Hawk's "egg-crate" grille. Packard Hawk has a smooth rear deck sloping from rear window light to bumper with a "dummy" continental tire housing in the center. Side trim is simpler than on the Studebakers and wheel discs have Packard's red hexagonal trade mark. Transmission options are standard synchromesh or automatic.

Rear deck sports a dummy spare a la the '57 Imperial.

Packard Station Sedan

CONTINUED FROM PAGE 13

drive works fine and makes highway cruising a breeze, but the Electromatic has been disconnected, as in so many Packards. When working properly, it did away with the need for depressing the clutch when idling or shifting gears. But short circuits and vacuum leaks made most Electromatics unreliable.

If Ultramatic had been available in 1948, this wagon would surely have had it. Development of Packard's 1949 automatic began near the

end of the war under chief research engineer Forest McFarland. Herbert L. Misch, who's now a Ford engineering v.p., was just 3½ years out of college at the beginning of the Ultramatic's development, yet Misch had the major responsibility of designing the torque converter, assisted by Warren Bopp. George Joly designed the gears.

Ultramatic became a particularly ambitious project for an independent automaker like Packard. They developed and built it without any outside help. Ford, in contrast, relied on Borg-Warner to develop Ford-O-Matic and Merc-O-Matic, and GM had Detroit Transmissions and later the Hydra-Matic Div.

Ultramatic used a torque converter similar in principle to Buick's Dynaflow but different in materials and construction. It had a direct-drive feature that engaged automatically above about 15 mph, the exact engagement speed being determined by load and pedal pressure. Once locked in direct drive, there was no more slippage, a fact that contributed to fairly good gas mileage. An accelerator kickdown kept Ultramatic from lugging and could be used for quick passing below 50 mph. In May 1951, CONSUMER REPORTS rated Ultramatic the best of all torque converters available at the time. It added $225 to the price of a 1949 Custom or Super Packard.

Packard cloistered a very GM-like front suspension under its 22nd and 23rd Series—coils with SLA and integral lever shocks as the upper A-arms. The Station Sedan also used stabilizer bars front and rear. These might lessen lean on hard corners, but the wagon still leans pretty much, although it's not uncomfortable. All Packards of that era moved along with a very mushy, floating ride, and a lot of owners liked it that way.

Steering is extremely light and surprisingly responsive, with no tendency to wander on high-crown roads or in crosswinds. Bill Geyer's 2-ton wagon isn't a hot dog when it comes to acceleration, but I never had to push it either.

Starting comes by flipping the key and depressing the gas pedal, same as in Buicks of that day. The Packard's instrument cluster, while uninspired, makes all gauges legible, and all buttons are integrated into a protective horizontal trim rail near the bottom of the dash. The four big vent and heater controls stand beneath those, and whole the regular buttons look almost Nader-inspired, the four heater knobs look positively lethal.

Because of the Station Sedan's high price and modest carrying capacity, it never became anything like a best-seller. A total of 1786 were produced in 1948, 1100 in the 1949 23rd Series, and an unknown number for the 1949 22nd Series and in 1950. After that, Packard offered no wagons until 1957, with the Studebaker merger. Which means Packard never did build another wagon after 1950.

Our thanks to Bill Geyer, Sacramento, Calif.; Burt Weaver and George L. Hamlin of Packard Automobile Classics, Box 2808, Oakland, Calif. 94618; John Reinhart and Herbert L. Misch, Ford Motor Co., Dearborn, Mich.; Forest McFarland, Flint, Mich.; William H. Graves, Ann Arbor, Mich.; and A.W. Prance, Bloomfield Hills, Mich.

PACKARD HAWK

Photos by Eric Rickman

Use of broad fiberglass nose section with simple bumper in opening permits smooth, sloping frontal appearance, complete lack of a grille.

PERFORMANCE TEST

A supercharged four-passenger coupe with handling and brakes that top the '58 crop—truly a tough competitor on the open road, more so through the hills.

by HRM Technical Editor Ray Brock

Do you remember when the ads for Packard said, "Ask the man who owns one"? We haven't seen that slogan around for quite some time but it might be a good idea for the Studebaker-Packard Corporation to revive it because a talk with the man who owns a Packard Hawk could be quite revealing. The Hawk is not a sports car but is a car with a certain amount of sports car styling and handling qualities.

We borrowed our test car from Rehwald and Danyluk, Studebaker-Packard dealer in Glendale, California, and fortunately got a Hawk being used for demonstration purposes so it was well broken in with better than 5,000 miles on the odometer. Slipping behind the wheel of a Packard Hawk for the first time will surprise you in many ways. First, the seating position, the feel and the smell of top grain leather upholstery are all very pleasant. The steering wheel is routed through the instrument panel at an angle of several degrees and the horn button is actually about 1½ degrees to the right of your belt buckle. This angular steering column also places the right side of the steering wheel a couple of inches farther forward than the left side so that when you sit with the hands on either side of the wheel, you are aware that something feels strange. A few miles behind the wheel with the left elbow on the well-placed arm rest, the left hand on the lower left side of the wheel, the right hand on the upper right side and the wheel angle is forgotten.

Unless you are accustomed to the Studebaker line of cars during the past few years, the nearness of your nose to the windshield will also cause momentary concern. This condition is easy to accept and vision through the curved but not "wrapped-around" glass is very good. By leaning forward over the wheel slightly, overhead signals are easily seen even if the car is sitting almost directly under them. Speaking of easy vision, take a look at the instrument panel. A 160 mph speedometer, 6,000 rpm tachometer, 240° temperature gauge, oil pressure, ammeter, fuel, combination vacuum and pressure gauge and a large clock with sweep second hand. All of these instruments are black with white numerals and easy to read.

BODY, CHASSIS

Both the body and the chassis components for the Packard Hawk are the same as those used in the Studebaker Hawk series with a few styling differences in the body and a few chassis differences for improved quality. To distinguish the Packard from the Stude Hawk, a couple of fiberglass body sections are attached to the front on the Packard and an amazing transformation is effected. The broad "shovelnose" is a fiberglass section and so is the hood. The frame uses box section side rails and is of the ladder type construction with box section crossmembers.

Repeated fast stops from high speeds did not affect the efficiency of the Hawk's very good brakes. In this picture, a panic stop is being made from 70 mph but nosedive is slight. 62% of brake efficiency is on front wheels but car stops in a straight line.

Interior of Packard is finished in real leather and seating is very comfortable. Rear seats are contoured in bucket style.

Large and easy-to-read instruments are grouped in front of the driver. Combination gauge shows vacuum, blower pressure.

SUSPENSION

Both front and rear suspensions on the Hawk are similar to the type that has been used successfully during the past several years by Detroit automobile manufacturers. The front suspension is independent with unequal length control arms to maintain constant tread and a spindle support arm is mounted between the control arms. The S-P company uses a tapered wire in the front coil spring which makes possible a variable rate spring instead of the common constant rate coil spring. This spring is mounted between the lower control arm and the frame rails with a tubular shock absorber in the center of the coil. A link type front stabilizer bar is fastened between the two lower control arms to eliminate excessive body roll.

The rear suspension is by means of a pair of semi-elliptical leaf springs mounted parallel to the frame rails and rubber bushed to a bracket at the front with compression type shackles at the rear. The rear axle housing is mounted ahead of the center of the spring so that the shorter front spring sections will absorb driving torque. The hypoid rear axle uses one of four gear ratios depending upon

PACKARD HAWK

the transmission. For Hawks equipped with the automatic transmission, a 3.31 ratio is used. For the overdrive transmission, a 4.09 ratio is standard with 3.92 or 4.27 ratios optional. All ratios are available with an optional limited slip differential called Twin Traction.

STEERING

The conventional steering used with the Hawk is a Ross unit with a ratio of 22 to 1. The overall ratio, gear ratio plus linkage ratio, is 24.5 to 1. This is not too fast but when compared to ratios of other U.S. cars, it is better than average. A Saginaw power steering unit is available as an option with a gear ratio of 19 to 1 and an overall ratio of 21.5 to 1. After driving other late model cars with slow steering ratios, we needed a little time to get used to the ratio of Packard's power steering on our test car but after we did, corner control was excellent.

BRAKES

Power brakes are standard equipment on the Packard Hawk and are the best of any '58 model we have tested. Lining area is a modest 172.4 square inches but through the use of finned cast iron drums and cooling flanges which extend past the backing plates to catch cool air, the Hawk's brakes are superb. Front drums are 11 inches in diameter with a lining width of 2¼ inches and the rear drums are 10 inches in diameter with a 2-inch lining. Throughout all of our testing, the Hawk brakes performed faultlessly and showed no signs of excessive fade even when purposely abused with repeated high speed stops. The temperature was in the high fifties on the day we made brake tests and the period required to accelerate back to high speed again after a brake test was just enough time to cool the brakes down for another hard stop. With the Hydrovac power assist, pedal pressure was never excessive, nor were the brakes over-sensitive at low speeds.

ENGINE

Only one engine is available in the Packard Hawk. It is a 289 cubic inch V8 with overhead valves and is basically the same engine used by Studebaker for the past several years. The Stude Golden Hawk uses the same engine for 1958. With 7.5 to 1 compression ratio and only 289 cubic inches in this day of high compression and large displacements, a supercharger is needed to provide the muscle for a 275 horsepower advertised rating. The supercharger, or blower, is made for S-P by McCulloch Motors and is the same basic design as when introduced by McCulloch about five years ago. The unit is mounted on top of the engine and is driven by a single wide belt from the crankshaft through a variable diameter pulley. Inside the centrifugal blower, a planetary ball bearing unit changes ratio as the drive pulley diameter is changed

Area beneath the fiberglass hood of the Hawk is well filled. Variable speed supercharger, center, feeds pressure to the cast aluminum box that encloses carburetor.

High speed cornering is easy with the Hawk. Car does not lean excessively, and goes exactly where placed. At all speeds, the car is very stable and is not affected by side winds or road dips. Hawk weighs 3680 pounds, full of fuel and with power extras.

to make possible impeller speeds in excess of 25,000 rpm. The impeller drive ratio changes are adjusted automatically by controls in the blower that are energized according to the engine demands.

A maximum manifold boost of approximately 5 pounds is provided by the blower under high rpm, full throttle use. The air is ducted to a cast aluminum housing which encloses a single Stromberg two-barrel carburetor with 1⅛ inch venturii. The fresh air supply to the blower is protected by a paper pack air cleaner.

This engine is rated 275 horsepower at 4800 rpm but as we have discovered while testing other '58 automobiles, twisting the engine to the advertised speed is not always possible. Adjustable lifters are used but valve spring pressures are 45-55 pounds closed and only 105-115 with the valve open so even when used with the Hawk's comparatively mild cam timing, valve float started at 4500 rpm with our test car. A couple of attempts to exceed 4500 rpm during acceleration tests brought clattering protests from the valve department and a definite power loss so we never did get to feel the 275 horses supposed to be lurking around at 4800.

The exceptionally low, 7.5 to 1, compression ratio of the Hawk engine is designed to prevent excessive pressure and detonation when the blower is providing a positive boost to the engine but it is also instrumental in knocking low speed power for a loop. Getaway speeds from a stop are on the mediocre side even in low gear and the engine only starts to feel strong when the tach nears the 3000 rpm mark and the blower gauge registers a positive manifold pressure. From 3000 to 4500 rpm, the blower starts to apply the pressure and the little engine feels healthy. From our viewpoint, it would appear more practical to start with a compression ratio of about 9 to 1 and then restrict maximum blower pressure the amount necessary to keep pressures within safe limits. The extra compression would not only provide better low speed power but also improve gasoline economy while cruising down the highway. A boost of 3 pounds should then do the job required by five with the present 7.5 c.r.

TRANSMISSIONS

Two transmissions are available with the Hawk, an optional overdrive equipped standard transmission and a three speed automatic unit with which the Packard Hawk is regularly fitted. The overdrive transmission has ratios of 2.49 in first, 1.59 in second, direct high, 3.15 in reverse and a ratio of .722 in overdrive. A Borg and Beck clutch and pressure plate are used with 2054 pounds of spring pressure and a 10½ inch diameter.

The Flightomatic transmission is standard equipment for the Hawk with a torque converter and planetary gears which give ratios of 2.40 in first, 1.47 in second, 1 to 1 in third and 2.00 in reverse. The torque converter provides a maximum stall ratio of 2.15 to 1 at an engine speed of 1800 rpm. There are only two positions on the selector quadrant for forward gears, low and drive. Drive is normally used with the car starting in the 1.47 ratio and shifting to direct. Full throttle starts will engage the 2.40 ratio with the selector in

SPECIFICATIONS

ENGINE	
Bore	**3.56 in.**
Stroke	**3.63 in.**
Displacement	**289 cu. in.**
Compression ratio	**7.5 to 1**
Horsepower	**275 at 4800 rpm**
Torque, ft/lbs	**333 at 3200 rpm**
Carburetion	**Stromberg 2 barrel**
Supercharger	**Variable, 5 lbs. max.**
CHASSIS	
Wheelbase	**120½ in.**
Tread, front	**57 5/16 in.**
Tread, rear	**56 5/16 in.**
Length	**205 in.**
Height	**55 in.**
Width	**71.3 in.**
Weight (test car)	**3680 lbs.**
PERFORMANCE	
0-60 mph acceleration	**9.2 secs.**
30-50	**5.3 secs.**
50-80	**9.5 secs.**
¼ mile	**17.5 secs.**
Top speed	**108 mph**

Despite compact appearance, the Packard Hawk is not a small car, having a 120½-inch wheelbase and 205-inch overall length. Driver vision is excellent in all directions.

Secret to Hawk's superior brakes is in the cast iron drums. Fins and cooling flange dissipate heat fast. Lining width, 2¼ in.

drive. The low position will give a 2.40 ratio until shifted into drive, at which time the 1.47 gear will be engaged and then an automatic shift into direct. Manual down-shifts into low range above 20 mph will give a 1.47 ratio for braking or permit holding second gear above the normal shift points for better acceleration.

HANDLING, RIDE

Our first ride in the '58 Packard Hawk was with the factory suggested tire pressures of 24 pounds front and 20 pounds rear so we weren't a bit surprised to discover that this car had a very comfortable ride when cruising down the highway. We were just a little surprised however when we took a few corners at moderate speeds with this low tire pressure because the Hawk didn't flounder like the normal automobile with soft tires, it was very positive and easy to control. Our next step was to increase tire pressure to 32 pounds at the front and 30 pounds at the rear. We were prepared to sacrifice the "boulevard ride" for better handling but such was not the case. The ride was firm but good and cornering ability was better than we thought possible.

The 3680 pounds of our test car, full of fuel but minus passengers, was spread out so that 55.7% or 2050 pounds rested on the front wheels and 1630 pounds on the rear. This ratio gives the Hawk a small amount of understeer at medium cornering speeds but this condition is not evident either at normal cornering speeds or during high speed cornering. High speeds through corners convince the driver that this car is as well balanced as any non-sports car on the road today and with the fast acting ratio of the power steering on our test car, a driver would have to be careless to get in real trouble. The Hawk stays quite level through the corners with the increased tire pressure and will "drift" evenly with all four wheels when pushed hard. Additional corner speed will bring the rear of the car around in a slide but the "quick" steering gives good correction and the car feels very secure. This car is definitely not the "breakaway" type that feels secure up until the moment

Outward canted fins on rear fenders can be useful when backing into tight parking place as they are visible to the driver.

it lets loose. There's plenty of warning.

Average highway driving discloses no weak points in the ride with either recommended or extra tire pressure. Gusty side winds do not affect the stability and neither do dips although the car is quite average when it comes to "bottoming out" the suspension system on the rubber frame snubbers when entering or leaving rolling dips at highway speeds. Our test car was equipped with the optional Twin Traction limited slip differential and there was a tendency for the rear of the car to "skate" on washboard roads as first one wheel and then the other got traction. This shouldn't be present with the standard differential.

ECONOMY

Mileage checks made during our test produced figures of 11.9 mpg for city and freeway driving plus a series of acceleration tests. High speed highway and hard mountain driving produced 11.4 mpg and a tankful of fuel restricted to normal freeway and highway speeds produced 14.1 mpg. None of these figures are outstanding but considering the blower and hard test driving, a minimum average of 11.4 mpg for a tank of gas isn't too bad. Any time the high pitched whine of the blower could be heard, it meant that extra fuel and air was being pumped into the engine and we heard it often.

PERFORMANCE

Take a look at the acceleration figures in the box on page 21 and you will notice that the Hawk is not the fastest car on the road. Zero to 60 mph in 9.2 seconds is not bad but there are several cars on the road that will do it in eight seconds or less. The figures do not disclose the whole story however. We mentioned earlier that the low engine compression hurt the low rpm power and this is quite noticeable when starting from a dead stop. Revving the engine while holding the brake didn't produce more than just a slight wheelspin on the start but once the engine reached the 3000 rpm mark, the car felt strong. Standing start quarter mile times of 17.5 seconds also fail to show that the start was slow but the engine was running very strong at the end of the quarter with a speedo correction showing 85 mph for the ¼ mile.

A single high speed run was made on a flat desert road and the speedometer indicated 115 mph but calculations made by tachometer readings indicated the true speed nearer 108 mph. At this speed the tachometer indicated 4600 rpm and the engine was "missing" badly enough to keep the engine rpm from increasing. This bore out our earlier findings that the valves started to float after 4500 rpm.

A strange condition exists with a variable speed centrifugal blower such as that used on the Packard Hawk with this condition noticeable only when all side windows are closed tightly so that the engine can be more easily heard. A centrifugal blower will cavitate when it is not pumping air and will therefore require less power to drive the blower. If the engine is being run at full throttle with full blower pressure being used and then the throttle suddenly closed, the blower will cavitate and speed up several hundred rpm as the load is relieved from the impeller, and the drive ratio increases. This condition also exists in the Hawk when top speed is reached and the engine will not take as much air as the blower is supplying. The blower rpm will increase slightly even though the engine speed remains constant.

The fact that this cavitation occurs at top speed indicates that a few modifications to the engine would permit it to use the blower pressure being wasted and probably produce a lot more power. Increased valve spring pressure together with increased cam timing and more carburetor venturi area should do wonders for this engine especially in the upper rpm range. With its streamlined design, the Hawk could have a pretty good top speed.

We leave the styling opinions up to the potential customer because buying a car is strictly a matter of personal taste but if it's mechanical opinions you want, we will say that the Packard Hawk is a fine car. It isn't the most powerful or the fastest but the brakes are excellent, handling is superb, ride is smooth and oh, that real leather interior! On the debit side of the ledger there aren't many entries but we do have to mention that the hood doesn't open wide enough to get at things and has to be propped up with a rod. The main gripe is the cramped engine compartment. Imagine an engine, battery, power steering pump, power brake booster apparatus, generator, supercharger, carburetor air box, air cleaner, oil filter, air ducts and a few other items all sitting on top and alongside the engine. We dare you to try to change a set of spark plugs. You can't get to them from the bottom either so plan on a healthy labor charge at the local garage or set aside a Saturday if you do the job yourself. You've heard about compact cars; well, that's the Hawk!